Grammatical Constructions

Grammatical Constructions

Their Form and Meaning

EDITED BY

Masayoshi Shibatani

AND

Sandra A. Thompson

CLARENDON PRESS · OXFORD

1996

Oxford University Press, Walton Street, Oxford OX2 6DP

Oxford New York
Athens Auckland Bangkok Bombay
Calcutta Cape Town Dar es Salaam Delhi
Florence Hong Kong Istanbul Karachi
Kuala Lumpur Madras Madrid Melbourne
Mexico City Nairobi Paris Singapore
Taipei Tokyo Toronto
and associated companies in
Berlin Ibadan

Oxford is a trade mark of Oxford University Press

Published in the United States
by Oxford University Press Inc. New York

© *The several contributors, and in this collection*
Oxford University Press 1996

British Library Cataloguing in Publication Data
Data available

Library of Congress Cataloguing in Publication Data
Data available

ISBN 0–19–823539–9

1 3 5 7 9 10 8 6 4 2

Typeset by Alliance Phototypesetters
Printed in Great Britain
on acid-free paper by
Biddles Ltd., Guildford and King's Lynn

To Chuck Fillmore

for being the model of a good linguist, and
for sharing his joy of doing good linguistics

Foreword

The last decade or so has seen the emergence of the investigation of grammatical constructions. This work has taken as a premise that grammatical constructions in a given language often have unique semantic, pragmatic, and grammatical properties, and that they therefore merit close study to determine their role in the complex interplay of linguistic resources that a speaker brings to a communicative situation.

The papers in this volume are dedicated to Charles J. Fillmore in recognition of his leadership in the study of constructions. Friends of Chuck's from all over the world have joined us in this project of expressing our appreciation of his contributions to our understanding of the way in which semantic, pragmatic, and grammatical factors come together in various constructions found in a variety of languages.

Several approaches to constructions are represented here. One approach is to study a relatively lexicalized construction, as does Goldberg in her study of the 'way' construction. Several other authors concern themselves with a traditional construction, such as conditionals (McCawley and Sweetser), possessor-raising constructions (O'Connor), relative clauses (Matsumoto), or *te*-clauses in Japanese (Hasegawa). The interactions among semantic verb types and argument types are discussed by Shibatani (applicatives and benefactives), Slobin (verbs of motion), Talmy (event frames), and Van Valin and Wilkins ('effector' roles), while constructions at the level of the noun phrase are the focus of the papers by Brugman (modified noun phrases) and Watters (deverbal nominals).

These papers reflect a range of perspectives on grammatical constructions. What they all share is a commitment to the study of language as an intricate set of cognitive and social skills exquisitely adapted for human communication, with all that this implies for the semantic, pragmatic, and grammatical richness of grammatical constructions.

Kobe and Santa Barbara　　　　　　　　　　Masayoshi Shibatani
April 1995　　　　　　　　　　　　　　　　Sandra A. Thompson

Contents

List of Contributors

Claudia Brugman is Lecturer in the Linguistics Section of the School of Language at the University of Otago, Dunedin, New Zealand. She is the author of *The Story of 'Over'* and other works on lexical semantics. She is interested in polysemy, the semantics of spatial expressions, pragmatics, and argument structure.

Adele E. Goldberg is Assistant Professor of Linguistics at the University of California at San Diego. Her work focusses on the various aspects of argument structure including constructional and lexical semantics, linking theory, and complex predicates. She had explored many of these topics in her 1995 book, *Constructions: A Construction Grammar Approach to Argument Structure* (University of Chicago Press). More generally, her interests include syntax/semantics, psycholinguistics, language acquisition, and cognitive science.

Yoko Hasegawa is Assistant Professor of Japanese Linguistics in the Department of East Asian Languages at the University of California at Berkeley. She has been working on various phenomena in syntax, semantics, pragmatics, and experimental phonology. Her recent studies include 'The (Nonvacuous) Semantics of TE-linkage in Japanese' (*Journal of Pragmatics*, forthcoming), 'Prototype Semantics: A Case Study of TE K-/IK-Constructions in Japanese' (1993, *Language and Communication*), and 'Fundamental Frequency as an Acoustic Cue to Accent Perception' (1992, *Language and Speech*). The topic of her chapter will be dealt with more extensively in her forthcoming book, *A Study of Japanese Clause Linkage: The Connective-TE in Japanese* (Center for the Study of Language and Information/Kurosio Publishers).

Yoshiko Matsumoto is Assistant Professor in the Department of Asian Languages at Stanford University. Her research interests are the intersection between pragmatics and the structure of language, and Japanese linguistics. Her publications on related topics include 'Japanese-Style Noun Modification . . . in English' (1989, *Proceedings*

of the Fifteenth Annual Meeting of the Berkeley Linguistics Society),
'The Role of Pragmatics in Japanese Relative Clauses' (1991, *Lingua*),
'Is It Really a Topic That is Relativized? Arguments from Japanese'
(1991, *Papers from the 27th Regional Meeting*, Chicago Linguistic
Society). A book-length manuscript on Japanese noun-modifying
constructions is in preparation.

James D. McCawley is Andrew McLeish Distinguished Service
Professor of Linguistics and of East Asian Languages and Civiliza-
tion at the University of Chicago. His research interests include syn-
tax, semantics, pragmatics, philosophy of science, Japanese, and
Chinese. Among his publications are *Everything that Linguists Have
Always Wanted to Know About Logic (But Were Ashamed to Ask)* (2nd
edn., 1993), *The Syntactic Phenomena of English* (1988), and *Thirty
Million Theories of Grammar* (1982).

Mary Catherine O'Connor is Assistant Professor in the Applied
Linguistics Program, and the Program in Literacy, Language, and
Cultural Studies at Boston University. Her research interests include
the interfaces of syntax, the lexicon, and discourse pragmatics; discourse analysis; and linguistics in education. She has conducted fieldwork on Northern Pomo for over fifteen years, receiving grants from
the National Science Foundation and the National Endowment for
the Humanities. Publications include *Topics in Northern Pomo
Grammar* (1992, Garland Press), 'Third Person Reference in Northern Pomo Conversational Narrative' (1990, *International Journal of
American Linguistics*), and Fillmore, Kay and O'Connor, 'Regularity
and Idiomaticity in Grammatical Constructions' (1988, *Language*).

Masayoshi Shibatani is Professor of Linguistics at Kobe University
and Visiting Professor of Japanese Linguistics at UCLA (1995–6). He
was one of the first students of Charles Fillmore's at Berkeley. His
interests include language typology, syntax, and Japanese linguistics.
He is the author of *The Languages of Japan* (1990, Cambridge University Press) and the co-editor of *Approaches to Language Typology*
(1995, Oxford University Press).

Dan I. Slobin is Professor of Psychology at the University of California at Berkeley, and a Research Psychologist in the Institute of
Cognitive Studies and the Institute of Human Development, at the
same university. He studies child language development in a cross-
linguistic and typological framework, and is interested in relations

between speaking and thinking in discourse contexts, with implications for both acquisition and grammaticalization. He has been involved in developmental psycholinguistic research in Israel, Italy, the Netherlands, Spain, Turkey, the United States, and Yugoslavia (Croatia). Relevant publications include *The Crosslinguistic Study of Language Acquisition*, i–iv, (Lawrence Erlbaum, 1992–), 'Learning to Think for Speaking: Native Language, Cognition, and Rhetorical Style' *Pragmatics* (1991), *Relating Events in Narrative: A Crosslinguistic Developmental Study* (with Ruth A. Berman) (1994, Erlbaum), 'Reference to Movement in Spoken and Signed Languages: Typological Considerations', *Proceedings of the Twentieth Annual Meeting of the Berkeley Linguistics Society* (with N. Hoiting) (1994).

Eve Sweetser is Associate Professor in Linguistics at the University of California at Berkeley, from which she received her Ph.D. in 1984 with Charles Fillmore as the Chair of her dissertation committee. She also teaches in the Cognitive Science Program and in the Celtic Studies Program at UCB. Her central research interests are semantics, metaphor, meaning change, and grammatical meaning within a cognitive theory of linguistics. She has published various articles on modality, lexical semantics, pragmatics, conditionals, metaphor, Middle Welsh poetics, and meaning change, and is the author of *From Etymology to Pragmatics: Metaphorical and Cultural Aspects of Semantic Structure* (1990, Cambridge University Press). She lately co-edited with Gilles Fauconnier *Spaces, Worlds and Grammar* (1996, University of Chicago Press), a volume of papers on the ways in which grammatical constructions represent mental space structure.

Leonard Talmy is Associate Professor in Linguistics and the Director of the Center for Cognitive Science at the State University of New York at Buffalo. His research interests center on natural-language semantics and its implications for cognitive theory. Within this area, his specific interests are: the relations between semantics and cognition— cognitive linguistics; typologies and universals of semantic structure; the relationship between semantic structure and formal linguistic structures—lexical, morphological, and syntactic; and the relation of this material to diachrony, discourse, development, impairment, and culture. Publications relevant to the topic of his chapter include 'Fictive Motion in Language and "ception" ', 'The Relation of Grammar to Cognition', 'Force Dynamics in Language and Cognition', and 'How Language Structures Space'.

Sandra A. Thompson is Professor of Linguistics at the University of California at Santa Barbara. She was one of Charles Fillmore's first students at Ohio State University. She specializes in discourse and language universals, and is particularly interested in the role of patterns of conversational discourse in shaping morphosyntactic regularities. She is the co-author with Charles Li of *Mandarin Chinese: A Functional Reference Grammar*, and with Paul Hopper of 'Transitivity in Grammar and Discourse'. She has co-edited *Studies in Transitivity* with Paul Hopper, *Discourse Description* with William C. Mann, and *Interaction and Grammar* with Elinor Ochs and Emanuel Schegloff.

Robert D. Van Valin, Jr. is Professor and Chair in the Linguistics Department at the State University of New York at Buffalo. His research is focussed on theoretical linguistics, especially syntactic theory (both formal and functional), theories of the acquisition of syntax, and neurolinguistics, especially aphasia and PET studies of language processing. He is the primary developer of the theory of Role and Reference Grammar. He has done research on two Native American languages, Lakhota (Siouan) and Yatee Zapotec (Oto-Manguean). He is the co-author of *Functional Syntax and Universal Grammar* (Cambridge University Press, 1984) and the forthcoming *Syntax: Meaning, Structure and Function* (Cambridge University Press); he is the editor of *Advances in Role and Reference Grammar* (John Benjamins, 1993) and has published articles on syntax, universal grammar, language typology, and language acquisition.

James K. Watters is a linguistic consultant and the translation coordinator for the Mexico branch of the Summer Institute of Linguistics. He and his wife, Juanita, are also assisting Tepehuas of the state of Veracruz in the development and promotion of Tepehua literature. He has written various papers on the phonology and morphosyntax of Tepehua. His interest in frame semantics began during his graduate studies at Berkeley, where Charles Fillmore was his advisor. The paper in this volume (which includes material from his dissertation) was written while he was a visiting researcher for the Seminario de Lenguas Indígenas in the Instituto de Investigaciones Filológicas, Universidad Nacional Autónoma de México.

David P. Wilkins is a Senior Research Fellow with Cognitive Anthropology Research Group of the Max Planck Institute for Psycholinguistics, Nijmegen. His major research interests are Australian Aboriginal languages, semantics, ethnopragmatics, and the relation between culture and cognition. He has done extensive fieldwork in Central Australia on Arrernte (Aranda), and his most recent publication (with Deborah Hill) is entitled 'When "go" means "come": Questioning the basicness of basic motion verbs (*Cognitive Linguistics* 6, 1995).

List of Symbols and Abbreviations

#	pragmatically deviant
%	idiolectal/dialectal variable acceptability
?	questionable acceptability
??	low acceptability
*	ungrammatical
*?	almost ungrammatical
1, 2, etc.	Bantu noun classes
1POSS, 2POSS, etc.	first person possessive, second person possessive, etc.
1S, 2P, etc.	first person singular, second person plural, etc.
3SF	third person singular feminine
3SM	third person singular masculine
ABL	ablative
ACC	accusative
ADV	adverbial clause-marker
ADVERS	adversative clause-marker
ALL	allative
APPL	applicative
ART	article
ASP	aspect
BEN	benefactive
CADV	controlled adverbial clause-marker
CAUS	causative
COMP	comparative
COMPL	complementizer
CONJ	conjunction
COP	copula
DAT	dative
DEM	demonstrative
DET	determiner
DIR	direction
DT	detransitivizer

EVID	evidential
FAM. DIM	familiar diminutive
FOC	focus
FV	final vowel
GEN	genitive
IMP. PASS	impersonal passive
IMPF	imperfect
IND	indicative
INST	instrumental
IRR	irrealis
LDR	long-distance reflexive
LOC	locative
NEG	negative
NMLZR	nominalizer
NOM	nominative
NPAST	non-past
OBL	oblique
PASS	passive
PAST	past tense
PFV	perfective
POSS	possessor
PRES	present tense
PROG	progressive
Q	question-marker
REFL	reflexive
TOP	topic
VIA	route-instrument
VOL	volitional

I

Inalienability and the Interpretation of Modified Noun Phrases

Claudia Brugman

INTRODUCTION

In his seminal work 'The Case for Case', Fillmore suggests that among the semantic distinctions which receive covert grammatical expression, in English and other languages, is the one between alienable and inalienable possession:

What is genuinely important about [1] is its paraphrasability as [4] (or [5]) and the fact that the construction exhibited by [1] is restricted to certain kinds of nouns. Note the ungrammaticality of [6].

1. I have a missing tooth.
2. I have a tooth.
3. I have a tooth and it is missing.
4. My tooth is missing.
5. One of my teeth is missing.
6. *I have a missing five-dollar bill.

Note that in sentences [1] and [4], three things are involved: (a) a possessor (an 'interested person', to use the traditional term), (b) a body part, and (c) an attribute—(a) *me*, (b) *tooth*, and (c) *missing* respectively—and that the sentences provide alternate ways of ascribing the attribute to the possessor's body

This paper was completed during a research fellowship funded by the National Endowment for the Humanities Fellowships for College and University Teachers Program. The endowment is herewith thanked for its support. Thanks also to Jeff Elman and Elizabeth Bates, directors of the Center for Research in Language, University of California, San Diego, for providing space, resources, and collegiality for that period. An early and brief mention of this phenomenon appears in Brugman (1988), completed under Professor Fillmore. Oral approximations to this paper were given at the 1989 meeting of the Linguistic Society of America, at the Purdue Linguistics Group, and at the UC San Diego Linguistics Department Colloquium. I thank the audiences at those meetings for their comments. Thanks to Michele Emanatian, Yuki Kuroda, George Lakoff, Catherine O'Connor, Matt Shibatani, and especially Farrell Ackerman for their comments.

part. They are two distinct superficial ways of expressing the same relationship among these three concepts. (Fillmore, 1968: 63)

Fillmore observes that sentence (1) does not entail (the usual reading of) sentence (2), nor is it equivalent in interpretation to sentence (3)—that the interesting relationship is not between the possessor and the body part, but between the body part and the 'attribute'. In a certain respect, it is that relationship which I will be exploring in this paper.

In placing the set of examples in (1–6) in a section headed 'The grammar of inalienable possession' (1968: 61), Fillmore implies that the difference in acceptability—on the intended reading—of (1) and (6) comes down to the fact that *tooth* denotes an inalienable possession and *five-dollar bill* denotes an alienable possession.

In the formalism by which he distinguishes sentences (1) and (6) and in the ensuing discussion, Fillmore suggests three things: first, that the relationship between the 'interested person' and his body part is the one expressed propositionally in sentences like (1), (4), and (5); second, that one may express this relation by using HAVE, as in (1), or by using the genitive marker, as in (4) and (5), but not both; and third, that HAVE and BE (at least in these constructions) are semantically bankrupt, since they are introduced by rule (Fillmore 1968: 64) rather than appearing in underlying structure.

In this paper I will explore alternatives to the first and third of these suggestions.[1] I will argue for the following points. First, the noncompositional reading of (1) which corresponds to (4) and (5) has nothing crucial to do with possession *per se* (though the semantics of inalienable possession does figure in, in an indirect way). Second, HAVE is only one among a class of predicators which allow a noncompositional reading of the modified NPs serving as their complements, but is sanctioned to fulfill this function on the basis of its semantics rather than by lexical stipulation—hence it cannot be semantically empty.[2]

---

[1] I do not dispute the claim that HAVE and the genitive are complementary in sentences which express a relation of possession or attribution between two individuals. There are acceptable interpretations of sentences like *He has his green eyes* (cf.(21) and (22)), but they seem not to express inalienable possession, even on the revised account I give below. Fillmore's general observation, that HAVE and the genitive marker do not co-occur in expressions of possession, seems indisputable.

[2] It would be disingenuous to evaluate by current standards the semantic implications of introducing HAVE and BE by rule, as Fillmore did in the 1968 model. These lexical insertions were part of a model in which semantic structures of a particular (rather abstract) sort constituted a large part of the underlying structure of a sentence. It might be more accurate to say that the implication of lexical insertion by rule in this model is

Finally, while there is a relationship of possession between the interested person and his body part (i.e. that the missing body part is one that 'properly' belongs to him) this relationship is inferred from the semantically expressed relationship, which is one of attributing to the interested person a state of lacking a tooth. In other words, the 'possession' relationship is an abstract one between the interested person and a state in which his tooth is missing. The attribution of missingness to the tooth is expressed by means of the parataxis of *missing* as a syntactic modifier of *tooth*; I will argue that semantically, *missing* is a predicate which takes *tooth* as its argument, which is why (1) is propositionally synonymous with (4) and (5), in which *missing* is also predicated of *tooth*. The relationship of 'inalienable possession' between the interested person and the tooth is determined on the basis of the entailment of the propositional content of the sentence in conjunction with extralinguistic knowledge, and is not the semantic basis for this construction.

I have paraphrased the preferred reading of (1), in a clumsy way, in (1'), and I will refer to the reading which it exemplifies as the 'state-of-affairs' or SOA reading, by contrast to a reading paraphrasable by (3) or (1"), which I shall call the 'entity' reading.

(1') 'I experience tooth-missingness'[3]
(1") 'I possess a tooth which is missing'

The analysis I will give as an alternative to Fillmore's is a very simple one: the normal reading of (1), corresponding truth-conditionally to (4) and (5), is a manifestation of a general principle of interpretation. That rule, which is stated more precisely in section 1.4.1, is that an NP (hereafter, the 'modified NP') which contains a modifier denoting a state or condition of the referent of the remainder of that NP can denote the state or condition of that individual, rather than the individual itself. In the service of this argument I will show, in section 1.2,

---

that these two lexemes have the function of case-markers. This is a claim with which I would also take issue.

[3] I will use the convention throughout of indicating the availability of a particular reading to a sentence by surrounding a sentence suggesting that reading with single quotation marks, and giving it a numeral co-indexing it with the sentence it is intended to paraphrase (e.g. (1') corresponds to a reading available to sentence (1)). As far as sheer grammaticality goes, all unprimed sentences will be considered unremarkably acceptable, unless marked by the conventional diacritics, while the grammaticality of sentences surrounded by single quotation marks will not be at issue, since they merely stand for readings and are not to be evaluated as idiomatic sentences of English. Attested examples are surrounded by double quotation marks.

that the proposed principle of interpretation operates on sentences involving neither the verb HAVE nor the semantics of inalienable possession. In section 1.1 I will settle some terminological and foundational matters.

By Fillmore's characterization, the unacceptability of (6) is due to the fact that *five-dollar bill* does not denote an inalienable possession: the syntactic schema (7) is apparently available only to the expression of an inalienable possession with an attribute.

(7) [$_S$ [$_{NP}$ 'interested person'] [$_{VP}$ HAVE [$_{NP}$ (spec) [$_{AP}$ 'attribute']
    'body-part']]]

Under my analysis the expression of inalienable possession is not a necessary condition of this sentence type, and therefore the difference in acceptability between (1) and (6) remains unaccounted for. I will attempt (with incomplete success) to account for its reduced acceptability in sections 1.3 and 1.4. Section 1.5 will summarize the findings and point to future avenues of investigation.

1.1. BACKGROUND AND FOUNDATIONS

1.1.1. *Some terminological notes*

Because my analysis rests on recognizing a discrepancy between the expected interpretation of a syntactic constituent and its actual interpretation, it is important to establish precisely how I will be using quite familiar and intuitive terminology. I will use 'predicator' to refer to *n*-place relations, reserving the term 'predicate' for one-place relations which are involved in the 'predication', or 'subject/predicate', relation. Here I am using both 'predicate' and 'predicator' as purely semantic constructs. Similarly, I will distinguish an argument, a semantic requirement of a predicator, from a complement—a syntactic constituent subcategorized-for by a predicator. I shall call the 'embedding predicator' the verb or other predicator which subcategorizes for the complement NP at issue, using it both for an argument-taking function and for a lexical item which subcategorizes for a number of complements, trusting to context to disambiguate between its syntactic and semantic senses. In the examples above, HAVE is the embedding predicator: it takes an NP complement, and a state-of-affairs argument, in example (1) on the reading (1′). The modifier in the NP may be a preposed AP, a postnominal phrase of any appropriate category, or a relative clause. When a sentence has an SOA (state-of-affairs) reading, I will call the 'embedded predicator' the constituent, syntactically a modifier, which takes the referent of the remainder of the NP (the syntactic head noun, any specifiers, and any other modifiers) as its argument. As the term 'embedded predicator' implies, I claim that the semantic function of the syntactic modifier is of secondary predication, not of modification. The proposition consisting of the secondary predicate and its argument I will call the 'embedded proposition'. In (1) *have* is the embedding predicator, which takes an NP complement, *a missing tooth*. The argument of *have* is 'the condition of being missing a tooth'. The embedded predicator is therefore *missing*, and its argument is 'a tooth'.

1.1.2. *A few words about 'predication' and 'modification'*

One thing that needs to be established is what is meant by 'modification' and 'predication' (and their derivatives)—in particular, whether these are basically syntactic constructs, basically semantic ones, or whether they are presumed to encode a one-to-one correspondence between syntactic form and semantic interpretation. There are many characterizations, but few definitions, of each in the literature. The characterizations are often not clear about whether they are to be taken as semantic or syntactic constructs; sometimes they confound or conflate semantic and syntactic criteria. Since what we are dealing with appears to be a lack of fit between what the syntactic form of the phrase implies about its semantics and the actual interpretation of a phrase, I will here summarize what others have said and what I mean by these terms.

Each approach to the characterization of 'predicate' and 'modifier' is taken by some linguistic scholars. For instance, Lyons (1977: 391) uses a syntactic characterization of modification (identifying it as an endocentric structure), though he appears to assume that there is some constant semantic function that (syntactic) modification accomplishes. By contrast, his definition of 'predicate' (given in his discussion of predicate calculus) is 'a term which is used in combination with a name in order to give some information about the individual that the name refers to: i.e. in order to ascribe to him some property' (p. 148). His phrase-structure rules indicate the presumption that predication involves an exocentric syntactic relationship, by contrast to the endocentric character of modification. Quine (1960: 96, 104 ff.)

similarly presumes that 'attribution' or modification and predication can be distinguished on syntactic grounds, though he claims a semantic distinction between them as well.

Jackendoff apparently presumes an isomorphism between semantic and syntactic criteria to distinguish predication from modification. (He discusses only restrictive modifiers.) He recognizes both predicates (or predicators) and modifiers as functors, and says that 'both display strong X-bar character' (1990: 56).

In her discussion of the difference between predication and modification, Napoli (1989: 20 ff.) distinguishes between them on the basis of what kind of expression can be the 'role-player' (roughly equivalent for current purposes to the argument) of each kind of functor. She discusses only noun modification, in which a modifier takes an expression of category N as its role-player, while a predicate takes an expression of category NP as its role-player. This corresponds essentially to Lyons's distinction between an exocentric and an endocentric function, though some confusion may result from Napoli's characterization, since it uses both semantic and syntactic constructs. Moreover, she assimilates certain forms of syntactic modification, such as the nonrestrictive epithet in *that madman George*, into her theory of predicate co-indexing (see Chs. 3, 4, and 5) and so threatens to reduce modification to a kind of predication.

Another invoked difference is that a predicate is situated in time, while a modifier is either not situated in time at all or is situated only relative to some externally specified temporal region. This point of difference is somewhat problematic when one attempts to use it to distinguish modification from secondary predication, which is the crucial distinction at issue in the present work. Secondary predicates are not temporally situated via tense-marking, as are main-clause or subordinate-clause predicates. They must nevertheless be given an interpretation with a specific temporal grounding based on their logical relation to the primary predicate: 'depictive' (Rothstein 1985) predicates like *raw* in (8)

(8) She eats meat raw

receive a temporal interpretation of simultaneity, while 'resultative' predicates like *breathless* in (9)

(9) She kissed him breathless

receive a temporal interpretation of immediate subsequence to, or temporal overlap with, the embedding predicator. However, the issue of temporal situatedness does not obviously distinguish depictive secondary predicates from modifiers: compare (10)

(10) She eats raw meat

where again *raw* must describe *meat* at the time the meat is eaten. Rothstein discusses the difference between the modifier in (10) and the depictive secondary predicate in (8) in terms of a nonlogical relation: the secondary predicate implicates a weak causative relationship between, in (8), the rawness of the meat and her eating it, while the modification semantics in (10) does not imply such a relation. I submit that the SOA readings of the modification structures discussed in this paper display the same 'nonlogical' aspects of interpretation which Rothstein claims hold in the case of secondary predication.

The most promising means of formalizing the difference between modifiers and predicates comes from categorial grammar. Bar-Hillel (1964: 71) distinguishes between endotypic and exotypic operators, the semantic analogue to endocentric and exocentric constructions: 'It is useful, in certain investigations, to distinguish between operators which out of their arguments form a string belonging to the same category as the arguments, and those which do not. The first kind might be called endotypic, the second exotypic. That type of *poor*, for instance, which belongs to the category $n/[n]$, is endotypic, while *sleeps*, which belongs to $s/(n)$, is exotypic.' (Notice that this characterization does not itself distinguish predicative uses of adjectives from attributive ones, and presumes an isomorphism between lexical category and functional category.)

Lehrberger (1974) takes up Bar-Hillel's distinction within Montague Grammar: 'Roughly, an endocentric construction corresponds to a phrase formed by an endotypic operator, and the argument of the operator is the head of the construction' (p. 36). All his examples of endotypic operators are (attributive) modifiers and specifiers. The Lambek calculus also treats modifiers as endotypic and predicates as exotypic (Lehrberger 1974: 39 ff.). Elsewhere, Lehrberger claims that 'modifiers . . . may be treated in the same way as predicates, although they may not be sentence forming. The modifier is taken as a functor and the modifier phrase as its argument' (1974: 78). Siegel (1976: 301 ff.) provides a Montague Grammar analysis of adjectives in attributive ('modifier') and in predicate position: according to that analysis, attributive adjectives are of the category CN/CN—that is, they take as input members of the category CN (mnemonic for 'common noun') and as output members of the same category (which will combine with a determiner to produce an NP). By contrast, predicate adjectives are members of either a simple or a derived category IV (mnemonic for 'intransitive verb'), which combines with terms to produce propositions. This distinction, which I will adopt informally here, amounts to saying that a modifier is a function whose output is of the same categorial type as its input, while a predicate is a function from an individual to a proposition.

The notional analogue of the Montague Grammar distinction is somewhat harder to characterize rigorously, intuitive as the distinction may be. I claim that the meaning of a predicative expression is a state of an individual, or an event in which an individual takes part. The meaning of a (nominal) modifying expression is an individual. The two kinds of expression correspond to two cognitive states: one in which a state of affairs or event is apprehended, and one in which an individual is apprehended, and any state or event which may be ascribed to that individual is backgrounded or taken for granted.[4]

Because of the lack of fit between the structure and the expected interpretation of constituents in the sentences at issue, I shall refer to the structures characteristic of each as a 'modification' structure' (that is, a structure dominated by an NP node whose head is a noun) and a 'predication structure' (a structure in which there are two sister nodes, an NP and an XP) respectively. I will talk about the semantic functions as 'modification semantics' and 'predication semantics (or interpretation)', respectively.

In the following, I will consider both prenominal and postnominal (phrasal and relative-clause) modifiers. On the semantic side, I will consider as 'predication' any function whose intension is a state of affairs (e.g. an event). 'Modification (of a noun)' will be a function whose intension is an individual. Accordingly, I will identify the

---

[4] It may not be a coincidence that we therefore do not find a 'referential' use of predicates corresponding to the 'referential' (in contrast to 'attributive') use of modifiers (Donnellan, 1966). While an inaccurate modifier may be employed in a successful act of referring—because it is the individual, and not its properties, which is at issue in such an act—we cannot find an analogous use of inaccurate, but successful, predication. The issue of what constitutes predication, and whether all declarative sentences correspond to acts of predication, is a much larger one than can be addressed here. In particular, I am not here considering the question of whether generic or impersonal sentences correspond to acts of predication. The characterization provided here is meant to cover cases of both the 'thetic' and the 'categorical' judgment as discussed by Kuroda (1972; 1990; cf. Sasse, 1987), with the exception of the above-mentioned generics and impersonals.

interpretation of 'modification semantics' with the 'entity reading' of a sentence in which it figures, and 'predication semantics' will be involved in the 'state-of-affairs' reading.

1.1.3. HAVE, *attribution, and secondary predication*

As Fillmore noted, the NP complement of HAVE in (1) includes a modifier which expresses a condition of the head of the NP. My claim is that, in fact, the proposition which predicates that condition of the entity, rather than the entity itself, is the argument of HAVE. HAVE subcategorizes for another complementation frame, one in which the 'attribute' which appears in the complement NP in (1) is instead found in a position characteristic of secondary predicates. This structure is exemplified in (11):

(11) I have a tooth missing

Examining secondary predicates raises a number of interesting issues, including the question of whether there is a syntactic constituent enclosing the NP and the predicate and, if so, what the phrasal type of that constituent is. There are also semantic questions such as whether subcategorized-for versus optional secondary predicates can be distinguished on the basis of their semantic role (see e.g. Rothstein, 1985). These questions are not directly relevant here.

The matter of the syntactic constituency of the string *a tooth missing* is part of a larger and continuing controversy about secondary predicates and the existence of 'small clauses' (see e.g. Williams, 1980; Rothstein, 1985; Napoli, 1989; Alsina, 1992). A small-clause analysis of (11) would produce the structure in (12):

(12) [$_S$ I [$_{VP}$ have [$_{SC}$ [$_{NP}$ a tooth] [$_{XP}$ missing]]]]

The analysis adopted in Brugman (1988) (and advocated for somewhat similar structures in e.g. Alsina, 1992) does not posit any constituent internal to the VP:

(13) [$_S$ I [$_{VP}$ have [$_{NP}$ a tooth] [$_{XP}$ missing]]]

The constituency of the string at issue is irrelevant, as long as it is not taken to be a single NP constituent (see Brugman, 1988). What is relevant for our purposes is that in (11), *missing* is a 'secondary predicate' (that is, a subcategorized-for predicative complement of the matrix verb HAVE), and its argument is *a tooth*.

In addition to the question of the status of expressions like *missing*, there are also questions about the object NPs in this structure. In (8), *meat* is an argument of the embedding predicator EAT as well as of the secondary predicate *raw*. By contrast, I argued (Brugman, 1988) that the NP *a tooth* is not an argument of HAVE, but only that the proposition expressed by the string *a tooth missing* is. In short, (11) expresses the same semantic relations as (1) on the reading (1'). There is no doubt that (1) and (11) are not completely equivalent sentences. Whatever semantic subtleties distinguish them, however, the two sentences are propositionally synonymous.

They are an interesting minimal pair in that (11) shows that HAVE can express a relationship between an entity and a state of affairs, as well as expressing a relationship between two entities, as it does in (2). Furthermore, whatever the points of nonsynonymy between (1) and (11), they are not due to a difference in the meaning of HAVE: in both sentences, HAVE expresses an abstract kind of attribution. In other words, I identify the attribution relation in (1) as one between me, the speaker-subject, and my tooth-missingness; the attribution of missingness to the tooth is ascribable to the predication (in (11)) or modification (in (1)) structure containing *missing* and *a tooth*. (Fillmore shows that this relation holds of sentences (4) and (5).)

This interpretation of HAVE is syntactically sanctioned and generally available, as examples (14)–(20) show.

(14) This bookshelf has too many books on it
(15) Bill has them coming to his house tomorrow
(16) Albany has an express bus running to it
(17) She has her husband to keep her honest

Examples (15), which has a pronominal head, and (17), which contains a marked infinitive VP, show that the postnominal material cannot be a modifier and must be a secondary predicate. This means that, whatever it is called, the XP after the nominal head is a separate constituent, that it functions as a predicate, and that it is predicated of the NP preceding it. In sentences with this structure, HAVE takes the proposition referred to by the NP–XP string as its argument, and presents that SOA as (if it were) an attribute of the referent of the subject NP.

The semantics of attribution expressed by HAVE need not involve an objective state of possession or attribution, but may impose such an interpretation on a particular situation. That it need not be an objective attribute of that entity is evident from the pair (18) and (19):

(18) She had her arms around me in a moment
(19) I had her arms around me in a moment

which can describe the same objective state of affairs but does it from
the point of view of different participants, perhaps implying the action
or responsibility of one participant as opposed to the other. It is
equally evident that the general function of this attributive use of HAVE
is often presentational—that is, that a situation may be presented by
means of this construction as if it were an attribute of some entity. It is
equally, perhaps better, suited for the predication of actual or objective attribution, as in (20), where the same structural and internal
semantic relations can be found.

(20) I have a scar running across my back

In (20), the speaker-subject predicates of herself the state of affairs
that a scar runs across her back. This proposition entails that the
speaker-subject has a scar.

(20) is structurally ambiguous, the other reading being one in which
a scar running across my back is an NP containing a postnominal
modifier, and where the sentence expresses a relationship between two
individuals. The two readings are truth-conditionally equivalent.
(This point will be taken up again in Section 1.3.2.) This ambiguity of
(20) can be eliminated by replacing the indefinite specifier with a genitive one (in accordance with Fillmore's observation that the genitive
does not co-occur with the possessive sense of HAVE):

(21) I have my scar running across my back

(21) has only the secondary-predicate structure and the SOA reading.
This shows that even inalienable-possession nouns can participate in
the abstract SOA attribution semantics—it is not the relation of the
body part to the 'interested person', but rather the relation of the condition of that body part to the 'interested person', that is being expressed in the matrix proposition.

To sum up, then, HAVE is a predicator which may express an attribution relationship between an entity and a state of affairs, as it does in
(14–20) (on the relevant reading), as well as in (11), or a relationship
between two entities, as it does in the entity reading of (20), as well as
in (22):

(22) I have green eyes

HAVE expresses attribution abstract enough to cover all these cases.[5] That conclusion is not too different from Fillmore's (1969), though I believe that having abstract semantics is not the same as being semantically empty, particularly when that abstract semantics is capable of imposing a specific perspective on a situation, in the sense of Fillmore (1977).

1.2. THE PROPERTIES OF THESE SENTENCES

1.2.1. *The entity and SOA readings*

Sentences like (23) do in fact have readings roughly corresponding to (24); i.e. (23) has an entity reading as well as a SOA reading.

   (23) I have a missing tooth (= (1))
   (24) I have a tooth and it is missing (= (3))

The entity reading of (23) is approximately equivalent to the reading of (24) when the deictic grounding of *missing* is taken to be the same 'interested person'.

   When *have a tooth* is taken as an expression of 'inalienable possession', both of these sentences express a logical contradiction, since they assert simultaneously that the speaker-subject has and lacks a tooth. It is difficult to interpret (23) as having this reading, since the SOA reading is available, just as the contradictory *de dicto* reading of *Dan thinks he's smarter than he is* is difficult to get in the context of the logically well-formed *de re* reading. Strictly speaking, however, both readings are possible, and pragmatic as well as semantic factors will determine which reading is preferred, as I will show below.

1.2.2. *Possession and alienability*

1.2.2.1. *Inalienability.* Fillmore hypothesizes that the data in (1)–(6) show a covert grammatical distinction between alienable and inalienable possession. One point which might be made in objection to this is that not all nouns which have traditionally been thought of as referring to inalienables easily receive the SOA reading in Fillmore's frame sentence. Notice, for instance, that (25) is not as good, out of context, as (23):

---

   [5] It also has other senses demonstrably different from this one: not all the uses of HAVE will reduce to attribution/possession. See Brugman (1988).

(25) ?I have a missing daughter[6]

In fact, this is not a real objection, since it is possible that English simply classes only body parts, and not kinfolk, as inalienable possessions. As Fillmore puts it, 'inalienability' is 'a "grammatical" rather than purely "notional" [construct]' (1968: 62). I shall show below that the difference between *tooth* and *daughter* in these sentences is revealing.

This brings us to the second point: the heads of modified NPs in sentences which allows the SOA reading are not all inalienables. Most are not even 'relational nouns', which, as Fillmore notes (1968: 61) constitute a set from which the 'inalienable possession' nouns are drawn. Example (26) is just as good as (23), for many speakers:

(26) Your paper has a missing question mark on p. 273

From this example, one might argue that an extended notion of inalienable possession is at work here. Perhaps punctuation marks are thought of as natural or integral parts of papers (in this sense of PAPER). In section 1.4.2.1 I will take up this point again. However, it is possible to show that no kind of possession, alienable or inalienable, is necessary for the SOA interpretation.

1.2.2.2. *Possession.* The SOA reading does not depend on the embedding predicator having semantics of possession of any kind, since it is available when the embedding predicator is not a predicator of possession. This is shown in (27) and its paraphrase, (27') (which also corresponds to an acceptable English sentence):

(27) The kids sat around all day watching TV and making dirty dishes
(27') 'the kids sat around all day watching TV and making dishes dirty'

On the favored SOA reading of (27), *dirty dishes* is not the argument of MAKE, in the way that *ceramic dishes* would be: the existence of the dishes is not brought about by the kids' action. Rather, some pre-existing dishes are made dirty by the kids' action; hence 'dish-dirtiness' is the SOA argument of MAKE, as the paraphrase (27') suggests.

1.2.3. *Secondary predication*

From (23), (12), and (27), (27'), it might be concluded that the apparent modifiers—*missing* in (23) and *dirty in* (27)—are actually

[6] Judgments are often slippery on these sentences, for reasons which should become apparent later. Many speakers find (25) no worse than (23); but many speakers find (6) no worse than either.

secondary predicates which have somehow become preposed. But if that were the case, only embedding predicators which sanction a secondary predicate in one of their subcategorization frames would appear in sentences with an SOA interpretation. (28) and (29) show that this is not the case, since, even though (28′) is the favored interpretation of (28), the presumed underlying structure is not acceptable:

(28)   The kids sat around all day watching TV and producing dirty dishes
(28′) 'the kids sat around all day watching TV and producing dish-dirtiness'
(29)   *The kids sat around all day watching TV and producing dishes dirty

Conversely, not all predicates which subcategorize for secondary predicates can appear as the embedding predicator in a sentence with an SOA reading: (30) does not receive a reading synonymous with that of (31) (i.e. (31′)):

(30)   They found the guilty party
(31)   They found the party guilty
(31′) 'they found the party to be guilty'[7]

Another argument against the hypothesis that these modifiers are preposed secondary predicates is that adjectives which can only be used attributively cannot appear with the function of the embedding predicator in a sentence with an SOA reading. For instance, (32) cannot receive the interpretation (32′):

(32)   She discovered the late president.
(32′) #'she discovered that the president was dead'

This shows also that the restriction on such adjectives is on their semantic function (of attribution), not on their position (prenominal).

1.3. MORE EXAMPLES, AND THE ANALYSIS

1.3.1. *More examples*

Attested examples verify that the embedding predicator need have neither the semantics of possession nor a subcategorization frame sanctioning a secondary predicate in order for that sentence to receive

---

[7] The unacceptability of the reading (31′) for (30) cannot be ascribed to a constraint against resultative secondary predicates appearing in modification structures: as *guilty* is a resultative predicate in (31), so is *dirty* in (27) and (28).

a SOA reading. (33–40) are all utterances I have collected, and the surrounding context of each confirms that the reading intended by the producer was the SOA reading, which for each is provided in (33′–40′).

(33) "With the level of housing starts that existed during the Carter administration, we could eliminate the people . . . that are homeless."

(33′) '. . . we could eliminate homelessness among the people'

(34) "I found a missing question mark on p. 240."

(34′) 'I found that there was a question mark missing on p. 240'

(35) "An older, more stable community contributes significantly to the low crime rate."[8]

(35′) 'An older, more stable community contributes significantly to the lowness of the crime rate'

(36) "Please forgive my tardy reply"

(36′) 'please forgive the tardiness of my reply'

(37) "I hate people who do that!"

(37′) 'I hate people doing that'

It is evident that in order to receive predication interpretation, a modified NP need not be headed by an inalienable possession noun or even by one which is semantically relational: none of *dishes, people, women, crime rate*, or *reply* is a relational noun. It is also evident that expressing possession is not a necessary condition for the embedding predicator: ELIMINATE, FIND, RESTRICT, CONTRIBUTE, FORGIVE, and HATE are among the embedding predicators found in sentences receiving this interpretation.

A few of the attested sentences have specific properties which are of interest in the current problem. Example (38) shows that the embedded proposition may fulfill the subject-argument requirement of the embedding predicator LAST, which shows that the SOA reading does not express a relation of possession or attribution to another individual.

(38) "With Epilady Ultra, your smooth and silky legs will last for weeks."

(38′) 'with Epilady Ultra, the smoothness and silkiness of your legs will last for weeks'

Example (39) is interestingly different from the other utterances considered so far.

(39) "But others have come to regret the perfection she longs for."

(39′) 'others have come to regret longing for the perfection she longs for'

[8] My terminology distinguishing the 'entity' reading from the 'SOA' reading is somewhat infelicitous since in this case the syntactic head noun of the NP denotes a state, rather than an individual proper.

This sentence, which appeared in a TV news story about botched cosmetic surgeries, was intended to convey that she longs for perfection and that others regret their own past longing for perfection. Context established that the others could not have regretted the perfection itself, since none of them had attained it. Here the situation which is the argument of the embedding predicator REGRET does not involve the referent of *she*, the subject NP in the relative clause. In this example, the relative clause both expresses the embedded predication and modifies its head noun, *perfection*. Though attested, this sentence is considered marked by speakers who accept the other examples without question.

1.3.2. *Structural ambiguity and the two interpretations*

In certain sentences the sequence [(spec)–(adj)*–N–XP] inside the VP headed by the embedding predicator is structurally ambiguous. While this fact does no damage to my main points, it does complicate the issue. (40) exemplifies this ambiguity:

(40) "The Florida legislature today eased restrictions on poor women seeking abortions."

(40′) 'the Florida legislature today eased restrictions on the seeking of abortions by poor women'

Here the relevant predicator is the nominalization *restrictions* and its complement is the phrase *poor women seeking abortions*. This string in (40) does have a possible analysis as in (41),

(41) $[_{NP} \ldots [_{AP}$ poor$] [_N$ women$] [_{VP}$ seeking abortions$] \ldots]$

and, on that analysis, has the SOA reading indicated in (40′). It also has the possible structure represented in (42), the 'small-clause' analysis, which would also receive this reading:[9]

(42) $[_{SC} [_{NP} \ldots [_{AP}$ poor$] [_N$ women$]] [_{VP}$ seeking abortions$]]$

Compare (43), which has two syntactic analyses and allows both the entity and the SOA reading (example (21) also displays this ambiguity):

(43) She had friends exposed to the gunfire

---

[9] The sentence was read aloud, and may have been written as *poor women's seeking abortions*, which is even more likely to have a small-clause analysis, cf. . . . *on their seeking abortions.*

The string *friends exposed to the gunfire* could be analyzed either as a NP containing a VP modifier or as a sequence consisting of the NP *friends* and the secondary predicate *exposed to the gunfire*. In the complex-NP parse, the sentence could obviously receive the entity reading, while the SOA reading is available to the secondary-predicate structure without the positing of any additional rule of interpretation. Such a sequence will be ambiguous only when, as in this case, the embedding predicator sanctions both subcategorization frames. In any event, the structural ambiguity exhibited by (20), (40), (43), and any NP which contains a postnominal VP or AP is not a precondition for the SOA reading.[10] But it seems important that many of these sentences, because of their structural and categorial properties, exhibit a kind of ambiguity in which both readings may be entertained simultaneously with no semantic conflict (see Norvig, 1988 for a discussion of this phenomenon).

1.3.3. *Pragmatic contributions to the availability of the reading*

As noted above, there are cases where the two readings are truth-conditionally equivalent; there are also cases where the difference in truth conditions of the two readings may be obscured by either general or contextually determined pragmatic principles. Let us take up (40) again. The entity reading would say that restrictions were placed on a certain class of women, namely poor ones who seek abortions. Presuming by general relevance principles that the modifiers are

---

[10] A further confounding phenomenon is the semantic and pragmatic effect of postposing a modifier when doing so is not grammatically required (viz. McCawley's observation (1988: 378) that a phrasal modifier is more acceptable when its head is adjacent to the head of the modified element). Bolinger (1967: 9–10) noticed that the identical modifier will have different semantic effects depending on whether it is prenominal or postnominal (similar effects can be observed in other languages, notably Romance): 'If an adjective names a quality that is too fleeting to characterize anything, it is restricted (with that reading) to predicative, or to post-adjunct, position. The meaning of *ready* in *The materials ready will be shipped* is excluded from *the ready man (and this has polarized *ready* to the extent that *a ready wit* is not easily interconvertible with ?*His wit is ready*.) Similarly with *handy*: *Are your tools handy?* normally means "Do you have them conveniently at hand?" whereas *a handy tool* normally means a useful one—a tool can hardly be characterized by the fact that it is momentarily within reach.' Bolinger implies here that predication, such as in *Are your tools handy?* produces the same, or a similar, effect as the postnominal modification found in *Just give me any tool handy* (contrast *Just give me any handy tool*). McCawley interprets Bolinger's discussion of these facts to signify that 'prenominal modifiers express "permanent" properties and postnominal modifiers express "ephemeral" properties' (1988: 383–4).

provided for communicative reasons other than simply identifying the relevant class of women, one might reasonably infer that the restrictions have something to do with the seeking of abortions. Given these pragmatic considerations, the entity reading and the SOA reading render essentially the same meaning. However, the inference about the entity reading on which this equivalence stands is cancellable, as (44) shows:

(44) The Florida legislature today eased restrictions on poor women seeking abortions, allowing them now to apply for low-income housing.

Sometimes it is easier to distinguish between the two readings, and pragmatics will favor one reading over the other. Take (45), which differs from (43) not in any properties of the object NP but in semantic properties of the subject:

(45) Gangs of restless youth contribute significantly to the low crime rate.
(46) An older, more stable community contributes significantly to the low crime rate. (= 35)

The preferred reading of (45) is that the youth contribute to a crime rate which is nonetheless low—i.e. the 'entity' reading. Contrast that with the preferred reading of (46), where what is affected is the level of the crime rate. ((45) may be pragmatically odd because of an implied, but not logical, contradiction between *contribute significantly* and *low*.) The same sort of manipulation of (34) can render the entity reading of the NP *people that are homeless:*[11]

(47) By closing up the soup kitchens and running a sweep of our city's parks, we could eliminate the people that are homeless.

The preferred reading of (47) is one in which the people, not the homelessness, are eliminated (from our city, at least). Since no part of the clause receiving the SOA reading in (33) has been altered, this contrast shows that the availability of the reading does not rest on lexical properties of the embedding predicator, the complement NP, or the modifier inside the NP.

---

[11] A radio-show host made a joke which depended on exactly this ambiguity, referring to Bush's criticism of the 'Great Society' programs in the wake of the Los Angeles riots: 'George Bush criticized Lyndon Johnson's policies for not eliminating enough poor people.'

1.4. THE ANALYSIS

1.4.1. *The principle of interpretation*

The examples discussed in Sections 1.3.1–3 show that a sentence including a modified NP can receive the SOA reading under circumstances in which Fillmore's analysis would preclude their acceptability. The availability of the reading does not crucially involve the lexeme HAVE; the head of the modified NP need not refer to an inalienable possession; and the nominal head is not an argument of the embedding predicator. As suggested above, I propose that the sentence that Fillmore discussed is in fact an instance of a type of expression in which the semantic interpretation—'predication semantics'—does not correspond to the interpretation expected on the basis of syntactic form—a 'modification structure'. The following interpretive rule gives a somewhat more formal statement of the relationship between the structure and its semantics.

In a proposition ρ_0 which is expressed by means of the syntactic structure

$$[_{SI} \cdots [_{XPo} \cdots X_0 \cdots [_{NPI} \cdots [_{N}' \cdots [XP_I] \cdots N_I \cdots] \cdots]]]$$

where X_0 is a lexeme which denotes a predicator, XP_I is an immediate constituent of N_I, N_I is the head of NP_I, and NP_I is a complement of X_0, if the X_0 denotes a predicator β in the semantic structure

$$\beta(n_i, \ldots n_k)$$

where n_k denotes a state of affairs (event, etc.), then XP_I may denote a predicate κ which takes the argument σ expressed by NP_I/XP_I (N_I and any additional specifiers and modifiers in NP_I). The result of this predication is a proposition ρ_I with the structure $\kappa(\sigma)$, denoting a state of affairs (event, etc.) which instantiates the argument of n_k of the predicator β.

So ρ_0 will have the predicate-argument structure

$$\beta(\alpha_i, \ldots, \rho_I)$$

where α_i instantiates the argument n_i, and ρ_I instantiates n_k.

1.4.2. *When the SOA reading is sanctioned*

1.4.2.1. *Properties of the argument of the embedded predicator.* So far, nothing I have said accounts for the unacceptability, on the SOA reading, of (48) compared to (49):

(48) *I have a missing five-dollar bill (= (6))
(49) I have a missing tooth (= (1))

I will have only a few comments to make about this question here. I have found only a small number of attested examples of the phenomenon in which a 'modification structure' receives 'predication semantics', and no generalization from such a small number can be made with any security. The small number of examples itself suggests that this discrepancy between syntax and semantics is not widely tolerated. On the other hand, while all the examples in (33–40) were orally produced, many of them involved scripted or otherwise planned speech, and so cannot be considered mere performance errors. Furthermore, people I have polled tend to find nothing remarkable about such sentences, and often find it difficult to discern the noncompositional nature of the SOA reading, even when the entity reading is pragmatically absurd, as it is in (28), (35), and (39). Unless the collection radically underrepresents the range of this phenomenon, there is a paradox between the unremarkability of these sentences and their relative rareness.

It may be misguided even to attempt to find semantic or syntactic factors to preclude the SOA reading, as it may be more a matter of construing the situation in a particular way or of contextualizing it to favor the reading. Farrell Ackerman (p.c.) has suggested that the predication semantics of the modification structure is more acceptable when the embedded proposition asserts or implies a disruption of a canonical situation. Recall that (6), repeated above as (48), is considered unacceptable by Fillmore, but (50) seems much better.

(50) I have a missing Indian-head nickel

This must be because an Indian-head nickel is easily construed as highly individuated and part of a normal state of affairs, as for instance if it belongs to a numismatist's collection. But (48) is equally acceptable when contextualized so that the referent of *five-dollar bill* can be seen as being part of the same kind of collection, especially if the individual denoted is a member of an established set, such as in a sentence like (51):

(51) I have a missing Denver Mint five-dollar bill

This leads us to reconsider Fillmore's hypothesis that inalienable possession is involved in the SOA reading. I have shown that inalienability *per se* is not involved; but if there is a condition on interpretation such as the one Ackerman suggests, sentences involving the disruption of a situation of inalienable possession should always be acceptable, since inalienable possession is a quintessential example of a canonical situation.

Another look at (52) supports this suggestion:

(52) ?I have a missing daughter (= (27))

While this sentence is questionable for some speakers out of context, its acceptability is improved by creating a context in which it describes a disruption of a canonical state or event:

> (53) I came home tonight hoping to have a quiet evening for once, and instead I have a missing daughter and a hysterical husband

It is not obvious that Ackerman's suggestion will work for all the examples I have found, or how it could be distinguished from the general tendency of people to talk about unusual or unexpected events. In particular, sentences like *I hate people who do that!* on the SOA reading do not conform to this condition, since no canonical state is being disrupted. It appears that Ackerman's condition is sufficient (barring independent factors), but not necessary, to make the reading available.

Another property of the embedded predication which appears to affect the availability of the SOA reading for some sentences is placing in the NP a specifier which increases the potential referential specificity of the NP. For instance, using the definite article or a numerical quantifier may interfere with the SOA reading:

> (54) I hate people who do that! (= (37))
> (55) I hate the people who do that!
> (55') #'I hate it when the people do that'
> (56) I've heard of people who do that
> (56') 'I've heard of people doing that'
> (57) I've heard of three people who did that
> (57') #'I've heard of three people doing that'

This fact, so far as it goes, accords with Kluender's (1991: ch. 3) general point that, as a NP acquires greater referential specificity, it achieves greater prominence as a possible argument and interferes with the interpretation of predication in material following it. Kluender claims that (58) is more acceptable than (59) because the increased referential specificity of the nominal precludes the complex structure's interpretation as a complex predicate:

(58) This is a paper that we really need to find someone who understands
(59) This is a paper that we really need to find a linguist who understands

This follows from his Principle of Predication:

Initial argument expressions must be as referentially specific as possible; all heads and specifiers occurring in complex expressions must be as non-specific in reference as possible. (p. 86)

I suggest in the same vein that the more referentially specific a NP is in a modified-NP sentence, the more likely it is to be interpreted as the argument of the embedding predicator, thereby interfering with the interpretation of the embedded proposition as the argument of the embedding predicator.

Still, it is readily apparent that high referential specificity of the nominal is not sufficient to rule out the SOA reading:

(60) I have three missing teeth

Among the attested examples, (33), (35), (36), (38), and (39) all have definite or genitive specifiers, and all receive the SOA reading. It may not be referential specificity itself, but how the increased specificity of the individual fits in with the canonical situation, that is critical. In general, the more sentence departs from Ackerman's condition, the more the increased referential specificity of the NP will interfere with the SOA reading.

If Kluender's Predication Principle is one condition affecting the availability of the SOA reading, then a number of other variables need to be considered, in particular the lexical semantic properties of the embedded predicator. When either the embedding predicator or the embedded predicator is such as to entail the nonexistence of the individual denoted by the noun (as *missing* does here), the entity reading is ruled out by semantic principles, and hence the SOA reading is more easily available irrespective of the potential referential specificity of the NP.[12] As Kluender notes, the effects of specific linguistic factors on the interpretation of a predication are often very subtle, and it may take an accumulation of such factors to render a noticeable effect on the availability of the SOA reading (cf. Kluender 1991: 91 ff.).

1.4.2.2. *Properties of the embedding predicator.* There do seem to be robust semantic constraints on the embedding predicator, if my small

---

[12] However, not all examples with definite specifiers in the NP display such predicators; therefore this cannot be the whole solution either.

sample is indicative. By necessity, all such predicators must be able to take SOA arguments. (That is, no predicator which can only denote a relation between individuals, such as EAT, can be an embedding predicator in a sentence receiving the SOA interpretation.) Additionally, they seem usually to be predicators which assert or entail the existence of that state of affairs, as do HAVE, FIND, LAST, etc., and factive predicators of emotion such as HATE and REGRET. Interestingly, there may be some restriction against the availability of the SOA reading to intensional predicators: most speakers do not readily give (61) the reading (61′):

(61) She imagined her brother's missing toe
(61′) 'she imagined that her brother's toe was missing'

This is despite the fact that (62) can have the reading (62′):

(62) She was born with her family's missing toe
(62′) 'she was born with her family's toe-missingness'[13]

Similarly, DREAM ABOUT, denoting a sleep-state, precludes the reading (63′), though it has the reading (63″):

(63) I dreamed about a female president
(63′) 'I dreamed that we had a female president'
(63″) 'I dreamed about one of our female presidents'

But DREAM OF, denoting a state of anticipation of a possible future situation, does allow the SOA reading:

(64) I dream of a female president
(64′) 'I dream that we will have a female president'

There is some cross-speaker variation among these examples, however, with some speakers finding (63′) a more acceptable interpretation of (63) than (64′) is of (64).

It is clear that conditions which affect the availability of the SOA reading deserve a great deal more study. Perhaps we need to tease apart two issues: first, the conditions under which speakers use a modification structure to express predication semantics, rather than using a structure which more directly mirrors that interpretation; and

[13] On the other hand, it may be that this difference exhibits another manifestation of Kluender's Predication Principles: even though the NPs in both (61) and (62) are formally definite, the one in (62) has type, or generic, reference while the one in (61) has token, or specific, reference; this difference in referential specificity may affect the availability of the SOA reading.

second, the factors which either improve or obscure the availability of that interpretation. There may very well be competing motivations for using or avoiding the modification structure with predication semantics, given the complexity of the structures involved.

1.4.3. *The discourse status of the NP referent*

An interesting fact about the meaning of the nominal in a SOA reading is that, though it does not refer to an entity which has been directly introduced into the discourse, it nevertheless has some intensional status: in particular, it may serve as the antecedent of a pronominal. Keeping in mind that these are constructed examples, we may nonetheless see that the expression denoting the individual can serve as an antecedent, in some cases more readily than others. In the following examples the (*a*) sentences contain a pronominal which refers to the individual denoted by the noun, while the (*b*) sentences contain a pronominal anteceded by the SOA.

(65*a*) I found a missing question mark and put it in
(65*b*) ?I found a missing question mark and fixed it
(66)   The ad said my smooth and silky legs would last for weeks, but
(66*a*) ?they didn't stay that way very long at all
(66*b*) *it didn't stay that way very long at all
(67)   The LSA is trying to eliminate unemployed linguists, but
(67*a*) there are still a lot of us around
(67*b*) ?there is still a lot of it around

I have argued above that the individual denoted by the noun head of the modified NP does not correspond to an argument of the embedding predicator—and indeed that individual need not even exist, as (65) shows; yet it has enough intensional status to serve as the antecedent of a pronominal, often more readily than does the SOA argument of the embedding predicator. In some ways this construction resembles possessor-raising, a construction which in many languages also favors nouns of inalienable possession, and which Fillmore also discusses in this connection (1968: 67 ff.). Perhaps nouns classified as 'inalienable' constitute an easily circumscribed subset of a class of nominals whose semantic properties contribute to the acceptability of various constructions exhibiting systematic discrepancies between syntax and semantics. It is likely that, in some cases at least, this modification structure is employed in preference to a secondary-predication structure (or an NP with a nominalized form of the embedded predicator as the head) in order to play up the thematic prominence in the embedding predication of an entity which bears no logical relation to it. In that respect, this construction is another example of the general possibility of rearranging elements in a sentence, out of strict accord with the predicate-argument structure, but to accommodate both semantic and discourse-pragmatic concerns. Such principles of rearrangement have been one focus of Fillmore's work from the time of 'The Case for Case' to the present.

I.5. CONCLUSION

I hope to have shown here that an apparent difference in the syntactic behavior of alienable and inalienable nouns is actually a small but instructive corner of a more general discrepancy between the semantic structure we expect, based on the syntax manifested by a sentence, and that which is actually found in the sentence. I have proposed that what Fillmore found is not a peculiar property of HAVE or of inalienable nouns, but rather a general possibility for modified NPs to denote a state of affairs rather than an individual or entity. I have only hinted at the conditions under which this discrepant interpretation is favored and those under which it is precluded; this remains a matter for detailed and careful investigation.

The examples I have discussed here are in fact a formally definable subset of the more general phenomenon that many constructions are not interpretable by compositional rules isomorphic to the syntactic structure. It is well known that modifiers do not always compose with their heads in a set-intersection fashion: *warm sweater* 'sweater that makes or keeps its wearer warm' is one kind of exception. But the examples I have discussed here do not simply require a sophisticated understanding of how linguistic expressions index knowledge structures, as *warm sweater* does: here we must make reference to the composition of the meanings of linguistic expressions when those expressions are not in the predicted structural relation to one another.

This oddness is not confined to 'predication semantics' of 'modification structures': it is a more general phenomenon, as we can see from (68) and (69) (collected, respectively, from the *Los Angeles Times* and the *New York Times*):

(68) "This summer, he and more than 2,000 others will lose their jobs when the long-threatened plant's operations are finally moved to Canada."

(68′) '. . . when the long-threatened move to Canada of the plant's operations takes place'
(69) "Some of the things they kept secret were just ridiculous."[14]
(69′) 'of some of those issues, it was ridiculous to keep them secret'

Continued attention to examples of this kind will surely reveal that a
variety of structures is subject to such discrepant readings, and that
what we have discovered is not a state of compositional chaos but the
principled result of the complicated interplay of a number of motivations for sentence construction.

REFERENCES

ALSINA, A. (1992). 'The Monoclausality of Causatives: Evidence from
    Romance,' paper delivered at the Annual Meeting of the Linguistic Society
    of America, Philadelphia.
BAR-HILLEL, Y. (1964). *Language and Information: Selected Essays on Their
    Theory and Application*. Reading, Mass.: Addison-Wesley.
BOLINGER, D. (1967). 'Adjectives in English: Attribution and Predication,'
    Lingua **18**: 1–34.
BRUGMAN, C. (1988). 'The Syntax and Semantics of HAVE and Its
    Complements.' Ph.D. dissertation, University of California at Berkeley.
DONNELLAN, K. (1966), 'Reference and Definite Descriptions,' *Philosophical
    Review* **75**: 281–304.
FILLMORE, C. (1968), 'The Case for Case,' in E. Bach and R. T. Harms (eds.),
    Universals in Linguistic Theory, 1–88. New York: Holt, Rinehart &
    Winston.
—— (1969). 'Toward a Modern Theory of Case,' in D. A. Reibel and S. A.
    Schane (eds.), *Modern Studies in English*. New York: Prentice-Hall, 361–75.
—— (1977). 'The Case for Case Reopened,' in P. Cole and J. Sadock (eds.),
    Syntax and Semantics viii: *Grammatical Relations*, 59–81. New York:
    Academic Press.
JACKENDOFF, R. (1990). *Semantic Structures*. Cambridge, Mass.: MIT Press.
KLUENDER, R. (1991). 'Cognitive Constraints on Variables in Syntax.' Ph.D.
    dissertation, University of California at San Diego.
KURODA, S.-Y. (1972). 'The Categorical and the Thetic Judgment: Evidence
    from Japanese Syntax,' *Foundations of Language* **9**: 153–85.
—— (1990). 'The Categorical and the Thetic Judgment Reconsidered,' in K.
    Mulligan (ed.), *Mind, Meaning and Metaphysics*, 77–88. Amsterdam:
    Kluwer Academic.

---

[14] Notice that the number of the verb agrees with the syntactic head of the NP, not
with the semantic 'head', the predicator RIDICULOUS.

LEHRBERGER, J. (1974). *Functor Analysis of Natural Language*. The Hague: Mouton.

LYONS, J. (1968). *Introduction to Theoretical Linguistics*. Cambridge: Cambridge University Press.

—— (1977). *Semantics*, ii. Cambridge: Cambridge University Press.

MCCAWLEY, J. D. (1988). *The Syntactic Phenomena of English*, ii. Chicago: University of Chicago Press.

NAPOLI, D. J. (1989). *Predication Theory: A Case Study for Indexing Theory*. Cambridge: Cambridge University Press.

NORVIG, P. (1988). 'Interpretation under Ambiguity,' in S. Axmaker and H. Singmaster (eds.), *Proceedings of the Fourteenth Annual Meeting of the Berkeley Linguistics Society*, 188–201.

QUINE, W. V. O. (1960). *Word and Object*. Cambridge, Mass.: MIT Press.

ROTHSTEIN, S. (1985). 'The Syntactic Forms of Predication'. Ph.D. dissertation, MIT. Distributed (1986) by the Indiana University Linguistics Club.

SASSE, H.-J. (1987). 'The Thetic/Categorical Distinction Revisited,' *Linguistics* **25**: 511–80.

SIEGEL, M. (1976), 'Capturing the Russian Adjective', in B. Partee (ed.), *Montague Grammar*, 293–310. New York: Academic Press.

WILLIAMS, E. (1980), 'Predication,' *Linguistic Inquiry* **11**: 203–38.

2

Making One's Way Through the Data

Adele E. Goldberg

INTRODUCTION

A semantic study of the particular clause-level construction which is exemplified by the expressions in 1 seemed to be appropriate for a Festschrift for Chuck Fillmore for a few reasons.

(1*a*) Pat pushed her way out of the room
(1*b*) Volcanic material blasted its way to the surface
(1*c*) The hikers clawed their way to the mountain-top

First, these expressions provide a good example with which to demonstrate the claim that extralexical grammatical *constructions* are required in the grammar, a central claim of Construction Grammar (cf. Fillmore *et al.*, 1988; Fillmore and Kay, 1993). Secondly, because the construction is partially lexically filled (by the noun *way*), it allows easy access to a wealth of corpora data, and Fillmore has been a strong advocate of supplementing speaker intuitions with corpora data for many years. Finally, the construction admits of a fine-grained semantic analysis, the general type of which Fillmore has championed for the last thirty years.

The construction can be skeletally represented as follows, (where V is a non-stative verb, and OBL codes a directional):

I would like to thank Farrell Ackerman, Charles Fillmore, Michael Israel, Rolf Johnson, Paul Kay, Suzanne Kemmer, Jean-Pierre Koenig, George Lakoff, Chris Manning, Eve Sweetser, Annie Zaenen, and the members of my graduate seminar at UCSD for helpful discussion on this topic. I also thank Patrick Hanks for compiling the Oxford University Press examples, and Annie Zaenen for forwarding them to me. All errors are solely my own. This paper was presented at a workshop on complex predicates at Stanford University May, 1993, and will appear in the proceedings of that workshop in a volume, *Complex Predicates*, published by the Center for the Study of Language and Information and edited by Alex Alsina, Joan Bresnan and Peter Sells. An edited version will also appear as Ch. 9 in *Constructions: A Construction Grammar Approach to Argument Structure*, published by University of Chicago Press. I thank both publishers for allowing me to reprint material here.

$$[SUBJ_i [V [POSS_i \, way] \, OBL]]$$

Several large corpora were searched for examples. The majority of the examples (1,050 out of 1,177) are from the Oxford University Press corpus (OUP). Additional examples have been culled from exhaustive searches of the *Wall Street Journal* 1989 corpus (*WSJ*), the Lund corpus consisting of various spoken dialogs (Lund), and the United States Department of Agriculture corpus (USDA).

2.1. THE EXISTENCE OF THE CONSTRUCTION

Instances of this construction entail that the subject referent moves along the path designated by the prepositional phrase. The construction's semantics cannot be fully predicted on the basis of the constituent parts of the construction. For example, (2) entails that Frank moved through the created path out of the prison.

(2) Frank dug his way out of the prison

Similarly, (3) entails that Frank managed to travel to New York.

(3) Frank found his way to New York

However none of the lexical items entails motion. To see this, compare (2) and (3) with (4) and (5) below:

(4) Frank dug his escape route out of prison
(5) Frank found a way to New York

The only interpretation for these examples is one in which the prepositional phrase modifies the direct object. Neither of these examples entails motion:

(4′) Frank dug his escape route out of prison, but he hasn't gone yet
(5′) Frank found a way to New York, but he hasn't gone yet

This is in contrast with examples (2) and (3), which do entail motion:

(2′) *Frank dug his way out of prison but he hasn't gone yet
(3′) *Frank found his way to New York, but he hasn't gone yet

The only difference between (4) and (2) is that *way* is replaced by *escape route*. Example (5) prevents us from postulating that *way* codes motion, because *way* is present in this example, and yet the sentence does not entail motion. Without belaboring the point, it should be noted that motion is not dictated by the combination of bound pronoun and *way* as (6) does not entail motion:

(6) He knows his way around town

Here the entailment of motion is not present because the verb *know* is stative, and the construction requires a non-stative verb.

Salkoff (1988) and Jackendoff (1990) also point out that this construction provides evidence for the claim that verbs do not exclusively determine complement configuration. One solution that Jackendoff proposes is that examples such as those in (1–3) instantiate a particular clause-level construction: a pairing of form and meaning that exists independently of the particular verbs which instantiate it. As he suggests, 'In a sense, the *way*-construction can be thought of as a kind of "constructional idiom", a specialized syntactic form with an idiomatic meaning, marked by the noun *way*' (1990: 221).

Levin and Rapoport (1988) suggest instead that each verb in the construction has a special motion sense, perhaps generated by a lexical rule, which predicts its occurrence in this pattern. However, this pattern occurs with an enormous variety of verbs. For example, we would need to posit such a motion sense for the each of the verbs in the following:

(7a) 'he'd *bludgeoned* his way through, right on the stroke of half-time' (OUP)
(7b) '[the players will] *maul* their way up the middle of the field' (OUP)
(7c) 'glaciers which had repeatedly *nudged* their way between England and Wales' (OUP)

That is, we would need a special sense of *bludgeon* 'to move, by bludgeoning', a special sense of *maul*, 'to move, by mauling', etc. These senses are intuitively implausible. The following examples involving metaphorical motion would be even more difficult to imagine as projections from a lexical subcategorization:

(8a) 'their customers *snorted and injected* their way to oblivion and sometimes died on the stairs' (OUP)
(8b) 'But he consummately *ad-libbed* his way through a largely secret press meeting.' (OUP)
(8c) 'I cannot inhabit his mind nor even *imagine* my way through the dark labyrinth of its distortion.' (OUP)
(8d) 'Lord King craftily *joked and blustered* his way out of trouble at the meeting.' (OUP)

If new senses *were* involved, then it would follow that each of the verbs above would be ambiguous, between its basic sense and its sense in this syntactic pattern. Therefore we would expect that there would be some language that would differentiate the two senses by having two independent verb stems. However, to my knowledge there is no language that has distinct verb stems for any of the meanings that would be required for the examples in (7–8).

In addition to being implausible, positing additional verb senses can be seen to be less parsimonious than associating the semantic interpretation directly to the construction. The reason for this stems from the fact that the proposed senses *only* occur in this construction; they are not available when these verbs are used with other valences:

(9) *Chris bludgeoned/mauled/snorted and injected into the room

The same is not true of verbs which clearly do *lexically* code literal or metaphorical motion, for example, *inch* and *worm*:

(10a) Lucky may have inched ahead of Black Stallion
(10b) He can't worm out of that situation

That is, both *inch* and *worm* can be used as (metaphorical) motion verbs even when they are not used specifically in the *way* construction. Therefore, not only would we need to stipulate the existence of additional senses for each of the verbs in examples (7–8), but we would have to further stipulate the fact that the new verb senses can only occur in this particular syntactic configuration. Instead, it is more parsimonious to attribute the motion interpretation directly to the construction itself. This idea is discussed more fully below.

Given that the interpretation of *way* expressions is not fully predictable from the semantics of the particular lexical items, a constructional analysis will be adopted here. In the theory of Construction Grammar, constructions play a central role in that grammar itself is claimed to consist of a structured inventory of constructions. A 'construction', or 'constructional idiom', can be defined as follows:

C is a Construction iff$_{defn}$ C is a form-meaning pair, $\langle F_i, S_i \rangle$ such that some aspect of F_i or some aspect of S_i is not strictly predictable from C's component parts.

That is, morphemes are instances of constructions in that their form is not predictable (Saussure, 1916), but so are larger phrasal patterns which associate syntax and semantics/pragmatics in an unpredictable way. See Langacker (1987; 1991) for a similar approach, and Goldberg (1995) for arguments in favor of this approach to argument structure.

An explicit statement of the construction will follow a more specific analysis of the construction's semantics, since it will be argued that the syntax of the construction is motivated by its semantics.

2.2. THE SEMANTICS OF THE *way* CONSTRUCTION

2.2.1. *Two different senses*

Both Levin and Rapoport (1988) and Jackendoff (1990) suggest two distinct paraphrases of this construction, one in which the verb designates the means of motion, the other in which the verb designates some other coextensive action or manner.[1] For example, Jackendoff notes that (11) is interpretable in either of the two ways given in (12):

> (11) Sam joked his way into the meeting.
> (12) *a.* Sam got into the meeting by joking. (*means*)
>   *b.* Sam went into the meeting (while) joking. (*manner*)

These paraphrases together are taken to constitute a disjunctive interpretation. However, logical disjunction is completely symmetric, and there are reasons to think that the means and manner interpretations do not have equal status in the grammar—that in fact the means interpretation is primary.

In the Oxford University Press, Lund, *Wall Street Journal*, and Department of Agriculture corpora, verbs which designated a coextensive action or manner, as opposed to the means of motion, were rare. In fact the total number of occurrences was 40 out of 1,177, or less than 4 per cent of the data (the proportion was no more than 4 per cent for any of the corpora).

---

[1] The distinction between means and manner that is used here is slightly different from Talmy's (1985) distinction between 'means' and 'manner' conflation patterns. Talmy used these terms to distinguish verbs which primarily designate an action performed by an agent (e.g. *push*) from those that primarily designate an action of the theme (e.g. *roll*) in sentences such as: (69a) *Joe pushed the barrel down the hill.* (69b) *Joe rolled the barrel down the hill.* Talmy refers to the former as a means conflation pattern and to the latter as a manner conflation pattern. However, both verbs in the above examples would be classified as designating the means of motion for our purposes. In particular, *roll* as well as *push* must designate the means of motion, and cannot designate a contingent coextensive manner. Notice that (69b) could not be used felicitously in the circumstance in which the barrel is being rolled between Joe's hands as Joe walked down the hill (cf. Pinker, 1989; Croft 1991 for further examples of this point). That is, the rolling must crucially be the means of motion (as well as designating a particular manner).

In addition, it is argued below that the syntactic form of the construction is motivated by the semantics associated with the means interpretation. The same cannot be said of the manner interpretation. That is, recognizing a cline of analyzability (or compositionality) of idiomatic expressions (cf. Nunberg *et al.*, 1994; Gibbs, 1990), the means interpretation will be argued to be more analyzable than the manner interpretation.

Finally, not all speakers find the purely manner interpretation acceptable. A case in point is (13), one of Jackendoff's examples:

(13) He belched his way out of the restaurant

When asked for judgments of this sentence, which was intended to have a manner interpretation (that the subject went out of the restaurant while belching), several speakers I checked with concocted situations in which the belching was instead the *means* by which motion was achieved. For example, one speaker suggested that the sentence would be acceptable in the context that the other diners found the belching so objectionable that they cleared a path through which the offending party could exit. Another speaker suggested that the sentence would be acceptable if the belching were understood to be a means of propulsion. Others, including myself, find the manner interpretation only marginal.

In a theory of grammar which postulates certain senses of grammatical constructions as more basic than other senses (e.g. Lakoff, 1987; Goldberg, 1992; 1995), parallel to the basic and extended senses often posited for morphemes and grammatical markers, these facts can be accounted for. We can analyze the manner interpretation as an extension of the more basic means interpretation. This analysis predicts, for example that there are no speakers who accept only the manner interpretation and not the means interpretation. And to date, I have found none.

Interestingly, there is diachronic evidence that the means interpretation of the construction pre-dates the manner interpretation by more than four centuries. The first citation of this pattern in the *OED* is 1400: 'I made my way . . . unto Rome.'[2] The first citation with any

---

[2] There existed other uses of *way* as a direct object previous to this date, e.g. (from the *OED*) *After the enterment the kyng tok his way* (1338), *childe fiet ne dar guo his way vor fie guos fiet blaufi* (1340). These cases are instances of a different construction: the path phrase is not obligatory as it is today, and the interpretation is quite different: these examples meant roughly either 'to go away' or 'to take one's leave'. Notice that the verbs TAKE and GO are no longer acceptable in the construction at all: **He went/took his way*

other verb is 1694: '[he] hew'd out his way by the power of the Sword.' These both encode the means interpretation. The first example cited in the *OED* that involves a purely manner interpretation, 'The muffin-boy rings his way down the little street,' is dated 1836, more than a century after the construction was used productively with a means interpretation, and more than four centuries after the first citation with *make*. The diachronic data, of course, do not directly support the claim that the means interpretation is synchronically more basic; however, they do provide evidence that the extension from means to manner is a reasonable connection for speakers to make, since at least one generation of speakers was willing to extend the pattern in just this way.

To summarize, it has been argued in this section that the means interpretation is the more central or *basic* interpretation of the construction. The manner interpretation has been argued to be a less basic extension, on the grounds that (i) manner examples were rare in each of the four corpora analyzed (ii) speakers' judgments as to the acceptability of the manner cases range from unacceptable to marginal to acceptable, while the means cases are all fully acceptable, and (iii) the means interpretation diachronically preceded the manner interpretation by several centuries. A fourth reason for claiming that the means interpretation is more basic follows from the observation, detailed below, that the syntactic form of the construction can be motivated by the means interpretation, but not by the manner interpretation. In the following, a particular semantic constraint on the means interpretation is proposed: that the motion must be through a literal or metaphorical self-created path. This constraint is argued to play a crucial role in motivating the syntactic form of the construction.

2.2.2. *The means interpretation: creation of a path*

Jespersen (1949) had the basic insight that the direct object, POSS *way*, was a type of 'object of result'. This can be interpreted to mean that the path (the *way*) through which motion takes place is not pre-established, but rather is *created* by some action of the subject referent. This observation can be used to account for the fact that, with the exception of the purely manner interpretation, the construction is used to convey that the subject moves despite some external difficulty,

to the beach. See Israel (forthcoming) for a detailed history of the origins of the construction.

or in some indirect way: the path is not already pre-established, but must in some sense be created by the mover. For example:

(14) Sally made her way into the ballroom.

This sentence is understood to imply that Sally moved through a crowd or other obstacles. It cannot be used to mean that Sally simply walked into an empty ballroom. In the case of metaphorical motion, the necessity of creating a path implies that there is some difficulty or metaphorical barrier involved. For example, notice also the difference in acceptability between the following:

(15a) ??Sally drank her way through the glass of lemonade.
(15b) Sally drank her way through a case of vodka.

Example (15b) is much more acceptable because it is much easier to construe drinking a case of vodka than drinking a glass of lemonade as requiring that some barrier be overcome.

In fact, the most common interpretation of this construction involves motion through a crowd, mass, obstacles, or other difficulty— i.e. there is some reason why a path needs to be created. The verb either lexically subcategorizes for the construction (e.g. *make*) or designates the *means* by which this motion is achieved. For example:

(16) 'For the record, Mr. Klein, as lead climber for the *Journal* team, pushed his way past the others, trampling the lunch of two hikers in his black army boots, and won the race to the summit.' (*WSJ*)
(17) 'In some cases, passengers tried to fight their way through smoke-choked hallways to get back to their cabins to get their safety jackets.' (*WSJ*)
(18) 'For hours, troops have been shooting their way through angry, un-armed mobs.' (*WSJ*)

Certain verbs, e.g. *thread, wend, weave*, encode a slightly different interpretation. They involve deliberate, careful, methodical, or winding motion. In these cases as well as in the cases which involve some external difficulty, the subject is not moving along a pre-established path. For example:

(19) 'This time, with no need to thread his way out, he simply left by the side door for a three-day outing.' (*WSJ*)
(20) 'A couple in fashionable spandex warm-up suits jogs by, headphones jauntily in place, weaving their way along a street of fractured and fallen houses.' (*WSJ*)

The fact that the construction entails that a path is created to effect motion, i.e. that the motion takes place despite some kind of external difficulty or is winding and indirect, accounts for why high frequency, monomorphemic (basic or superordinate level) motion verbs are typically unacceptable in this construction:

(21) *She went/walked/ran her way to New York (Napoli, cited by Jackendoff, 1990)
(22) *She stepped/moved her way to New York

These basic motion verbs do not normally imply that there is any difficulty or indirect motion involved, an implication which is required by the means interpretation of the construction. (Note that the manner interpretation is also unavailable since these verbs do not code any salient manner.) If a context is provided in which a basic-level motion verb is understood to imply motion despite difficulty, these cases are decidedly better:

(23*a*) The novice skier walked her way down the ski slope
(23*b*) The old man walked his way across the country to earn money for charity.

Another case in which a (metaphorical) path may need to be created is given if there are social obstacles standing in the way. Contrast the following examples:

(24*a*) #Welcome our new daughter-in-law who just married her way into our family
(24*b*) Welcome our new daughter-in-law who just married into our family

Example (24*a*) is pragmatically odd because it implies that the daughter-in-law in question managed to get herself into the family by marriage, and such an implication is incongruent with a sincere welcome. The following example is relevantly similar:

(25) Joe bought his way into the exclusive country club

This example entails that Joe managed to get himself into the country club despite social obstacles. The necessity of the metaphorical creation of one's own path despite social obstacles can account for the implication that the subject referent used some unsanctioned means to attain his goal. That is, if there are social obstacles preventing one from attaining a goal, the only way to attain the goal is to violate the social constraints. Attested examples of this class included *bribe, bluff, crapshoot, wheedle, talk, trick, con, nose, sneak, weasel, cajole, inveigle*.

Several lexical items seem to lexicalize this sense, for example: *worm, weasel*, and *wrangle*.

The claim then is that *way* is analyzable as a literal or metaphorical path that is created by the action denoted by the verb. This accounts for the semantic constraint that the motion is effected despite some external physical or social obstacle, by forging a path through or around these external obstacles.

Support for the claim that *way* is analyzed as a meaningful element comes from the fact that it can appear with modifiers. The following examples are attested:

> (26*a*) 'the goats wending their familiar way across the graveyard' (OUP)
> (26*b*) '[he] decided from then onwards that he could make his own way to school' (OUP)

In (26*a*) *familiar* is a modifier of *way*—i.e. the path is familiar. Similarly, in (26*b*) *way* is internally modified by *own*. These facts argue that the phrase POSS *way* is not an arbitrary syntactic tag of the construction, but rather plays a role in the semantics of the construction.

Further support for the claim that the construction, at least historically, was associated with the creation of a path comes from the fact noted above that the verb *make*, a verb which normally means 'create,' has had a privileged status with respect to this construction: this verb was used in the construction for almost three centuries before the construction was extended to be used with other verbs, according to citations in the *OED*.

Make continues to be closely associated with the construction insofar as it is used with greater frequency than any other single verb, accounting for 20 per cent of the tokens. This suggests that *make* may well have a privileged status synchronically as well.

Finally, the recognition that the *way* is an effected entity motivates the syntactic form of the construction. As stated at the beginning of this chapter, Jackendoff notes that there are reasons to assign the construction the structure:

$$[\text{SUBJ}_i\,[\text{V}\,[\text{POSS}_i\,way]\,\text{OBL}]\,],$$

He argues that the NP, POSS *way* is argued to be a direct object, rather than some kind of syntactic adjunct or measure phrase, because nothing can intervene between the V and this phrase (Jackendoff, 1990: 212):

> (27) *Bill belched noisily his way out of the restaurant

The OBL phrase coding the path is argued to be a sister of the verb, and not a modifier of *way* on the grounds that an adverb may intervene between the two complements, indicating a constituency break:

(28*a*) Bill belched his way noisily out of the restaurant (Jackendoff, 1990: 212)

(28*b*) 'He made his way cautiously along the path beside the lake.' (OUP)

Given the semantics of the means interpretation described above, the construction can be viewed as a kind of conventionalized amalgam which combines the syntax and semantics of creation expressions such as (29) which have two arguments, a *creator* and a *created entity*,

(29) He made a path

with the intransitive motion construction exemplified by (29) which has two arguments, a *mover* (*theme*) and a *path*:

(30) He moved into the room

The *way* construction syntactically and semantically amalgamates these two constructions into a structure with three complements: the *creator–theme*, the *created–way*, and the *path*. That is, the *way* construction can be viewed as inheriting aspects of both the creation and the motion constructions, but as existing as an independent construction in its own right.

The semantics involves both the creation of a path and movement along that path. As has been argued to generally be the case for clause-level constructions (Goldberg, 1995), the verb may, but need not necessarily, code the semantics associated with the construction directly. Cases in which the verb does directly code the semantics of the construction include *worm*, *inch*, and *work*. In other cases, the verb may designate the means of effecting the action designated by the construction; that is to say, the verb may code the means of effecting motion through a self-created path. This is represented in Fig. 2.1 by the means link between PRED, representing the verb sense and the CREATE–MOVE predicate.

$$
\begin{bmatrix}
\text{Sem.:} & \text{CREATE–MOVE} & \text{(creator–theme,} & \text{created–way,} & \text{path)} \\
 & |\,\text{means} & | & | & | \\
 & \text{PRED} & (& &) \\
 & \Downarrow & \Downarrow & \Downarrow & \Downarrow \\
\text{Syn.:} & \text{V} & \text{SUBJ}_i & \text{OBJ}_{\text{way}_i} & \text{OBL}
\end{bmatrix}
$$

Fig. 2.1.

Any argument that the verb obligatorily expresses must be 'fused' (in the sense of Jackendoff, 1990 or Goldberg, 1995) with one of the arguments associated with the construction. This possibility is notated by the vertical lines between the construction's argument structure array and the verb's (PRED's) argument array. For example, the verb *push* has one obligatory argument, the 'pusher'. This argument is fused with the creator–theme argument of the construction, (a pusher can be construed as a type of creator–theme). Both the createe–way and the path phrase are contributed by the construction.

The fused composite structure represented in Fig. 2.2 yields expressions such as *The demonstrators pushed their way into the building*.

$$
\begin{bmatrix}
\text{Sem.:} & \text{CREATE–MOVE} & \text{(creator–theme,} & \text{created–way,} & \text{path)} \\
& |\ \text{means} & | & | & | \\
& \text{push} & \text{(pusher} & &) \\
& \Downarrow & \Downarrow & \Downarrow & \Downarrow \\
\text{Syn.:} & \text{V} & \text{SUBJ}_i & \text{OBJ}_{way_i} & \text{OBL}
\end{bmatrix}
$$

Fig. 2.2.

The verb *lurch* has two obligatory arguments, a lurcher, and a path. These two arguments are fused with the creator–theme and path arguments of the construction, respectively. In this case the direct object argument, the created–way, is contributed by the construction. The fused composite structure licenses expressions such as *The drunk lurched his way out of the betting shop*.

$$
\begin{bmatrix}
\text{Sem.:} & \text{CREATE–MOVE} & \text{(creator–theme,} & \text{created–way,} & \text{path)} \\
& |\ \text{means} & | & | & | \\
& \text{lurch} & \text{(lurcher} & & \text{path)} \\
& \Downarrow & \Downarrow & \Downarrow & \Downarrow \\
\text{Syn.:} & \text{V} & \text{SUBJ}_i & \text{OBJ}_{way_i} & \text{OBL}
\end{bmatrix}
$$

Fig. 2.3.

The syntactic form of the construction, although given in Figs. 2.1–2.3, does not actually require much stipulation. The fact that the construction takes the syntactic form it does is strongly motivated by general principles. That is, the POSS *way* phrase is linked to direct object, because effected entities are generally direct objects. The fact that the path argument is linked to an adverbial directional follows from the fact that it is coding a path. The fact that the creator–theme is linked to subject follows from the fact that creators and self-propelling themes are generally linked to subject. It is only necessary to state that the created–way argument must be realized in a particular fixed way: by the bound pronoun plus *way*. Thus, little needs to be stipulated about the syntax of the construction, once its special semantic properties are captured.

To summarize, the recognition that the path of motion is not pre-established and must be created by the mover accounts for the fact that the means interpretation of the construction always entails that the subject referent moves despite external difficulty or in some indirect way. This observation allows us to analyze *way* as a meaningful element, designating the path of motion. It also allows us to account for the fact that *make*, a verb which in its basic sense means 'create', has a privileged status both diachronically (in being the first verb to be used in the construction) and synchronically (in being the most frequently used verb in this construction). Finally, recognition that *way* designates an effected entity allows us to motivate the syntactic form of the construction.

2.2.3. *The manner interpretation*

The following attested examples do not admit of a means interpretation:

(31) '[They were] clanging their way up and down the narrow streets' (OUP)

(32) 'the commuters clacking their way back in the twilight towards' (OUP)

(33) 'She climbed the stairs to get it, crunched her way across the glass-strewn room' (OUP)

(34) 'He seemed to be whistling his way along.' (OUP)

(35) 'he was scowling his way along the fiction shelves in pursuit of a book.' (OUP)

For example, (31) does not entail that the clanging was the *means* of the motion, only that it was the co-occurring manner. Again, not all speakers accept this type of example, but many do, at least marginally.

While many of the attested manner cases involve motion in the face of some external difficulty or obstacles, just like the means cases, this does not seem to be a general constraint on the interpretation of the manner cases. Examples (32) and (34), for instance, do not imply any external difficulties. It is because of this that the syntax is claimed to be less analyzable in the case of the manner interpretation: there is no necessary implication that a path must be created. The manner interpretation only entails that the the subject referent moves along a (possibly pre-established) path. Thus the *way* phrase in direct object position is not motivated. It is predicted that internal modification of *way* in the manner interpretation should be less acceptable than in the means interpretation. And in fact this prediction seems to be borne out:

(36a) ??Joe whistled his own way to the street (*manner*)
(36b) Joe dug his own way to the street (*means*)

The interpretation associated with this sense can be represented as in Fig. 2.4. The construction designates a two-place relation; the *way* phrase is not represented in the semantics of the construction, but is instead encoded as a syntactic stipulation about the form of the direct object complement.

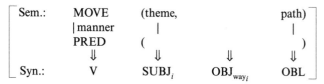

Fig. 2.4.   The *way* construction: manner interpretation.

2.2.4. *Constructional polysemy*

It has been argued that the manner interpretation is an extension of the more basic means interpretation. The relationship between the two senses is represented in Fig. 2.5. The arrow between the two constructions, notated as an I_p link, is a special type of inheritance link: a polysemy inheritance link. The arrow specifies that there is a systematic relationship between the two senses, in that the form is inherited

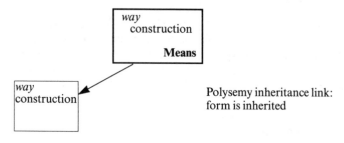

Fig. 2.5.

from the means case by the manner case. The same link can be used between different but related senses of the same lexical item, and in fact captures what we mean by polysemy: the same form is identified with different but related senses (see Goldberg, 1995 for discussion of this and other types of inheritance link).

The claim that this is a case of constructional polysemy raises a question: what is the relationship between means and manner that allows manner to become an extension? Note that the means and manner of a motion event are often coextensive in that the means of motion often determines the manner of motion. For example, consider the use of *roll* in (37):

(37) Joe rolled the ball into the room

In this example the verb specifies not only the means of motion (Joe caused the ball to move by rolling) but also the manner of motion (Joe caused the ball to move while rolling). The same is true of many motion verbs, e.g. *float, wiggle, jump, skip*. It is likely that the polysemy was created when speakers began to decouple these two often co-occurrent features. This type of decoupling is in fact a known source of *lexical* polysemy (cf. Traugott, 1989).

In order to further motivate the link between means and manner, note that this construction does not provide the only instance of this particular polysemy in the language. English *with* is used both as an instrumental or means marker and as a marker of manner:[3]

(38) Bob cut the bread with a knife (*means*)
(39) Bob cut the bread with care (*manner*)

How is similarly polysemous:

(40) How did you cut the turkey? *Answer*:
(40*a*) with a knife (*means*)
(40*b*) carefully (*manner*)

Interestingly, the noun *way* itself is polysemous between means and manner senses. An example in which *way* is used to mean 'means' is:

(41) Pat found a way to solve the problem

Way is used to mean 'manner' in (42):

(42) He had a pleasant way about him

---

[3] I thank Michael Israel for this observation.

It is possible that this latter fact has encouraged the use of this particular construction with a strict manner interpretation, although it is somewhat unclear how this parallelism between the polysemy of *way* and the polysemy of the construction may be represented.

To summarize, attested examples involving a manner interpretation—that is, a purely coextensive activity, not causally related to the motion—while rare, do exist. These cases do not necessarily involve motion despite obstacles or indirect motion. Therefore there is no reason to think that these examples indicate the creation of a path, and thus the syntactic expression of POSS *way* is not motivated directly by the semantics of the manner extension. Instead, the manner sense of the construction was argued to be an extension of the more basic means sense. The link between means and manner was motivated by noting several instances of similar lexical polysemy, including the polysemy of the noun *way* itself.

2.3. SEMANTIC CONSTRAINTS

2.3.1. *Unbounded activity*

There is a constraint that the verb necessarily designate a repeated action or unbounded activity (Jackendoff, 1990):

- (43*a*) Firing wildly, Jones shot his way through the crowd
- (43*b*) *With a single bullet, Jones shot his way through the crowd
- (44*a*) Bill punched his way through the crowd by pummelling everyone in his path
- (44*b*) *Bill punched his way through the crowd by leveling the largest man and having everyone else step aside

For the same reason, we find the following to be unacceptable:

- (45) *She dove her way into the fire
- (46) *She jumped her way over the ditch

This constraint also seems to hold of the manner interpretation. For example, consider (47):

- (47) He hiccupped his way out of the room

This sentence entails that there were a series of hiccups occurring over time, rather than a single hiccup.

2.4.2. *Self-propelled motion*

A further constraint on the means interpretation is that the motion must be self-propelled:[4]

(48) *The wood burns its way to the ground

(49) *The butter melted its way off the turkey

This constraint serves to rule out the use in the construction of verbs which are commonly classified as unaccusative (Perlmutter, 1978; Burzio, 1986), since unaccusativity has been argued to be correlated with the lack of agentivity or lack of self-initiation (Van Valin 1990; Levin and Rappaport Hovav 1990; Zaenen, 1993). However it seems that the relevant constraint is semantic, insofar as the normally unaccusative verbs *grow* and *shrink* are attested in the data, with an agentive interpretation:

(50) 'The planned purchase furthers Bull's strategy of trying to grow its way out of its extensive computer-marketing problems.' (*WSJ*)

(51) 'The bank-debt restructuring is the centerpiece of Lomas Financial's months-long effort to shrink its way back to profitability after two straight years of heavy losses.' (*WSJ*)

The subject referent need not be volitional, or even human as long as the motion is construed as self-propelled:[5]

(52) 'sometimes it [the cyst] forces its way out of the ((plumpton)) at the top.' (USDA)

(53) 'The large seeds sprout quickly and dependably and the strong seedlings can push their way through crusted soil.' (USDA)

There are two lexical exceptions to the constraint that the motion must be self-propelled: *work* and *find*:

(54) 'The spending bills working their way through Congress don't present much of a problem in terms of the Gramm–Rudman law.' (*WSJ*)

(55) 'Bolivia estimated that about half its sacred textiles had been smuggled out of Bolivia and had found their way into American collections.' (*WSJ*)

---

[4] It seems that for some speakers, myself included, this constraint is strengthened in the case of human movers to a constraint that the motion must be volitional (although the motion may terminate at an unintended location): (70) % *She tripped her way down the stairs.*

[5] Jackendoff, however includes the following example: (71) *The barrel rolled its way up the alley* (1990: 212). I find this example unacceptable, and I suspect that Jackendoff may have had a personification interpretation in mind because he further includes the following: (72) *The barrel rolled its ponderous way up the alley*, which he paraphrases as (73) 'The barrel, ponderous (as an elephant), went up the alley rolling' (p. 217).

Find in this use is further distinguished from the general case in that only the goal or endpoint of the path can be made explicit—the route itself may not be expressed.[6] This is evident from the fact that examples with an explicit path are unacceptable:

(56) *The textiles found their way through customs
(57) *The statements found their way toward the right people

The constraint that the motion must be self-propelled does not seem to hold of the manner interpretation, as attested by the following manner example, which does not involve self-propelled motion:

(58) ' "I knitted my way across the Atlantic," he reveals.' (OUP)

However, even in this case, the action designated by the verb, i.e. the knitting, is performed agentively. Speakers only accept manner examples in which the action designated by the verb is self-initiated (otherwise such speakers would be able to give examples (48) and (49) a manner interpretation, and they do not).

2.3.3. *Directed motion*

Related to the constraint that the motion must be self-propelled is the fact that the motion must be directed: it cannot be aimless motion. This accounts for the unacceptability in some dialects of the following examples.

(59) *She wandered her way over the field
(60) *She meandered her way through the crowds

Notice that it is actually not possible to state the constraint as a constraint on a class of verbs *per se*, because the constraint applies to nondirected motion expressed by means of prepositions such as *among* as well:

(61) *Joe shoved his way among the crowd
      (Joe shoved his way through the crowd)

This constraint also does not strictly hold of the manner interpretation, although there may be a tendency to prefer directed motion. Dialects which allow the purely manner interpretation differ as to the acceptability of (59–61), with some accepting them fully and others marginally.

---

[6] I thank Charles Fillmore for this observation.

2.4. *The lexical complex-predicate approach*

In addition to suggesting a constructional analysis of the *way* expressions, Jackendoff (1990) proposes an alternative solution. He does not decide between the two proposals. The alternative proposal is that verbs which appear in the construction undergo a lexical rule, turning e.g. *push* into *push* POSS *way*. The complex predicate *push* POSS *way* could then be argued to select for a path argument.

The problem with this proposal is that POSS *way* is not only an N, but an NP. Therefore the complex predicate analysis would have to posit a maximal phrase internal to a word. Recent incorporation proposals (e.g. Baker, 1988) have allowed incorporated proforms, but not full NPs complete with determiners and optional modification.

One might argue that the NP is unanalyzed, and is therefore simply a string that forms part of the complex predicate. Support for this idea might be drawn from the fact that, as Jackendoff notes, modifiers of *way* often have only an external (adverbial) interpretation:

(62a) Bill joked his insidious way into the meeting (Jackendoff, 1990)
(meaning) 'Insidiously, Bill joked his way into the meeting'

(62b) '[They] make their noisy way along the Rue Saint Antoine' (OUP)
'They noisily make their way along the Rue Saint Antoine'

(62c) 'They made their weary way home.' (OUP)
'They wearily made their way home'

However, there is reason to think that POSS *way* is analyzed syntactically and semantically as a maximal noun phrase. First, it has the normal internal structure of a noun phrase, and is not idiosyncratic syntactically in any way. Also, the possessive phrase is controlled by the subject, and thus its realization is not predetermined.

The fact that internal modification of *way* is possible, as in examples (26a–b) repeated here, further supports the claim that the noun *way* is meaningful, since being meaningful is a prerequisite to being available for modification:

(63a) 'the goats wending their familiar way across the graveyard' (OUP)
(63b) '[he] decided from then onwards that he could make his own way to school' (OUP)

That is, if *way* were simply a semantically empty syntactic marker of the construction, modifiers such as *familiar* or *own* would be impossible to interpret.

To summarize, the fact that the postverbal NP is analyzed as a maximal noun phrase argues against the move to treat the verb + POSS *way* phrase as a complex predicate formed by a lexical rule. One could admittedly take the tack of looking such cases in the eye and calling them lexical items, or perhaps 'functional words' (in the sense of Ackerman and Webelhuth, forthcoming, or Mohanan, 1990; cf. also Zwicky, 1990), but this move would in effect equate 'lexical item' with what we are here calling 'construction.' That is, a 'lexical item' would be any item that must be listed, i.e. a *listeme* in the sense of DiSciullo and Williams (1987). If this were done, it would become impossible to distinguish the complex predicate analysis from the alternative proposal made by Jackendoff, and defended here, that the *way* examples are instantiations of a particular extralexical construction.

2.5. RELATION TO RESULTATIVES

Marantz (1992) points out that the *way* construction bears a certain similarity to the so-called 'fake' object resultatives exemplified by:

(64*a*) He cried his eyes red
(64*b*) He talked himself hoarse

In both the *way* construction, and this construction, the direct object complement is not normally an argument of the verb. In addition, both constructions disfavor unaccusative verbs (cf. Section 2.3). Marantz does not propose a specific account of 'fake' object cases, but in fact they also admit of a constructional analysis (cf. Goldberg, 1991).

Specifically, Marantz claims that 'the path named by *way* . . . is the person named by the possessor of *way* extended in space (and time)' (1992: 185). This proposal allows Marantz to predict the existence of what I am calling external modification (cf. examples (62*a–c*)), since on Marantz's account these examples would actually involve normal internal modification. For example, (62*c*), *They made their weary way home*, involves *weary* modifying *way*, and *way*, on Marantz's account, is claimed to designate the movers. That is, the *way* = 'the movers' are weary.

It is possible to reinterpret Marantz's claim to make it stronger. 'Fake' object cases have been argued to preferentially involve reflexives or inalienably possessed terms, specifically body-part terms (Jackendoff, 1990). It might be argued that *way*, while in fact coding the path (and not the mover), designates an inalienably possessed entity; i.e. wherever a person's *way* is, the person must travel. Support for this idea might be drawn from a certain finding in Guaraní (Velásquez-Castillo, 1993). Guaraní has a special noun-incorporation construction that, with few exceptions, only allows the incorporation of inalienably possessed terms, primarily body-part terms. Interestingly, one of the few non-body-part terms that is allowed is the term *hape*, translated as 'way.' (Other non-body part terms include the terms for 'talk,' 'house,' and 'clothes'.) This fact supports the idea that 'way' is interpretable as an inalienably possessed path.

What exactly does it mean to say that a path is inalienably possessed? The interpretation that the path (the way) is created by the mover as the mover travels provides an answer: the path exists only where the the mover travels because it is created by the traveler. The path is therefore inalienable.

On this reinterpretation of Marantz's proposal, we can no longer directly account for the fact that external modification is allowed in this construction, a fact that was predicted by Marantz. While a full explanation will have to be postponed, it is possible to reduce this problem to a previously unsolved problem. It seems that *way* can occur with external modification, even when appearing in another construction, a construction in which *way* clearly does not designate the mover:

(65) 'Rearmament proceeded on its gentle way.' (OUP)

It is likely that the use of external modification is motivated by the use of *way* meaning 'manner' as in:

(66) He spoke in his amusing/eloquent/interminable way

While it is important to recognize the relationship between the *way* construction and 'fake' object resultatives, it is nonetheless necessary to posit a distinct, albeit related, construction in the grammar to account for the *way* examples. In particular, the following differences between the two constructions remain; these differences prevent us from claiming that the two are actually the *same* construction. As observed above, the *way* construction is available for use with a wide variety of verbs, whereas resultatives in general, and 'fake' object resultatives in particular, are highly restrictive. For example, the 'fake' object resultative analogs of the examples in (7) and (8) are unacceptable:

(67a) *He bludgeoned himself crazy
with a 'fake' object interpretation whereby he bludgeoned (people in general) until he went crazy

(67*b*) *He mauled himself silly
        (meaning) 'He mauled (people) until he became silly'
(67*c*) *He snorted and injected himself dead

Another difference between the *way* construction and 'fake' object resultatives is that the former at least marginally allows a manner interpretation, whereas resultatives do not:

(68) *Joe whistled himself out of the room
      'Joe whistled his way out of the room'

Moreover, the resultative construction cannot be used to predict the interpretation of a path being created in the *way* expressions, i.e. that the speaker must construe there to be difficulty or obstacles to the motion. Finally, Dutch is a language which has fake object resultatives, and yet does not have the *way* construction (Annie Zaenen, p.c.). Because of these various differences, the *way* expressions cannot be directly assimilated to the resultative construction.

2.6. CONCLUSION

This paper has argued that it is necessary to posit an extralexical grammatical construction in the grammar to account for *way* expressions, since the sentential semantics is not naturally attributed to any of the lexical items' inherent semantics. In particular, no single lexical item can be plausibly assigned responsibility for the motion interpretation, or the other semantic constraints detailed in sections 2.2.1 and 2.3. It is claimed, therefore, that the *way* construction is directly associated with a certain semantics independently of the lexical items which instantiate it. This then goes against the current trend of placing an increased emphasis on lexical, particularly verbal, semantics and trying to predict overt complement configuration exclusively from the lexical semantics of the main verb (cf. e.g. Levin and Rapoport, 1988; Bresnan and Kanerva, 1989; Pinker, 1989; Grimshaw, 1990).

The analysis of the *way* construction given here extends Jackendoff's similar proposal insofar as the extralexical constructional analysis was argued to be more appropriate than a complex predicate analysis. In addition, the noun *way* has been argued to contribute to the semantics of the means interpretation, instead of being simply a syntactic flag of the construction. On this basis it was suggested that the *way* construction is a conventionalized amalgam of two constructions: the creation construction and the intransitive-motion construction. The *way* construction demonstrates the need to recognize *constructional polysemy*, parallel to the polysemy often posited for lexical items and grammatical morphemes.

It has been argued that we need to allow for certain senses of constructions to be more basic (or prototypical) than others. In particular, the means interpretation of the construction was argued to be more basic than the manner interpretation, in that (i) it is accepted by all speakers, while judgments about the manner interpretation vary widely, (ii) it accounted for 96 per cent of the cases in the database analyzed, and (iii) it was argued to motivate the syntactic form of the construction. Motivation for the manner interpretation was given by noting a similar pattern of polysemy in certain lexical items. In a theory of grammar such as Construction Grammar, which posits no strict division between the lexicon and the rest of grammar, such a parallelism between lexical and constructional polysemy is natural and, indeed, expected.

REFERENCES

ACKERMAN, F., and WEBELHUTH, G. (forthcoming). *Wordhood and Syntax: The Theory of Complex Predicates*. Stanford, Calif.: Center for the Study of Language and Information.

BAKER, M. C. (1988). *Incorporation: A Theory of Grammatical Function Changing*. Chicago: University of Chicago Press.

BRESNAN, J., and KANERVA, J. (1989). 'Locative Inversion in Chichewa,' *Linguistic Inquiry* **20**: 1–50.

BURZIO, L. (1986). *Italian Syntax: A Government and Binding Approach*. Dordrecht: Reidel.

CROFT, W. (1991). *Syntactic Categories and Grammatical Relations*. Chicago: University of Chicago Press.

DI SCIULLO, A.-M. and WILLIAMS, E. (1987). *On the Definition of Word*. Cambridge, Mass.: MIT Press.

FILLMORE, C., and KAY, P. (1993). 'Construction Grammar.' MS, University of California at Berkeley.

—— —— and O'CONNOR, C. (1988), 'Regularity and Idiomaticity in Grammatical Constructions: The Case of *Let Alone*,' *Language* **64**: 501–38.

GIBBS, R. (1990). 'Psycholinguistic Studies on the Conceptual basis of Idiomaticity,' *Cognitive Linguistics* **1**: 417–52.

GOLDBERG, A. E. (1991). 'A Semantic Account of Resultatives'. *Linguistic Analysis* **21/1–2**: 66–96.

—— (1992). 'The Inherent Semantics of Argument Structure: The Case of the English Ditransitive Construction,' *Cognitive Linguistics* 3/1: 37–74.

—— (1995). *Constructions: A Construction Grammar Approach to Argument Structure*. Chicago: University of Chicago Press.

GRIMSHAW, J. (1990). *Argument Structure*. Cambridge, Mass.: MIT Press.

ISRAEL, M. (forthcoming). 'The Way Constructions Grow', in A. Goldberg (ed.), *Conceptual Structure, Discourse, and Language*. Stanford, Calif.: Center for the Study of Language and Information.

JACKENDOFF, R. (1990). *Semantic Structures*. Cambridge, Mass.: MIT Press.

JESPERSEN, O. (1949). *A Modern English Grammar on Historical Principles*, vi: *Syntax*. Copenhagen: Munksgaard.

LAKOFF, G. (1987). *Women, Fire, and Dangerous Things: What Categories Reveal About the Mind*. Chicago: University of Chicago Press.

LANGACKER, R. (1987). *Foundations of Cognitive Grammar*, i. Stanford, Calif.: Stanford University Press.

—— (1991). *Foundations of Cognitive Grammar*, ii. Stanford, Calif.: Stanford University Press.

LEVIN, B., and RAPOPORT, T. (1988). 'Lexical Subordination,' *Chicago Linguistic Society* 24/1: 275–89.

—— and HOVAV, M. (1990). 'The Lexical Semantics of Verbs of Motion: The Perspective from Unaccusativity,' MS, Northwestern University and Bar Ilan University.

MARANTZ, A. (1992). 'The *Way*-construction and the Semantics of Direct Arguments in English: A Reply to Jackendoff,' in *Syntax and Semantics* xxvi: *Syntax and the Lexicon*, 179–188. New York: Academic Press.

MOHANAN, T. (1990). 'Arguments in Hindi.' Dissertation, Stanford University.

NUNBERG, G., SAG, I. A., and WASOW, T. (1994). 'Idioms,' *Language* 70/3: 491–538.

PERLMUTTER, D. M. (1978). 'Impersonal Passives and the Unaccusative Hypothesis,' *Proceedings of the Fourth Annual Meeting of the Berkeley Linguistics Society* 157–89.

PINKER, S. (1989). *Learnability and Cognition: The Acquisition of Argument Structure*. Cambridge, Mass.: MIT Press.

SALKOFF, M. (1988). 'Analysis by Fusion,' in *Lingvisticae Investigationes* 12/1: 49–84.

SAUSSURE, F. DE (1916). *Cours de Linguistique Générale*. Repr. Paris: Payot, 1973. Translated by W. Baskin, New York: McGraw-Hill, 1976.

TALMY, L. (1985), 'Lexicalization Patterns: Semantic Structure in Lexical Forms,' in T. Shopen (ed.), *Language Typology and Syntactic Description*, iii: *Grammatical Categories and the Lexicon*, 57–149. Cambridge: Cambridge University Press.

TRAUGOTT, E. (1989), 'On the Rise of Epistemic Meanings in English: An Example of Subjectification in Semantic Change,' *Language* 65/1: 31–55.

VAN VALIN, R. D., JR. (1990). 'Semantic Parameters of Split Intransitivity,' *Language* **66/2**: 221–60.

VELÁSQUEZ-CASTILLO, M. (1993). 'The Grammar of Inalienability: Possession and Noun Incorporation in Paraguayan Guaraní.' Dissertation, University of California at San Diego.

ZAENEN, A. (1993). 'Unaccusativity in Dutch: Integrating Syntax and Lexical Semantics,' in J. Pustejovsky (ed.), *Semantics and the Lexicon*, 129–61. Dordrecht: Kluwer.

ZWICKY, A. (1990). 'Syntactic Words and Morphological Words, Simple and Composite,' *Yearbook of Morphology* **3**: 201–16.

3

Toward a Description of *Te*-linkage in Japanese

Yoko Hasegawa

INTRODUCTION

Since the work of Grice (1975), it has been widely accepted that there are two types of meaning for any given utterance: what is *asserted* and what is *implicated*. One salient example of the assertion/implication distinction involves the English conjunction *and*. In *and*-linked sentences, the *and–then* reading emerges naturally if the first conjunct can be interpreted as perfective. The same temporal sequentiality can also arise, however, even when the two clauses are copresent paratactically without *and*. The semantic relation of Temporal Sequence, accordingly, should not be attributed to the conjunction *and per se* (i.e. asserted), but to such pragmatic principles as the iconicity between clause order and intended temporal order (i.e. implicated). It is commonly accepted that the first type of meaning (assertion) is strictly a property of the sentence and hence is a subject for semantics proper, while the second (implication) should be accounted for by pragmatics. The present study challenges this prevailing view of linguistic meaning by examining *te*-linkage in Japanese, a translational equivalent of English *and*-linkage.[1]

I would like to thank Charles Fillmore, Seiko Y. Fujii, Orin Gensler, Derek Herforth, Kyoko Hirose, Katsuya Kinjo, Minoru Nakau, Masayoshi Shibatani, and Robert Van Valin for their comments and criticism. This study was supported in part by a grant to the Department of Linguistics, University of California, Berkeley, from Nippon Telegraph and Telephone Corporation.

[1] In the present study, those grammatical constructions in which *te* appears as a linking device are referred to as '*te*-constructions' or, collectively, as '*te*-linkage'. *Te* is attached to the stem of a verb or adjective, making it and its grammatical dependents part of a complex construction. The resulting 'Verbal + *te*' has sometimes been referred to as *gerund* (Bloch, 1946), *gerundive* (Kuno, 1973), or *te-form* (most textbooks of Japanese). Although 'Verbal + *te*' exhibits similarities to the gerund in Indo-European and other languages, it cannot in general function as a nominal, and some occurrences

Japanese *te*, like *and*, is used to express a diverse range of semantic relations—e.g. Temporal Sequence, Cause–Effect, Means–End, Contrast. When such a relation is understood to be intended by the speaker, it is always inferable solely from the conjuncts themselves. Furthermore, these relations are cancellable and thus can be regarded as implicatures. Most researchers, therefore, have considered that *te*-linkage has no meaning of its own: all semantic relations associated with *te*-linked sentences are worked out from the meanings of conjuncts alone.

However, the contrary does not hold: not all semantic relations that can be implicated by two paratactic clauses are possible with clauses linked by *te*. For example, if the clauses equivalent to *I sat down* and *The door opened* are presented paratactically in Japanese, the interpreter naturally reads in a Temporal Sequence relation, just as in English. But this relation is not an available interpretation when the clauses are linked by *te*. That is, among the relations potentially implicated by two copresent clauses, some are filtered out by *te*-linkage. This indicates that *te*-linkage cannot be a mere syntactic device. It must have some meaning that excludes Temporal Sequence from the range of possible interpretations.

The fact that not all implicated semantic relations are compatible with *te*-linkage also indicates that, while one can accurately *understand* the intended semantic relation solely from the meaning of the conjuncts, one cannot accurately predict when to *use te* correctly—not without further explicit stipulation. Therefore, the semantic relations compatible with *te*-linkage need not be stated as such for *decoding*, but this information is indispensable for *encoding*. Fillmore (1979: 67) notes: 'It is important to distinguish the *decoding*, or hearer's point of view, from the *encoding*, or speaker's point of view. Applying these two perspectives in the case of compositionality, we can talk about *semantic transparency* in the decoding case, and *semantic productivity* in the encoding case' (emphasis in original).

The distinction between what is asserted and what is implicated is certainly an important one in the theory of meaning. However, the reductionism inherent in attributing all semantic relations to pragmatic principles in the description of *te*-linkage appears to be a case of what Fillmore (p. 63) has called a theory of the 'language-understanding

of *te* function much more like the English conjunction *and*. In this study, I adhere to the traditional analysis of *te* as a connective suffix. See Shibatani (1990: ch. 10) for further discussion.

abilities of the idealized innocent speaker/hearer'. He points out that in addition to the 'ideal speaker/hearer that knows its language perfectly' (Chomsky 1965: 3), there is a second idealization—the idealization of innocence—in most traditions of semantics. This idealized innocent language-user knows

'the morphemes of its language and their meanings, it recognizes the grammatical structures and processes in which these morphemes take part, and it knows the semantic import of each of these. As a decoder, or hearer, the innocent language user calculates the meaning of each sentence from what it knows about the sentence's parts and their organization . . . The innocent speaker/hearer is in principle capable of saying anything sayable'. (Fillmore, 1979: 64)

However, the innocent speaker/hearer does not know about anything that falls outside a purely compositional semantics. If we teach some pragmatic principles to this language user, it can interpret all *te*-linked sentences—but still cannot use *te* correctly. It will, for example, wrongly conjoin the Japanese equivalents of *I sat down* and *The door opened* with *te* to indicate the sequence of the two situations, thinking that because of the congruence between clause order and intended sequence of situations the sentence has indeed been appropriately uttered.

Fillmore considers that while the idealization of innocence need not be abandoned, it must be kept pure: 'The nature of the fit between predictions generated by a theory and the phenomena within its domain can sometimes be assessed only when different sources of explanation can be isolated through one or more idealizations' (p. 63). However, he cautions, it is important to distinguish real innocence from pretended innocence. The present study was inspired by this envisaged limitation of the idealized innocent speaker/hearer when it is to use *te*-linkage.

The organization of this chapter is as follows. Section 3.1 provides a brief survey of semantic relations compatible with *te*-linkage. In Section 3.2 I demonstrate that such relations can be analyzed as implicatures. In Section 3.3 I then discuss the constraints on *te*-linkage *vis-à-vis* the Temporal Sequence and Cause relations. In Section 3.4 I argue that the notion of *grammatical construction* (Fillmore, 1986; Fillmore *et al.*, 1988), i.e. a pairing of a syntactic pattern with a meaning structure, is needed for an adequate description of *te*-linkage because many constraints apply neither to the syntactic structure of the *te*-linkage alone nor to the semantic relation between the conjuncts alone, but to the syntax and semantics coupled together. The conclusion follows in section 3.5.

3.1. CONVENTIONAL CATEGORIZATION OF *te*-CONSTRUCTIONS

Traditionally, *te*-constructions have been divided into three categories according to the function of *te*: (i) as a non-productive derivational suffix (1*a*); (ii) as a linker joining a main verb with a so-called auxiliary to form a complex predicate (1*b*); and (iii) as a linker connecting two phrases or clauses (1*c*).[2]

(1*a*) **hazimete**   kyooto ni   itta.
for the first time (begin-*te*)   LOC   went
'(I) went to Kyoto for the first time.'

(1*b*) hito   ga   takusan   **hasitte**   iru.
people NOM   many   **run-te**   be-NPAST
'(There are) many people running'

(1*c*) itami o   **koraete**   hasiri-tuzuketa.
pain ACC   **endure-te**   run-continued
'Enduring pain, (I) kept running'

In the first category, *te* functions as a derivational suffix, forming an adverb from a verb. *Hazimete* in (1*a*) could be analyzed as *hazime-* 'begin' (transitive) + *te*; however, *hazimete* in this usage does not have its own valence, i.e. it lacks a subject and/or object. In general, verbs in this category lose part of their verbal nature when *te* is attached. Furthermore, the meaning of a derived adverbial is not always predictable from the meaning of the base verb. Therefore, *hazimete* 'for the first time' as expressed in (1*a*) must be listed as such in the lexicon.[3] (When *hazimete* takes overt or covert arguments, on the other hand, it belongs to the second or third category.) Because the derivational process associated with *te* is semantically irregular and nonproductive,

---

[2] As with other /t/-initial verbal suffixes in Japanese, *te* participates in a number of morphophonemic processes that depend on the final consonant of a consonant-final verb stem, e.g. *aw-* 'meet' + *te* > *atte*, and *kak-* 'write' + *te* > *kaite*. When the verb stem ends in a voiced obstruent, *te* is voiced, e.g. *yob-* 'call' + *te* > *yonde*, and *oyog-*'swim' + *te* > *oyoide*. The morphophonemic details are irrelevant in this study, but it is crucial for the reader to recognize the presence of *te* in each example.

[3] Other examples of this category follow: *aratame-* 'renovate' + *te* > *aratamete* 'on another occasion', *hatas-* 'accomplish' + *te* > *hatasite* 'really', *itar-* 'reach' + *te* > *itatte* 'extremely', *sitagaw-* 'follow' + *te* > *sitagatte* 'therefore'.

and in particular because *te* does not function here as a connective *per se*, this first category will not be considered further here.

In the second category, exemplified by (1*b*), the verb preceding *te* is semantically the main predicate of the clause, and the verb or adjective that follows *te* is a so-called auxiliary. For example, 'Verb-*te i-*' in (1*b*) is the grammatical means for expressing imperfective aspect. In this second category the semantic relations between the linked constituents are relatively fixed compared with the third category, and are determined in large measure by the second constituent. Syntactically, on the other hand, some *te*-constructions in this category raise serious questions. For example, when *ar-* 'be (located)' is the second constituent, the construction as a whole becomes intransitive even if the 'main' verb is transitive. The current trend in syntactic theories is to treat such grammatical-function-changing processes as lexical, i.e. to consider 'Verb-*te ar-*' as a lexical unit; however, there is no syntactic evidence to support such an analysis (Lee, 1989; Matsumoto, 1990; Hasegawa, 1992). I shall not further address these problems here. Although *te* does function as a connective suffix, this category too will be excluded from the present investigation.

The semantic relations between the linked constituents in the third category, on the other hand, are so diverse that no single subtype can be considered central. In (1*c*), the first clause holds a Circumstance relation to the second; however, as shown in (2–8), many other relations can also be expressed by *te*-linked constituents, e.g. Additive, Temporal Sequence, Cause–Effect, Means–End, Contrast, and Concession.[4]

(2) Additive
zyoon   wa   ***akarukute***   kinben   da.
Joan   TOP   ***be-cheerful-te***   diligent   COP-NPAST
'Joan is cheerful and diligent'

(3) Temporal Sequence
gogo   wa   tegami o   ***kaite***,   ronbun   o yonda.
afternoon   TOP   letter   ACC   ***write-te***   thesis ACC   read-PAST
'In the afternoon, (I) wrote letters and read the thesis'

(4) Cause–Effect
taihuu   ga   ***kite***,   ie   ga   hakai-sareta.
typhoon   NOM   ***come-te***   houses   NOM   destroy-PASS-PAST
'A typhoon came, and houses were destroyed'

---

[4] These relations are provided here solely for purposes of exposition; whether or not the description of *te*-linkage must provide a list of all such relations is a separate issue.

(5) Means–End
   okane   o   ***karite,***   atarasii   kuruma   o   kau.
   money   ACC   ***borrow-te***   new   car   ACC   buy-NPAST
   '(I) will borrow money and buy a car'

(6) Contrast
   zyoon   wa   ***syuusyoku-site,***   tomu   wa   kekkon-sita.
   Joan   TOP   ***get-a-job-te***   Tom   TOP   marry-PAST
   'Joan got a job, and Tom got married'

(7) Concession
   kare   wa   okane   ga   ***atte,***   kasanai.
   he   TOP   money   NOM   ***there-be-te***   lend-NEG-NPAST
   'Although he has money, (he) won't lend (it to anyone)'

The prevailing view is that because of this diversity of semantic relations *te*-linkage has no intrinsic meaning, and that the interpreter must rather infer the intended semantic relationship on the basis of extralinguistic knowledge (e.g. Alfonso, 1966; Teramura, 1981; Endo, 1982; Himeno, 1984; Ogoshi, 1988). I discuss the validity of this claim in the next section.

3.2. MEANING OF CONNECTIVES

Most, if not all, linguistic expressions are semantically underspecified, but potential ambiguities rarely emerge if an expression is embedded in a larger context—for example, if a word appears in a sentence and the sentence is uttered/written in discourse. The word and the intrasentential, intersentential, and/or extrasentential context contribute jointly to the final interpretation.

Although *te*-linkage exhibits an extreme degree of semantic non-specificity, it is nonetheless very common in actual usage[5] and does not cause problems in communication. This leads to questions about how much of the meaning is attributable to the *te*-linkage itself, how much to the properties of the conjuncts, and how much to the

[5] On the basis of a corpus of 3,330 multi-predicate sentences sampled from various types of text, Saeki (1975: 81) reports a total of 26 connectives (1, 047 tokens altogether), of which *te* holds the foremost rank: it occurs 512 times, while the second most frequent connective, *ga*, occurs only 141 times. According to Inoue (1983: 128–30), *te* appears most frequently in spontaneous speech (34.5% of all connectives) and in informal writing (27%). In formal writing such as newspaper editorials, *te* ranks second (17.2%) after *ren'yoo* linkage (36.9%). The actual occurrence of *te* is much more frequent than these numbers suggest, because these data do not include cases in which the second predicate is a so-called auxiliary.

interpreter's extralinguistic knowledge of the described situation. Before proceeding, let me clarify the notion of *meaning* as utilized in this study.

3.2.1. *Independent and dependent semantic aspects*

Following Reichling's methodology, Dik (1968: 257–8) divides linguistic information into *semantic information* and *grammatical* (i.e. syntactic/morphological) *information*. All expressions have grammatical information associated with them by virtue of being usable in larger syntagms.

Semantic information is further divided into *independent* and *dependent semantic aspects*. The independent semantic aspects are immediately obtainable from the expression with no further linguistic context. By contrast, the dependent semantic aspects of the expression are obtained only within a larger whole of which the expression is a part. For example, speakers of English know the semantics of *table* without any further context, whereas they need some context, e.g. *table__*, to conceptualize the semantics of the plural suffix -*s*; plurality, as a relational notion, cannot be defined without essential reference to some noun. Thus *table* is said to have an independent semantic aspect of its own, whereas -*s* has only a dependent one. Not surprisingly, grammatical morphemes in general have only dependent semantic aspects.

Henceforth I will use the expression *meaning of the connective X* to refer to X's *dependent* semantic aspects. Connectives have grammatical information associated with them; they also indicate certain relationships between the semantic information of the conjuncts. Crucially, however, connectives do not carry independent semantic aspects of their own. Even with a 'semantically loaded' connective, such as *before*, it is necessary to mention the clauses that *before* links in order to describe the semantic information it conveys—namely, that the occurrence of the referent of the clause to which *before* is attached temporally follows the occurrence of the referent of the other clause.

Viewed in this light, the common claim that *te* does not have its own meaning is justified only if *meaning* is restricted to independent semantic aspects, since indeed no semantic description of *te* is possible without recourse to the larger constituent of which *te* is a part. However, advocates of this claim appear to contend that *te* lacks even dependent semantic aspects: they assert that the contingent semantic relations associated with *te*-linkage are so diverse that the interpreter only *infers* the specific sense intended by the speaker. In order to discuss this issue, it is necessary to clarify the distinction between what is asserted and what is implicated.

3.2.2. *Implicature*

One of the basic requirements for understanding discourse is recognizing how each clause coheres with its predecessor. Our linguistic and pragmatic competence enables us to read in conceivable relation(s) even when two clauses are copresent without any overt cues, i.e. in parataxis. Thus, certain aspects of interpretation are not part of the conventional force of the uttered sentence but rather part of what Grice (1975) has named *conversational implicatures*. For example, one automatically perceives a Cause relation when one hears *My cat died last night. I'm sad*; it therefore seems superfluous to attribute a Cause relation to *and* in *My cat died last night, and I'm sad*. Another such example is *They had a baby and got married* (Wilson, 1975: 151). As Horn (1985: 146–7) points out, a Temporal Sequence relation (as in the *and–then* reading) is present even when these two clauses are in mere parataxis. Rather than attributing the Temporal Sequence relation to the meaning of *and* itself, researchers therefore appeal to certain auxiliary theories, such as the iconicity between clause order and intended temporal order (Haiman, 1980) and the Gricean maxim of manner that stipulates, 'Be orderly.'

In the Gricean theory of linguistic pragmatics, the Cause relation observed between conjuncts linked by *because* and the Temporal Sequence relation between those linked by *before* are considered *conventional* (not conversational) *implicatures*. They involve the lexical meaning of some element and are attached to particular expressions by convention, not by pragmatic principles. Conventional implicatures are non-truth-functional inferences; as such, they cannot have any 'meaning' in the logical sense. However, if we do not adhere to the dogma of truth-functional semantics and instead adopt what Fillmore (1985) refers to as the *semantics of understanding*, there is no obstacle to considering Cause and Temporal Sequence as the meaning of *because*- and *before*-linkage, respectively.

The difference between *and*-linked and *because*- or *before*-linked sentences emerges sharply in the following pairs.

(8*a*) One plus one is two, and I'm sad.

(8*b*) Because one plus one is two, I'm sad.

(9*a*) John eats apples, and six men can fit in the back seat of a Ford.

(9*b*) John eats apples before six men can fit in the back seat of a Ford.

If the *b*-sentences were uttered, the interpreter would at least try to make sense out of them in such a way that a relation of Cause (8*b*) or of Temporal Sequence (9*b*) holds between the conjuncts; the connectives *because* and *before* force these interpretations. As Lakoff (1971) points out, success or failure in interpreting these sentences depends on one's deductive abilities. One might interpret (9*b*), for example, as describing John dieting so that he will be thinner and take up less space. With the *a*-sentences, on the other hand, the word *and* does not demand any particular interpretation. Indeed the most likely interpretation of *and* here is simply as a signal that the speaker has something more to say, i.e., intends to keep the floor. Halliday and Hasan (1976: 233), who draw a strict line between structural and cohesive (semantic) relationships, note, 'The "and" relation is felt to be structural and not cohesive, at least by mature speakers; this is why we feel a little uncomfortable at finding a sentence in written English beginning with *And*, and why we tend not to consider that a child's composition having *and* as its dominant sentence linker can really be said to form a cohesive whole.' They contend that *and* has a syntactic function, but that it provides little information about the semantic relation between the conjuncts.

3.2.3. *Cancellability test*

Grice proposes several diagnostic tests for conversational implicature, of which the so-called *cancellability* test is the most prominent.[6] Conversational implicatures can be cancelled without yielding contradiction, as with *and* in (10*a*). On the other hand, if something is

---

[6] Conversational implicatures are characterized as *calculable, cancellable, nondetachable, nonconventional,* and *indeterminate* (Grice, 1975). However, Sadock (1978: 295) claims that 'There are no sufficient tests for conversational implicature and no group of tests that together are sufficient.' He argues that nondetachability fails to be a necessary feature, nonconventionality is completely circular, and indeterminacy is not unique to conversational implicatures (cf. demonstratives). '[C]alculability is trivially necessary since nearly anything can be 'worked out' with the aid of the Cooperative Principle' (ibid.). Finally, cancellability, although necessary, fails to be sufficient 'for recognizing conversational implicature because, in the very important case of grammatical ambiguity, any one sense is obviously cancellable' (ibid. 296).

asserted, denying (part of) it will result in contradiction, as with *before* in (10*b*).

> (10*a*) They had a baby and got married, but not necessarily in that order.
> (10*b*) #They had a baby before they got married, but not necessarily in that order.

Te is in this respect similar to *and*.[7] The Cause relation associated with a *te*-construction is cancellable and hence can be taken as an implicature.

> (11) kaze o   hite   atama ga   itai atama ga   itai no
>   cold ACC catch-*te* head NOM ache head NOM ache NMLZ
>   wa   itumo no   koto   dakedo.
>   TOP always GEN thing   though
>   '(I) caught a cold, and (my) head aches. I always have a headache, though.'

If only the first sentence is supplied, it is naturally implicated that the cold is a cause of the speaker's headache. This implicature is cancelled by the second sentence, indicating that the speaker always has a headache anyway. In a typical such scenario the speaker, after uttering the first sentence, realizes the potential implicature and cancels it explicitly.

The Temporal Sequence relation is also cancellable, and hence it, too, can be regarded as an implicature.

> (12) maki wa oosaka e   itte hiro wa oosaka kara kaette   kuru
>   TOP   ALL go-*te* TOP   ABL return-*te* come
>   hiro ga   kaette   kuru no   ga   saki dakedo.
>   NOM   return-*te* come NMLZ NOM first though
>   'Maki will go to Osaka, and Hiro will return from Osaka. Hiro's return comes first, though.'

To recapitulate, in both *and*- and *te*-linkage, the perceived semantic relation would be present even if the linked constituents were in pure parataxis without *and* or *te*, and it would not be perceived otherwise. Accordingly, many researchers have claimed that *te*, like *and*, does not

---

[7] Of the 4 logical operators (conjunction, disjunction, material implication, and equivalence), *te* is equivalent to logical conjunction: the *te*-conjuncts must be compatible in their truth condition, i.e. neither of the conjuncts can entail the negation of the other. By contrast, logical disjunction allows the conjuncts to be contradictory, e.g. 'Mary is a Christian, or Mary is not a Christian.' *Te* is clearly not equivalent to material implication, for neither the falsity of the first proposition nor the truth of the second proposition linked by *te* guarantees the conjoined proposition to be true. Finally, *te* cannot be used to state that the conjuncts are logically equivalent.

have a meaning of its own, and that all semantic relations that the hearer perceives are implicated by the conjuncts themselves and the context. Let us call this claim the *implicature-only reductionist analysis*.

3.3. IDIOMATICITY OF *te*-LINKAGE

The implicature-only reductionist analysis is challenged by the fact that not all semantic relations potentially implicated by parataxis can be expressed by *te*-linkage—i.e. *te* is *not* absolutely transparent. As already remarked, some conceivable relations are filtered out when constituents are linked by *te*, and *te*-constructions have many arbitrary (and idiomatic) constraints, both on possible semantic relations and on the semantic nature of the conjuncts, that cannot be attributed to any pragmatic principles. In other words, *te*-linkage restricts the universe of possible semantic relations implicated by the conjuncts.

This section elaborates on such constraints imposed by *te*-linkage, focusing on the semantic relations of Temporal Sequence and Cause. It is demonstrated that the constraints are associated neither with *te*-linkage nor with semantic relations in isolation. In order to state such constraints, rather, linguistic descriptions need to employ the notion of grammatical construction—a pairing of a form and a meaning.

3.3.1. *Temporal Sequence relation and te-linkage*

Given appropriate pairs of clauses, the Temporal Sequence relation can always be implicated when two clauses are in parataxis, as in (13).

(13*a*) watasi   wa   tatiagatta. mado   ga   aita.
       I   TOP   stood-up   window   NOM   opened
      'I stood up. The window opened.'

(13*b*) watasi wa   kaizyoo   ni   tuita.   kooen ga   hazimatta.
      I   TOP   meeting-place loc   arrived lecture NOM began
      'I arrived at the meeting place. The lecture began.'

However, the same Temporal Sequence cannot be implicated when such pairs of clauses are linked by *te*, as illustrated in (14).[8]

---

[8] In order to express a Temporal Sequence with (14), such adverbials as *sugu ni* 'soon' or *5-hun-go ni* '5 minutes later' must be inserted between the clauses. That is, *te*-linkage by itself is not sufficient here to implicate Temporal Sequence.

(14a) #watasi ga tatiagatte   mado ga aita. (Yoshikawa, 1980)
            stand-up-*te*
        'I stood up, and the window opened.'

(14b) #watasi ga kaizyoo ni tuite   kooen ga hazimatta.
                              arrive-*te*
        'I arrived at the meeting-place, and the lecture began.' (Endo, 1982,
        modified)

Significantly, there would be no unnaturalness here if the connective
to or -*tara* were used instead of *te*, and the resultant sentences would
then permit Temporal Sequence interpretations.[9] There is thus
nothing *inherently* anomalous about conjoining the two clauses in
each pair in (14)—i.e. the anomaly is not purely pragmatic, as it would
be in *Joan ate sushi, and the tower collapsed*.

On the other hand, substituting (15a–b) for (14a–b) enhances the
acceptability.

(15a) watasi ga   oogoe   o   dasite   mado   ga   aita.
        I   NOM   loud-voice ACC emit-*te* window NOM   opened
        'I screamed, and the window opened.'
(15b) koosi   ga   kaizyoo   ni   tuite   kooen ga   hazimatta.
        lecturer NOM meeting-place LOC arrive-*te* lecture NOM began
        'The lecturer arrived at the meeting-place, and the lecture began.'

Changing *tatiagar-* 'stand up' in (14a) to *oogoe o das-* 'scream' in (15a)
improves the naturalness somewhat because an extremely loud sound
might, in principle, cause a window to open. In (15b), replacement of
the subject *watasi* 'I' with *koosi* 'lecturer' makes the sentence perfectly
natural because it is precisely the arrival of the lecturer that enables the
lecture to begin.[10] The key here is the notion of causation. If native
speakers of Japanese are forced to interpret (14), they read in some
sort of Cause relation, rather than mere Temporal Sequence—e.g. the
speaker has the magical power to open windows by standing up (14a).

Matsuda (1985) has pointed out that *te* links two constituents more
'tightly' than does *to* or -*tara*. If we interpret *tightly* as the involvement
of some notion of causation, his characterization provides a partial

---

    [9] The fact that the 'synonymous' connectives *to* and *tara* do allow the Temporal
Sequence relation in this example can be taken as evidence that the relation is detach-
able and thus not a conversational implicature. However, as Sadock points out (cf. n. 6
above), nondetachability may not be a necessary property of implicature. I do not pursue this idea further in the present study.
    [10] Even if the speaker him/herself is the lecturer, (14b) is still anomalous. See
Hasegawa (1992) for further discussion.

account of the inappropriateness of *te* in (14), in which the clause pairs fail to show any obvious Cause relations. From the anomalies observed in such sentences as (14), I conclude that mere incidental sequence of events—i.e. Temporal Sequence proper—cannot be expressed by the use of *te*-linkage, and that what makes events non-incidental is our recognition of causation.[11]

3.3.2. *Agentivity*

This requirement of causation between the referents of the linked clauses does not apply when the subject is shared by both clauses and the subject bears the semantic role of *agent vis-à-vis* both predicates. For example, *zyon* is the agentive subject of both *oki-* 'get up' and *araw-* 'wash' in (16), and the sentence is natural even though there is no Cause relation. The linked clauses are normally interpreted as having a Temporal Sequence relation. (One may perceive an Enablement relation between the clauses in (16). This issue will be discussed later in this section.)

(16) zyon wa asa   okite   kao o   aratta.
      TOP morning get-up-*te* face ACC washed
      'John got up in the morning and washed (his) face.'

If the shared subject has two distinct semantic roles in the two clauses, on the other hand, the sentence is awkward. For example, *zyon* in (17) is the theme subject of *me o samas-* 'wake up', but the agentive subject of *araw-*.

(17) #zyon wa asa   me o samasite kao o   aratta. (Kuno, 1973)
       TOP morning wake-*te*   face ACC washed
       'John woke up in the morning and washed (his) face.'

Kuno (pp. 196–7) contends that in a *te*-linkage with the same subject, both clauses must be either self-controllable (agentive) or

---

[11] Humans do not perceive the physical world as a constantly changing stream of co-incidental and arbitrary happenings but rather as situations occurring in organized patterns over specific spans of time. The fundamental basis whereby humans establish boundaries of discrete situations is 'provided by our tendency to perceive or infer cause–effect relations' (Bullock *et al.* 1982: 209). It is widely accepted that causation exists not as part of objective reality but as part of our interpretation of reality, and there is little dispute that the idea of causation is indispensable to understanding the human cognitive faculty. However, there is no universally accepted sense of causation (Hart and Honoré, 1959).

non-self-controllable (nonagentive).[12] He considers (18) to be anomalous because of the violation of this controllability constraint, since *zyon* is the theme in the first clause but the agent in the second.

(18) #zyon wa hikoozyoo ni   tuite,   ie   ni   denwa   sita.
        TOP airport   LOC arrive-*te* home LOC telephone did
     'John arrived at the airport and called home.' (Kuno, 1973)

As Kuno's theory predicts, when the subject is the theme in both clauses, anomaly does not emerge, e.g. (19) below.

(19) zyon wa hikoozyoo ni tuite, nimotu no   kensa   o
                                luggage GEN inspection ACC
     uketa
     underwent
     Lit. 'John arrived at the airport and underwent the inspection of (his) luggage.'
     'John arrived at the airport and had (his) luggage inspected.'

However, note that in (19) some non-incidental relation between the two events is necessarily assumed. The acceptability of (19) cannot, therefore, be attributed purely to agreement in agentivity. Also, *contra* Kuno, many speakers do consider (17) and (18) natural if they are interpreted with an Enablement relation—i.e. John's waking up enabled him to wash his face, and his arrival enabled him to call home. Furthermore, as mentioned above, (16) also has an Enablement interpretation, and hence cannot count as definitive evidence that causation is not required when there is a common agentive subject. One can, however, easily construct an example where a link of causation is all but impossible. In an example like (20), the first event clearly does not enable the second.

(20) zyon wa sinbun   o   yonde   heya o   soozi sita.
        TOP newspaper ACC read-*te* room ACC cleaned
     'John read a newspaper and cleaned the room.'

There is no question of cause and effect here; yet the two clauses are certainly not chosen at random. I maintain that what is expressed by *te*-linkage in (20) is not the mere fact of Temporal Sequence *per se*, nor the fact of causation, but that both actions were *intentionally performed* by the same person. Humans perceive, and in turn describe,

---

[12] The anomaly of (17) is not due solely to the lack of agreement in agentivity. In the event sequence implicit in (17), an intermediate action—'getting up'—is missing. If the second clause in (17) were to be replaced by, say, 'looked around', the sentence would be perfectly natural, despite the inconsistency in agentivity.

sequences of events that involve voluntary actions differently from those that do not (Hart and Honoré, 1959; Donnellan, 1967; Buss, 1978);[13] we do not normally consider a series of actions by a rational being to be mere coincidence. It is not surprising, then, that Japanese should reflect this difference grammatically, in choosing to encode a non-incidental sequence, but not an incidental one, with *te*. The non-incidental sequentiality, in effect, 'substitutes' for true, prototypical causation. This is all rather abstract, however; at a more 'concrete' level of semantics, it can simply be stated that the Temporal Sequence relation is indeed compatible with *te*-linkage if the conjuncts share an agentive subject.

3.3.3. *Cause relation and te-linkage*

We have referred in passing to causation, which in fact is one of the major semantic relations commonly attributed to *te*-linkage. One of the central aspects of causation is temporal sequentiality: cause must precede its effect. As we will soon see, this has interesting implications for the grammar of *te*-linkage.

As Sweetser (1990) has shown, some conjunctions (including causal conjunctions) may function in two domains, the content (real-world) domain and the epistemic domain, as illustrated in (21).[14]

[13] Investigating causation in judicial contexts, Hart and Honoré (1959: 39–40) note that 'a voluntary human action intended to bring about what in fact happens, and in the manner in which it happens, has a special place in causal inquiries . . . when the question is how far back a cause shall be traced through a number of intervening causes, such a voluntary action very often is regarded both as a limit and also as still the cause even though other later abnormal occurrences are recognized as causes . . . If unusual quantities of arsenic are found in a dead man's body, this is up to a point an explanation of his death and so the cause of it: but we usually press for a further and more satisfying explanation and may find that someone deliberately put arsenic in the victim's food. This is a fuller explanation in terms of human agency; and . . . we speak of the poison's action as the cause of the death; though we do not withdraw the title of cause from the presence of arsenic in the body—this is now thought of as the "mere way" in which the poisoned produced the effect. Once we have reached this point . . . we have something which has a special *finality* at the level of common sense: for though we may look for and find an explanation of why the poisoner did what he did in terms of motives like greed or revenge, we do not regard his motive . . . as the cause of the *death* . . . We do not trace the cause *through* the deliberate act' (emphasis in original).

[14] In addition to the content and epistemic domains, Sweetser also posits a third domain, viz. the speech-act domain, exemplified by the following sentence: Since {we're on the subject/you're so smart}, when was George Washington born? (I ask you because we're on the subject, or because you're so smart—the fact that we're on the subject, for example, enables my act of asking the question.) Although the Cause relation in the speech-act domain is certainly an interesting subject of investigation, I do not consider it here.

(21*a*) Since John wasn't there, we decided to leave a note for him.
         (His absence caused our decision in the real world.)
(21*b*) Since John isn't here, he has (evidently) gone home.
         (The knowledge of his absence causes my conclusion that he has gone
         home.)

When Cause applies in the epistemic domain, it is quite possible for
the event sequence to be distinct from the temporal sequence. (Of
course, we may conceive sequentiality metaphorically; but then the sequence is *logical*, not temporal.) For example, one may say, *My daughter will begin college soon, and I had to quit the gym* [*to save money for
tuition*]. Japanese can express equivalent clauses in the same order by
using the fully explicit conjunction *node* or *kara* (roughly 'since/be-
cause').

(22) musume   ga   moo-sugu gakkoo ni   hairu   node
      daughter NOM   soon   school LOC   enter-NPST because
      zimu o   yamenakereba naranakatta
      gym   ACC   had-to-quit
      'Because my daughter will begin school soon, I had to quit the gym.'

As shown in (23*a*) below, this epistemic Cause relation can also be implicated by parataxis with the same clause order as (22). It cannot,
however, be expressed by *te*-linkage while maintaining the same clause
order, as shown in (23*b*).

(23*a*) musume ga moo-sugu gakkoo ni   hairu.   zimu o
                                         enter-NPAST
         yamenakereba naranakatta.
         'My daughter will begin school soon. I had to quit the gym.'
(23*b*) #musume ga moo-sugu gakkoo ni haitte   zimu o
                                         enter-*te*
         yamenakereba naranakatta.
         'My daughter will begin school soon, and I had to quit the gym.'
         (Intended reading)

One apparently natural way to account for the phenomenon seen in
(23*b*) would be to propose (*contra* my own position) that the basic
function of *te*-linkage is to express a pure Temporal Sequence relation, and that the Cause relation is parasitic on this fact. Sentence
(23*b*), then, would be anomalous because (i) morphologically *te* does
not permit the preceding verb to be tensed, (ii) *te*-linkage expresses
that the referent of the first conjunct temporally precedes that of the
second, (iii) the tense of the second clause in (23*b*) is in the past, and

thus (iv) the event referred to by the first conjunct must also have occurred in the past. In other words, Cause relations can be expressed by *te*-linkage only when they are in accordance with the Temporal Sequence relation; and in (23*b*) this does not hold.

However, this seemingly attractive explanation depends crucially on the assumption that *te*-linkage does express Temporal Sequence *per se*; yet, as shown earlier, this is not an adequate characterization. Rather, the anomaly of sentences like (23*b*) seems to require an explicit statement in the grammar—a point to which we will return.

A second example of a Cause relation that is not compatible with *te*-linkage involves the notion of modality, i.e. the speaker's attitude toward the proposition. Here *te* cannot be used even when the two clauses do maintain an iconic temporal order. For example, the first sentence in (24*a*) is naturally interpreted as the Cause of the speaker's emotion, and this relation can be expressed by the use of *node* 'because', (24*b*); yet linking these two sentences by *te* will result in an anomaly, as shown in (24c).

(24*a*) kutu o   katta.   uresii.
     shoe ACC bought am-happy
     '(I) bought shoes. I am happy.'
(24*b*) kutu o katta node   uresii.
              because
     'Because (I) bought shoes, I am happy.'
(24c) #kutu o katte   uresii.
          buy-*te*
     'I bought shoes, and (so) I'm happy.' (Intended)

The reason for this pattern of anomaly lies in the interaction between the construction and modality, the latter defined as the speaker's mental attitude toward the proposition or speech act *at the time of utterance, conceived as the speaker's instantaneous present* (Nakau, 1979; 1992). Verbals in Japanese such as *uresi-* 'be happy' in (24), which denote human feeling or mental activity, are called *psych-predicates* and are considered to be modality expressions when occurring in the non-past tense.[15] With psych-predicates, a Cause relation can indeed be expressed by *te*-linkage when the predicate is in the past tense—cf. (25), where the sentence reports an event which is divorced from the speech situation. As Nakau convincingly argues, when the speaker describes

---

[15] Psych-predicates constitute a closed grammatical class in Japanese; membership in this class is thus sometimes arbitrary and not always purely a matter of semantics. See Aoki (1986) for details.

a past event, the sentence can no longer be taken as a modality expression.

(25) kutu o katte   uresikatta.
                     was-happy
      '(I) bought shoes, and (so) I was happy.'

But such a Cause relation is not possible in (24c), where the fact of being happy is coterminous with uttering the sentence. The two situations (24c, 25) are fundamentally different.

As was the case with the epistemic type discussed earlier, here too we have an arbitrary *constraint* which must be imposed on *te*-linkage.

3.4. GRAMMATICAL CONSTRUCTIONS

We have not yet addressed the question of where in the description of a language constraints like those just discussed should be stated. The constraints are neither on syntactic structures alone nor on semantic relations alone; they apply only when a particular syntagm (the *te*-construction) is used to express a certain semantic relation. Such a pairing can be stated through the notion of *grammatical construction*. As Fillmore (1986: 3) notes, Construction Grammar 'aims at describing the grammar of a language directly in terms of a collection of *grammatical constructions* each of which represents a *pairing of a syntactic pattern with a meaning structure*' (emphasis in original). This notion of grammatical construction, similar to that found in traditional and pedagogical grammars, is indispensable for explaining the subtle constraints on *te*-linkage.

If we represent a particular syntactic subtype of *te*-linkage as Syn-*te*,[16] and a particular semantic relation that *te*-linkage can denote as Sem-*te*, then the grammatical construction [Syn-*te*, Sem-*te*] is the appropriate descriptive unit for expressing the constraints on that particular pairing. For example, the grammatical construction [Syn-*te*, Temporal Sequence] has the following constraint:

(26) Constraint on [Syn-*te*, Temporal Sequence]
      When two events which are linked solely by temporal sequentiality are expressed via *te*-linkage, the conjuncts must share an agentive subject.

---

[16] There in fact exist several syntactically distinct *te*-constructions; however, as such syntactic subtypes are not directly relevant to the theme of the present article, I have ignored the matter here. See Hasegawa (1992) for further discussion.

This constraint does not apply to Syn-*te* alone: *te* can also link clauses with distinct subjects, e.g. (12, 15). It does not apply to the Temporal Sequence relation alone either: the connectives *to* and -*tara* can denote Temporal Sequence with distinct or nonagentive subjects. On the other hand, the constraint that the first conjunct must be interpreted as perfective in [Syn-*te*, Temporal Sequence] need not be stated specifically here, for it applies to the Temporal Sequence relation *per se* rather than to the particular construction at hand and thus is 'inherited' by the construction from the description of the Temporal Sequence relation.

Within this framework, the two constraints (epistemic and modality) discussed in the previous section can be stated as follows:

(27) Constraint 1 on [Syn-*te*, Cause]
The Cause relation is compatible with *te*-linkage only in the content domain, not in the epistemic domain.

(28) Constraint 2 on [Syn-*te*, Cause]
When two clauses are causally linked by *te*, the second conjunct must be in the past tense if it involves a psych-predicate.

3.5. CONCLUSION

To sum up, the reductionism of the implicature-only analysis—with its over-attribution of semantic relations to pragmatics—is not tenable. As demonstrated in this paper, *te*-linkage cannot be used to express all Temporal Sequence or Cause relations that are implicated by the bare juxtaposed conjuncts, but only certain subtypes of them. If a theory claims these semantic relations are to be derived by a pragmatic principle, it will then have to employ some filtering mechanism to eliminate those subtypes of the relations that do not persist through *te*-linkage. But such filtering will be impossible unless the theory has attributed potential semantic relations to *te*-linkage in the first place,[17] because the constraints apply only to instances where the linkage is understood to have a *particular* semantic value—e.g. to involve a nonincidental course of events, in the case of Temporal Sequence when the conjuncts do not share an agentive subject. The implicature-only

[17] This claim, however, does not exclude the possibility that some constraints on *te*-linkage may have more general application and therefore need not be (re)stated in the description of this particular construction.

reductionist analysis imagines that the whole problem can be solved through the agency of pragmatic implicature. However, when one seeks to actually articulate such pragmatic principles, there is no way to avoid an explicit statement of *te*-compatible semantic relations.

REFERENCES

ALFONSO, A. (1966). *Japanese Language Patterns: A Structural Approach.* Tokyo: Sophia University.

AOKI, H. (1986). 'Evidentials in Japanese,' in W. Chafe and J. Nichols (eds.), *Evidentiality: The Linguistic Coding of Epistemology*, 223–38. Norwood, NJ: Ablex.

BLOCH, B. (1946). 'Inflection,' *Journal of the American Oriental Society* **66**: 97–109.

BULLOCK, M., GELMAN, R., and BAILARGEON, R. (1982). 'The Development of Causal Reasoning,' in W. Friedman (ed.), *The Developmental Psychology of Time*, 209–54 (New York).

BUSS, A. R. (1978). 'Causes and Reasons in Attribution Theory: A Conceptual Critique,' *Journal of Personality and Social Psychology* **75**: 1311–21.

CHOMSKY, N. (1965). *Aspects of the Theory of Syntax.* Cambridge, Mass.: MIT Press.

DIK, S. C. (1968). *Coordination.* Amsterdam: North-Holland.

DONNELLAN, K. S. (1967). 'Reasons and Causes,' in P. Edwards (ed.), *The Encyclopedia of Philosophy* vii: 85–8 New York: Macmillan.

ENDO, Y. (1982). 'Setuzoku-zyosi *te* no yoohoo to imi,' *Onsei-gengo no kenkyuu* **2**: 51–63.

FILLMORE, C. J. (1979). 'Innocence: A Second Idealization for Linguistics,' *Proceedings of the Fifth Annual Meeting of the Berkeley Linguistics Society*, 63–76.

—— (1985). 'Frames and the Semantics of Understanding,' *Quaderni di Semantica* **6**: 222–53.

—— (1986). 'On Grammatical Constructions.' Unpublished paper.

—— Kay, P., and O'Connor, M. C. (1988). 'Regularity and Idiomaticity in Grammatical Constructions,' *Language* **64**: 501–38.

GRICE, H. P. (1975). 'Logic and Conversation', in P. Cole and J. Morgan (eds.), *Syntax and Semantics iii: Speech Acts*, 41–58. New York: Academic Press.

HAIMAN, J. (1980). 'The Iconicity of Grammar,' *Language* **54**: 565–89.

HALLIDAY, M. A. K., and HASAN, R. (1976). *Cohesion in English.* London: Longman.

HART, H. L. A., and HONORÉ, A. M. (1959). *Causation in the Law.* Oxford: Clarendon Press.

HASEGAWA, Y. (1992). 'Syntax, Semantics, and Pragmatics of TE-linkage in Japanese.' Ph.D. dissertation, University of California at Berkeley.

HIMENO, M. (1984). 'Doosi "te" kei no rentaisyuusyoku-koozoo,' *Kokugogaku ronsetu siryoo* **21**: 151–9 (Tokyo).

INOUE, K. (1983). 'Bun no setuzoku,' in Inoue (ed.), *Kooza gendai no gengo I: Nihongo no kihon koozoo*, 127–51. Tokyo: Sanseidô.

KUNO, S. (1973). *The Structure of the Japanese Language*. Cambridge, Mass: MIT Press.

LAKOFF, R. (1971). 'Ifs, Ands, and Buts about Conjunction,' in C. J. Fillmore and D. Langendoen (eds.), *Studies in Linguistic Semantics*, 114–49. New York: Holt, Rinehart, & Winston.

LEE, N. I. (1989). 'Complementation in Japanese: A Lexicase Analysis.' Ph.D. dissertation, University of Hawaii.

MATSUDA, T. (1985). '*To, te, tara* ni tuite', *Kokugogaku ronsetu siryoo* **22**: 98–103.

MATSUMOTO, Y. (1990). 'On the Syntax of Japanese "Intransitivizing" -*te aru* Construction: Non-lexical Function Changing,' *Papers from the Twenty-Sixth Regional Meeting of the Chicago Linguistic Society* i: 277–91.

NAKAU, M. (1979). 'Modaritii to meedai,' in *Eigo to nihongo to: Hayashi Eiichi kyoozyu kanreki kinen ronbunsyuu*, 223–50. Tokyo: Kurosio.

—— (1992). 'Modality and Subjective Semantics.' Unpublished paper.

OGOSHI, N. (1988). 'Ren'yookei to tekei ni tuite,' *Kokugo kenkyuu* **6**: 62–71 (Yokohama).

SADOCK, J. M. (1978). 'On Testing for Conversational Implicature,' in P. Cole (ed.), *Syntax and Semantics ix: Pragmatics*, 281–97. New York: Academic Press.

SAEKI, T. (1975). *Gendai nihongo no gojun*. Tokyo: Kasama Shobô.

SHIBATANI, M. (1990). *The Languages of Japan*. Cambridge: Cambridge University Press.

SWEETSER, E. (1990). *From Etymology to Pragmatics: Metaphorical and Cultural Aspects of Semantic Structure*. Cambridge: Cambridge University Press.

TERAMURA, H. (1981). *Nihongo no bunpô*. Tokyo: National Language Research Institute.

WILSON, D. (1975). *Presupposition and Non-truth-conditional Semantics*. New York: Academic Press.

YOSHIKAWA, T. (1980). ' "-te kara" o meguru syomondai,' *Kokugogaku ronsetu siryoo* **17**: 69–75.

4

Conversational Scorekeeping and the Interpretation of Conditional Sentences

James D. McCawley

In this paper I develop ideas that are aimed at answering the first of the three basic questions about conditional sentences that Fillmore (1987: 163) poses ('To what extent are facts about the form and interpretation of a conditional sentence predictable from knowledge about its constituent elements?'). If I were writing a considerably longer paper, I would attempt also to answer Chuck's third question ('To what extent must an account of the meaning and function of a conditional sentence of a given type be sensitive to subtle structural patterns whose total effects cannot be seen as the *compositional product* of its parts but must be described in terms of separate *grammatical constructions*?'), which would require me, for example, to show how the diverse uses of indicative conditionals that Chuck tabulates differ in the set of possible worlds that fit into the scheme 'In (all) worlds [of such-and-such set] in which A, B' that serves below as an analysis of the semantics of *if*.

I will begin with exposition and illustration of one of the most important and fruitful notions of pragmatics, namely David Lewis's notion of 'conversational scorekeeping', which I will exploit in the body of the paper in an account of the interpretation of *if*-clauses that aims at a uniform treatment of both indicative and counterfactual *if*-clauses, whether unadorned or combined with such words as *only* and *even*.

Lewis's (1979) term 'score' is suggested by the lists of parameter values that sports announcers give in informing their listeners of the

Versions of this paper were read at the 15th Annual Minnesota Linguistics Conference, 13–14 Oct. 1989, the 28 Jan. 1991 session of the Pragmatics Workshop, University of Chicago, and the 13th Annual Conference of the Cognitive Science Society, Chicago, 7–10 Aug. 1991. For valuable comments on it, I am grateful to John Dolan, William Hanson, Josef Stern, and Alice ter Meulen.

present situation of the game: 'Orioles batting in the top of the fourth, one out, runners on first and third, one ball, two strikes, Cal Ripken at bat; White Sox 4, Orioles 2,' or 'second down and five to go, the Bears have the ball on their own 20 yard line, 4 minutes to go in the third quarter; Steelers 28, Bears 14.' Lewis's notion of a conversational score is a set of values of parameters that shares two important characteristics of these parameters relating to the progress of baseball and football games: first, the settings of the various parameters change as the game or the conversation progresses, reflecting what the participants have just done, and second, the settings of the parameters determine what the participants are allowed to do and what various things that they might do will count as. For example, whether the 'strike' count is 2 or not determines whether a foul ball counts as a strike or does not count as anything; it also determines whether a strike will cause the number of outs to be increased by 1, the strike count to be reset to 0, and a new batter to be the one who is at bat, and whether the number of outs is 2 determines whether the next out is to be accompanied by changing the value of the 'team at bat' parameter and resetting of the 'strike', 'ball', 'out', and 'runners on base' parameters to 0.

Some of the parameters in a 'conversational score' are close analogs to parameters in sports scores. For example, 'person whose turn it is to speak' is analogous to 'team at bat' or 'team having the ball', and a culture's rules of conversational turn-taking are roughly analogous to the rules for when each team bats in a baseball game or when a team takes possession of the ball in football. Other parameters relate to social and epistemological matters that have no close analog in sports. The treatment of pragmatic presupposition proposed in Karttunen (1974) is in terms of something that Karttunen calls a 'context', which would be one of the parameters in a Lewis-type conversational score. The *context*, in Karttunen's technical sense, is the set of propositions that are 'mutual knowledge' of the participants in the discourse; it includes propositions that the participants in the discourse can for some reason or other take to be 'common background knowledge' that they share, propositions that one or other of them has asserted during the discourse and which the other participants have not challenged, and propositions corresponding to anything that the participants have jointly witnessed as the discourse has progressed, including propositions relating to who said what in the discourse. (The context thus typically grows rapidly as the discourse progresses.)[1] Karttunen treated pragmatic presuppositions as demands that linguistic elements make on contexts, e.g. a clause of the form *x regrets S* demands that the context relative to which it is interpreted entail the proposition that S expresses, and thus a clause such as *Bush regrets that he seduced Raisa Gorbacheva* is felicitous only at a point in a discourse at which the proposition that Bush seduced Raisa Gorbacheva is mutual knowledge of the participants, e.g. one of them has already said that and the others have not challenged his statement.[2]

One of the uses that Lewis makes of the notion of 'score' relates to the interpretation of imprecise predicates. Is the sidewalk on Woodlawn Avenue flat? One can answer this question only relative to particular settings of a threshold for how large a deviation from perfect planarity it takes for something to fail to be flat. When a person disputes your affirmative answer to this question, he probably isn't disputing your factual claims but is rather demanding that the threshold for flatness be set to a value that would yield a negative answer when it is combined with your factual claims. An example somewhat similar to this one figures in McCawley (1986), where I noted that while according to Russell's analysis of definite descriptions, ($1a$) is a valid argument form, it is easy to find apparent instances of it such as ($1b$) that seem to be invalid:

($1a$) a is the X
        $b \neq a$
        Therefore b is not the X
($1b$) New York is the place where John lives
        Queens $\neq$ New York
        Therefore, Queens isn't the place where John lives

The second premise of ($1b$) is trivially true, and if John in fact lives in Queens, that fact would be grounds for saying that the first premise of ($1b$) was true and that the conclusion was false. There are a number of things that one can identify as wrong with ($1b$), and one of them relates to a component of the conversational score, namely the

[1] For some specific details of what entitles participants in a discourse to take various propositions as 'shared background knowledge', see Prince (1978).
[2] The especially original feature of Karttunen's analysis is that he treats the parts of various complex sentences as evaluated at appropriate derived contexts; e.g. in the interpretation of a conditional sentence *If A, then B*, the proposition expressed by A is added to the context relative to which B is interpreted. Thus, *If Bush has seduced Raisa Gorbacheva, he regrets that he seduced her* is felicitous even relative to contexts that do not contain the proposition that Bush seduced Raisa.

geographical level that one takes as determining the values of variables that range over 'places'. The setting of that component that would make the first premise a normal thing to say would be one in which it took cities rather than boroughs or districts as its values, and that would make the conclusion not a normal thing to say. In going from the premises to the conclusion in (1*b*), one has surreptitiously changed the score. Extending the metaphor of Lewis's title, 'Scorekeeping in a language game,' one might say that in offering the argument (1*b*) a person was committing a foul in a language game. Scores can of course be changed as a discourse proceeds, as when one demands a finer distinction among places, but changing the score may change the truth value of premises in an argument, and the foul that a speaker would commit in offering the argument (1*b*) would be in starting with a score that made his premises true and stating his conclusion in a form that forces one to change the score to one relative to which one of the premises was neither true nor even relevant to the conclusion.

Lewis also relies on the notion of 'score' in his treatment of the interpretation of definite descriptions. How an NP such as *the dog* can be interpreted at a given point in a discourse depends on two components of the score. The first of these is what I have called (McCawley, 1979; 1981) the **contextual domain**: the set of entities whose identities count as 'already established' at the given point in the discourse. (Roughly speaking, a contextual domain is to the entities that constitute it as a context is to the propositions that constitute it: entities get into the contextual domain either on the basis of background knowledge that the participants are entitled to take one another as sharing or on the basis of what is said during the conversation—when one of the participants asserts an existential proposition, an entity corresponding to what he says exists is added to the CD unless his assertion is challenged—or on the basis of events that the participants jointly witness as the discourse proceeds.) The second of the components of the score that plays a role in the interpretation of definite NPs is a relationship of relative salience among the members of the CD. In a sentence such as *The dog wants to go for a walk*, the definite NP *the dog* is interpreted as referring to the most salient dog in the contextual domain. The most salient dog in the CD won't necessarily remain the most salient one for very long, and it is easy to construct stretches of discourse in which two occurrences of a definite NP are assigned different referents, as a result of the addition to the CD of a new entity that takes on higher salience than the referent of the first occurrence of the NP:

(2) When I took the dog out for a walk last night, another dog started barking at him. I was afraid the dog would attack him, but fortunately its owner and I were able to keep them apart.

	When S_1,	S_2.	S_3,	but S_4.	$\ldots S_9$
CD	a, b, ...	a, b, ...	a, b, r, ...	a, b, r, ...	
Context	a is a dog, b is a dog,	a is a dog, b is a dog,	a is a dog, b is a dog, r is a dog,	a is a dog, b is a dog, r is a dog,	
Salience	a > b	a > b	r > a > b	r > a > b	a > r > b
Referent of *the dog*	a	a	r	r	a

Here the first occurrence of *the dog* is interpreted as whatever dog was initially the most salient one in the discourse (most plausibly, the speaker's dog); the second clause of the first sentence refers to a dog that is not hitherto in the CD, and an entity corresponding to it is added to the CD and the proposition that that entity is a dog is added to the context. New additions to the CD automatically achieve high salience, though not necessarily higher salience than entities that are already high in salience; what this amounts to in this case is that the participants in the discourse have the option of treating the new dog in the discourse as more salient than hitherto most salient dog, and I assume in (2) that they have exercised that option. Thus, the first occurrence of *the dog* will be interpreted as having *a* as its referent and the second occurrence will be interpreted as having *r* as its referent. In the next couple of sentences, the relative salience of *a* and *r* could be reversed and *the dog* could again have *a* as its referent.

I now turn to the interpretation of conditional sentences. I will start with a revision of some recent proposals for the semantics of counterfactual conditional sentences, with a view towards separating out specific semantic contributions by particular linguistic elements that recur in other types of sentence; e.g. I seek analyses of sentences like (3*a*) that not only correctly account for their truth conditions but derive the truth conditions from semantic analyses of the items listed in (3*b*), which can safely be assumed to combine in some compositional fashion in sentences like (3*a*):

(3*a*) If Bush had promised to legalize drugs, I would have voted for him
(3*b*) i. the *If A, B* sentence form

    ii. the counterfactual (subjunctive?) form of the two constituent sentences
    iii. *would* (versus *might*)

Accounts by logicians of the truth conditions of sentences like (3*a*) generally simply treat them as wholes rather than dealing with their various parts individually. For example, the most influential account of the logic of *would*-counterfactuals is probably that of David Lewis (1973), who simply introduces a connective □→ that is to formalize the *would*-counterfactual and for which he gives the truth conditions in (4):

(4) A □→ B is true in a world w if either (i) there is a world w′ such that A is true in w′ and for every world w″ in which A is true that is at least as close to w as w′ is [symbolized Cww″w′ by Lewis], B is also true in w″, or (ii) there is no world in which A is true. (Loosely speaking: A □→ B is true in w if B is true in the closest worlds to w in which A is true.) (See Fig. 4.1.)

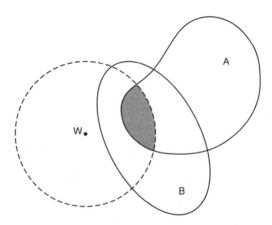

Fig. 4.1.

Before attempting to improve on Lewis's account, let me first summarize its rationale and its virtues. Lewis's invocation of a relationship of relative closeness among worlds (for which he provides postulates that I will not reproduce here) is intended to capture the widely accepted intuition that counterfactuals make reference not to arbitrary (and possibly outlandish) alternatives to the real world but only to alternatives that are as different from the real world as is necessary to accommodate the counterfactual protasis (in this case,

worlds in which Bush promised to legalize drugs but which otherwise are as much like the real world as possible). I have suggested
(McCawley, 1976) the name *local entailment* for the relationship
defined by these truth conditions for □→: to say that A entails B is to
say that B is true in all logically possible worlds in which A is true, and
to say that it locally entails B is to say that B is true in those worlds in
which A is true that are closest to the given one.

Lewis's formalization of the *would*-counterfactual has the virtue
of accounting for the invalidity of some counterfactual analogs of
arguments that are usually thought to be valid for indicative conditionals, e.g.[3]

(5a) Transitivity (If A, then B; if B, then C; therefore, if A, then C)
 If Bush had been born in Palestine, he would be a PLO agent
 If Bush were a PLO agent, he would be sending American defense se-
 crets to Saddam
 Therefore, if Bush had been born in Palestine, he would be sending
 American defense secrets to Saddam

(5b) Strengthening the protasis (If A, then B; therefore, if A and A′, then B)
 If you had gone to the party, you would have had a good time
 Therefore, if you had gone to the party and you had broken your leg,
 you would have had a good time

(5c) Contraposition (If A, then B; therefore, if not B, then not A)
 If Willie Mays had played in the American League, he would have
 been elected to the Hall of Fame
 Therefore, if Willie Mays hadn't been elected to the Hall of Fame, he
 wouldn't have played in the American League

(5a) is invalid because the two premises refer to sets of worlds that
need not overlap; the closest worlds to our world in which Bush was
born in Palestine are worlds in which he become a PLO agent but
never had any opportunity to become President of the USA, because
he did not meet the constitutional requirement of being a native-born
American citizen; the closest worlds to our world in which Bush is a
PLO agent are worlds in which he was born in the United States and
managed to become President of the USA despite secret membership
in the PLO; what Bush does in the latter worlds tells nothing about
what he does in the former worlds and does not warrant drawing any
conclusion (such as that of (5a)) about what he does in them. (5b) is

---

[3] I do not mean this to be taken as implying that I think Strengthening the Protasis
and Contraposition are valid even for indicative conditionals. I just think their invalidity is more blatant for *would*-counterfactuals than for indicatives.

invalid because the worlds that figure in the conclusion are much further from the real world than those that figure in the premise and hence the premise gives you no information about them. Finally, the proposition that in the closest worlds to the real world in which Mays played in the American League he was elected to the Hall of Fame does not rule out the possibility that among the closest worlds in which he wasn't elected to the Hall of Fame there are both worlds in which he played in the AL and worlds in which he didn't.

In addition, Lewis's truth conditions are set up so as to accommodate a class of cases that had previously been overlooked in accounts of counterfactuals, namely those in which for every world in which A is true there are closer worlds to w in which A is true, which he illustrates with such sentences as

(6) If David Lewis were over 7′ tall, he would have trouble shopping for clothes

If one takes worlds in which Lewis is 7′ 1″ tall to be closer to the real world than worlds in which he is 7′ 2″, worlds in which he is 7′ 0.5″ tall to be closer to the real world than worlds in which he is 7′ 1″, etc., then there would be an infinite sequence of worlds in which he is over 7′ tall, each closer to the real world than the preceding one, but no absolutely closest worlds to the real world in which he is over 7′ tall. Lewis's semantics deals with this case in exactly the same way as it deals with cases in which there *are* absolutely closest worlds to w in which A is true.

Like most logicians who have talked about counterfactuals at all, Lewis has lavished attention on *would*-counterfactuals but given little attention to *might*-counterfactuals. While his analysis of *would*-counterfactuals does not in itself force on one any particular analysis of *might*-counterfactuals, it readily suggests two possible ways of giving truth conditions for sentences of the form *If A were the case, B might be the case*. One is to do as Lewis himself does and analyze the *might*-counterfactual in terms of □→ and negation, and the other is to replace the universal quantifier of (4) by an existential quantifier:

(7a) 'If A were the case, B might be the case' is true in w if and only if $\neg(A \mathbin{\Box\!\!\rightarrow} \neg B)$ is true in w. (Lewis, 1973: 21)

(7b) 'If A were the case, B might be the case' is true in w if there is a world w′ in which A is true and for some world w″ for which Cww″w′ and A is true in w″, B is true in w″, which (in virtue of the postulate that ensures that Cww′w′) is equivalent to:

(7*b'*) 'If A were the case, B might be the case' is true in w if there is a world w' such that A and B are both true in w'

Neither of these two versions of truth conditions for *might*-counterfactuals is satisfactory, since the one makes it disconcertingly hard for a *might*-counterfactual to be true, and the other makes it ridiculously easy. Suppose that B is false in all of the very closest worlds to w in which A is true, but true in some worlds only slightly less close to w in which A is true (e.g. A = Dukakis hired competent advisors, B = Dukakis beat Bush). Then (7*a*) makes (8*a*) false, even though it would widely be held to be true. (7*b*) would make it true, but it would also make virtually any *might*-counterfactual true since the mere consistency of the protasis with the apodosis would make it true; e.g. (8*b*) would come out true according to (7*b*):

> (8*a*) If Dukakis had hired competent advisors, he might have beaten Bush
> (8*b*) If the Cubs had won the 1988 NL playoffs, Dukakis might have beaten Bush

I will return shortly to the problem of finding satisfactory truth conditions for a *might*-counterfactual. First, however, I wish to take up a couple of additional problems for Lewis's truth conditions for the *would*-counterfactual that will suggest a small but important revision in Lewis's proposal that will not only solve those problems but also yield a more satisfactory treatment of *might*-counterfactuals. As Lewis sets up his truth conditions, if A is true in w, then the truth conditions for the *would*-counterfactual fall together with the classical truth conditions for an indicative conditional: if A is true in w, then the truth value of A $\square\!\!\rightarrow$ B is the same as that of B. Arguing about the truth conditions of counterfactuals with a true protasis is difficult because such sentences often sound very odd, e.g. (9*a*), although there are rare instances, such as (9*b*), in which an author has used a counterfactual conditional whose protasis and apodosis he knew to both be true:

> (9*a*) ??If Deng Xiaoping had been born in China, he would speak Chinese
> (9*b*) If Shakespeare had written a play about Antony and Cleopatra, he probably would have called it *Antony and Cleopatra* (Geoffrey K. Pullum)

The usual bizarreness of counterfactual conditionals whose protases are true has led many authors (e.g. Lakoff 1971: 571) to claim that counterfactuals presuppose the falsehood of their protases. However,

Alan Ross Anderson (1951) refuted this claim in advance on the basis of sentences such as (10), which can be perfectly normal parts of discourses in which the speaker is attempting to demonstrate that the protasis is true (here, that the patient is suffering from yellow fever):

(10) If this patient were suffering from yellow fever, he would be displaying exactly the symptoms that we have just observed

The normalness of sentences like (10) might at first suggest that Lewis is correct in taking a counterfactual with a true protasis to be true just as long as the apodosis is true. However, that conclusion is premature. There is a case in which one could plausibly claim that (10) was false, even though its protasis and apodosis both were true, namely that in which the patient has an atypical case of yellow fever and is displaying symptoms that yellow-fever patients rarely display. To restate that in Lewis's terms, the relation C of relative closeness among worlds would be such that there were worlds very close to w in which A was true and B false, namely worlds in which the patient had yellow fever but was exhibiting something closer to the normal symptoms. My opinion is that such worlds make (10) false. However, Lewis has set up his truth conditions in such a way that they would play no role in determining the truth value of (10): since w is the only world that is at least as close to w as w is, if A is true in w then truth of B in all the worlds in which A is true that are at least as close to w as w is amounts to just the truth of B in w. I thus conclude that Lewis's truth conditions make it too easy for a *would*-counterfactual to be true when its protasis is true.[4]

A second problem is the following, adapted from an example discussed by Nute (1984: 407–8). Suppose that you have an economy-class reservation on a flight on which the economy-class section is badly overbooked but there are two unsold first-class seats. When you

---

4 The following is another case in which one could plausibly hold that a *would*-counterfactual with true protasis and true apodosis was false. Suppose that Smith, who cannot be counted on to get up before noon, is supposed to take an 11 a.m. flight to get here for a lecture. I am under the mistaken impression that to catch the necessary flight Smith needs only to get up by 10 a.m. and catch a certain bus (actually, the schedule has been changed, and he would need to get up by 9 a.m. to be sure of getting to the airport in time); I am also under the mistaken impression that Smith is not yet here (he actually has just entered the lecture hall, unbeknownst to me, having got up at 10 a.m. and, through several strokes of luck, managed to board his plane before it took off). I express my belief that Smith got up too late and missed the flight and say *If Smith had got up at 10 a.m., he would be here now*. My statement about Smith is false, even though he did get up at 10 a.m. and is indeed here now.

check in, you are assigned the last economy-class seat. You later discover that some passengers who had economy-class tickets and who
checked in after you (in fact, the two persons who were immediately
behind you in line, one of whom joined the line only a split second
after you did) were upgraded to first class. You might then say

(11) Damn it! If I had checked in later, I would have gotten an upgrade

You would have been wrong: if you had checked in more than about a
minute later, you wouldn't have even gotten onto the flight, let alone
gotten an upgrade; but what you said would come out true according
to Lewis's truth conditions, at least if one treats times the way Lewis
treated heights: there would be a world w' in which you checked in
later (specifically, a world in which you were at most two places further back in the line) such that in all of the worlds at least as close to
the real world as w' in which you checked in later you got an upgrade.
Here, as in the preceding case, a counterfactual is given a dubious
assignment of the value 'true' because Lewis's truth conditions rule
out of consideration worlds that would normally be regarded as relevant to the truth of the counterfactual (here, worlds in which you were
three places further back in line).

A third problem, noted by Nollaig MacKenzie, is reported in
Harper (1981: 9). Lewis's treatment of sentences such as (6), repeated
here as (12a), has the bizarre consequence that all sentences of the
form (12b) should then be true:

(12a) If David Lewis were over 7' tall, he would have trouble shopping for
      clothes (= (6))
(12b) If David Lewis were over 7' tall, he would be under 7' + ε tall

Specifically, no matter how close to zero ε is, all the worlds in which
Lewis's height is between 7' and 7' + ε/2 are worlds in which he is over
7' tall, and in all of them his height is less than 7' + ε. Thus, according
to Lewis's truth conditions (plus his stipulation about how his height
in the different worlds relates to the closeness relation C), if Lewis
were over 7' tall, he would be over 7' tall by less than any conceivable
amount.[5]

---

[5] In McCawley (1981), I took up another problem with Lewis's analysis that I will
ignore here, namely that it treats alike all counterfactuals with a necessarily false protasis, notwithstanding some fairly clear differences in people's judgments of their truth:
If 3 were an even number, 4 would be odd (true). *If 3 were an even number, 5 would be odd*
(false).

There is a proposal for the truth conditions of *would*-counterfactuals that provides an easy way out of these problems while retaining the virtues of Lewis's account, and in the process makes it easy to extend one's account to *might*-counterfactuals. Suppose that, following Nute (1975), we replace 'local entailment' in (4) by what I will call **uniform** local entailment. Specifically, suppose that we

(13a)   assume that there is a function Ψ (w, A) that associates to each world w and proposition A a 'sphere' around w that takes in all alternatives to w that are 'worth considering seriously' if A is being considered as a serious possibility. [A set W of worlds is a *sphere* around w if for every world w' in W, W also contains all worlds w" for which Cww"w', i.e. whatever worlds it contains, it also contains all worlds that are at least as close to w]. NB: the specific choice of Ψ varies with context and is in the realm of 'scorekeeping'.[6] Ψ is subject to the condition that Ψ (w, A) contain worlds in which A is true; the case in which there are no worlds (in the ordinary sense) in which A is true might be handled by treating Ψ (w, A) in that case as containing all ordinary worlds and, in addition, the 'absurd world' in which all propositions are true.

(13b)   adopt the following truth conditions:
'If A were the case, B would be the case' is true in w if and only if in all worlds of Ψ(w, A) in which A is true, B is also true.
'If A were the case, B might be the case' is true in w if and only if in some worlds of Ψ(w, A) in which A is true, B is also true.

With (13b) as the truth conditions, it is neither implausibly difficult nor implausibly easy for a *might*-counterfactual to be true. For example, (14) will be true as long as the possibility of your drinking the water brings into serious consideration worlds in which you drink it and get sick, even if there are worlds in which you drink it and don't get sick that are closer to the real world than any world in which you drink it and get sick:

(14)   If you had drunk that water, you might have gotten sick

Thus, if A is the proposition that you drank the water and B is the proposition that you got sick, a world w' in which you drank the water and got sick is enough to make (14) true as long as w' belongs to

---

[6] i.e. it is subject to negotiation among the parties to a discourse; worlds that would otherwise not be considered as serious possibilities can be made to count as serious possibilities if one of the parties to the discourse insists on loosening the standards of what worlds are 'serious possibilities', i.e. insists on taking Ψ(w, A) to be large enough to include the worlds in question.

Ψ(w, A), even if you didn't get sick in any of the closest worlds to w in which you drank the water. However, really outlandish worlds in which you drink the water and get sick aren't enough to make the sentence true: only worlds that belong to Ψ(w, A) can serve to verify a *might*-counterfactual or to refute a *would*-counterfactual.

In addition, while the two versions of truth conditions for *might*-counterfactuals suggested by Lewis's treatment of *would*-counterfactuals are nonequivalent with a real vengeance, their analogs in Nute's approach in fact define the same truth conditions: 'it is not the case that in all worlds of Ψ(w, A) in which A is true, B is false' is equivalent to 'in some worlds of Ψ(w, A) in which A is true, B is true,' at least under the supposition that in every world every proposition is either true or false.

Lewis's account of the invalidity of the arguments in (5) goes through equally well with Nute's (13*b*) as the truth conditions: the only difference is that the classes of worlds that figure in the various steps would generally be larger, since Ψ(w, A) generally takes in more worlds in which A is true than the very closest ones to w. Nute's truth conditions likewise don't require that there be any absolutely closest worlds to w in which 'Lewis is over 7′ tall' is true, but this is just because (13*b*) operates in terms of spheres: the condition that the sphere Ψ(w, A) contain worlds in which A is true is noncommittal with regard to whether any of those worlds is closest to w. MacKenzie's problem, then, is no problem for Nute: since Ψ(w, Lewis is over 7′ tall) is a sphere about w and contains worlds in which Lewis is over 7′ tall, there will be values of ε for which it is false that 'If Lewis were over 7′ tall, he would be under 7′ + ε tall,' namely any value of ε for which Lewis's height is at least 7′ + ε in some world of the given sphere, though what values they are will depend in an indeterminate way on context, because of the indeterminate way in which Ψ depends on context.

For Lewis, when A is true in w, one need not look outside of w to tell whether A $\square\rightarrow$ B is true; however, for Nute, even when A is true in w, Ψ(w, A) will generally contain more worlds than just w, and so the falsehood of B in other worlds of Ψ(w, A) in which A is true can make the counterfactual false (see Fig. 4.2). Thus, Nute's truth conditions allow (10) to be false in cases such as the one described above in which A and B are both true in the real world but A is true and B false in close alternatives to the real world. In addition, (13*b*) lets the over-booked-airliner example (11) come out false, as it should: as long as

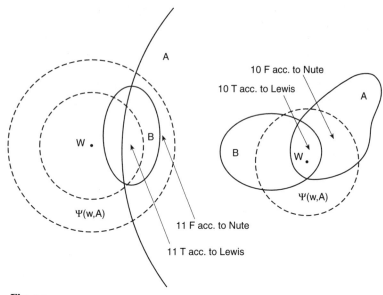

Fig. 4.2.

$\Psi(w, A)$ is large enough to take in at least some worlds in which the speaker got in line more than two places behind his actual place, there will be worlds of $\Psi(w, A)$ in which he checked in later and didn't get an upgrade, and thus the counterfactual comes out false.

So far, I have been speaking only about counterfactual conditionals; let me now bring indicative conditionals into the picture. As I indicated at the beginning, I want to develop an analysis in which each of the linguistic elements that can figure in conditional sentences makes its own contribution to the interpretation of a sentence. If I am to make Nute's analysis of counterfactual conditionals a part of that research program, I must factor out from it specific contributions to the interpretation that are made by the *if* and by the subjunctive mood, in such a way that the *if* makes the same contribution to the interpretation of indicative conditionals but combines with indicative rather than subjunctive mood. Since the 'selection function' $\Psi(w, A)$ is clearly something that is specific to subjunctive rather than indicative conditionals (i.e. it's only in subjunctive conditionals that there is reason to consider worlds that differ from the real world by enough to make the protasis a real possibility), the most obvious way to separate out the contributions of *if* and the subjunctive mood to the interpretation of subjunctive conditionals is to suggest that *if A, B*, whether indicative or subjunctive,[7] says that in all worlds of such-and-such class in which A is true, B is true, with indicative and subjunctive conditionals differing with regard to what that class of worlds is.

Actually, I wish to claim that indicative conditionals are not a homogeneous class and that there are simply a number of different kinds of *if*-sentences, some with an indicative form and some with a subjunctive form, all saying something of the form 'In all worlds of such-and-such class in which A is true, B is true,' and differing with regard to what sort of 'worlds' serve as values of the world variable, whether worlds that are in some sense epistemically possible, temporal slices of possible continuations of the way the actual world is up to now, or hypothetical alternatives to the real world:

- (15a) If John took the 2:00 plane, he is in Toronto by now
- (15a′) If John took the 2:00 plane, he'll be in Toronto in time for the meeting
- (15b) If Mary wins the lottery, she'll buy a new house
- (15b′) If the phone rings at an inconvenient moment, I don't answer it
- (15c) If Dukakis had replaced his advisors by competent people, he might have been elected

In the remainder of this paper, I will concentrate on indicative conditionals such as (15a) and a treatment of them close to that of Geis and Lycan (forthcoming), according to which the relevant set of worlds is, roughly speaking, the set of epistemically possible worlds, that is, the worlds that are consistent with 'what is known.' I will interpret the notion of 'epistemically possible world' in a way that will make it fit the general approach of this paper, in which conversational scorekeeping influences the interpretation of many elements of meaning and scorekeeping is done on the basis of the mutual knowledge of the participants in a discourse. I will make the following four assumptions:

(i) As I will use the term here, an 'epistemically possible world' has to be consistent with the mutual knowledge of the participants in the

---

[7] In saying this, I am tacitly assuming that *if A, B* is indicative or subjunctive as a whole, rather than the two pieces being independently indicative or subjunctive. While sentences in which one part is subjunctive and the other indicative are rare, they do occasionally occur, as in the following example, adapted from Johnson-Laird (1986): *If you had needed money, there was plenty in my bank account.* Perhaps such examples can be fit into the indicative/subjunctive dichotomy by claiming that they convey a subjunctive apodosis ('If you had needed money, you could have had some of the money that was in my bank account').

discourse, though not necessarily with knowledge in general. Thus, relative to a given discourse taking place in 1991, there may be epistemically possible worlds in which Elvis Presley is still alive or in which early human beings hunted dinosaurs. There is only a loose connection between what worlds are epistemically possible in the sense in which I use the term here and what worlds are possible in relation to the full corpus of human knowledge, or even in relation to the full corpus of propositions that any of the participants in the discourse knows.

(ii) However, not all worlds consistent with the mutual knowledge of the participants in the discourse will count as epistemically possible: only some of them will be 'live' enough possibilities to count.

(iii) Co-operativity demands that the sentences uttered in a discourse be given nonvacuous interpretations. And

(iv) For conditionals to be nonvacuous, the set of worlds under consideration has to be large enough to take in at least some worlds in which the protasis is true.

These conditions imply that, if it is necessary in order to make nonvacuous an indicative conditional that someone utters, the set of epistemically possible worlds will be enlarged sufficiently that there will be some in which the protasis of the conditional is true, possibly deleting propositions from the mutual knowledge if that is necessary to make such worlds epistemically possible. Thomason (1973) argues that the words *may* and *must* are commonly used to (respectively) broaden or narrow the class of epistemically possible worlds, e.g. in a discussion about lost baggage, a person might say (16a) to stipulate that worlds in which his bag was loaded onto the wrong plane or was stolen before being loaded will not count as epistemically possible in what is to follow, and he might say (16b) to stipulate that worlds in which the bag destined for Portland was unloaded at Kansas City or at Salt Lake City will count as epistemically possible in what is to follow:

(16a) The bag must have been loaded onto my flight
(16b) It may have been unloaded at one of the intermediate stops

Any set of truth conditions of the general form under consideration here makes it harder for a conditional to be true than it is under the classical truth table. According to the classical truth table, the only thing that can make a conditional false is for the protasis to be true and the apodosis false in the given world. However, according to truth conditions such as are under consideration here, the conditional will be false as long as the protasis is true and the apodosis false in *some* world of the class in question, not necessarily the actual world. Thus, according to my version of the Geis–Lycan truth conditions, (17) will be false as long as, as far as the participants in the discourse mutually know, it may be that it's raining in Santo Domingo right now and Morry's Deli hasn't just run out of chopped liver:

(17) If it's raining in Santo Domingo right now, Morry's Deli has just run out of chopped liver

The classical truth table is the degenerate special case of these truth conditions in which only the actual world counts as an epistemically possible world.[8] Correspondingly, the argument (18), which is valid according to 'standard' logic, is invalid according to the Geis–Lycan truth conditions:

(18) It is not the case that if God is dead, everything is permissible
Therefore God is dead and not everything is permissible

In fact, inferences of the form in (18) will be invalid relative to any system of truth conditions of the general form considered here, other than the classical truth table, since except for that degenerate case there will always be instances in which the protasis of some conditional is true and the apodosis false in some world of whatever the privileged class is but not in the actual world.

---

[8] One important implication of this claim that needs to be tested is that it should be possible to say later that the speaker who uttered (17) was right or wrong on the basis of the mutual knowledge of the time rather than the way the facts have turned out, e.g. (i) should be a normal thing to say and (ii) shouldn't: (i) You said that if it was raining in Santo Domingo, Morry's had just run out of chopped liver, but you were wrong—for all we knew, Morry's could still have had some chopped liver, regardless of what was going on in Santo Domingo. (ii) You said that if we caught the 2:00 plane, we'd be in time for the meeting, but you were wrong: the meeting started half an hour ago and here we are sitting in the middle of a traffic jam on the Kennedy Expressway. My immediate reaction to these sentences is that the first implication is correct but the second isn't: both sentences are reasonable ways for the speaker to dispute what his interlocutor had said. The best that I can do to reconcile my claims with this apparent fact is probably to suggest that the speaker who utters (ii) revises *ex post facto* the score relative to which his interlocutor had asserted the conditional, so as to include (what turned out to be) the actual world among the epistemically possible worlds. He is entitled to do that, since the set of epistemically possible worlds is supposed to include the actual world, even if the participants in the discourse, through ignorance or error, have inadvertently excluded the actual world from what they are taking to be the epistemically possible worlds.

All the various kinds of conditionals allow such words as *only* or *even* to be combined with the *if*-clause:

(19a) John will be at the meeting only if he managed to catch the 2:00 plane

(19a′) John will be late for the meeting even if he managed to catch the 2:00 plane

(19b) John gets angry only if people make fun of him

(19b′) Agnes stays calm even if everyone else is going crazy

(19c) Bush would fire Baker only if Baker were convicted of a felony

(19c′) Bush wouldn't fire Baker even if Baker were convicted of a felony

The truth conditions proposed here for conditional sentences make it possible to treat *only if* and *even if* as simply combinations of *only* or *even* with an *if*-clause, rather than the idioms that logicians have commonly but erroneously treated them as. To the arguments that Geis (1973) and I (McCawley, 1974) have already given that the *only* and *even* of these examples are the ordinary *only* and *even*, I add the observation that *only if* and *even if* allow *only* and *even* to be separated from their foci just as *only* and *even* normally can be:

(20a) John only eats *organic foods*. (focus italicized)

(20a′) John will only be at the meeting *if he managed to catch the 2:00 flight*

(20a″) John only gets angry *if people make fun of him*

(20a‴) Bush would only fire Baker *if Baker were convicted of a felony*

(20b) John even lied about *his place of birth*

(20b′) John will even come to the meeting *if he's running a fever*

(20b″) John doesn't even get angry *if people make fun of him*

(20b‴) Bush wouldn't even fire Baker *if Baker were convicted of a felony*

The focus must be *if A* and not just *if*, in virtue of the acceptability of substitutions for *if A* but not of substitutions for just *if*:

(21a) John eats only *organic* foods; for example, he doesn't eat Twinkies.

(21b) John gets angry only *if people make fun of him*; for example, he doesn't get angry if people waste his time

(21b′) ??John gets angry only *if* people make fun of him; for example, he doesn't get angry although/because people make fun of him

Treating *if A* as the focus of course requires that one give up the constituent structure implicit in most logicians' treatments of *if*, in which *if* is a sister of two Ss that it combines with (22a), in favor of one in which *if* and the sentence with which it combines make up a syntactic unit (22b), a move that logicians will find shocking and linguists boring:

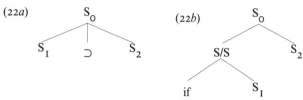

The truth conditions that I am developing here in fact treat *if S₁* as a syntactic unit modifying S_2.

In giving the examples (21), I have implicitly assigned to *only* a logical form 'nothing that is not', so that e.g. *John eats only organic foods* will have a logical form 'For all foods x such that x is not an organic food, John doesn't eat x.' ((21*a*) has an understood extra premise: Twinkies aren't an organic food.) As long as *if A* is given an interpretation of the form 'in worlds of such-and-such class in which A,' it can be combined with the suggested logical form for *only*: *only if A* will mean 'in no worlds of such-and-such class other than those in which A.' For an indicative conditional, the class of worlds will be the epistemically possible worlds, and (19*a*) will be interpreted as saying that in no epistemically possible worlds other than those in which John managed to catch the 2:00 flight will he be at the meeting; likewise, (19*b*) will be interpreted as saying that in no temporal slices of possible histories other than ones in which people make fun of John does John get angry.

I will not present a detailed analysis of the *even if* sentences here, but will merely state that the approach to *only if* that I sketch here can be adapted to *even if* as long as *even* is given an analysis in which it binds a variable that ranges over elements that contrast with its focus, as in the analysis of *only* as 'nothing other than . . .' For example, if (23*a*) is assigned a logical structure '{x: x passed the exam} includes not only the values of x that are unremarkable but also Ted' and (23*b*) a logical structure '{x: x voted for Bush} takes in not only unremarkable values of x but also values for which x is a Southerner', (23*c*) would be assigned one of the form '{w': (Bush keeps Baker in his cabinet) in w'} includes not only unremarkable members of Ψ(w, Baker is convicted of a felony) but also worlds in which Baker is convicted of a felony:[9]

[9] Here I am hinting at an analysis of *even* in terms not of the quantifiers that figure in the analyses of Fraser, Horn, and others but rather of the image that *even* suggests to me: that of the set of verifying instances expanding from the least remarkable ones, through ever more remarkable ones, until the instances corresponding to the focus of *even* are reached; an analysis of *even* that I find highly congenial is developed in Kay (1990).

(23*a*) Even Ted passed the exam

(23*b*) Even Southerners voted for Bush

(23*c*) Bush would keep Baker in his cabinet even if Baker were convicted of a felony

(23*d*) Dukakis would have lost even if the Republicans had nominated Pat Robertson

(23*d'*) Dukakis would have lost even if the Republicans had nominated Charles Manson

Both (23*d*) and (23*d'*) say that Dukakis lost in all of some large set of possible worlds, and they differ with regard to how large that set is: since worlds in which the Republicans nominated Manson are more remote from the real world than worlds in which they nominated Robertson, the world variable ranges over a larger domain in (23*d'*) than in (23*d*).

Only if can be treated as *only* plus *if*, irrespective of which kinds of 'world' the world variable takes as its values. There is an illusion that different cases of *only if* differ in what paraphrases they allow, but this is simply because different cases differ with regard to how blatant the differences between the truth conditions of the putative paraphrases are. Compare the generic indicative conditionals in (24) with the counterfactuals in (25):

(24*a*) My pulse goes over 100 only if I do heavy exercise

(24*b*) If my pulse goes over 100, I do heavy exercise

(24*c*) My pulse doesn't go over 100 if I don't do heavy exercise

(24*c'*) My pulse doesn't go over 100 unless I do heavy exercise

(25*a*) Dukakis would have been elected only if he had replaced his advisors by competent people

(25*b*) If Dukakis had been elected, he would have replaced his advisors by competent people

(25*c*) Dukakis wouldn't have been elected if he hadn't replaced his advisors by competent people

(25*c'*) Dukakis wouldn't have been elected unless he had replaced his advisors by competent people

In both cases, the sentence form that logic textbooks usually offer as an equivalent of *A only if B*, namely *If A, B* (24*b*, 25*b*) turns out to be a wretched paraphrase, in part because it reverses the temporal and causal connections between A and B. (Logicians have gotten away with paraphrasing *A only if B* as *If A, then B* only because they have usually restricted themselves to conditional sentences whose parts didn't stand in any significant temporal and causal relations, so that there was nothing for the substitution to reverse.) The indicative *only if* conditional (24*a*) is quite well paraphrased by both (24*c*) and (24*c'*); however, in the counterfactual case these paraphrases diverge, the *not . . . unless* version (25*c'*) being a much better paraphrase of (25*a*) than the *not . . . if not* version (25*c*). Many of the arguments given by Geis (1973) and Geis and Lycan (forthcoming) that *unless* does not mean 'if not' but rather 'except if' can be used to bring out not only differences between the meaning of an indicative conditional with *unless* and one with *if not*, as in (26*a*, 26*a'*) but also between counterfactuals such as (26*b*, 26*b'*):

(26*a*)   I give students low grades only if they don't do their assignments
(26*a'*) *I give students low grades only unless they do their assignments
(26*b*)   Bush would fire Baker only if Baker didn't support his policies
(26*b'*) *Bush would fire Baker only unless Baker supported his policies
(26*c*)   *Sam works out at the gym only except on Tuesdays

If can combine with any kind of sentence, negative or affirmative, irrespective of whether an *only* is attached to it, as illustrated in (26*a*, 26*b*), and *only* can combine with an *if*-clause irrespective of the latter's internal structure, but *if* cannot combine with an *unless*-clause, since *unless* means 'except if' and *only except* is incoherent, as illustrated in (26*c*).

However, there is something special to counterfactuals that makes the difference between *unless* and *if not* bigger in the counterfactual than in the indicative case. Specifically, the sets of worlds from which the world variables are chosen in the counterfactual case are distinct, except that that for *not . . . unless* coincides with that for *only if*. Specifically, the sets of worlds from which the world variables for (25*a–c*) take their values are:

(27*a*) $\Psi(w, A)$ A = Dukakis replaced his advisors by competent people
(27*b*) $\Psi(w, B)$ B = Dukakis was elected
(27*c*) $\Psi(w, \neg A)$

In most cases, no two of these sets will be identical, and that in itself will be enough to allow the corresponding sentences to differ in truth value. For example, $\Psi(w, A)$ generally is distinct from $\Psi(w, \neg A)$, because whichever of A and $\neg A$ is true in w, a smaller sphere will be needed to accommodate all the worlds that it makes worthy of consideration; here, $\Psi(w, \neg A)$ is much smaller than $\Psi(w, A)$, and thus it is easier for (25*c*) than for (25*a*) to be true. (I overlook here something that makes (25*c*) a less normal thing to say than (25*a*), namely its false suggestion that Dukakis did replace his advisors by competent people.) According to Geis's analysis of *unless* as 'except if', $(25c') =$ 'except in worlds of $\Psi(w, A)$ [NB: not of $\Psi(w, \neg A)$!] in which Dukakis replaced his advisors, he wasn't elected,'[10] and thus the truth conditions of $(25c')$ agree with those of $(25a)$ and not of $(25c)$.

Let me finally return again to conversational scorekeeping. By treating the set of epistemically possible worlds that figures in the interpretation of conditionals as part of Lewis's conversational score, we can show that various questionable instances of supposedly valid patterns of inference involve conversational fouls, though the inferences in themselves may be perfectly valid. George Lakoff, among others, has offered as evidence that Strengthening the Protasis $(28a)$ is not generally valid even for indicative conditionals examples such as $(28b)$:

($28a$) If A, B.
     Therefore, if A and A', B.
($28b$) If they went to Hawaii, they had a pleasant vacation
     Therefore, if they went to Hawaii and went to Greece, they had a
     pleasant vacation

For the premise of $(28b)$ to be true, it would have to be evaluated relative to a set of epistemically possible worlds that is sufficiently narrow to exclude various things that would have made their vacation unpleasant, e.g. doing more traveling than they could comfortably fit into a vacation. However, given some plausible assumptions about how much time they had for their vacation and how much traveling they could comfortably endure, the conclusion would be nonvacuous only relative to a score in which the set of epistemically possible worlds included worlds in which they did more traveling than they could comfortably do, and relative to that score the premise would be false. In that case, one who offered the argument $(28b)$ would be committing a foul.

---

[10] An important difference between *unless* and *if not* that I am not taking up here relates to the possibility of truth-value gaps. If A is neither true nor false in a world w', then w' is among the worlds taken in by 'except in worlds in which A' (because w is not a world in which A is true) but is not among the worlds taken in by 'in worlds in which not A' (because 'not A' likewise is not true in w'). This difference is reflected in the different acceptability of the following sentences relative to a context in which students are not assumed to all have living mothers: *I won't excuse a student from the exam unless his mother is on her deathbed. ??I won't excuse a student from the exam if his mother isn't on her deathbed.* Not surprisingly, the *only if* version is just as acceptable as the *not . . . unless* version: *I will excuse a student from the exam only if his mother is on her deathbed.*

This point is fairly trivial, since there are obviously many cases in which a proposition A is true relative to some score, while a conjunction A & A' in which it figures is true only relative to a score in which the set of epistemically possible worlds is larger. It is somewhat more difficult to come up with examples in which contraposition would be anomalous in virtue of such a foul, since having a score that would make *If A, B* true does not usually exclude epistemically possible worlds in which B is true. There are, however, cases in which the most plausible scores that make *If A, B* true are ones that exclude from epistemic possibility worlds in which B is not true, e.g.

(29a) If she wrote a letter to Santa Claus, he didn't send her an answer
??Therefore, if Santa Claus sent her an answer, she didn't write him a letter

(29b) If he said anything, he said something that we can ignore
??Therefore, if he didn't say anything that we can ignore, he didn't say anything

The most plausible scores relative to which the premise of (29a) would be true and a co-operative thing to say are scores in which there is no Santa Claus in any epistemically possible world; however, for the conclusion to be a co-operative thing to say, the score must include epistemically possible worlds in which Santa Claus sent her an answer and in which thus there is a Santa Claus, and relative to that score, the grounds for evaluating the premise as true have vanished.

As a last illustration of the role of conversational scorekeeping in this treatment of indicative conditionals, I turn to a puzzle about indicative conditionals that has been discussed in such recent works as Jackson (1987). Arguments such as (30) have been suggested occasionally as counterexamples to a pattern of inference that is almost universally regarded as valid for indicative conditionals, namely Transitivity:

(30) If it rained, it didn't rain heavily
If it rained heavily, it rained
Therefore, if it rained heavily, it didn't rain heavily

There are a number of possible responses to (30). A defender of the analysis of *if* as a connective with the classical truth table could simply claim that (30) is really valid: according to the classical truth table (plus the assumption that it can't rain heavily unless it rains), the first premise of (30) is true if and only if it didn't rain heavily, and that would be sufficient to make the conclusion true according to the classical truth table. The response that I prefer, however, is the following. For the first premise to be true, the score has to be such that there are no epistemically possible worlds in which it rained heavily. But for the second premise to be a co-operative thing to say, there have to be epistemically possible worlds in which it did rain heavily. And if one altered the score so as to make the second premise co-operative, one would have changed it to something relative to which the first premise was false: only relative to a score in which there aren't any epistemically possible worlds in which it rained heavily is the first premise true. Therefore, if one were to offer (30) as an argument, one would commit a foul by surreptitiously changing the score in mid-argument to one that would make the first premise false. Relative to the new score, the conclusion would be false (indeed, it would be false relative to any score that would make it a co-operative thing to say), but that is immaterial, since the new score would not make all the premises true.

REFERENCES

ANDERSON, A. R. (1951). 'A Note on Subjunctive and Counterfactual Conditionals,' *Analysis* **12**: 35–8.

FILLMORE, C. J. (1987). 'Varieties of Conditional Sentences,' *Eastern States Conference on Linguistics* **3**: 163–82.

GEIS, M. (1973), '*If* and *unless*,' in B. Kachru *et al.* (eds.), *Issues in Linguistics*, 231–53. Urbana, Ill.: University of Illinois Press.

—— and LYCAN, W. (forthcoming). *A Treatise on Conditionals.*

HARPER, W. (1981). 'A Sketch of Some Recent Developments in the Theory of Conditionals,' in Harper *et al.* (1981: 3–38).

—— PEARCE, G., and ROBERT STALNAKER, R. (1981) (eds.). *Ifs.* Dordrecht: Reidel.

JACKSON, F. (1987). *Conditionals.* Oxford: Oxford University Press.

JOHNSON-LAIRD, P. N. (1986). 'Conditionals and Mental Models,' in E. Traugott *et al.* (eds.), *Conditionals*, 55–75. Cambridge: Cambridge University Press.

KARTTUNEN, L. (1969). 'Presupposition and Linguistic Context', *Theoretical Linguistics* **1**: 182–94.

—— and PETERS, S. (1979). 'Conventional Implicature,' in Oh and Dinneen (1979: 1–56).

KAY, P. (1990). '*Even*,' *Linguistics and Philosophy* **13**: 59–111.

LAKOFF, G. (1971). 'Linguistics and Natural Logic,' in D. Davidson and G. Harman (eds.), *Semantics of Natural Language*, 545–665. Dordrecht: Reidel.

LEWIS, D. (1973). *Counterfactuals*. Oxford: Blackwell.

—— (1979). 'Scorekeeping in a Language Game,' *Journal of Philosophical Logic* **8**: 339–59.

MCCAWLEY, J. D. (1974). '*If* and *only if*,' *Linguistic Inquiry* **5**: 632–5.

—— (1976). 'Remarks on What Can Cause What,' in M. Shibatani (ed.), *The Grammar of Causative Constructions*, 117–29. (New York Academic Press. Repr. in McCawley, *Adverbs, Vowels, and Other Objects of Wonder*, 101–12. Chicago: University of Chicago Press, 1979).

—— (1979). 'Presupposition and Discourse Structure,' in Oh and Dinneen (1979: 371–88).

—— (1981). *Everything that Linguists Have Always Wanted to Know About Logic (But Were Ashamed to Ask)*. Chicago: University of Chicago Press.

—— (1986). 'Actions and Events Despite Bertrand Russell,' in E. LePore and B. McLaughlin (eds.), *Actions and Events*, 177–92. Oxford: Blackwell.

NUTE, D. (1975). 'Counterfactuals and the similarity of worlds,' *Journal of Philosophy* **72**: 773–8.

—— (1984). 'Conditional Logic,' in D. M. Gabbay and F. Guenthner (eds.), *Handbook of Philosophical Logic* ii, 387–439. Dordrecht: Reidel.

OH, C.-K., and DINNEEN, D. (1979) (eds.). *Presupposition*. New York: Academic Press.

PRINCE, E. (1978). 'On the Functions of Existential Presupposition in Discourse,' *CLS* **14**: *Papers from the Fourteenth Regional Meeting of the Chicago Linguistic Society*, 362–76.

THOMASON, R. (1973). 'Semantics, Pragmatics, Conversation, and Presupposition.' MS.

5

Interaction of Factors in Construal: Japanese Relative Clauses

Yoshiko Matsumoto

INTRODUCTION

The idea that syntax, semantics, and pragmatics are interdependent is clearly stated in Fillmore (1981): 'I also believe that some syntactic facts require semantic and pragmatic explanations and that some semantic facts require pragmatic explanations. Put differently, inter-preters sometimes use semantic and pragmatic information in making judgements about the syntactic structure of a sentence, and they sometimes use pragmatic facts in making semantic judgements' (p. 144). In this spirit, the goal of this paper is to consider what various factors serve to determine the interpretation of the relative-clause construction in Japanese, and to examine how such factors interact. This goal would appear to be unnecessary if one assumed that the interpretation of Japanese relative-clause constructions could, like their English counterparts, be unambiguously based on their syntax. However, a careful examination of the Japanese constructions reveals that such a parallelism between English and Japanese relative clauses is not supported. In the following sections I will illustrate that it is semantics and pragmatics, but not syntax, that play the central role in the construal of Japanese relative-clause constructions, and that a multitude of factors, rather than a single rule or principle, are crucial for construal.

This chapter is a revised and expanded version of a paper presented at the Annual Meeting of the LSA at Philadelphia in January, 1992. I would like to thank Susumu Kuno for his comments on my research project, and Peter Sells for reading and com-menting on versions of this paper. My thanks are also due to Adele E. Goldberg, Yasunari Harada, Masayo Iida, Michio Isoda, and Ivan Sag for their discussion and encouragement. This research was partially supported by a Seed Grant from the College of Humanities at the Ohio State University during 1990–1.

5.1. THE ROLE OF SEMANTICS AND PRAGMATICS IN JAPANESE RELATIVE CLAUSES

5.1.1. *Contrast between Japanese and English relative clauses*

Japanese relative clauses appear prenominally with their predicate typically in a finite form.[1] The feature most relevant to the discussion here is that the grammatical role of the target of relativization is not overtly marked, regardless of whether or not that target is a sub-categorized argument of the relative-clause predicate. That is, there is no structural indication as to how the head noun is linked with the target of the relativization. Moreover, it cannot be assumed that a missing complement in a relative clause is necessarily bound to the head noun. In accord with the well-known general characteristic of Japanese—that there is no requirement that all the complements of a predicate be present in a sentence—it is perfectly possible to have a relative-clause construction in which an adjunct is the target of relativization while one or all complements are missing. This char-acteristic gives rise to a multiplicity of possible interpretations for a single construction; to construe the construction as intended, hearers must actively employ available clues from the linguistic and non-linguistic context and from their knowledge of the world (Matsumoto, 1988; 1990; in preparation). The point is illustrated by the follow-ing example, which lists a subset of the possible interpretations of a complex NP consisting of a relative clause and the noun that it modifies.

(1)   [[hon o katta] gakusee]
       book ACC bought student
(1a) 'the student (who) bought a book'
(1b) 'the student (from whom) (   ) bought a book'
(1c) 'the student (for/to whom) (   ) bought a book'

The translation given in (1a), in which the subject of the predicate *katta* 'bought' is the target of the relativization, is not the only possible interpretation of the complex NP given in (1). For instance, (1) would be in all likelihood interpreted as (1b) when used in a main clause con-text such as (2).

---

[1] An exception to this general characteristic is that, when the predicate is an adject-ival noun or a noun + copula in the non-past form, it assumes an adnominal form.

(2) [[Hon o katta] gakusee] kara pasokon mo kau
    book ACC bought student from PC. also buy
    koto ni sita.
    NMLZR DAT did
    '(I) decided to buy a PC too from the student (I) bought books from.'

Similarly, in a context in which someone has been buying various gifts for students, (1) could be used to convey the interpretation given in (1c).

It should be noted that, although (1a) represents the only one of the three suggested interpretations in which the missing complement is bound with the head noun, it is not necessarily preferred over other interpretations if the context specifically suggests a plausible reading. In other words, the 'syntactically motivated' interpretation, in which the head noun is bound to a 'missing' complement of the relative-clause predicate, does not preclude other possible interpretations.[2]

The point that syntactic factors such as the subcategorization of the predicate in the relative clause cannot be the sole basis for the determination of the grammatical role of the target of the relativization comes into clearer focus when we contrast Japanese relative clauses with English counterparts.

It seems to be uncontroversial in English that a missing subcategorized argument must be construed as bound with the head noun of a relative clause. Therefore, *the restaurant that John ate* only has a pragmatically strange interpretation, within a normal understanding of the world: the *restaurant* is the object that was eaten. The location role for *restaurant* is not available in this example, unlike in the Japanese counterpart (as we will discuss later in (22)), since English requires a preposition to indicate such a role, as, for example, in *the restaurant at which John ate*. However, this requirement can be circumvented if the head noun is *place*, which can function as an adverbial, as exemplified in the complex NP in *This is the kind of the place I want to eat everyday*.

Similarly, the interpretation of the *place* in (3a) is as taking an adverbial role, specifically, the location role.

(3a) Is the place John plans to construct a memorial hall expensive?

---

[2] Na (1986) claims in her analysis of Korean relative clauses that there is a hierarchy among 'subcategorized elements', 'semantically entailed elements', and 'pragmatically entailed elements', in that order. Matsumoto (1990) discusses the inapplicability of such a hierarchy to Japanese relative clauses.

In contrast, the head noun *place* in (3*b*) is only interpretable as the building to be constructed, rather than as the location of the construction activity.

(3*b*) Is the place John plans to construct expensive?

That is, because of the subcategorization of the relative clause predicate *construct*, the object-role interpretation takes precedence over the location-role interpretation, even though it involves some amount of reasoning to facilitate the construal of (3*b*) by interpreting 'the place' as a blueprint or a model rather than an actual product of construction.

One could attribute the contrast between (3*a*) and (3*b*) to the general requirement for relative-clause constructions that the subcategorization of the relative clause predicate be satisfied. If Japanese had a similar constraint, we would expect to find similar contrasts in the data. This is not supported, however. To be sure, there is a construction corresponding to (3*a*) in Japanese, given in (4*a*).

(4*a*) [[Nomura-san ga   kinendoo   o   kentikusi-yoo to
         Mr Nomura NOM memorial hall ACC construct-VOL COMPL
         keekakusite-iru] basyo] wa   takai   desu ka
         is-planning   place   TOP expensive   is   Q
         'Is the place Mr Nomura plans to construct a memorial hall expensive?'

The Japanese construction corresponding to (3*b*), however, also has the location interpretation for the head noun, but not the object interpretation, unlike (3*b*), as given in (4*b*).

(4*b*) [[Nomura-san ga   kentikusi-yoo   to   keekakusite-iru]
         Mr Nomura NOM construct-VOL COMPL is-planning
         basyo] wa   takai   desu ka
         place   TOP expensive   is   Q
         'Is the place (at which) Mr Nomura plans to construct (   ) expensive?'

The acceptability of (4*b*)[3] can be viewed as resulting from the *pro*-drop property. It can, however, also be seen, from the point of view of the construal, as showing that the head noun can be construed as linked with an adjunct even in relative-clause constructions in which a complement is not expressed.

---

[3] The acceptability would be the same for the sentence if the modifying clause predicate were replaced by another verb denoting 'construct', *tate-yoo* 'build/construct— VOL', which may be more clearly transitive.

The examples in the remainder of this section also illustrate that the determination of the grammatical role of the target of the relativization does not crucially depend on the subcategorization of the predicate in the relative clause. For instance, two of the most likely interpretations for the complex NP in (5) are those given in (5a) and (5b).

(5) [[Nomura-san ga   katta]   basyo] wa   doko   desu ka
       Mr Nomura NOM bought place TOP where is   QP
(5a) 'Where is the place (in which) Mr Nomura bought (it)?'
(5b) 'Where is the place (which) Mr Nomura bought?'

The choice between (5a) and (5b) largely depends on the interlocutors' knowledge about Mr Nomura and about the place.

In contrast, the corresponding English example in (6) offers no flexibility in the interpretation of the complex NP.

(6) Where is [the place [Mr Nomura bought]]?

Although *place* in principle allows a locative interpretation, the only acceptable interpretation of the complex NP in (6) is the one in which 'the place' is the object of buying.

We have observed above that different interpretations are potentially available in Japanese, depending on the possible semantic and pragmatic relationships between the head noun and the clause. It is also important to note that, although syntax provides the structural basis for these constructions, it does not offer a useful tool for determining interpretations by itself. (See also 5.1.3.) In other words, in a syntactic analysis, the Japanese relative-clause construction is underdetermined from the surface form. Granted this, the question remains of how such constructions are successfully construed. Clearly the answer cannot be solely in terms of the predicate–argument structure of the relative-clause predicate. We will see more examples that support this point in the following sections.

5.1.2. *Construal of Japanese relative clauses*

Examples (7) and (8) illustrate more closely how construal is effected in Japanese.

(7a) [[tomo-tyan   ga   katta] mise] wa   doko
       Tomo-FAM.DIM NOM bought store TOP where
       'Where is the store (in which) little Tomo bought (it)?'
(7b) [[donarudo toranpu ga   katta]   mise] wa doko
       Donald Trump   NOM bought store TOP where
       'Where is the store (which) Donald Trump bought?'

(8) [[Kookoo   nyuusi   ni   zettai   ukaru]
      high school entrance examination DAT   absolutely pass
      katei-kyoosi]   o   sagasite-imasu
      tutor   ACC is-searching-for

(8a) '(I) am searching for a tutor (with whose asistance) (one) can be sure
      to pass the high-school entrance exam'

(8b) '(I) am searching for a tutor (who) can be sure to pass the high-school
      entrance exam'

For examples (7a) and (7b), the most natural interpretations are those
given in the translations. In explaining (5), I mentioned that the choice
between (5a) and (5b) depends on the interlocutors' knowledge of the
real world. This is even more visible in (7) and (8). For example, in (7),
depending on the identity and the social standing of the buyer, the role
of *mise* 'store' is likely to be interpreted either as a location, as in (7a),
or as the object, as in (7b). In (8), the preferred interpretation is (8a),
although the head noun is then an adjunct of the relative-clause
predicate *ukaru* 'pass'. This can be explained by the real-world background information that generally, when tutors are hired, it is of
particular relevance that the students whom they teach should pass
the examinations.

In examples (7) and (8), the most appropriate interpretation has to
be based on semantic and pragmatic information. While speakers of
Japanese would generally agree with the interpretations given in (7a)
and (8a), that does not imply that, in a specific context, (8b), for
example, may not be selected as an interpretation of (8). Thus, in
(9a), the store referred to by the complex NP is likely to be interpreted
as Trump's favorite location of buying, rather than as the object, as
in (7b).

(9a) [[donarudo toranpu ga   itumo   kau] mise]   wa   doko
      Donald Trump   NOM always buy   store   TOP   where
      'Where is the store (at which) Donald Trump always buys (things)?'

Note that, in the English example (9b), the syntax determines the
interpretation regardless of the pragmatic unnaturalness.

(9b) Where is [the store [Donald Trump always buys]]?

The complex NP in (9b) is interpreted consistently with the syntax
only as referring to a building that Trump repeatedly buys. The contrast between (9a) and (9b) reaffirms the point that, in English relative clauses, syntax takes precedence in construal over pragmatic

plausibility, while in Japanese counterparts, semantic coherence and pragmatic plausibility guide the construal. This also explains why the targets of relativization in (10a) and (10b) would normally receive assignments of different grammatical and semantic roles with regard to the relative clause verb *utta* 'hit'.

(10a) [[beebu ruusu ga utta] batto] wa asoko desu
     Babe Ruth NOM hit   bat TOP there is
    'The bat (with which) Babe Ruth hit is there'
(10b) [[beebu ruusu ga utta] booru] wa asoko desu
     Babe Ruth NOM hit   ball TOP there is
    'The ball (which) Babe Ruth hit is there'

The examples we have seen show that a gap, or missing complement, in the relative clause is not necessarily bound with the head noun. I claim that the existence of a syntactic binding relationship between the complement gap and the head noun is therefore a less useful criterion for determining the acceptability of relative-clause constructions than the condition that the relative clause and the head noun be semantically coherent. Coherence in this sense is best understood in terms of fitting into the frame or scene of the action described in the relative clause, since frames accommodate a wider variety of roles than does the subcategorization of a predicate. (See Fillmore, 1977; 1982; 1985 for an account of frame semantics, and Matsumoto, 1988; in preparation for an application of frame semantics to relative-clause constructions.) In order for the construction to be coherent, the semantic role of the head noun in the relative clause should be recoverable from structural, semantic, and pragmatic information available to the addressee; moreover, the semantic relation between the relative clause and the head noun should be pragmatically plausible. Plausibility in this sense depends on the 'world-view' or background knowledge of the interlocutors. For example, (11) is a perfectly acceptable construction although the role of the head noun in the relative clause is an obscure sort of adjunct, while (12) is generally impossible to construe without a special context. The interpretation of (11) is supported by the experience shared by people in Japan that they miss a chance to visit the bathroom during a commercial break since some TV commercials have recently become fun enough to watch. In contrast, there is no readily available world-view to support a connection between a pencil and bathroom-going; hence the construction is hardly considered semantically coherent.

(11) [[toire   ni   ike-nai]   komaasyaru]
         bathroom   GOAL cannot-go   commercial
      'commercials (because of wanting to watch which) (one) cannot go to
      the bathroom'
(12) ??[[toire   ni   ike-nai]   enpitu]
         bathroom   GOAL cannot-go   pencil
      'pencils (that) (one) cannot go to the bathroom',
      'pencils (that) cannot go to the bathroom', etc.

5.1.3. *Syntactic accounts and the 'aboutness relation'*

I claimed above that the interpretation of Japanese relative clause constructions is syntactically underdetermined, and that what syntax offers in the analysis of the constructions is therefore limited. Even
within syntax-based accounts such as Saito (1985), it is acknowledged
that Japanese relative clauses need not involve any syntactic movement internal to the relative clause (p. 291). This is based on two
observations: that the bound element in the clause may be a resumpt-
ive pronoun in a position inaccessible to movement, and that there
may in fact be no bound position at all within the relative clause. In
Saito's view, it seems, the syntax is responsible for generating a clause
as sister to the head noun, but has no role in the interpretation of the
relative-clause construction; interpretation, if it is to fit within his account at all, follows from the so-called 'aboutness relation' which
should hold between the relative clause and its head.

Consideration of a wide range of examples, however, suggests that
there is no obvious sense of 'aboutness' which can cover all the acceptable instances of relative-clause constructions. While it will always be
possible after the fact to describe any relative clause which can be successfully construed in a given context as being 'about' its head, there have
been no suggested properties of the 'aboutness relation' which would
predict in advance which relative-clause constructions are construable.

In this regard, it should also be noted that, notwithstanding Kuno's
claim (1973; 1976) to the contrary, the notion of 'aboutness' that describes the relation between the topic and the comment of the topic
construction in Japanese cannot be identified with the 'aboutness
relation' for relative-clause constructions. There are many instances of
well-formed relative-clause constructions which do not have a topic-
construction counterpart, some of which are presented by Kuno as
counterexamples to his hypothesis.[4] (13*a,b*) is such a pair (taken from

----

[4] Muraki (1970) is the original source of the counterexamples given in Kuno (1973).

Kuno, 1973: 260); (14*a*,*b*) represents another counterexample, showing the unnaturalness of a topic-construction counterpart to (11), given as (14*a*).[5]

   (13*a*) [[Taroo   ga   kessekisita]   riyuu]
           Taro   NOM was-absent   reason
          'the reason (for which) Taro was absent'
   (13*b*) *(Sono) riyuu   wa   Taroo   ga   kessekisita
           that   reason TOP Taro   NOM was-absent
   (14*a*) [[toire ni ikenai] komaasyaru] (= (11))
   (14*b*) ??(Sono) komaasyaru wa   toire   ni   ikenai
             that   commercial TOP   bathroom GOAL cannot-go

Intuitions about the nature of 'aboutness' that come from the topic construction cannot therefore be assumed to shed light directly on relative clauses. In a sense, the present paper can be seen as an investigation of the factors that contribute to the 'aboutness relation' observed in relative-clause constructions, while in fact denying that there is such a unitary relation.

While I agree with Saito that syntax should account for the formation but not the interpretation of relative clauses, I cannot agree that there is a 'condition' which controls well-formedness at some relevant interpretive linguistic level. Rather, various clues are used by hearers in the interpretation of particular utterances of relative clauses. This is not to imply, however, that the construal process should be considered random or nonsystematic, since native speakers consistently agree on the interpretation of the constructions. A complete analysis of Japanese relative clauses should start with what the syntax gives, namely an S and a sister N, and provide an account of what interpretations actually arise, what influences those interpretations, and how different factors interact in construal. I would now like to turn to the issue of the factors that determine or help recover the semantic role of the head noun in the relative clause.

5.2. FACTORS IN CONSTRUAL AND THEIR INTERACTIONS

In the examples given in the last section, I indicated that the lexical semantics of the head noun, the elements in the relative clause, and

For more discussions on the discrepancies between relative clause and topic constructions and the reason for such discrepancies, see Matsumoto (1991).

  [5] Romanization and the gloss are slightly modified to retain the stylistic consistency of examples in this paper.

general knowledge of the world associated with them strongly suggested the interpretation given to each. In this section I will attempt to pinpoint what semantic and pragmatic factors are crucial to the determination of the semantic role of the head noun and how those factors may interact with one another.

A successful construal of a relative-clause construction may involve information given externally to the construction, such as that provided in the prior discourse or in the main clause (although a relative-clause construction can be used simply as an independently standing noun phrase). There will also be interactions with factors that are internal to the construction. In the following I will consider six factors that can contribute to the determination of the role of the head noun.

5.2.1. *Core roles*

The first factor to be considered is the influence of the core roles associated with the relative-clause predicate as shown in (15), (16), and (17). In these examples, the absence of any indication to the contrary leads to the construal of the semantic role of the head noun as most likely being a core role of the predicate.

(15) [[x   ga   tabeta] y]
       NOM   ate
    'y (which) x ate' (y is food or some eaten thing)

(16) [[x   o   katta] y]
       ACC   bought
    'y (which) bought x' (y is the buyer)

(17) [[x   ga   y   o   utta] z]
       NOM   ACC hit
    'z (at/in/. . . which) x hit y' (z is location, time, etc.; see below)

In (15), the structural information that is provided by the nominative case-marking following *x* indicates that *x* is the subject of the verb *tabeta* 'ate' designating, in this case, the role of the Eater. The other core role for the verb is the object of the verb, the Food, identified with the semantic role of the head noun *y*. In the maximally generalized situation of (15), there is then a strong tendency for linking the head noun with the object of the verb. Similarly, (16) gives the interpretation with the head noun *y* linked with the subject of *katta* 'bought', the Buyer. In (17), on the other hand, where there are no uninstantiated core roles in the relative clause, there is no single strongly preferred reading. Therefore, *z* can be the Location, the Time, the

Instrument, or any role that is circumstantially associated with the verb *utta* 'hit'.

The core roles mentioned here can be considered the same as the elements that are linked with a predicate within the Nucleus of a sentence, as opposed to those in the Periphery, in the sense of Fillmore (1977). These notions are intuitive in that for an action or event of eating, for example, the Eater and the Food (or the agent and the patient) are more central to the meaning of the verb *tabeta* 'ate' than, say, the instrument or the location. Another notion which bears some similarity to that of core roles is the notion of the subcategorized arguments of a predicate; however, the two can be distinguished in that the former is a less restricted notion. In particular, subcategorization[6] is intrinsically associated with a surface completeness requirement, whereas core roles do not impose such a condition.

It should be pointed out that interpretations based on core roles, although they are often the only interpretations discussed in the literature, are merely 'default readings', preferred only where the context is maximally generalized. Any such tendency of preference can be overridden by factors that depend on more specific information provided within and/or outside the complex NP. I will discuss such overriding factors in the following sections.

5.2.2. *Semantics of the head noun*

A factor that influences the interpretation of a relative clause is the specific lexical semantics of the head noun. The head nouns in (15)–(17) are intended to be particularly uninformative. The given interpretation in (15) would be probably unaltered if x were replaced by the personal name *Taroo* and y by *mono* 'thing', which conforms with our knowledge of eating, as shown in (18). A similar observation can be made about (16) if we replace x with *hon* 'book' and y by *hito* 'person', as given in (19). In the absence of a specific context, the most accessible interpretation for the head noun would be that of the Buyer. As for (17), one cannot find a semantically general lexical item to replace z, since there is no obvious semantic property shared among possible circumstantial roles. Therefore, as in (20), if x, y and z were

---

[6] It is open to question whether there is enough evidence in Japanese to assume a clear distinction between subcategorized arguments and adjuncts as is assumed in English, or whether the number of subcategorized arguments for a predicate in Japanese should be assumed to be the same as that of the English counterpart. I do not, however, attempt to answer these questions, as they go beyond the scope of this chapter.

replaced, for example, by *Taroo*, *hoomuran* 'home run', and *mono* 'thing', respectively, it is still difficult to determine the preferred interpretation; the Instrument interpretation may be the least awkward since it is compatible with the meaning of *mono* 'thing' and with the scene of hitting.

(18) [[Taroo ga   tabeta] mono]
     Taro NOM ate   thing
     'the thing (which) Taro ate'

(19) [[hon o   katta]   hito]
     book ACC bought person
     'the person (who) bought the book'

(20) [[Taroo ga   hoomuran o   utta] mono]
     Taro NOM home run ACC hit   thing
     ?'the thing (with which) Taro hit the home run'

If, however, *mono*, or *hito* is replaced by a semantically more specific noun, different preferred interpretations can arise, as shown in (21)–(25).

(21) [[Taroo ga   tabeta] otyawan] o   aratte-okimasita
     Taro NOM ate   bowl   ACC washed
     '(I) washed the bowl (from/with which) Taro ate'

(22) [[Taroo ga   tabeta] resutoran] wa oisikatta soo desu
     Taro NOM ate   restaurant TOP was tasty EVID is
     '(I) heard that the restaurant (at which) Taro ate was good'

(23) [[Hon o   katta]   sakka] ga   syoo o   moraimasita
     book ACC bought writer NOM prize ACC received
     'The writer (whose) book (   ) bought received a prize'

(24) [[Taroo ga   hoomuran o   utta] batto] wa kodomo-yoo desu
     Taro NOM home run ACC hit   bat   TOP children-use is
     'The bat (with which) Taro hit the home run is for children'

(25) [[Taroo ga   hoomuran o   utta] yunifoomu] wa
     Taro NOM home run ACC hit   uniform   TOP
     takara-mono desu
     treasure   is
     'The uniform (in which) Taro hit a home run is his treasure'

The semantics of the specific lexical items supported by real-world knowledge strongly suggest the interpretations of the role of the head noun as the utensil in (21) and the location in (22), rather than the core role of the object of eating, even though both *otyawan* 'bowl' and *resutoran* 'restaurant' are 'things', as in (18). That is, the knowledge that the referent of *otyawan* '(rice-) bowl' in (21), for example, is normally used to hold food provides a preferred interpretation of the role of the head noun with respect to the relative clause verb *tabeta* 'ate' as being that of a utensil. In (22), given that the meaning of *resutoran* 'restaurant' is a commercial establishment where meals are served, the most natural interpretation of the semantic role of the head noun with regard to the relative clause predicate is as the location. In (23), the knowledge associated with the professional activities of writers makes the given interpretation possible, if not preferred. The interpretation of (24) is essentially the same as that of (10*a*), discussed in Section 5.1.2. In comparison to (20), the Instrument interpretation is more clearly accessible. A successful interpretation of (25) relies on the (sociocultural) knowledge that the persons who hit home runs are playing baseball, and that baseball players wear uniforms. With such knowledge, the head noun *yunifoomu* 'uniform' is understood in relation to the scene of hitting a home run.

The reason why (8*a*), given in section 5.2.2, is normally preferred to (8*b*) as an interpretation for (8) is similarly explained in terms of the semantic content of the head noun. If a more general noun such as *hito* 'person' is used in the place of *kateekyoosi* 'tutor', (8*a*) ceases to be the preferred reading; instead we get the interpretation (8*b*), in which the head noun takes a core role of the verb *ukaru* 'pass'.

What these examples show is that if the lexical semantics and pragmatics of the head noun strongly indicate a non-core role of the relative-clause predicate that is compatible with the scene activated by that predicate,[7] then that more semantically and pragmatically guided interpretation is likely to be preferred over one which results from simply assigning an available core role to the head noun. Since this point has been neglected in many accounts of relative clauses, it bears repeating that it is not only the valence of the relative clause predicate that determines the semantic role of the target of the relativization, but also the meaning of the head noun and the real-world knowledge associated with it. The fact that such semantic and pragmatic information plays a crucial role in the interpretation of relative-clause constructions in Japanese points to the advantage of a frame-semantic account of the construal.

5.2.3. *Aspectual information in the relative clause*

In terms of interactions with the specific lexical semantics of the head noun, one factor that could assist in determining a preferred construal

---

[7] Fillmore (1977) discusses the idea of a scene activated by a predicate.

for a construction is the aspectual information given by a predicate in the relative clause. As is well known, when an action verb in a relative clause is in the past form, it indicates the completion of the action designated by the verb (e.g. Teramura, 1971).

(26*a*) [[tabako   o   *katta*] oturi]
       cigarette ACC bought change (= balance of money)
    'the change (from) buying cigarettes'
(26*b*) [[tabako o *kau*] oturi]
              buy
    'the change (for) buying cigarettes'
(27*a*) [[beekingu paudaa to   abura o   *mazekonda*] koromo] o
      baking powder   and oil   ACC mixed-in   batter   ACC
    tukete   ageru node . . .
    attach   fry   so
    '(It is) fried with the batter (which is made by) mixing baking powder
    and oil (into the flour), so . . .'
(27*b*) [[beekingu paudaa to   abura o   *mazekomu*] koromo] o . . .
      baking powder   and oil   ACC mix-in   batter   ACC
    '(It is) fried with the batter (into which) baking powder and oil will be
    mixed, so . . .'

In (26), the semantics of the head noun *oturi* 'change' points to a commercial transaction prior to the existence of the change, since *oturi* 'change' specifically refers to the money that the buyer receives after a purchase when the buyer gave a larger amount of money for the goods than its price. The past form of the relative predicate *katta* 'bought' in (26*a*) is in accord with this situation and indicates that the change came into being by buying cigarettes. In contrast, the non-past form given in (26*b*) suggests that the event expressed in the relative clause is yet to be conducted and that *oturi* 'change' is therefore the by-product of some other prior transaction, and is to be used to effect a future action of buying cigarettes. In (27*a*), because of the past form of the verb in the relative clause, the head noun *koromo* 'batter' is construed as the product of the action described in the relative clause, while in (27*b*) the action described in the relative clause has the batter as an ingredient or precursor. As these examples show, when the head noun can be understood to denote some product (of an action), a perfective aspectual encoding in the relative predicate assists in the construal as the product of the action described in the relative clause.

    The roles at issue in (26) and (27) are non-core roles, but aspectual information can also influence the determination among core roles of the relative clause predicate. The effect may not be quite so strong, yet it functions to provide a clue. The interpretations given in (28a) and (28b) are not the only possible ones; however, all other things being equal, the given interpretations would be more likely, since the past form of the verb *suisensita* 'recommended' in (28a) indicates that the recommendation has already been given, and hence that the recommended person is known, while the non-past form in (28b) does not provide a particular clue toward such an implication.

(28a) [[suisensita]   hito]
        recommended   person
      'the person (whom) (   ) recommended'
(28b) [[suisensuru]   hito]
        recommend   person
      'the person (who) recommends (someone)'

5.2.4. *Empathy-loaded predicate in the relative clause*

Among other factors associated with the relative-clause predicate, we can include the phenomenon of empathy-loaded predicates (in the sense of Kuno and Kaburaki, 1977; Kuno, 1978, etc.).[8] For example, *kureta* 'gave' in (29a) puts the center of empathy on the non-subject (dative) NP (Kuno, 1978). This empathy factor influences the construal of the relative clause. In (29a) the head noun is semantically very general; it follows that the head noun is not the empathy focus, since the referent of the empathy focus should be already familiar to the speaker. This fact, combined with the absence of an explicit expression of any argument in the relative clause, supports the interpretation of the head noun as taking the non-empathy-focus subject role.

(29) [[kureta]   hito]
       gave (DAT-centered) person
     'the person (who) gave (   ) (to 'Empathy Focus')'

In other words, in (29) the factor of empathy affects the choice of one core role over another; the role of the head noun is understood as the Giver rather than the Receiver. The interpretation that *hito* 'person' is the object of giving would also be possible if (29) were used in an appropriate context.

---

[8] 'Empathy' is defined in Kuno (1987: 206) as 'the speaker's identification, which may vary in degree, with a person/thing that participates in the event or state that he describes in a sentence', and is slightly revised from Kuno and Kaburaki (1977).

This does not imply that the empathy-focused position can never be the target of relativization. In (30a) the head noun *imooto* 'younger sister' is the empathy focus (dative NP of *kureta*).

(30a) [[tonari-no-hito ga   okasi o   kureta]   imooto]
      neighbor   NOM sweets ACC gave (DAT) younger sister
      'my younger sister (to whom) a neighbor gave sweets'

It is more natural, however, to express the same situation as (30b), with *moratta* 'received', a Subject-focused verb.

(30b) [[imooto   ga   okasi o   moratta] tonari-no-hito]
      younger sister NOM sweets ACC received   neighbor
      'the neighbor (from whom) my younger sister received sweets'

If the relative verb assigns a weaker empathy focus than do dative-centered verbs such as *kureru* in (29), then, the interpretation will be more flexible (or ambiguous) as shown in (31), which contains the weakly subject-centered verb *ageta* 'gave'.[9]

(31) [[ageta]   hito]
     gave   person
     'the person (who) gave ( )( )',
     'the person (to whom) ( ) gave ( )'

The effect of empathy-loaded predicates on relative-clause construal may be seen more clearly in their interaction with the main clause environment.

(32a) Watasi wa [[oseebo   o   *okutta/yokosita] yuuzin] ni
      I   TOP winter-gift ACC sent   friend DAT
      reezyoo   o   kaita
      thank-you-letter ACC wrote
      'I wrote a thank-you letter to the friend (who) sent (me) a winter-gift'

(32b) Watasi wa [[oseebo   o   okutta/*yokosita] yuuzin] ni
      I   TOP winter-gift ACC sent   friend DAT
      okurizyoo   o   kaita
      letter-notifying-sending ACC wrote
      'I wrote a letter to the friend (to whom) (I) sent a winter-gift notifying (him/her) of the sending'

---

[9] Kuno (1978: 141–2) describes *kureru* and *yaru*, two verbs of 'giving and receiving', in terms of the requirement of Empathy. *Kureru* is used when the degree of the speaker's empathy with referent of the Dative Object (Receiver) is greater than that with the referent of the Subject (Giver), while *yaru* is used when the degree of the speaker's empathy with the referent of the Subject (Giver) is either greater than or equal to (or neutral with) that of the Dative Object (Receiver). The verb *ageru* (*ageta*) used in (29b) is equivalent to *yaru* with regard to the Empathy requirement, but is traditionally used when the Receiver is either equal to or higher in status than the speaker. Recently, *ageru* has been more widely used even in contexts where *yaru* may once have been preferred.

Given that *yokosu* 'send' is a dative-focus predicate whereas *okuru* 'send' is subject-focus, *yuuzin* 'friend' in (32*a*) would be construed as the sender of the winter-gift to whom the speaker wrote a thank-you letter, while *yuuzin* 'friend' in (32*b*) is the receiver or the addressee of the gift, to whom the speaker wrote to inform him/her of the sending of the gift. The restrictions on the role of the head noun that are implied by the use of empathy-loaded predicates interact with the information provided in the main clause. In the unstarred versions of the examples, the main-clause information is pragmatically consistent with the sense given by the empathy factor and reinforces that interpretation; in the starred versions, it provides a pragmatic contradiction, and the construction will not be acceptable.[10]

5.2.5. *'Role-adding' elements in the relative clause*

Another factor contributing to a successful construal of a relative clause construction is the presence of some phrase that would potentially add and 'highlight' a role, and facilitate the construal:

(33*a*) #[[Yumi   ga   tabeta]   hito]
       Yumi   NOM   ate   person
      'the person (with whom) Yumi ate'
(33*b*) [[Yumi   ga   *issyoni*   tabeta]   hito]
       Yumi   NOM   together   ate   person
      'the person (with whom) Yumi ate together'
(34*a*) *[[Yumi   ga   wakai]   hito]
       Yumi   NOM   is young   person
      'the person (who) Yumi is young(er) (than)'
(34*b*) [[Yumi   *no*   *hoo*   ga   wakai]   hito]
       Yumi   GEN   side   NOM   is young   person
      'the person (who) Yumi is younger than'

(33*a*) is difficult to construe in the intended sense, short of a very specific context. In contrast, with the adverbial phrase *issyoni* 'together', the co-actor role is made accessible in (33*b*). In (34*b*), the target of the comparison is brought into more specific attention by attaching *no hoo* '(lit.) of side/x's side' to the subject, which is the canonical way of expressing comparison in Japanese. A ramification of this factor is that it brings to light the inaccuracy of the common claim (e.g. Kuno, 1973; Okutsu, 1974; Inoue, 1976) that a comitative

---

[10] Kuno (1976; 1978) discusses the conflict of empathy foci created between main and subordinate clauses.

NP or an object of comparison cannot be the target of relativization. A more accurate statement would be that those roles need be highlighted lexically or contextually in order for them to felicitously become the target of relativization.

It should be mentioned that having such highlighting elements does not necessarily force the interpretation in which the the role of head noun in the relative clause is either the comitative (co-actor/partner) or the object of comparison. Factors that we have considered earlier, such as the lexical semantics of the head noun, interact with the elements mentioned here. In (35), the denotatum of the head noun would be most likely construed as the Food rather than the Co-actor, and in (36), it is a kind of sports rather than a person that is compared with Yumi.

(35) [[Yumi ga   issyoni tabeta] kudamono] wa   ringo desu
         Yumi NOM together ate   fruit   TOP apple is
     'The fruit (which) Yumi ate together (with someone) is an apple'
(36) [[Yumi no   hoo   ga   umai]   supootu] wa   tenisu desu
         Yumi GEN side NOM is good at sport   TOP tennis is
     'The sport (which) Yumi is better at (than someone) is tennis'

5.2.6. *Prior discourse context*

Prior linguistic and nonlinguistic context, as well as the main-clause information, form an important factor in achieving a particular construal. I will briefly consider this kind of influence on the determination of the role of the head noun in the following examples.

When the prior context indicates that (37) is described from the point of view of the speaker (writer), it becomes most likely that the speaker, who is not explicitly referred to in (37), takes the role of the Arranger (the subject of *mati-awasete-ita* 'arranged to meet'), while the role of the head noun is that of Partner of the arranged meeting (which would be expressed as a comitative NP). The preference of this particular interpretation is congruent with the observation made by Kuno (e.g. 1976) that 'it is easiest for the speaker to empathize with the referent of the subject.'[11]

[11] This is from Kuno's 'Surface Structure Empathy Hierarchy': 'It is easiest for the speaker to empathize with the referent of the subject; it is next easiest for him to empathize with the referent of the object . . . It is most difficult for him to empathize with the referent of the by-passive agentive' (1976: 432). The 'Topic Empathy Hierarchy' that Kuno proposes is also relevant: 'It is easier for the speaker to empathize with an object (e.g., person) that he has been talking about than with an object that he has just introduced into discourse for the first time' (1976: 434).

(37) [[mati-awasete-ita]   onna-no-ko]   wa   kaette-simatta
     arranged-to-meet   girl   TOP   has-gone-home
     'The girl (with whom) (I) arranged to meet has gone home'

However, if a different prior context such as that in (38) is given, the role of the head noun is easily construable as the Arranger (as given in the translation in (39)), even though the sentence structure of (39) is identical to that of (37). (38) provides a neutral context as to the point of view (i.e. the boy's or the girl's) from which the event is described.

(38) Otoko-no-ko   to   onna-no-ko   ga   mati-awasete-ita.   Sikasi
     boy   and   girl   NOM   arranged-to-meet   however
     zikan   ga   kita   noni   aite   ga   araware-nakatta
     time   NOM   came   although   partner   NOM   did-not-appear
     'A boy and a girl had arranged to meet. However, the partner (the person to meet with) did not show up.'
(39) [[mati-awasete-ita]   onna-no-ko]   wa   kaette-simatta
     arranged-to-meet   girl   TOP   has-gone-home
     'The girl (who) arranged to meet (him) has gone home.'

The influence of the factors external to the relative-clause construction, such as the prior discourse and the matrix sentence in which the relative clause is used, is worthy of further study, as the above discussion suggests. In this regard, the work of Fox and Thompson (1990*a*; 1990*b*) on relative clauses in conversation offers one interesting approach.

5.4. CONCLUSION

I have discussed five factors internal and one external to relative-clause constructions, and have considered some interactions among them. This account was not intended to be exhaustive, and it is possible that there are factors and interactions other than those I have discussed. I have shown that interpretations predicted from the core roles of the predicate in the relative clause are not necessarily preferred; they can be overridden unless supported by semantic coherence and pragmatic plausibility. The fact that the syntax does not provide an absolute rule for predicting acceptable relative constructions means that Japanese relative clauses are controlled primarily by factors other than syntax. The nonsyntactic factors that I have discussed can conspire with structural characteristics of the construction to contribute

to the successful construal. If all the information provided points to
one interpretation, the specific construal will be successful; if not, the
construal will be problematical.

As noted above, the factors that are discussed in this paper are not
exhaustive, as can be seen in the contrasts in (40).

(40a) ?[[tabako   o   katta]   gan]
          cigarettes ACC bought cancer
          'the cancer (from) buying cigarettes'
(40b) [[tabako o   sutta]   gan]
                smoked cancer
          'the cancer (from) smoking cigarettes'

The combination of the aspectual information of the relative predicate and lexical meaning of the head noun should provide a construal
for both head nouns as denoting the outcome of the action described
in the relative clause. Yet, while (40*b*) is readily interpretable, (40*a*)
does not provide a clearly preferred interpretation, and is indeed questionable in its acceptability on account of the lack of any apparent
semantic role for the head noun with respect to the predicate *katta*
'bought' in the relative clause. The difference seems to originate in the
number of reasoning steps needed to connect the head noun and relative clause. The difficulty of construal in (40*a*), however, does not imply
that it can never be successfully interpreted. Although coherence between the clause and the head noun is difficult to obtain with normal
background assumptions, if the speaker and the hearer share some
special information (or relation) that would allow stronger coherence,
the construction should become felicitous. This flexibility in acceptability judgement is also evidence of the pragmatic nature of the construction.

Although there is much room for further investigation, this study illustrates that any simple hierarchy of influence of syntactic and ex-
trasyntactic factors is not supported. It also provides an example of
how semantics and pragmatics pervade the grammar. More generally,
given that constructions whose interpretation is syntactically underdetermined, such as the relative clause in Japanese, are commonplace,
the analysis in this paper suggests that a comprehensive grammatical
theory of Japanese should allow for the incorporation of extrasyn-
tactic factors as integral parts of the system.

REFERENCES

FILLMORE, C. J. (1977). 'Topics in Lexical Semantics,' in R. Cole (ed.), *Current Issues in Linguistic Theory*, 76–138. Bloomington: Indiana University Press.

—— (1981). 'Pragmatics and the Description of Discourse,' in P. Cole (ed.), *Radical Pragmatics*, 143–66. New York: Academic Press.

—— (1982). 'Frame Semantics,' in *Linguistics in the Morning Calm*, 111–38. Seoul: Hanshin Publishing Co. for Linguistic Society of Korea.

—— (1985). 'Frames and the Semantics of Understanding,' *Quaderni di Semantica* 6: 222–54.

FOX, B., and THOMPSON, S. (1990a). 'A Discourse Explanation of the Grammar of Relative Clauses in English Conversation,' *Language* 66: 297–316.

—— (1990b). 'On Formulating Reference: An Interactional Approach to Relative Clauses in English Conversation,' *Papers in Pragmatics* 4: 183–95.

INOUE, K. (1976). *Henkei Bunpoo to Nihongo* (Transformational Grammar and Japanese). Tokyo: Taishukan.

KUNO, S. (1973). *The Structure of the Japanese Language*. Cambridge, Mass.: MIT Press.

—— (1976). 'Subject, Theme and Speaker's Empathy: A Reexamination of Relativization Phenomena,' in Charles Li (ed.), *Subject and Topic*, 419–44. New York: Academic Press.

—— (1978). *Danwa no Bunpoo* (Discourse Grammar). Tokyo: Taishukan.

—— (1987). *Functional Syntax: Anaphora, Discourse and Empathy*. Chicago: University of Chicago Press.

KUNO, S., and KABURAKI, E. (1977). 'Empathy and Syntax,' *Linguistic Inquiry* 8: 627–72.

MATSUMOTO, Y. (1988). 'Grammar and Semantics of Adnominal Clauses in Japanese', Ph.D. dissertation, University of California at Berkeley.

—— (1990). 'The Role of Pragmatics in Japanese Relative Clause Constructions,' *Lingua* 82: 111–29.

—— (1991). 'Is It Really a Topic That Is Relativized? Arguments from Japanese,' *Papers from the Twenty-Seventh Regional Meeting of the Chicago Linguistic Society*.

—— (in preparation). *Noun-Modifying Constructions in Japanese: A Frame Semantics Approach*.

MURAKI, M. (1970). 'Presupposition, Pseudo-Clefting, and Thematization', Ph.D. dissertation, University of Texas at Austin.

NA, Y. (1986). 'Syntactic and Semantic Interaction in Korean: Theme, Topic, and Relative Clauses,' Ph.D. dissertation, University of Chicago.

OKUTSU, K. (1974). *Seisei Nihongo Bunpoo Ron: Meishi-ku no Koozoo* (On Generative Japanese Grammar: The Structure of Noun Phrases). Tokyo: Taishukan.

SAITO, M. (1985). 'Some Asymmetries in Japanese and Their Theoretical Consequences,' Ph.D. dissertation, MIT.

TERAMURA, H. (1971). '-*Ta* no Imi to Kinoo: Aspect, Tense, Mood no Koobunteki Itizuke (The Aspectual, Temporal, and Modal Functions of -*ta*)', in Festschrift Committee for Professor T. Iwakura (ed.), *Gengogaku to Nihongo-mondai* (Linguistics and the Problems of Japanese), 24–89. Tokyo: Kurosio.

6

The Situated Interpretation of Possessor-Raising

Mary Catherine O'Connor

INTRODUCTION

In a relatively small number of languages, there appears to be an alternation between clauses containing an intact NP argument with a possessor and corresponding 'possessor-raised' clauses, in which the possessor NP and the possessed object both appear as independent constituents. Pairs like the following Northern Pomo[1] examples are typical of the construction. In (1a) the unremarkable NP 'his knee' is the direct object of the transitive verb 'burn.' In (1b), the possessor NP is no longer marked with the Oblique case, is no longer adjacent to the nominal 'knee,' and is marked in the accusative case.[2]

(1a) man   moːw-aʔ yasis -nam phaley-ka
    3SF-NOM 3SM-OBL knee   -DET burn-CAUS
    'She burned his knee'

The data collection and analysis reported here was partially supported by National Science Foundation grant DBS-9111264, and grants from the Phillips Fund of the American Philosophical Society. Their support is gratefully acknowledged. I also extend thanks to Claudia Brugman, Paul Kay, Jean-Pierre Koenig, Joan Maling, Sandra Thompson, and Andrea Zukowski for good advice and comments (not invariably heeded, but invariably appreciated). As always, special acknowledgement is due to Edna Campbell Guerrero, who has generously shared with me her knowledge of the Northern Pomo language and her insights about it. Finally, I acknowledge a largely unpayable debt to Charles Fillmore, whose ways of seeing and talking about language have permanently shaped my own.

[1] Northern Pomo is an indigenous language of Northern California spoken fluently by a small number of elderly speakers. Central aspects of the morphology and syntax are presented in O'Connor (1992). The topic of possessor-raising is introduced there, and a very preliminary version of the analysis presented here can be found in Ch. 7 of that work.

[2] In O'Connor (1992) the problems associated with choice of traditional labels for this case system are discussed. For ease of exposition in this paper, I will use Accusative and Nominative for the cases that are called 'P' and 'A' respectively in the work cited.

(1*b*) mo:w-al   man   yasis-nam   phaley-ka
      3SM-ACC   3sf.NOM   knee-DET   burn-CAUS
'She burned his knee'

Unlike other alternations—e.g. dative movement (Gropen *et al.*, 1989; Goldberg, 1992) and the object-oblique 'spray-load' alternation (Dowty, 1991)—the possessor-raising (PR) construction is not limited to a small set of verbs, but appears to be available to any verb with an absolutive[3] NP argument. Cross-linguistically, the alternation is licensed just in cases where the absolutive argument is an inalienably possessed nominal (Baker, 1988: 103). In Northern Pomo, the possessed object must further be a body part.[4]

A full characterization of the differences between the regular expression of possession and the PR construction in any particular language requires an account of the nature of the syntactic relationship between the 'raised' possessor and the verb, between the possessed object nominal and the verb, and between the possessor and possessed nominals themselves. Also to be determined is the semantic contribution of each constituent in the PR construction to utterance interpretation. In most descriptions, the alternants are assumed to be truth-conditionally equivalent. How are the lexical semantics of the verb distributed over the altered set of clausal constituents in the PR sentence schema? And are there further interpretive differences that distinguish sentences like (1*a*) from (1*b*), as there are in the dative alternation and in the object-oblique pairs?

A number of syntactic analyses have been posed for similar constructions in a variety of languages (Aissen, 1987; Davies, 1986; Baker, 1988; Maling and Kim, 1992), but rarely is a detailed account given of the construction's interpretation. Since a complete account of the construction within any framework will encompass the necessary linkages between semantic and pragmatic interpretation and syntactic structure, however, a close examination of the interpretive details would seem to be warranted. These are particularly interesting in Northern Pomo: the construction is obligatory in the case of certain

---

[3] It has been widely observed that the possessor may be 'raised' only out of an Absolutive argument, i.e. the object of a transitive verb, or the subject of some (unaccusative) intransitive verbs (Baker, 1988: 274–6). I will not discuss this aspect of the construction in this paper, and will use the traditional term 'absolutive' for these arguments, acknowledging the unsolved mystery of this constraint.

[4] Thus in Northern Pomo the constraint is more specific than just 'inalienability.' Kinship nominals, for instance, display case-marking patterns that differ from alienably possessed objects, but do not participate in the possessor-raising construction.

combinations of body part, possessor, and predicate and is avoided in others. Moreover, there are rich conversational implicatures that can be drawn from a speaker's decision to use or avoid the construction in cases where it is optionally available.

In this paper I will expand and develop the semantico-pragmatic account of the PR construction begun in O'Connor (1992). (See also O'Connor 1994.) In section 6.1 I will briefly review the syntax and morphology associated with the construction in Northern Pomo. This will be followed in section 6.2 by a detailed analysis of the semantics and pragmatics of PR in that language. I will offer conclusions and brief comments on some implications in section 6.3.

6.1. MORPHOLOGY AND SYNTAX OF NORTHERN POMO POSSESSOR-RAISING

6.1.1. *Basic characteristics of the PR and non-PR variants*

The simple sentence in Northern Pomo given in (2) exemplifies the canonical structure of the noun phrase and sentence word order. A possessor NP precedes the head noun, and the entire possessed nominal is followed by a definite determiner. A case-marker clitic may occur at the right margin of the NP (although it does not in sentence 2). Unmarked word order is SOV.

(2) $_S$[[[[mo:w-aʔ]$_{NP}$ [xabe   tiy-ay]]   nam]   —]$_{NP}$ [[ma-ɪ]
　　　　3SM-OBL　　rock   large-PL   DET   [case]   ground-DIR
　　kadokado]$_{VP}]_S$
　　roll
　　'His large rocks rolled to the ground'

The (*a*) examples in the following pairs of Northern Pomo sentences are ordinary, non-PR sentences: the absolutive[5] argument of the verb consists of a structurally ordinary noun phrase containing a body-part nominal head, and a possessor NP that, like the possessor in (2), is obligatorily marked in the Oblique case and obligatorily appears to the left of the body-part nominal. The (*b*) sentences are Possessor-Raising sentences, and display several kinds of syntactic

---

[5] PR is permitted in some cases where the possessed NP would not traditionally be called an Absolutive; I have found a few cases of PR where the possessed NP occurs within a postpositional phrase that is not an obligatory complement of the verb, e.g. 'The cat is sitting on her legs.' I will not discuss these cases further here.

and morphological evidence of this. First, the possessor no longer appears in the Oblique case, but is marked with the Accusative case (the case category associated with objects of transitive verbs and some subjects). (See O'Connor 1992 for details of the case system.) Second, the determiner—cliticized to the end of the entire possessed noun phrase in the (*a*) examples—is disfavored, though in some cases it may appear cliticized to the body-part nominal. Third, any case-marking which might appear on the full possessed NP in the (*a*) sentences disappears. (NPs with inanimate heads tend to receive zero case allomorphs, as in (2) above; thus this property is rarely observed but can sometimes be elicited.) Fourth, the body-part nominal tends in the PR sentence to appear immediately to the left of the verb but, as seen in example (4*b*), may appear elsewhere. The possessor may now precede or follow the body-part nominal, and is no longer necessarily adjacent to it (see 6.1.2 for further discussion of this aspect).

(3*a*) *khe   ʔuy-nam   šikišiki-m-a*
        IS-OBL   eye -DET   twitch-ASP-PRES
        'My eye is twitching'

(3*b*) *ʈoː   ʔuy   šikišiki-m-a*
        IS-ACC   eye   twitch-ASP-PRES
        'My eye is twitching'

(4*a*) *moːwaʔ   xamabuːsa-nam   šit'ay-miti*
        3SM OBL   big toe-DET   crooked-lie
        'His big toe is crooked'

(4*b*) *xamabuːsa   moːwal   šit'ay-miti*
        big toe   3SM-ACC   crooked-lie
        'His big toe is crooked'

6.1.2. *Constituency and lexicalized versus syntactic possessor-raising*

Possessor-raising has been treated as an incorporation process (both descriptively and within theoretical frameworks such as that proposed by Baker, 1988). In discussions of noun incorporation in general (Mithun, 1986; Sadock, 1986; Baker, 1988)[6] a central issue is the

---

[6] Baker makes a distinction between 'possessor-stranding' that results from 'overt' noun incorporation (where the possessed object is clearly part of a phonological word including the verb) and 'possessor-raising' that results from 'abstract N(oun) I(ncorporation)' or 'noun reanalysis' where many signs of word formation are missing. Northern Pomo displays both sorts of construction, but my point does not depend on making the distinction. Thus I will simply refer to 'P-R' as a cover term for both types.

extent to which a nominal argument (here the possessed body-part nominal) is incorporated into the verb, and is thus rendered inaccessible to further syntactic processes that normally operate on the arguments of the verb.

In Northern Pomo there are clear examples of fixed, even idiomatic instances of PR, where the possessed body part appears adjacent to the verb, and both appear to be part of a phonological word. At the same time there are many clearly novel instances of a productive process where the body-part nominal may appear anywhere in the sentence. There are several ways to distinguish these two ends of the continuum. In the discussion that follows, I will use the term 'lexical PR' to refer to those cases that are clearly formulaic or fixed (as evidenced below). I will use the term 'syntactic PR' to refer to those examples that appear to be the output of a productive process, or novel application of a general schema. (This terminology is not intended to imply anything about the form of representation the construction might require within a fully theorized grammar of the language.) In section 6.2 I will focus only on syntactic PR examples.

In lexical PR example (5), the body-part nominal *must* occur immediately to the left of the verb, the expected position for incorporation in a head-final language. In syntactic PR, the body-part nominal may (and frequently does) appear immediately to the left of the verb, but it need not, as demonstrated in both (6) and (7).

(5) mul   kay   mițo   *ʔuy-dalušam*   -khe nakan
    DEM   also   2S-ACC   *eye-fade*   -FUT CONJ
    'Because from that also your eyes will fade [you will go blind]'

(6) nan   mo:wal   *ṭhana*   kay   mo:wal   *čhok*-na -n -way
    and   3SM-ACC   hand   also   3SM-ACC   shoot-COP-PROG-DISC
    khap-nam mo:w
    COP-DET. 3SM. NOM
    'And he shot him in the hand, too, the cop'

(7) *xama. bu:sa* . . .   mo:w-al   šit'ay-miti
    big toe (pause)   3SM-ACC   crooked-lie
    'His big toe is crooked'

The meaning of a lexical PR predicate, as in (8*a*) below, is often idiomatic or non-predictable. One might expect that the regular possession alternant of such lexical PR examples would simply convey the non-idiomatic meaning of the verb plus body-part combination, but this frequently is not the case. Often, the non-PR version of such a sentence is deemed unacceptable under any interpretation, as in (8*b*).

(8*a*) *mo:w-al   šina:*-čamalu?-ye
    3SM-ACC   head-turn around-PERF
    'He got confused'
    (does not mean 'his head turned')

(8*b*) **mo:w-a?   šina:-nam*   čamalu?-ye
    3SM-OBL   head-DET   TURN around-PERF
    (does not mean 'his head turned'; seems to have no other interpretation)

In the discussion that follows, examples that are termed *lexical PR* will have met the diagnostic criteria of obligatory adjacency between the body-part nominal and the incorporating verb, and non-availability of the non-PR variant as a paraphrase.

Word formation in the lexicon is widely considered to create linguistic objects that are opaque to sentence-level processes of reference. The 'anaphoric island condition' has been used as a test for the lexical versus syntactic (or post-syntactic) status of incorporation processes (Sadock, 1986; Shibatani and Kageyama, 1988). In Northern Pomo, there is a clear contrast between the referential potential of the lexical PR body part nominal, as in (9),[7] and that found in the syntactic PR construction, as in (10). These differences are illustrated in examples (11) and (12).

(9) mo:wal mul *ha-w*-čam-a
    3SM-ACC DEM mouth-DIR-jump
    'It just popped into his mouth'
    (means he said it before thinking)

(10) ma:d-al *ha*   dac'ap-am
    3SF-ACC mouth slap-IMP
    'Slap her on the mouth!'

Example (11*a*) demonstrates that the lexically incorporated body-part nominal in (9) is not available as an antecedent to the demonstrative pronoun 'it', *mul*. Instead, the nominal *ha* 'mouth' would have to be repeated explicitly, as in (11*b*) below. (Unlike the long-distance reflexives mentioned below, this antecedency is not an obligation imposed by the grammar, but is simply optional discourse-based co-reference.)

(11*a*) **čano ṭiyiš ma:d-al   ha-w-čam-kan   ?a: ma:d-al*
    word ugly 3 SF-ACC   mouth-dir-jump-ADV IS NOM 3SF-ACC
    mul   dac'apa
    it   slap
    *'Bad words "jumped into" her mouth, so I slapped it (her mouth)'

---

[7] The incorporated body part nominal *ha* 'mouth' appears inflected with a directional suffix found in a few other lexicalized incorporation examples involving non-body-part nominals such as *ča-w—hu* (home-DIR-go) 'go home'. It is also a productive verbal element (O'Connor, 1992).

(11*b*) čano   ṭiyiš ma:d-al   *haw*—čam-kan   ʔa: ma:d-al
      word ugly 3SF-ACC   mouth-DIR-jump-ADV IS NOM 3SF-ACC
      ha   dac'apa
      mouth slap
      'Bad words "jumped into" her mouth, so I slapped her mouth'

When the PR predicate is *not* lexicalized, however, the body-part nominal is available to anaphoric processes.

(12) man   mo:w-al ʔ*uy* datoy sili ʔa: *mul* dasey
     3SF NOM 3SM-ACC face design after IS NOM DEM wash
     'After she painted him on the face, I washed it (his face)'

Another indication of the referentiality and independent constituency of the body-part nominal is its availability to focus constructions. In syntactic PR examples it is possible to move the body-part nominal into the focus position at the beginning of the sentence. The body-part nominal in a lexical PR example is, not surprisingly, not accessible to focus or movement. The examples below all involve explicit markers of focus. Example (13*a*) is an unmarked syntactic PR example and (13*b*) is the same sentence with the body-part nominal marked as a focus of contrast.

(13*a*) *mo:w-al šina:* phidal-ʔa   (13*b*) *šina: yɛʔ* mo:w-al phidal-ʔa
       3SM-ACC head split-pass   head only 3SM-ACC split-pass
       'They split his head open'   'Only his head got split open'

The focus construction marked with *yɛʔ* signals in this case that the speaker presupposes the proposition that some unspecified part of the man's body was split open. The focussed element fills in the unspecified value. Further, the focus marker *yɛʔ* indicates that the constituent to its left is being offered in contrast to other possible values for that variable, either previously stated or contextually available. On the other hand, in lexical PR examples such as (14), we can see that the body-part nominal is not available to be explicitly focussed.

(14) **šina: yɛʔ* mul ṭo: čam-a
     head only DEM IS. ACC jump-PRES
     [presumably this would mean something like 'Only into my head did it pop']

There are other constructions which explicitly pick out some element of the sentence for foregrounding or contrastive focus. Syntactic PR sentences are hospitable to these focus elements or constructions, as the examples below demonstrate, while lexical PR sentences are not. In each syntactic PR sentence below, the body-part nominal is subject to further modification, comparison, or direct questioning.

(15) *sit'ay*   *ṭa*   moːw   maːd-al *ʔoh* phac'am-yɛ
     how many Q   3SM NOM 3SF ACC tooth break-PERF
     'How many of her teeth did he break?'

(16) šibah-nam yax   t̪hin na-nṭe   moːw-al *yaː dul*
     body-DET   strong NEG   COP-ADVERS   3SM-ACC leg FOC
     yax   na-n
     strong COP-PROG
     'Even though his body is not strong, his *legs* are strong'

(17) *k'o*   *ṭa*   moːwal čaxaː-ya
     thing   Q   3SM-ACC cut-PASS
     'What (body part) did they cut him on?'

The possessor is also accessible to WH-questions and to focus constructions:

(18a) *čibaː-l*   *ṭa*   xama čaxaː-ya
      who-ACC   Q   foot   cut-PASS
      'Whose foot did they cut?'

(18b) *moːw-al yɛ?* xama čaxaː-ya
      3SM-ACC only   foot   cut-PASS
      'It was only him whose foot they cut'

In contrast, the possessor NP inside a regular possessed NP cannot be extracted or focussed.

(19a) *čiba-?*   *ṭa*   *šina-nam* ma   čadi
      who-OBL Q   head-SPEC   2S NOM see
      'Whose head do you see?'

(19b) *čiba-?*   *šina-nam* *ṭa*   ma   čadi
      who-OBL head-SPEC   Q   2S NOM see
      'Whose head do you see?'

In summary, in 'lexical' PR the body-part nominal does not form a separate constituent, but is incorporated into the verb; it is not referential, and thus is not available for modification, focus, questioning, etc. Meanings of verb–body-part combinations are often idiomatic. In 'syntactic' PR, both possessor and possessed nominals appear to be independent, fully referential constituents. Sections that follow on the interpretive properties of the construction will rely only on examples of syntactic PR, which will henceforth be referred to simply as 'PR'.

6.1.3. *Grammatical function status of possessor and possessed nominals*

The literature suggests that the raised possessor takes on the grammatical function of the constituent out of which it ascended. The case-marking displayed by the raised possessor in the examples above (accusative) does not uniquely identify it with a particular grammatical relation, as many intransitive subjects (and even a few transitive subjects) may receive the accusative case, while all direct objects receive accusative case. When the PR sentence features an intransitive verb, as in (3) and (4), the raised possessor NP does take on the behavioral properties of subjects, including control of anaphors of several kinds and of null subjects in controlled adverbial adjuncts.

In (20a), the (unequivocal) subject of a comparative can serve as antecedent to the long-distance reflexive prefix on the kinship stem 'mother.' These anaphoric prefixes (see O'Connor, 1992 for discussion) require subject antecedents. In example (20b), the raised possessor can successfully serve as antecedent for this anaphoric prefix.

(20a) *ma-*   the -ʔ   ʔanu   t'iko   *man*   na
      LDA POSS- mother-OBL COMP   short   3SF NOM COP
      'She_j is shorter than her_j mother'

(20b) *ma-*   the -ʔ   ya: ʔanu   t'iko-ṭay   *ma:d-al* ya: na
      LDA POSS- mother-OBL leg COMP   short -PL   3SF-ACC   leg   COP
      'Her_j legs are shorter than her_j mother's legs'

Still other evidence is given by two types of controlled adverbial adjunct clause. The null subjects of these adjuncts must be construed as coreferent with the subject of the matrix clause. As shown below, a raised possessor in the matrix clause can control the interpretation of these adjunct subjects. The sentence below would be ungrammatical if the regular possessed NP headed by 'knee' and containing an oblique possessor were the subject of the main clause.

(21a) wa:d-en   wa:d-en   wa:d-en   *ma:dal*   yasis čatoh
      walk-COR   walk-COR   walk-COR   3SF-ACC   knee   swollen
      '(After) walking, walking, walking, she had a swollen knee'

(21b) *wa:d-en   wa:d-en   wa:d-en   *ma:daʔ yasis nam* čatoh
      walk-COR   walk-COR   walk-COR   3SF-OBL knee DET swollen
      *'(After) walking, walking, walking, her knee was swollen'

When the possessor 'raises' out of a direct object NP, it is difficult to find unambiguous evidence of its grammatical function status. There is only one diagnostic for direct objects, and it is of limited use: the direct-object reflexive element *k'aye*. This morpheme is not a part of the long-distance reflexive system, and occurs only as the direct object of a reflexive verb and in a few adjuncts (e.g. *k'aye khe* 'by (her)self'). In all cases it must be bound by a subject in its own clause. Consider the contrast in examples (22*a* and *b*). In (22*a*), the NP 'her arm' is the direct object, and the possessor appears as the Oblique long-distance reflexive *t̰i?*, a form that is never used for the direct object. (There is a member of the LDR paradigm that may instantiate a direct object, but it must be bound by a subject outside of its minimal clause. The binding conditions on these LDRs are given in O'Connor 1992. It will suffice here to say that the possessor in (22*a*) must be an NP determiner of the head noun inside the direct object NP.) In (22*b*), on the other hand, the possessor NP appears to be the direct object of 'burn', now instantiated as the local reflexive element *k'aye*.

(22*a*) *t̰i?*   ša: -nam   *me:di*   phaley-ka-?a
      LDA-OBL arm -SPEC Mary NOM burn-CAUS-REFL
      'Mary$_j$ burned her$_j$ arm'

(22*b*) *k'aye* *me:di*   ša: phaley-ka-?a
      self   Mary NOM arm burn-CAUS-REFL
      'Mary$_j$ burned herself$_j$ on the arm'

The available tests suggest that the grammatical function of the raised possessor is the same as that of the NP headed by the body-part nominal in the unmarked, 'unraised' version of the sentence. Unfortunately these tests are not compatible with the animacy features of the body-part nominal itself, so no evidence is available about its grammatical function status. In what follows the semantic interpretation of each constituent will be discussed.

6.2. SEMANTICS AND PRAGMATICS OF THE POSSESSOR-RAISING CONSTRUCTION

6.2.1. *Framing the problem*

The facts described in section 6.1 suggest that the raised possessor has the status of a canonical grammatical relation: it is arguably a subject in intransitive clauses, and while there is minimal evidence for objecthood, there is no evidence that it is not an object in transitive sentences. Given that the paired PR and non-PR sentences are truth-conditionally equivalent, and starting with the assumption that the verb assigns thematic roles of some sort[8] to nominal arguments, we can assume that the same set of thematic roles is available in both (*a*) and (*b*). The question arises, what roles are assigned to the raised possessor and the body-part nominal? More neutrally, we can ask how the verbal semantics is realized over the nominal participants.

First, consider the following pair of sentences, in which the (*b*) sentence is the PR version of the (*a*) sentence. (Glosses in single quotes are the first interpretation offered by the native-speaker consultant. Parenthesised glosses are native speaker's explanatory comments.)

(23*a*) man	*mo:w-aʔ*	*xama:-nam*	čaxa
3SF NOM	3SM-OBL	foot-DET	cut
'She cut his foot'			
(23*b*) *mo:w-al*	man	*xama:*	čaxa
3SM-ACC	3SF NOM	foot	cut
'She cut his foot'			

In (23*a*), presumably *mo:w-aʔ* 'his' is assigned the Possessor role in virtue of its constituency with 'foot.' The NP 'his foot' is understood as the participant that undergoes the action of cutting; many researchers would label it a Patient.

In (23*b*) the interpretation indicates that both these roles still obtain, in the sense that we must understand *mo:w-al* 'him' to be the possessor of the foot, and we must understand the foot to have been cut. Yet here the possessor NP, 'him,' is not case-marked as a possessor, is not necessarily adjacent to the possessed object, and appears moreover to be case-marked as the direct object of the verb. On this basis we might ask (i) how it gets assigned the Possessor role, and (ii) whether it is also understood as a Patient, either instead of or along with the complement 'foot.'

Two further sets of observations must also be accounted for. First, as will be discussed in section 6.2.3, the PR construction is obligatory in some cases, and strongly dispreferred in others. Moreover, a speaker's use or avoidance of the construction sometimes triggers strong, contextually specific conversational implicatures. These provide useful evidence concerning the underlying interpretive contents of the construction, as will be demonstrated below in section 6.2.6.

---

[8] Thematic role names are used as a labelling convenience only; no commitment to a particular semantic ontology is implied. This issue is discussed further in sections 6.2 and 6.3.

6.2.2. *Distribution of verbal semantics over NP constituents*

Example (23*b*) suggests a simple way to compute the role of the raised possessor. Both the possessor and the possessed body part are compatible with the role of the object that has been cut: both are causally affected and undergo a change of state. This is due to an entailment of the verb in combination with a fact about the nature of body-part possession: if you cut my foot, it is entailed that you cut me, by virtue of the many biological linkages between me and my foot. One might expect that similar entailments will explain the interpretive relationship between the verb and the raised possessor in all other cases. However, the next examples suggest that entailments like these will not always be reliable, or even available.

(24*a*) mi?   ?e:-nam   k'edi   phiṭ'a
        2S OBL   hair-DET   good   appear
        'Your hair looks nice'
        ("That would mean that its color, or something about the hair was pretty")

(24*b*) miṭo   ?e: k'edi   phiṭ'a
        you-ACC   hair   good   appear
        'You look nice with that hairstyle'
        ("That would mean it *looked* pretty *on* her, not particularly the color or anything, just that it looked nice")

The fact that my hair looks nice does not necessarily entail that my whole self looks nice. But the predicate 'look nice' means that the appearance of its principal argument receives a positive aesthetic judgment. Perhaps in PR sentences that property is simply extended to the possessor.

In the next example, however, it is difficult to see in what sense the property conferred on the body part is shared by the possessor. The verb *lok'* 'to fall or collapse', if predicated of a whole person, e.g. 'the man', would mean that the man fell down or collapsed. If predicated of a body part, as in the examples below, it means that the body part fell off, either through disease or accident. Thus in (25b), if the possessor shared the properties conferred by the predicate upon its theme argument, hearers would understand that the possessor *and* the toe fell or dropped. Example (25b), however, continues to mean that the person's toe fell off, not that he himself fell or collapsed, with or without the toe.

(25*a*) moːw-a?   xamabuːsa-nam   lok'-a
        3SM-OBL   big toe-SPEC   fall/drop
        'His big toe fell off'

(25*b*) *mo:w-al   xamabu:sa*   lok'-a
　　　3SM-ACC big toe   fall/drop
　　　'His big toe fell off'

Examples (3*a*) and (3*b*) ('my eye is twitching') provide a similar example. The PR version does not imply that the possessor is twitching anywhere except the eye.

What, then, is the interpretive contribution of the raised possessor? The next example suggests that, like the dative direct object and the direct object of spray/load-type predicates, there is heightened affectedness associated with the raised possessor:

(26*a*) *hayu yaču? ?uy-nam*   mo:w   xabe-with baneh
　　　dog OBL   eye-DET   3SM NOM   rock-INST hit
　　　'He hit the dog's eye with a rock'
(26*b*) *hayu yačul*   mo:w   xabe-with *?uy* baneh
　　　dog ACC   3SM NOM   rock-INST eye   hit
　　　'He smashed the dog's eye with a rock'
　　　("That means the eye might be destroyed")

Heightened affectedness does not constitute an adequate characterization of previous examples, however. The target of a global compliment, as in (24*b*), is not precisely more *affected* than the target of a specific compliment, although perhaps some analogue of affectedness can be proposed, its interpretation depending upon the predicate, the body part, and the possessor. Examples (25*a*) and (25*b*), however, suggest that the account must be somewhat more complicated than this. Here the Northern Pomo consultant asserts that there is no straightforward sense in which the possessor is more greatly affected by his toe falling off in (25*b*) than in (25*a*). In both cases, the toe is interpreted as having fallen completely off, through disease or accident. Examples (3*a*) and (3*b*) receive a similar interpretation: (3*b*) is not taken to mean that the speaker's eye is twitching more severely.

Notice that in every example reviewed so far, the body-part nominal receives the same interpretation in the PR version as in the regular possession construction: the foot is cut, the hair looks nice, the toe drops off, etc. So in each case, the verbal entailments (in the sense of Dowty, 1991: 572, n. 16) for the unmarked (non-PR) set of arguments persist in the PR version and are distributed as we would expect. The raised possessor contributes something extra to the interpretation of the utterance.

Given the interpretive arguments of this section, we can see that there is evidence that the raised possessor retains its thematic status as a Possessor. On the other hand, it does not invariably hold the same thematic status as the body part. Therefore, it seems reasonable to view the raised possessor not as a semantic argument, but as an adjunct. It is generally assumed that adjuncts contribute a constant meaning to any clause that allows them (Dowty, 1991: 577): benefactive, instrumental, temporal and other adjuncts add a predictable meaning that is not dependent on the verbal semantics. (Furthermore, assigning the raised possessor adjunct status avoids another problem: if it is viewed as a complement, it is an unselected complement, ruled out by the Projection Principle and other variants of the same idea.)

What remains to be specified is whether there is an interpretation of the raised possessor adjunct that is generalizable to all instances of the construction. Croft (1985: 46) has observed that, in general, PR constructions are limited to benefactive or malefactive relationships between the raised possessor and the predicate. There are many examples that are compatible with this observation as a first approximation, but the data in the following sections will demonstrate that it is possible to develop a more fine-grained analysis, one that preserves the particularistic nature of each utterance interpretation while still providing generality across instances of the construction.

6.2.3. *Factors affecting use and avoidance of PR*

In both elicitation and in textual examples, there are observable patterns of preferred use and avoidance of the PR construction in Northern Pomo.

6.2.3.1. *Possessor nominal effects.* Some verb–NP combinations require use of the PR construction if the possessor is human, whereas if the possessor is nonhuman the construction is optional or even dispreferred. Within the referential domain of human possessors, the more well-known the possessor is to the speaker, the more the PR construction is preferred, all other things being equal. This is shown in (27a–d). The PR construction is strongly preferred for (27a)— a human possessor with kinship ties to the speaker; it is available but not as strongly preferred for 'the boy' (27c–d), and is slightly dispreferred for a nonhuman possessor. (I will return to example (27d) below.)

(27a) ʔaːmi-deː-l   ʔuy-nam moːw   xabe-wih baneh
       my-older sister ACC eye -DET 3SM NOM rock-INST hit
       'He hit my older sister's eye with a rock'

(27b) *kawiya ba-nam moːwal ʔuy-nam* moːw   xabe-wih baneh
       child   boy -DET 3SM ACC eye-DET   3SM NOM rock-INST hit
       'He hit the boy's eye with a rock'

(27c) *kawiya ba-nam   moːw-aʔ ʔuy-nam* moːw   xabe-wih baneh
       child   boy -SPEC 3SM-OBL eye-DET   3SM NOM rock-INST hit
       'He hit the boy's eye with a rock'

(27d) *hayu yačuʔ ʔuy-nam* moːw   xabe-wih   baneh
       dog OBL   eye-SPEC 3SM NOM rock-INST   hit
       'He hit the dog's eye with a rock'

6.2.3.2. *Predicate effects.* Within the realm of human possessors, there is a greater tendency for speakers to prefer use of the PR construction when the predicate is one of high impact or high effect on the whole person. The (*a*) examples below (which display the PR construction) would thus be preferred to the (*b*) examples (regular possession).

(28a) *moːwal xama* dithal-e   (28b) #*moːw-aʔ xama-nam* dithal-e
       3SMACC foot hurt -PRES   3SM-OBL   foot -DET hurt-PRES
       'He has foot pain'   'His foot hurts'

(29a) *toː   ʔuy* dithal-e   (29b) #*khe ʔuy-nam* dithal-e
       1S ACC eye hurt-PRES   1S OBL eye -DET hurt-PRES
       'My eye hurts'   'My eye hurts'

(30a) *čon ṭuh*   man   *ʔuymo* dac'ap-a
       John ACC 3SF NOM face   slap-PRES
       'She slapped John in the face'

(30b) #*čon wih ʔuymo-nam* man   dac'ap-a
       John OBL face-DET   3SF NOM slap-PRES
       'She slapped John's face'

When possessor nominal and body part are held constant, this effect of verb type is evident. Contrast (29*a*–*b*) 'My eye hurts,' where PR is preferred, with (3*a*–*b*), 'My eye is twitching', where either construction is equally acceptable.

However, no single verbal feature seems to predict the preference for the construction. A contribution is also made by the nature of the body part itself. In example (31) below, the physical impact of the verbally encoded event seems minimal and causes the possessor no pain; nevertheless, the PR construction seems to be preferred.

(31a) ba-de: *ma:dal ?uymo* datoy
      3's older sister NOM 3SF ACC face   design
      'Her older sister₍ᵢ₎ painted her₍ⱼ₎ face'
(31b) #ba-de: *ma:da? ?uymo-nam* datoy
      3's older sister NOM 3SF OBL face-DET   design
      'Her older sister₍ᵢ₎ painted her₍ⱼ₎ face'

On the other hand, if the nominal *thana-heč* 'fingernails' is substituted for the nominal 'face' in (31), either construction is perfectly acceptable.[9] A similar contrast is found if one compares sentences like 'A fly is sitting on her face' and 'A fly is sitting on her knee.' The former shows a strong preference for the PR construction, while the latter is open. In general, the body-part nominal 'face' contributes to the preference for the construction.

Nonhuman animate possessors do not seem to trigger these predicate and body-part-related patterns of preference to anywhere near the same degree: nonhuman animates can occur freely in the construction, but there seems to be less semantically and pragmatically sponsored variation in the examples I have found. (Part–whole relationships of inanimates are not expressed using the possession construction (e.g. 'the jar's lid', 'the table's leg').)

6.2.4. *The phenomenology and linguistics of body-part possession*

By now the reader will probably have observed that the continuous and subtle nature of these effects is not easily characterized in terms of the standard categories of thematic role types, or even in terms of the more fine-grained verb entailments proposed by Dowty (1991) as constitutive of thematic proto-roles. Yet the effects are far from surprising, and suggest an underlying systematicity. In discussing the nature of that systematicity I will rely in particular on work by Fillmore (1977; 1982) in which it is argued that semantics must be grounded in complex understandings of whole events and their parts. Words and more complex expressions 'represent categorizations of experience, and each of these categories is underlain by a motivating situation occurring against a background of knowledge and experience' (Fillmore, 1982: 112). The job of the empirical semanticist is therefore to discover precisely what categorization of experience a word represents, and in

---

[9] The preference for the PR construction in (31) should not be construed as stemming from the process of lexicalization. Example (12) above demonstrates that 'face-paint' is not a fixed or frozen lexical item.

addition to understand the experiential and institutional background against which that categorization arose (p. 135). For example, the meanings of verbs of judging ('accuse,' 'criticize,' etc.) involve 'a schematization of human judgment and behavior involving notions of worth, responsibility, judgment, etc., such that one would want to say that nobody can really understand the meanings of the words in that domain who does not understand the social institutions or the structures of experience which they presuppose' (p. 116).

Fillmore asserts that, to understand the contribution of words—and larger units—to the texts in which they occur, the semanticist must be prepared to make reference to irreducibly rich sets of related concepts and facts, or 'scenes' and 'frames.' Speakers' interpretations rely on scenes and frames, and linguists' accounts can usefully be posed in those terms, he argues. Many of the examples that Fillmore discusses (among the best known being the commercial-event scene and verbs of buying and selling) involve the capacity of a verb to index a complex scene. In contrast, I have shown that interpretation of the PR construction is not mediated solely by verbal semantics, nor even by the use of a body-part nominal *per se*. Rather, the elements of the cognitive 'scene' involving a self and that self's body parts (activated by the body-part lexeme, presumably) must be integrated with the scene activated by the use of the predicate. The construction as a whole imposes a perspective, or frame, in which the experience of the body-part possessor is foregrounded, in ways that I will elaborate upon below.

6.2.4.1. *The body-part possession 'scene'.* First, consider the components of a special 'scene' of possession; in particular, in this case the special relation between body parts and their possessors. I will argue that, for the purposes of setting out a semantics of this construction, at least three facets of human experience must be considered:

(A) *The nature of possible relationships between any body part and the possessor of the body part.* This will include more than simply the neurophysiological and neuromuscular linkages between a body part and the 'self' or conscious possessor of that body part. Although these neurological linkages are highly varied (consider the differences between one's experienced relationship to one's lips versus one's big toe), there are also other, non-neurally mediated experiences indexed by the PR construction. Relationships between body parts and their possessors are also socially and culturally constructed (compare the sociocultural significance of one's hair to that of one's elbow). They vary as well in terms of functional significance (compare the significance of loss of hands to that of loss of hair).

(B) *The nature of the relation between a particular body part and a particular event.* Just as body parts differ in their absolute significance to a possessor, they differ in terms of how they figure within a particular event. It is one thing to tie up someone's hair, another to tie up his hands. Observing that someone's hair is grey is quite different from observing that her face is grey; and painting one's nails has quite different social consequences from painting one's nose. (This relationship must also be discussed in strictly linguistic terms; see below.)

(C) *The nature of the relation between the <u>effect</u> of an event on a particular body part and the <u>consequences</u> of that effect for the possessor of the body part.* This aspect of experience derives from (1) and (2). Given an intact nervous system in a state of wakefulness, any impingement on a body part will be perceptually accessible to the possessor. Moreover, due to the normal undetachability of a body part, any affect on a body part will have consequences—neural, pragmatic, social, cultural, or otherwise—for the possessor. If someone ties a weight to one's leg, the whole self is constrained. If somebody paints a sign on one's back, the whole person must deal with the consequences. If one's hair is grey, there are many potential consequences for the social self.

These experientially based, 'real-world' aspects of possession make up the scene that forms the sociocognitive background to a hearer's interpretation of the PR construction. Now these aspects of experience must be linked specifically to the linguistic construction under consideration. What follows is an attempt to make explicit the interactions between components—linguistic and nonlinguistic—that play a constitutive role in the semantic interpretation of PR sentences.

6.2.4.2. *Mapping between experience and language structure*

(1) There is a (nonlinguistic) relation, call it Possession$_{bp}$, that holds between a sentient being and a part of that being's body. It consists of neurological, physiological, mechanical, social, and cultural linkages between a particular body part and the whole person, or self. Because

the nature of these linkages (neurological, social, etc.) varies by body part, each body part has a unique Possession$_{bp}$ relation to the whole self, or the possessor. We can say that *a body part nominal evokes a particular cognitive scene that schematizes this complex relationship, Possession$_{bp}$.*

(2) As proposed by Fillmore, a verb evokes a scene, and may also index a particular framing of that scene. The verb evokes a scene in part by evoking the participant roles that are featured in such a scene. For purposes of this analysis, I will therefore posit a (linguistic) *semantic relation, R, that holds between a verb and each of its direct arguments.*[10] This semantic relation highlights a conventionalized part of the scene evoked by the verb. Although one can think of thematic role assignment as a first-order approximation of this relation, it is clearly insufficient. For example, Searle (1980) argues that interpretation of the truth conditions for a literal use of 'cut' (as in 'cut the grass' and 'cut the cake') depends upon a set of conventional understandings about both the object being cut and the nature of the contextualized scene (a suburban lawn and a sod farm require different kinds of grass-cutting, the latter being much like cake-cutting).

Yet in spite of the fact that cutting a watermelon and cutting a finger may share little in the way of physical, social, or experiential outcomes, both constitute tokens of what is conventionally understood as an instance of the meaning of the linguistic predicate 'cut'. So the relation R holding between the predicate 'cut' and the argument NP 'my finger' is, in this view, interpreted by integrating both the verbal meaning and the contextually appropriate consequences of that meaning for the type of entity denoted by the argument NP, in this case 'my finger'. The specific interpretation of a PR sentence will thus derive in part from integrating the relevant verbal scene and the relevant 'scene' of body part possession, Possession$_{bp}$—*mediated by the semantic relation R.*

(3) By virtue of the nature of the experiential relation Possession$_{bp}$, any experience that affects a body part may have effects that propagate through the neurological, physiological, mechanical, social and cultural linkages between that body part and the whole person, or possessor. So *every category of experience E affecting a body part generates a corresponding <u>set</u> of events and experiences (sensory, social,*

---

[10] I am limiting myself here to arguments of a verb which are conventionally thought of as directly subcategorizing the verb (but cf. nn. 3 and 5). Transitive and agentive intransitive subjects are thus excluded from this preliminary statement.

functional etc.) E′ that may affect the possessor, or whole self. The actual content of the set E′ will depend upon the particular content of the experience and the particular instantiation of Possession$_{bp}$.

So for any verb used with an argument denoting a body part, there will be an interpretation of the meaning of that verb predicated of that particular body part, and there will also be a set of implications or consequences of that meaning for the body-part possessor. The set will include physical, social, functional, and cultural consequences of that verb–body part combination for the body-part possessor. As such, these consequences will be highly context-specific.

As laid out thus far, this account provides all the cognitive contents and linguistic relationships needed to provide an interpretation for sentences such as (24*a*) and (24*b*), 'His big toe fell off.' However, this account does not distinguish *between* (24*a*) and (24*b*). Elements A, B, C and 1, 2, and 3 above would all combine to give these two sentences exactly the same interpretation. Yet I am claiming that, while they are truth-conditionally the same, they do not have exactly the same situated interpretation. What creates the interpretive difference?

(4) Fillmore suggests that the particular choice of a verb—such as 'buy'—frames a commercial event scene in terms of a particular point of view, in this case that of the buyer. Our knowledge of the rich domain of commercial transactions will be brought to bear in order to interpret the relevant text, but the choice of the verb 'buy' structures or frames that knowledge in a particular way, such that we will schematize our envisionment of the scene from the perspective of the buyer. I suggest that the PR construction (as identified by its morphosyntactic characteristics) similarly frames the hearer's envisionment of the scene evoked by the verb: it causes the hearer to foreground the consequences for the body part possessor. The hearer is tacitly directed to find some consequence or consequences in the set E′ and to understand the speaker as implicating those consequences. Which consequence or consequences is not given, and may remain vague or diffuse, but the construction directs the hearer to find some such consequence as having intended relevance.

We can now describe the interpretation of an example like the following, taken from a conversation in which two friends are discussing the hospitalization of the hearer due to an auto accident in which the back of her hand was nearly severed. In (32), the speaker is asserting that the addressee's skin was hanging off of her hand, and is implicating that she intends to foreground some set of consequences for the possessor.

(32) nan *siyan-nam   miţo*   phidima-n
     and skin -DET   2S ACC   hang-PROG
     'So your skin was just hanging there'

The intended consequences might include the addressee's fear, her pain, her confusion, her feelings of vulnerability, or all of these. The hearer is simply alerted that, by choosing this construction, the speaker means to foreground the consequences. In essence, she is saying that the consequences of the event for the possessor rank more highly in her current concerns than the consequences for the body part itself.[11]

These interpretive effects are accomplished, I propose, through the existence of a *conventional implicature* that is attached to the construction itself. It is the conventional implicature that directs the hearer to understand the speaker as foregrounding the consequences for the possessor and ranking them above those of the body part itself. Conventional implicatures are usually said to be a property of lexical items (Grice, 1981), adding meaning without changing truth conditions. However, in recent work that investigates particularistic linkages between pragmatic interpretation and units larger than a word (Fillmore *et al.*, 1988; Fillmore, 1988; Kay, 1987; Lambrecht, 1990; Dowty, 1991: 609, Zwicky, forthcoming), it has been argued that nonpredictable semantics and pragmatics may be part of particular constructions beyond the contributions of single lexical items (but cf. Akmajian, 1984). In the case of Northern Pomo PR, no single verb or other morpheme heads the construction, yet there are morphosyntactic regularities that allow us to recognize it, specifically the presence of a grammatical function that is not a subcategorized argument (the raised possessor) and a constituent necessarily headed by a body-part nominal.

Taken in its entirety, this account is both more precise and more predictive than one which asserts only that a benefactive or malefactive

---

[11] Note that framing the scene from the perspective of the possessor is not identical with saying that the possessor is in focus or is somehow new or activated information. Evidence for this is provided by the fact that either the raised possessor or the body part can be the target of a focus construction or a WH-question, as described in section 6.1. The PR construction is a backdrop to other information-structuring elements in the clause in both cases. Nevertheless, as pointed out to me by Knud Lambrecht, the discourse status of the possessor (as topic, etc.) needs further investigation.

role is assigned to the raised-possessor nominal. This account requires that the interpretive contribution of the PR construction be a function of several factors: (*a*) the nature of the relation between the predicate and the body part, (*b*) the nature of the relation between the body part and the possessor, (*c*) the nature of the possible consequences of (*a*) for the body-part possessor, and (*d*) contextual factors that might favor the highlighting of some subset of consequences in E'. While the labels benefactive and malefactive may provide a rough approximation of the contribution of PR to many utterances, they underspecify the interpretation of the examples given above, and they provide no explanation for the preference effects discussed in section 6.2.3. The conventional implicature account, on the other hand, predicts that the construction will be favored in those cases where the possessor's concerns, feelings, or experiences are to be foregrounded for any reason.

This account, then, requires that we factor in the speaker's contextually specific construal of a situation or state of affairs. The speaker is the one who decides whether to cast the event in the regular possession construction or in the PR construction. This provides a fairly straightforward explanation for the effects reported in section 6.2.3, where human possessors, high-impact predicates, and highly innervated or socially significant body parts all contribute to the likelihood that the speaker will want to foreground or highlight the consequences for the possessor. Cross-linguistically, there is a general tendency to accord privileged status to the physically mediated experiences of other humans, and to mark that status linguistically (Brown and Levinson, 1987). In other words, the preference for the PR construction with human possessors, important body parts, and high-impact verbs (or the avoidance of the *non*-PR construction in such situations) is due, on this view, to socioculturally specific beliefs, values, or conventions that assign conversational significance to the consequences of some event for the body-part possessor. Although Northern Pomo displays grammaticized animacy hierarchy effects in its case-marking morphology (such as those described in Silverstein, 1976), the PR preference effects are largely not grammaticized, but rather are a reflection of the social and cultural status of the beings denoted by linguistic expressions. These effects are thus part of the situated interpretation of this construction, and many are subject to contextual variation.

In the next section I will review further data which supports the conventional implicature account, and which shows that the construction is a resource actively used by speakers to generate social meanings in face-to-face interaction.

6.2.5. *Conversational implicatures arising from the PR construction*

I have argued that use of the PR construction signals to the hearer that the consequences of the event for the possessor are currently import-ant or relevant. As described in section 6.2.3, in certain circumstances the PR construction is the default, or heavily favored, choice. In just these contexts, when the PR construction is the default choice, if the speaker *avoids* use of the PR construction, a robust *conversational* implicature may result.

Specifically, avoidance of the PR construction with high-impact verbs and human possessors may cause the hearer to infer that *the speaker is trying to communicate that the consequences of the event for the possessor (the set E') are not significant*. This particular conversa-tional implicature is then further specified in light of the details of the speech situation and the event being described. For example, in (33) below, the speaker has avoided using the PR construction, although the human possessor and predicate would usually call for it. The result is that the utterance constitutes an insult to the possessor.

(33) ṭi-ʔ   *xama-nam*   dithal-kan   moːw   khemane-nha
       LDR-OBL   foot -DET   hurt-ADV COMP   3SM NOM   dance-NEG
       'He's not dancing because his foot hurts'
       ("Sounds like you're belittling him")

On the account proposed here, the explanation is as follows. The situ-ation described (a well-known human is suffering pain) should norm-ally be encoded so that the consequences for the possessor are foregrounded. They are not so encoded in this utterance, so the hearer infers that the speaker avoided that option for some reason. An easily available reason is that the speaker is demeaning the experience of the possessor, either implying that his foot doesn't hurt much, and so should not warrant non-participation in the dance, or implying that whether his foot hurts or not, his internal experiences do not warrant regard in any case.

A general demeaning of the possessor is a common interpretation of PR avoidance, but there are many others. For example, when the speaker avoids the PR construction in contexts like the following (human possessor, high-impact verb and body-part extremity), the hearer may assume that the relationship of possession (Possession$_{bp}$) does not hold at all. If the body part is detached from the body-part possessor, the set of possible consequences for the possessor (E') is greatly attenuated.[12]

(34) *moːw-aʔ   šaː-nam*   man   phaley-ka
      3SM-OBL   arm-DET   3SF NOM   burn-CAUS
      'She burned his arm'
      ("Sounds like his arm is detached")

In fact, the PR construction is not usable when the body part is detached, particularly when the possessor is no longer alive. The following example comes from a Pomo traditional narrative, in which Bear Woman has killed her daughter-in-law and is getting ready to roast and eat her eyeballs. The PR construction is unacceptable here, according to the native speaker consultant.

(35) so-nam   mil   mina   *ma-ʔod-aʔ*   *ʔuy-xabe -nay*
      clover-SPEC   OBL   on   *LDR*'s d.-in-law-OBL   eye-stone-DET
      mul   mičam-hɛ
      DEM   put-ADV
      '[Bear woman] . . . having put her daughter-in-law's eyeballs on top of the clover'

There are a number of other examples in which the speaker avoids the PR construction because she wants to avoid responsibility for some contextually specific implication that she might otherwise be taken to imply or endorse. For example, the speaker may want to avoid implicating some unflattering or negative consequence about the possessor. In (36) below, the speaker avoids the PR construction because, although the possessor's feet are deemed to be ugly, she does not want to go further and implicate that he himself suffers from this in any global way.

(36) *moːw-aʔ   xama -nam*   tiyiš na
      3SM-OBL   foot -DET   ugly COP
      'His feet are ugly'
      ("Well, his *feet* may be ugly, but he looks pretty good")

---

[12] The requirement to avoid the use of the PR construction when the body part is detached is also mentioned by Michelson (1991) in her discussion of possessor stranding in Oneida.

The same strategy with different intentions can be seen in example (24a), repeated here. Suppose the speaker has been asked to render a judgment: the hearer has asked, 'How do I look?' The speaker replies with (24a), implying that she does not wish to commit herself to the implicature that the hearer's appearance is globally pleasing, and thus communicating off-record lack of enthusiasm.

(24a) *mi?*   *?e:-nam*   k'edi   phiṭ'a
      2S OBL   hair-DET   good   appear
      'Your hair looks nice'
      ("Well, your *hair* looks nice . . .")

A similar but more contextually specific example was related to me as having taken place in an encounter between two Pomo women. One was carrying her great-granddaughter, a blond child with blue eyes, but with significant Pomo heritage. The other woman commented on how Caucasian the child looked, implying that perhaps she was not really Pomo and thus indirectly challenging her membership in the community. The response, given below as example (37), contradicts that unspoken challenge. By limiting the predication to the girl's eyes, the speaker implicated that one salient consequence of having blue eyes did not hold for her great-granddaughter. Through avoiding the PR construction, she was saying in effect that although some of her features were Caucasian, the child was Pomo.

(37) *kawi -yaču?* *?uy* c'axat'? -ay   na
     child-OBL   eye   blue-PL   COP
     'The kid's *eyes* are blue . . .'

The examples above are all instances in which a speaker derived an inference from the fact that the construction was expected, but avoided. There are converse examples also, where the construction is used when not expected. These also provoke inferences. An earlier example can be reinterpreted using the elements of the proposed model. The relevant pair of sentences is repeated here.

(38a) *hayu yaču?* *?uy-nam* mo:w   xabe-wih   baneh
      dog OBL   eye -DET   3SM NOM rock-INST   hit
      'He hit the dog's eye with a rock'
(38b) *hayu yačul* mo:w   xabe-wih *?uy* baneh
      dog ACC   3SM NOM rock-INST eye   hit
      'He smashed the dog's eye with a rock'
      ("That means the eye might be destroyed")

At first this pair seemed to indicate that the use of the PR construction (38*b*) conveyed heightened affectedness of the possessor. A more precise analysis is now available. Since the possessor is not a human, the PR construction is not preferred. When the speaker chooses to use it in this case, the hearer derives a conversational implicature that the speaker has a reason for using the construction. In this case, where the possessor is a dog, the choice between the non-PR construction and the PR construction will not be motivated by the logic of social deference; it will instead be motivated by other kinds of reason the speaker might have for highlighting the consequences of that event for the canine possessor. The pairing of 'hit' and 'eye' could result in a wide range of consequences for the possessor, from the minimal to the traumatic. With all of this as background, the hearer seeks to assign a motivation to the speaker's choice of PR. Perhaps the most obvious possible inference is that the event was particularly intense, complete, or affecting.

The animal counterpart to (35), where expected deference is withheld, is (39), where unexpected deference is given. Here, the speaker uses the PR construction for a predication about a cat's eyes. Since animals are generally not accorded raised possessor status, the choice to use the construction results in an inference that the cat has a special status, or is a valued companion.

(39) *xadalom-nam yačul* ʔ*uy*   c'axat'ʔ -ay   na
      cat -DET   ACC   eye   blue-PL   COP
      'The cat's eyes are blue' [The cat has a special status]

6.3. CONCLUSIONS

This description of Possessor-Raising in Northern Pomo poses several interesting puzzles for grammarians. The first concerns the complex semantic and pragmatic regularities involved in the interpretation of PR sentences. These regularities must be associated with the PR syntactic pattern if we are to explain patterns of preference in using the construction (section 6.2.3), and, in turn, situated interpretations based on use or avoidance of the construction in particular settings (section 6.2.5). The first question that arises is how these facts can be incorporated into any particular theoretically coherent account of the phenomenon: where in the grammar is the association between the syntax and the semantico-pragmatic features? Linguists of a variety of theoretical persuasions are coming to agree that an adequate description of human language competence requires a rich and heterogeneous lexicon including at least formulaic phrases, idioms, and their associated non-predictable semantics and pragmatics. Yet there is no invariant lexical or morphological element associated with PR that could carry the necessary semantico-pragmatic features as a lexical property. Neither are the effects associated with a verb class. Speaking descriptively, the semantics and pragmatics described above are associated with any sentence containing both (*a*) an absolutive argument headed by an (unpossessed) nominal denoting a body part and (*b*) a nominal adjunct denoting an individual that can be construed as the possessor of the body part. Moreover, the patterns of preference and implicature described here suggest that much of the interpretation depends upon a cognizance of *both* syntactic possibilities: the PR version and the non-PR version.

One well-known account of PR, Baker (1988), would in principle be unable to incorporate many of these facts. Baker proposes that PR is the result of syntactic movement: like a variety of relation-changing alternations, PR for Baker is simply an instance of the general syntactic process of Incorporation, or movement of X^0 (lexical) categories. The syntactic process of PR involves movement of the body-part nominal into the verbal complex. The syntactic requirements on the process are said to explain the cross-linguistic restriction of PR to absolutive arguments mentioned above (p. 126). However, Incorporation is only constrained by general syntactic constraints on movement, and there is no sense in which the resulting syntactic configuration has any independent status, much less that of a stable construction. Therefore it is difficult to see how speakers' knowledge of this construction, described here as an amalgam of syntactic, semantic, and pragmatic regularities (that do not depend upon lexicalization), could be represented within Baker's framework. Furthermore, the widely observed restriction of PR to sentences containing body-part nominals (or other inalienably possessed nouns) is unexplained within his framework. There are only a few reported instances in the literature of PR involving alienably possessed objects. It is not clear how a general syntactic process such as his Incorporation could be constrained to act only on body part (or other inalienably possessed) nominals, as he himself notes (1988: 103), yet this constraint is one of the most striking cross-linguistic regularities of the phenomenon.

An account featuring constructions in the sense of Fillmore *et al.* (1988) could easily incorporate these specificities: the construction might consist of a schematic slot for a verb and its lexically specified arguments, one of which would be an absolutive (necessarily) headed by a body part nominal. The construction would also include the nominal adjunct (the 'raised possessor'), thematically specified as a (body-part) possessor. The possessor adjunct would be assigned the grammatical function of the absolutive argument, whether Subject or Direct Object, as required by the evidence presented in section 6.1.3. Finally, the conventional implicature (indicating current relevance of the consequences of the event for the possessor) could be associated with the construction as a whole, thus explaining the preference patterns and the implicature effects.

Yet what this approach offers in the linking of syntactic, semantic, and pragmatic information it loses in explanatory power in two important respects: it can only stipulate, not explain, the restriction to absolutives, and, like Baker's account, it cannot explain the fact that all known instances of PR cross-linguistically are limited to inalienable possession.

I will focus here only on the latter problem, phrased in a slightly different way: why should the nominal adjunct be limited to the role of Inalienable Possessor? The original motivation for calling the 'raised' possessor an adjunct is that it makes a constant contribution to the interpretation of the sentence and that otherwise it would be an unselected complement—a problem in any theory. (Baker's objections to the traditional account of PR follow these lines: the 'raised' possessor cannot actually be a fully fledged direct object (or subject) because that would violate the Projection Principle—the requirement that all lexical selection properties of predicates be satisfied at all syntactic levels. The 'raised' possessor would be an unselected complement of the verb. Moreover, he claims, the raised possessor cannot simply be base-generated as an NP direct argument of the verb, since the PR sentence is a 'thematic paraphrase' of the non-PR counterpart, and thus for him both must have the same D-structure (p. 273). This problem does not arise with the adjunct solution.)

So the question can be rephrased in this way: why should a nominal adjunct that is assigned the role of Possessor be required to be an Inalienable Possessor? Notice that this adjunct contains no morphology indicating this role—it is an Accusative NP. It looks like an unselected complement. Why are unselected complements generally ruled out? Whether one attributes the problem to syntactic recoverability constraints on theta role assignment or to parsing problems, the problem is that the hearer cannot easily assign an interpretation to the NP—it is unaccounted for, however we think about it.

Viewed from this perspective, the question changes once more. Under what conditions can the general prohibition against extrathematic nominals be eased? This is the form of the question posed recently by Shibatani (1994 and the current volume). He deals with the small inventory of types of extrathematic nominals encountered in the world's languages, including subjects of adversative passives, benefactives, malefactives, and inalienable possessors.[13] (The account I will offer is consistent with his independently conducted study, although his conclusions are more far-reaching.)

It is widely assumed that in regular possession (e.g. 'Kim's car') the role of Possessor is conferred upon the possessor NP via the structural configuration within NP, and obviously, in this configuration there is no restriction to inalienability. But when the possessor is an independent NP constituent, its status is unclear. Whether viewed as a parsing problem or as a syntactic problem, its thematic status is difficult to reconstruct in the absence of morphosyntactic cues. Here, only the relation of *inalienable* possession can be reconstructed. Using Fillmore's notion of 'scene' once again, we might say that the rich experiential grounding of body-part nominals is robust enough to evoke a scene that provides an interpretation for the adjunct nominal possessor.

Other researchers, who have focused more on syntax than on interpretation of the construction, have noted that body-part nominals are 'relational' (have an implicit possessor argument) and thus license a possessor adjunct (see Maling and Kim, 1992 and references cited there). The present account is consistent with such a statement but goes further in considering the content of that claim. What is the basis of this 'relationality', if not the kinds of knowledge described in section 6.2.4? Such knowledge begins to accumulate at birth, and continues to grow in complexity and subtlety throughout life. It is perceptually multimodal and culturally significant in multiple ways. It is for these reasons that the presence of a body-part nominal can

---

[13] Maling and Kim (1992: 58) propose that for a similar construction in Korean, the whole NP (possessor) is an argument of the part NP, since the (inalienable) part NP is a 'relational' noun that always has an implicit possessor. They construct an account of theta role assignment in these terms which covers the data they report and captures some of the phenomena reported here.

license the highly specific interpretation of a nominal adjunct that is in no clear lexical or configurational relationship to it. The empirical semantics suggested by Fillmore and carried out here provides the underpinnings for a statement about the 'argument structure' of body part nouns.

A scene-based account is also able to encompass the few examples in the literature in which PR occurs with alienably possessed objects. The example given by Baker from Mohawk ('He stole my car', p. 103) encompasses two aspects of the account given here. Although 'car' is not a relational noun in the same way 'knee' is, ownership of cars is a culturally central notion in many parts of the world. In this language, the word 'car' and the verb 'steal' together evoke a scene with such clear and salient consequences for the possessor that the construction is licensed. 'He saw my car' would presumably fail to occur in the PR construction. Fillmore's notion of a lexically evoked scene is the substance that supports the rich and complicated process of situated interpretation.

This account, then, supports a claim that the constraints on PR are not merely lexical constraints but derive from limits on the domains of experience that can support interpretation of unmarked nominal adjuncts, or 'extrathematic nominals', to adopt Shibatani's term.[14] This is not to deny that it may be possible to state such a constraint in terms of lexical classes; rather it is to emphasize what might underlie such constraints. This position leads to a rather low-risk conjecture: if a language has a PR construction at all, it will allow the construction with body-part nominals. If it extends beyond body-part possession, it will first extend to cases where the particular combination of verb and possessed object results in a salient, conversationally relevant outcome for the possessor.

Depending upon one's theoretical concerns, such knowledge may be seen as outside the purview of linguistics, or at least of syntax. But empirical semantics and pragmatics of this type may support current efforts to decompose thematic role types in search of grammatical explanation (e.g. Ladusaw and Dowty, 1988; Dowty, 1991), or even efforts to separate what is syntactically motivated from what is cognitively given without the superimposition of unnecessary semantic machinery (e.g. Emonds, 1991).

[14] Thanks to Paul Kay, Jean Pierre Koenig, and Joan Maling, who also brought related 'extrathematic' constructions (ethical datives, adversative passives, etc.) to my attention.

Finally, this analysis supports the supposition that in order to further understand the interface of syntax, semantics, and pragmatics it is worth going beyond the semantics of thematic role assignments and the pragmatics of information structuring, and to consider both in light of the particulars of speakers' situated interpretations of specific syntactic structures.

REFERENCES

AISSEN, J. (1987). *Tzotzil Clause Structure*. Dordrecht: Reidel.

AKMAJIAN, A. (1984). 'Sentence Types and the Form–Function Fit,' *Natural Language and Linguistic Theory* 2/1: 1–23.

BAKER, M. (1988). *Incorporation: A Theory of Grammatical Function Changing*. Chicago: University of Chicago Press.

BROWN, P., and LEVINSON, S. (1987). *Politeness: Some Universals in Language Usage*. Cambridge: Cambridge University Press.

COLE, P. (1981) (ed.), *Radical Pragmatics*. New York: Academic Press.

—— and SADOCK, J. (eds.) (1977). *Syntax and Semantics viii: Grammatical Relations*. New York: Academic Press.

CROFT, W. (1985). 'Indirect Object "Lowering",' *Proceedings of the Eleventh Annual Meeting of the Berkeley Linguistics Society*, 39–51.

DAVIES, W. D. (1986). *Choctaw Verb Agreement and Universal Grammar*. Dordrecht: Reidel.

DIXON, R. M. W. (ed.) (1976). *Grammatical Categories in Australian Languages*. Canberra: Australian Institute of Aboriginal Studies.

DOWTY, D. (1991). 'Thematic Proto-Roles and Argument Selection,' *Language* 67/3: 547–619.

EMONDS, J. (1991). 'Subcategorization and Syntax-Based Theta-Role Assignment,' *Natural Language and Linguistic Theory* 9: 369–429.

FILLMORE, C. J. (1977). 'The Case for Case Reopened,' in Cole and Sadock (1977: 59–82).

—— (1982). 'Frame Semantics', in Linguistic Society of Korea (ed.), *Linguistics in the Morning Calm*, 111–37. Seoul: Hanshin.

—— (1988). 'The Mechanisms of "Construction Grammar",' *Proceedings of the Fourteenth Annual Meeting of the Berkeley Linguistics Society*, 35–55.

—— KAY, P., and O'CONNOR, M. C. (1988). 'Regularity and Idiomaticity in Grammatical Constructions,' *Language*, 64/3: 501–38.

GOLDBERG, A. (1992). 'The Inherent Semantics of Argument Structure: The Case of the English Ditransitive Construction,' *Cognitive Linguistics* 3/1: 37–74.

GRICE, P. (1981). 'Presupposition and Conversational Implicature,' in Cole (1981: 183–98).

GROPEN, J., PINKER, S., HOLLANDER, M., GOLDBERG, R., and WILSON, R. (1989). 'The Learnability and Acquisition of the Dative Alternation in English,' *Language* **65**: 203–57.

KAY, P. (1987). 'EVEN,' Berkeley Cognitive Sciences Report No. 50. Berkeley: University of California.

LADUSAW, W., and DOWTY, D. (1988). 'Towards a Non-Semantic Account of Thematic Roles,' in Wilkins (1988: 61–73).

LAMBRECHT, K. (1990). ' "What, Me Worry?": "Mad Magazine Sentences" Revisited,' *Proceedings of the Sixteenth Annual Meeting of the Berkeley Linguistics Society*, 215–28.

MALING, J., and KIM, S. (1992). 'Case Assignment in the Inalienable Possession Construction in Korean,' *Journal of East Asian Linguistics* **1**: 37–68.

MICHELSON, K. (1991). 'Possessor Stranding in Oneida,' *Linguistic Inquiry* **22/4**: 756–61.

MITHUN, M. (1986). 'On the Nature of Noun Incorporation,' *Language*, **62/1**: 32–7.

O'CONNOR, M. C. (1992). *Topics in Northern Pomo Grammar*. New York: Garland.

—— (1994). 'The Marking of Possession in Northern Pomo: Privative Opposition and Pragmatic Inference,' *Proceedings of the Twentieth Annual Meeting of the Berkeley Linguistics Society*, 387–401.

SADOCK, J. (1986). 'Some Notes on Noun Incorporation,' *Language* **62/1**: 19–31.

SEARLE, J. (1980). 'The Background of Meaning,' in Searle *et al.* (1980: 221–32).

——, KIEFER, F., and BIERWISCH, M. (eds.) (1980). *Speech Act Theory and Pragmatics*. Dordrecht: Reidel.

SHIBATANI, M. (1994). 'An Integrational Approach to Possessor Raising, Ethical Datives and Adversative Passives', *Proceedings of the Twentieth Annual Meeting of the Berkeley Linguistics Society*, 401–56.

—— and T. KAGEYAMA (1988). 'Word Formation in a Modular Theory of Grammar,' *Language* **64/3**: 451–84.

SILVERSTEIN, M. (1976). 'Hierarchy of Features and Ergativity,' in Dixon (1976: 112–71).

WILKINS, W. (ed.) (1988). *Syntax and Semantics xxi: On the Nature of Thematic Roles*. New York: Academic Press.

ZWICKY, A. (1994). 'Dealing out Meaning: Fundamentals of Syntactic Constructions,' *Proceedings of the Twentieth Annual Meeting of the Berkeley Linguistics Society*.

7

Applicatives and Benefactives:
A Cognitive Account

Masayoshi Shibatani

INTRODUCTION

My early readings in linguistics included one of Chuck Fillmore's earliest writings, *Indirect Object Constructions in English and the Ordering of Transformations* (originally written in 1963), which took as its primary goal 'to construct and incorporate within the grammar of English the means for correctly generating sentences containing indirect objects'—the sentence types exemplified by *He gave me an umbrella* and *He bought me an umbrella*. In his 1977 paper 'The Case for Case Reopened,' Chuck dealt with, among others, sentence alternations exemplified by *Bees were swarming in the garden/ The garden was swarming with bees* and *I loaded hay onto the truck/ I loaded the truck with hay.* What is common to these phenomena is the pattern of grammatical coding of apparently peripheral event participants or physical settings as central clausal arguments.

During the decade that separated these two papers, Chuck's theoretical orientation shifted from that of transformational grammar to that of cognitive grammar, but his interests in these phenomena and

Earlier versions of this paper were presented at the 103rd meeting of the Linguistic Society of Japan at Nanzan University on 26 Oct. 1991 and at the linguistic colloquia at the University of California, Irvine (31 Jan. 1992), Stanford University (7 Feb. 1992), and the University of California, Berkeley (29 Apr. 1992). I am grateful to the participants of these meetings for comments and discussions. Thanks are also due to John Haig, Talmy Givón, Jan Nuyts, and Sandra Thompson, who read earlier versions and provided me with valuable comments. In addition, I must acknowledge the help of the following individuals for providing me with and discussing with me the relevant data: Dileep Chandralal (Sinhala), Noritaka Fukushima (Spanish), Katia Lancelotti (Italian), Akio Ogawa (German), Zhāng Qíng (Chinese), Lawrence Schourup (English), Lú Tāo (Chinese), and Yatna Yuwana Wartawirya (Indonesian, Javanese). The present work was partly supported by a grant (04301059) from the Japanese Ministry of Education, Science, and Culture.

his concern for the proper ways of handling them seem unchanged even today (see Fillmore and Kay 1992: ch. 8). It thus appears highly fitting for me to deal with similar phenomena as a way of expressing my admiration and gratitude to one of the most insightful linguists of our time, whose teaching and writings have had profound impacts well beyond the circle of those lucky enough to have come into direct contact with him.

In the 1977 paper mentioned above, Chuck outlined the possibility for developing a theory of grammatical coding that was founded upon the notion of "perspective". He concluded the paper with the following summary (p. 80):

We recognize scenes or situations and the functions of various participants in these scenes and situations. We foreground or bring into perspective some possibly quite small portion of such a scene. Of the elements which are foregrounded, one of them gets assigned the subject role . . . and one of them if we are foregrounding two things gets assigned the direct object role in the clause. Something like a SALIENCY HIERARCHY determines what gets foregrounded, and something like a CASE HIERARCHY determines how the foregrounded nominals are assigned grammatical functions.

In this paper I wish to develop Chuck's idea one step further and bring into focus the role of grammatical schemata in the coding of complex situations. What I am exploring is the possibility of a theory in which speakers are thought to view scenes or situations in terms of specific schemata. A schema provides a template, so to speak, through which a particular situation is viewed. When the scene matches or approximates the schema, it is coded according to the structural pattern of the schema; otherwise, such coding results in a deviant expression. This theory, when fully developed, places the speaker in his rightful position with an active role in the apprehension and grammatical coding of events, and at the same time provides a framework in which grammaticality judgments are naturally characterized in terms of the match between situations and the schemata through which they are viewed.

The central topic dealt with below is benefactive constructions, which, covering what Chuck called 'indirect object constructions,' encode beneficiaries either as direct objects or as indirect objects. But as a way of showing their nature as a unified phenomenon, it is necessary first to contrast them with another type of construction, called applicatives, in which locations, instruments, and other peripheral elements are coded as direct objects.

7.1. APPLICATIVES AND BENEFACTIVES: A DISTINCTION

The terms 'applicative' and 'benefactive' are normally used in reference to specific grammatical elements—verbal affixes that increase valence in the former case and nominal forms expressing beneficiaries in the latter—but for the sake of convenience, we shall be using them in reference to the grammatical constructions exemplified in the (*a*) versions of (1–3) and those of (4–6). Notice that by 'benefactives' or 'benefactive constructions' we mean specifically those constructions in which beneficiaries are coded as arguments, as in (4*a*), rather than as adjuncts, as in (4*b*). In constructions in which beneficiaries are coded as true adjuncts, the kind of syntactic and semantic restrictions central to the discussion of the present paper do not hold, and therefore they are excluded from our consideration other than for the purpose of contrasting the true benefactive constructions with them, as in (4–6) below.

Applicatives

(1) Indonesian

    (1*a*) Saya menduduk-i kursi
           I   sit-APPL   chair
           'I sit in the chair'
    (1*b*) Saya duduk di kursi
           I   sit   in   chair
           'I sit in the chair'

(2) Ainu

    (2*a*) Poro cise   e-horari
           big house APPL-live
           'He lives in a big house'
    (2*b*) Poro cise   ta horari
           big house in live
           'He lives in a big house'

(3) Chicheŵa (Alsina and Mchombo, 1990)

    (3*a*) Anyǎni a-na-yénd-ér-a   ndōdo.
           2-baboon 2S-PAST-walk-APPL-FV 9-stick
           'The baboons were walking with the stick'
    (3*b*) Anyǎni a-na-yénd-a   ndî   ndōdo
           2-baboon 2S-PAST-walk-FV with 9-stick
           'The baboons were walking with the stick'

Benefactives
(4) English

- (4a) John bought Mary a book
- (4b) John bought a book for Mary

(5) Indonesian

- (5a) Dia membuat-kan saya kursi itu
  he make-BEN I chair this
  'He made me this chair'
- (5b) Dia membuat kursi itu untuk saya
  he make chair this for I
  'He made this chair for me'

(6) Japanese

- (6a) Boku wa Hanako ni hon o kat-te yat-ta
  I TOP DAT book ACC buy-CONJ give-PAST
  'I bought Hanako a book'
- (6b) Boku wa Hanako no tame ni hon o kat-te yat-ta
  I TOP GEN sake DAT book ACC buy-CONJ give-PAST
  'I bought a book for Hanako's sake'

Since Baker's (1988) incorporation analysis of applicatives and benefactives, these two constructions have in general been collapsed, and they are collectively called applicatives. But we maintain that applicatives and benefactives are two distinct constructions. Although some languages, such as Chicheŵa, use the same verbal affix for both applicatives and benefactives, there is an important difference between the two: applicatives generally allow intransitive bases, while benefactives seldom admit intransitive bases. The contrast is rather clearly seen in the following data, in which it is observed that in contrast to intransitive-based applicatives, intransitive-based benefactives are barred in one language after another. The telling minimal pair is Chicheŵa examples (7e) and (8g).

(7) *Intransitive-based applicatives*

- (7a) Otto be-wohnt ein altes Haus (German)
      APPL-live a old house
  'Otto lives in an old house'
  (Cf. Otto wohnt in einem alten Haus 'Otto lives in an old house')
- (7b) Saya menjatuh-i kucing (Indonesian)
  I fall-APPL cat
  'I fell on the cat'

(7c) Poropet   kotan   e-arpa (Ainu)
           village   APPL-go
           'He goes to Horobetsu village'
(7d) kaa   kuus-ne   pee-x-yuu-ye (Nez Perce)
           and   water-DO   3TR-go-APPL-ASP
           'And he went to the water' (Rude, 1986)
(7e) Msōdzi   a-ku-phík-ír-a   mthîko (Chichewâ)
           1-fisherman   1S-PRES-cook-APPL-FV   3-ladle
           'The fisherman is cooking with a ladle' (Alsina and Mchombo, 1990)

(8) *Intransitive-based benefactives*

    (8a) *Otto ging Karin   auf   den   Marktplatz (German)
              went   to   the   market
         'Otto went to the market for Karin'
    (8b) *Saya   datang-kan Ana   ke   pasar (Indonesian)
           I   come-BEN   to   market
         'I came to the market for Ana'
    (8c) *I went Mary to the market (English)
    (8d) *Boku   waHanako ni   itiba   e   it-te   yat-ta (Japanese)
           I   TOP   DAT   market   to   go-CONJ   give-PAST
         'I went to the market for Hanako'
    (8e) *Ranjit Chitra   -ṭa pola-ṭa   gihin   de-nawa (Sinhala)
                     DAT market-DAT   go.PP   give-PRES IND
         'Ranjit goes to the market for Chitra'
    (8f) *Wǒ gěi   māma   qù   shì-chǎng   le (Chinese)
           I   to   mother   go   market   ASP
         'I went to the market for Mother'
    (8g) *Msōdzi   a-ku-phík-ír-a   aná (Chichewâ)
           1-fisherman   1S-PRES-cook-BEN-FV   2-children
         'The fisherman is cooking for the children' (Alsina and Mchombo,
         1990)

It is important to notice that, though morphosyntactic properties
vary, the intransitive-based benefactives are ungrammatical in various languages. English, German, and Chinese use no benefactive affix
to mark verbs, whereas Indonesian and Chichewâ involve benefactive
verbal markings. Japanese benefactives make use of compound verbal
forms with the main verb marked by the conjunctive particle. Sinhala
also uses compound forms for benefactives but with the main verb in
the past participial form. The beneficiaries are realized either as primary objects of the double object constructions (English, Indonesian,
Chichewâ) or as indirect objects (Japanese, Chinese, German) (see
(11c), (11d), and (22a) below for grammatical benefactive forms in

these languages). The fact that, despite this structural diversity, intransitive-based benefactives are all ungrammatical indicates that what we call benefactives are a unified phenomenon that goes beyond the characterization in terms of 'Dative Shift' as in transformational grammar or '3-to-2 advancement' in Relational Grammar (more on this below).

I conclude this section by reiterating my earlier point that applicatives and benefactives are distinct constructions, though they both fall under the overarching domain of voice, defined as alternations of the nominal status with respect to the core/periphery or argument/-adjunct distinction.

7.2. PROBLEMS WITH FORMAL ACCOUNTS: A PRELIMINARY[1]

In many languages both applicatives and benefactives have semi-paraphrases, like the (*b*) forms in (1–5), which contain simple prepositional phrases that typically express semantically oblique elements. Again, in many languages both applicatives and benefactives contain verbal markings of either affixal or compound form that signal an increase in the verbal valence. These characteristics have provided enough evidence for transformational grammarians to derive applicatives and benefactives from corresponding plain forms with prepositional phrases. Oddly, this analysis was first practiced, under the name of 'Dative Shift,' with respect to English benefactives, where there is no additional verbal marking indicating their marked status.

Treating applicatives and benefactives as transformationally derived constructions poses a number of serious problems. This is especially clear in the case of benefactives. For example, in languages such as Japanese, no simple transformational operation is possible in relating benefactives and their semi-paraphrases (see (6*b*), in which Hanako is a genitive modifier of the head *tame* 'sake'). Furthermore, rule-based analyses fail to characterize the constructions and their restrictions (see below) in a uniform manner, for, as pointed out above, actual syntactic forms vary from one language to another. These considerations suggest that applicatives and benefactives arc better considered in their own right independently from their semi-paraphrases.

---

[1] By 'formal' accounts I mean those analyses that are couched in the autonomous theory of syntax that makes no recourse to pragmatic matters.

Besides these formal considerations, the basic motivation for a cognitive account comes from the fact that neither applicatives nor benefactives are categorically definable in terms of lexical information. Thus, despite the similarity in verb forms, we find that while the applicatives in (9) are possible, those in (10) are not. Likewise, the benefactives in (11) are acceptable, but those in (12) are at best rather bizarre.

(9a) Otto be-wohnt ein   altes Haus (German)
   APPL-live one   old   house
  'Otto lives in an old house'

(9b) Saya meninggal-i rumah-nya (Indonesian)
  I   stay-APPL   house-his
  'I am staying in his house'

(10a) *Otto be-wohnt Berlin (German)
    APPL-live
  'Otto lives in Berlin'
  (Cf. Otto wohnt in Berlin 'Otto lives in Berlin')

(10b) *?Saya   meninggal-i Jakarta (Indonesian)
  I   live-APPL
  'I am staying in Jakarta'
  (Cf. Saya tinggal di Jakarta 'I am staying in Jakarta')

(11a) I opened Mary a can of Coke.

(11b) I cleared him a place to sleep on the floor (Langacker, 1991)

(11c) Boku wa Hanako ni   to   o   ake-te
  I   TOP   DAT   door ACC open-CONJ
  yat-ta (Japanese)
  give-PAST
  'I opened the door for Hanako'

(11d) Wǒ gěi Lǐsì shā le   jī (Chinese)
  I   to   kill ASP   chicken
  'I killed a chicken for Lisi'

(12a) ??I opened Mary a jar of mayonnaise

(12b) *I cleared him the floor. (Langacker, 1991)

(12c) *?Boku wa Hanako ni   mado   o   ake-te
  I   TOP   DAT   window ACC open-CONJ
  yat-a (Japanese)
  give-PAST
  'I opened the window for Hanako'

(12d) *Wǒ gěi Lǐsì shā le   hào zi (Chinese)
  I   to   kill ASP   rat
  'I killed a rat for Lisi'

These contrasts are problematic to those analyses that explain away the distinctions between possible applicatives and benefactives on the one hand and impossible applicatives and benefactives on the other, in terms of the formal distinction between VP internal and VP external adjuncts, or in terms of theta-marking (cf. Baker, 1988). For example, how can one avoid circularity in deciding that *ein altes Haus* in (9a) is VP internal, whereas *Berlin* in (10a) is not, or that the verb *bewohnt* in (9a) theta-marks its object, while the same verb in (10a) does not?

The situations observed above are highly analogous to the case of English prepositional passives, where we obtain the following contrasts.

(13a) This house was lived in by Winston Churchill
(13b) *England was lived in by Winston Churchill
(13c) England has been lived in by the people of many different nations
(14a) Martha was rushed to by George, because he needed advice
(14b) *The countryside was rushed to by George, because he needed a rest
        (Rice, 1987)

Again the situation above is problematic to the theta-theoretic account or to the one involving reanalysis made contingent on the concept of 'semantic unit' or 'natural predicate'. That is, while it is true that *This house was lived in by Winston Churchill* contrasts with *This house was died in by Winston Churchill*, the contrast is also observed between (13b) and (13c), where both involve presumably the same 'natural predicate', *live in*.

In fact, the same kind of problem is seen even in the regular passive, as shown, for example, by the contrasts observed by Bolinger (1977).

(15a) I was approached by the stranger
(15b) *I was approached by the train
(16a) The Pacific has been sailed by the mightiest fleets in history
(16b) *The Pacific was sailed by my brother Joe

Bolinger (1977: 77) makes the point that the difficulties that grammarians have had with these cases 'have been due partly to too much insistence on immanent rather than transcendental features.' Our cognitive account offered below takes this point seriously, and attempts to characterize the acceptability in terms of the match between the situations and the entire features of the schemata through which they are construed.

7.3. THE NOTION OF SCHEMA

The cognitive account offered here departs from the previous formal accounts most straightforwardly in the assumption that certain expressions take their formal characteristics because situations expressed are construed in terms of particular schemata with specific formal characteristics. The ungrammaticality of an expression is to be explained in terms of the mismatch between the schema and the situation described, or in terms of the difficulty informants encounter in construing the situation along the lines of the schema upon which the construction in question is based.

The notion of schema is familiar to those who are exposed to the rudiments of cognitive psychology. The idea is that we tend to interpret the world according to preconceived notions or principles, sometimes imposing information or a particular structure that is not even there. The figure below illustrate the effects of two Gestalt principles of organization, namely the principle of good continuity and the principle of closure or good form.[2]

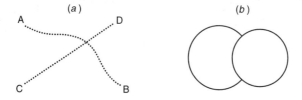

We perceive (17*a*) as being composed of two lines, one from C to D and the other from A to B, although the figure could have been construed some other ways—e.g. as involving two lines stretching from A to C and from B to D. Likewise, (17*b*) is construed specifically as one circle being occluded by another, although there is no way of knowing the actual shape of the occluded object.

Now, our claim is that applicatives and benefactives are based on two different schemata; the former on the prototype of transitive clauses and the latter on more specific 'give' constructions. That is, applicatives and benefactives are distinct constructions based on distinct schemata, and the distinction between the two noted earlier and others follow from this. However, rather than dwelling on the contrasts

---

[2] Adapted from Anderson (1980).

between the two constructions, we shall in this paper concentrate on benefactives, which show intriguing interplays between their grammaticality patterns and the syntactic and semantic properties of the schema upon which they are based.

7.4. BENEFACTIVES

7.4.1. *Problems*

A comprehensive study of benefactives requires a number of problems to be addressed. They divide into two groups: those concerned with the grammaticality of various benefactive expressions and those having to do with the semantics of benefactive constructions. A first problem includes language-specific restrictions on benefactives that have been taken up by those dealing with English benefactives, most recently by Pinker (1989). English benefactives are restricted both morphophonologically and semantically, such that while *I gave the library a lot of books* is possible, **I donated the library a lot of books* is not, and while *I told Mary the story* is acceptable, **I whispered Mary the story* is not.[3] What interests us with regard to this problem is Pinker's (1989: 103 ff.) discussion of 'an important dissociation between semantics and cognition,' which he illustrates by the contrast shown by the following classes of verbs:

(18) Verbs of instantaneous causation of ballistic motion; *throw, toss, kick, slide, fling*, etc. (e.g. *She tossed him the puck*).

(19) Verbs of continuous imparting of force in some manner causing accompanied motion; *carry, push, schlepp, lift, lower*, etc. (e.g. **I pulled John the box*).

Pinker's point is that, though the verbs in (19) can be cognitively construed as resulting in a change of possession—i.e. the verbs in (18) and (19) are cognitively similar—they are not associated with the semantic structure necessary for the benefactive expressions, for such an association is sensitive to narrowly defined semantic classes of verbs. Our position is that, while language internal semantics cannot be ignored—as pointed out by Pinker and others, verbs with strong manner semantics, e.g. *whisper, scream, yell*, do not yield benefactive constructions—and while degrees of conventionalization or

---

[3] See Wierzbicka (1988) for an attempt to explain away these and similar contrasts on a semantic basis.

generalization must be recognized, semantic distinctions are rooted in cognition. In other words, we want to be able to offer a cognitively based explanation for such a contrast as seen between (18) and (19). We shall return to this point below.

Another related problem has to do with language-internal variations reflected in the native speakers' reactions to various benefactive expressions. This has been a constant problem running through such discussions of English benefactives as Green (1974), Oehrle (1977), and Goldsmith (1980), where authors do not agree as to what is and what is not acceptable. Allerton's (1978) survey of British speakers indicate the gradual decline of acceptability ranging from a high degree of acceptability for forms like *Could you pour me a cup of coffee?* and *Could you cook me a meal?* to the highly marginal status of *Could you taste me this wine?* and *Could you watch me a television programme?* with medially acceptable forms such as *Could you wash me the dishes?* and *Could you phone me the hospital?*

Grammarians need to respond to this kind of language-internal variation and restrictions on the range of possible benefactives, which give rise to cross-linguistic variation. Languages differ with respect to the ranges of acceptable benefactive expressions. For example, whereas English does not allow a form such as *John opened Mary the door*, the German counterpart *Otto öffnet Karin die Tür* is perfectly well formed. Cross-linguistic variations of this type are examined in Section 7.4.3 below, where English appears to be among the most restrictive languages, whereas Indonesian, Javanese, and Spanish allow far wider ranges of benefactive expressions. Again, cross-linguistic variations pose problems for purely lexically based formal analyses, for it does not seem to be the case that the semantics of the verbs, e.g. 'open', or their Case-marking properties differ from one language to another.

The cognitive account offered here deals with these grammaticality problems not in terms of any formal principle of grammar but in terms of the construability of a situation. That is, there is nothing grammatically wrong about expressions such as *Could you watch me a television program?* or *Could you taste me this wine?* What is wrong with them is that the situation of someone's watching a television program or tasting wine for someone else's sake is not construable in terms of the schema underlying benefactive constructions; i.e. situations do not match the relevant schema. We will be dealing with the problem of cross-linguistic variation along the same line.

The most basic semantic problem associated with benefactive constructions has to do with the meaning difference between a benefactive expression such as *John bought Mary a book* and its paraphrase *John bought a book for Mary*. Specifically, whereas the former implies that the book was meant to be given to Mary, the latter has no such specific reading associated with transfer of goods to a third party. The same difference is observed in other languages that possess benefactive constructions with beneficiaries in an argument position and paraphrases in which beneficiaries are coded as adjuncts. The problem here for languages like English and German, in which verbs of giving do not overtly occur, is that verbs such as *buy, make, bake* which are usable in benefactive constructions do not inherently have this notion of transfer of goods to a third party in their semantic specifications, as attested by their regular transitive use. In other words, what is being discussed here is a meaning specifically associated with benefactive constructions (see Goldberg, 1995). The task for us then is to identify the source for this constructional meaning. Our answer is that it is to be sought in the schema that underlies benefactive constructions (see section 7.4.4.2).

7.4.2. *RG and PI analyses*

The discussion above already points up various aspects of the problems that formal treatments encounter in offering cross-linguistically valid analyses of benefactive constructions. Indeed, past formal analyses have fallen far short of this goal.

Aissen (1983) analyzed benefactives in Tzotzil in the framework of Relational Grammar, characterizing the construction as an instance of indirect object to direct object (i.e. 3-to-2) advancement. This analysis is clearly limited in its applicability in that it leaves out a large number of languages, including German, Italian, Japanese, Korean, and Sinhala, whose beneficiaries are difficult to construe as final direct objects—beneficiaries in these languages occur in the dative. The same problem applies to Baker's (1988) P (preposition/postposition) Incorporation analysis, since incorporation of adpositions is not observed in the set of languages, e.g. Japanese, Chinese, Sinhala, and Italian, that code beneficiaries as indirect objects marked by dative adpositions.[4]

---

[4] Baker (1988: 471 n. 36) recognizes this limitation inherent in his approach.

Another problem these analyses face has to do with what is known as the transitivity effect. As pointed out earlier, intransitive bases generally resist benefactive conversion. The same holds true in Tzotzil, and Aissen (1983) is forced to stipulate that the relevant 3-to-2 advancement is restricted to transitive clauses. This kind of stipulation, which has no explanatory power, is insufficient, since the transitivity effect is operative even in those languages in which benefactive constructions involve no advancement.

Baker (1988) tries to account for the inability of intransitives to convert to benefactives in terms of Case theory. That is, since intransitive verbs do not assign Case, P-incorporated beneficiaries (coded as direct objects) fail to be Case-marked. This solution is strange in view of Baker's analysis of locative and instrumental applicatives, in which intransitive verbs are assumed to assign Case. Furthermore, the solution in terms of Case-marking is problematic for those languages in which beneficiaries are marked by the dative case forms.

Perhaps the problem most damaging to these two formal analyses is the failure to capture a continuum of acceptability that cuts across the transitivity line. Certain benefactive expressions with transitive verbs are not permissible, despite the fact that they have the same Case-marking properties as other transitive verbs (see (20b–e) below). On the other hand, languages like Javanese allow benefactives based on intransitive verbs (see (27) below).

Though, as we shall see below, the transitivity effect plays a crucial role in benefactive formation, what is at issue is not a simple matter of the transitive/intransitive distinction or the Case-marking ability of verbs. Rather, the problem has to do with how easily the situations expressed are construable in terms of the schema for benefactive constructions. Whether the verb involved is transitive or intransitive, a benefactive expression is possible to the extent that is construable according to the schema; intransitive benefactive forms just happen to express those situations that are not construable according to the schema for benefactives.

7.4.3. *Cross-linguistic variation*

Before we turn to the discussion of the schema for benefactives, let us examine the nature of cross-linguistic variation seen in benefactive constructions. In order to save space, our discussion of the relevant cross-linguistic variations will be carried out in reference to the following English examples, which are arranged according to the degrees of ease of benefactive formation.

(20*a*) I bought Mary a book
(20*b*) *I opened Mary the door
(20*c*) *I closed Mary the door
(20*d*) *I swept Mary the garden
(20*e*) *I killed Mary the centipede (*a–e*: transitives)
(20*f*) *I danced Mary
(20*g*) *I sang Mary (*f–g*: intransitive cognate object verbs)
(20*h*) *I went Mary to the market (true intransitive)

The transitions from the most restrictive languages to more liberal ones are observed at several cut off points. English draws the line between (20*a*) and (20*b*), and another major cut off point, observed by German, Japanese, and Italian, is between (20*b*) and (20*c*), where while 'opening someone the door' is a viable expression, 'closing someone the door' is not. Both are permitted by more liberal languages such as Sinhala, Indonesian, and some others. The following data show the transitions in question.

(21) English

(21*a*) *John opened Mary the door
(21*b*) *John closed Mary the door

(22) German

(22*a*) Otto öffnet Karin   die Tür
             open   the door
'Otto opens the door for Karin'
(22*b*) *Otto schliesst Karin   die Tür
             close   the door
'Otto closes the door for Karin'

(23) Sinhala

(23*a*) Ranjit Chitra- ṭa   dora   æra-la   dun-na
                      DAT   door   open-PP   give-PAST.IND
'Ranjit opened the door for Chitra'
(23*b*) Ranjit Chitra- ṭa   dora   waha-la   dun-na
                      DAT   door   open-PP   give-PAST.IND
'Ranjit closed the door for Chitra'

Sinhala differs from Indonesian in that the former draws the line between (20*d*) and (20*e*), while both are permitted by Indonesian.

(24) Sinhala

(24a) Ranjit Chitra- ṭa   midula atung-la   dun-na
                    DAT garden sweep-PP give-PAST.IND
      'Ranjit swept the garden for Chitra'
(24b) *Ranjit Chitra- ṭa   pattæææya mara-le dun-na
                      DAT centipede kill-PP give-PAST. IND
      'Ranjit killed the centipede for Chitra'

(25) Indonesian

(25a) Saya membersih-kan Ana halaman
      I   clean-BEN   garden
      'I cleaned up the garden for Ana'
(25b) Saya membunuh-kan Ana lipas
      I   kill-BEN   centipede
      'I killed the centipede for Ana'

Indonesian, however, does not allow intransitive cognate object verbs to form benefactives, thus drawing the line between (20e) and (20f). Javanese, on the other hand, permits such intransitives to convert to benefactives.

(26) Indonesian

(26a) *Saya menari-kan Ana
       I   dance-BEN
      'I danced for Ana'
(26b) *Saya menyanyi-kan Ana
       I   sing-BEN
      'I sang for Ana'

(27) Javanese

(27a) Aku narek-ne Ana
      I   dance-BEN
      'I danced for Ana/on behalf of Ana'
(27b) Aku nyanyue-ne Ana
      I   sing-BEN
      'I sang for Ana/on behalf of Ana'

Languages show a great deal of variation and inconsistency in benefactive formation based on intransitive verbs. Intuitively one feels that intransitives of cognate object verbs are easier to form benefactives than true intransitives, and this is the case in Javanese, where (28a–c), based on true intransitives, are all ungrammatical in opposition to the grammatical forms in (27), which are based on intransitive forms of cognate object verbs.

(28) Javanese

(28a) *Aku lungo-ne Ana   meng   pasar
      I   go-BEN   to   market
      'I went to the market for Ana'
      (Cf. Aku lungo meng pasar kangu Ana 'I went to the market for Ana')
(28b) *Yesus mate-ne kapeh wong
      'Jesus died for all people'
      (Cf. Yesus matei kangu kapeh wong 'Jesus died for all people')
(28c) *Aku mlayuk-ne Ana
      'I ran for Ana'
      (Cf. Aku mlayu kangu Ana 'I ran for Ana')

But certain languages seem to allow benefactives of true intransitives, while barring those based on intransitive cognative object verbs. This appears to be the case in Chicheŵa, where the following are said to be grammatical, while the ones based on intransitive cognate object verbs are not (see (8g)).

(29) Chicheŵa (Baker, 1988; Alsina and Mchombo, 1990)

(29a) Yêsu   a-ná-f-ér-s   anthu   ônse
      1-Jesus   IS-PAST-die-APPL-FV   2-people   all
      'Jesus died for all people'
(29b) Mtolankhâni a-na-thámáng-ir-á chíphadzûwa
      1-journalist IS-PAST-run-APPL-FV 7-beauty queen
      'The journalist ran for the beauty queen'

Yet certain other languages indicate that no consistent line is drawn between true intransitives and those of cognate object verbs. Thus, in Spanish certain intransitive cognate object verbs yield acceptable benefactives, e.g. (30a), while some others, e.g. (30b, c), do not. Benefactives based on true intransitives seem to be generally rejected by the native Spanish speakers, but some of them, e.g. (30d), appear to be easier to accept than others, e.g. (30e).

(30) Spanish

(30a) Le   canté
      she.DAT sang
      'I sang for her'
(30b) *La mamá   me   casió
      the mother me   sewed
      'Mother sewed for me'

(30*c*) *Le   comí a María
       she.DAT ate   to
       'I ate for Maria'
(30*d*) %Le   fui a María al   mercado
       she.DAT went to   to.the market
       'I went to the market for Maria'
(30*e*) *Jesús les   murió a   todos
               them.DAT died to all
       'Jesus died for all of them'

Thus, the pattern of cross-linguistic variation is such that those expressions similar both in form and meaning to the basic benefactive expression instantiated by *John gave Mary a book* are consistently grammatical cross-linguistically, whereas those that deviate further and further from this basic form show a gradual decline in acceptability, finally reaching the level of intransitive-based expressions, where no clear cross-linguistic consistency is observable. It is this overall cross-linguistic pattern that a successful account for benefactives must capture. Toward this end, we shall now turn to our cognitive account based on the notion of schema.

7.4.4. *The 'give' construction as a schema*

Our account for benefactives is extremely simple. It involves no transformation of the 'dative shift' type. It neither stipulates a restriction on the 3-to-2 advancement rule nor makes recourse to Case theory. Our solution instead is in terms of a schema based on the 'give' construction, e.g. *John gave Mary a book*. That is, situations are construed according to the 'give' construction in the language. Those situations construable are expressed according to the structural pattern of the 'give' construction, whereas those that are remote from the schema resist 'coercion' into the benefactive construction.

Let us now enumerate the properties of the 'give' schema and examine their roles in the formation of benefactives.

(31) *The 'give' schema*
    Structure: [NP1 NP2 NP3 GIVE]
        NP1 = coded as a subject
        NP2 = coded either as a primary object or as a dative indirect object
        NP3 = coded either as a secondary object or as a direct object
    Semantics: NP1 CAUSES NP2 TO HAVE NP3; i.e.
        NP1 = human agent, NP2 = human goal, NP3 = object theme

NP2 exercises potential possessive control over NP3
NP1 creates the possessive situation on behalf of NP2

7.4.4.1. *The syntax of benefactive constructions.* Structurally, the schema consists of three NPs. There are two different methods of encoding the recipient NP2, yielding either the double object construction, as in English, Indonesian, and Bantu[5], or the direct- and indirect-object pattern as in German, Japanese, Italian, Spanish, and Sinhala. These two instantiations of the schema are illustrated below:

(32) *Instantiations of the schema*
1st pattern: NP2 = primary object, NP3 = secondary object
a. English: John gave Mary a book
NP1 GIVE NP2 NP3
b. Indonesian: Saya memberi Ana pisang
NP1 GIVE NP2 NP3
'I gave Ana a banana'
2nd pattern: NP2 = indirect object, NP3 = direct object
a. Japanese: Taroo ga Hanako ni hon o yatta
NP1 NP2 NP3 GIVE
'Taro gave Hanako a book'
b. German: Otto gibt dem Kind Brötchen
NP1 GIVE NP2 NP3
'Otto gives the child pieces of roll bread'

The initial syntactic motivation for our analysis that benefactives are based on 'give' constructions comes from the fact that many languages actually use the verbs meaning 'give' in their benefactive constructions. This is the case, for example, in Japanese (*yaru*, see below), Chinese (*gěi*), Korean (*cwu-ta*), Sinhala (*denawa*, see (23)), where the verbs meaning 'give' function as the second member of the benefactive verbal compounds, and in Chinese, where *gěi* has also become a dative preposition (see (11*d*)).[6]

The second motivation is that the basic syntax of benefactives is the same as that of 'give' constructions. Thus, when the language instantiates the first pattern of coding double objects in its 'give' construction, then its benefactives also follow the first pattern, e.g. Indonesian. Likewise, if the language opts for the second direct-/indirect-object

[5] See Dryer (1986), Bresnan and Moshi (1990), and Hudson (1992) on the nature of double object constructions.

[6] See Matisoff (1991) for other languages in which the verb 'give' has given rise to the benefactive morpheme.

pattern in the coding of the 'give' expression, then its benefactives also show the second pattern, e.g. Japanese.

This similarity between 'give' constructions and benefactives, however, can be deceptive. As is well known from Fillmore (1965), in English the benefactive nominals behave differently depending on whether they are those of the 'give' construction or those found in the benefactive construction. Observe the following contrast, where (34*b*) is rejected by a fairly large number of English speakers.

(33*a*) They gave me an umbrella
(33*b*) I was given an umbrella

(34*a*) They bought me an umbrella
(34*b*) %I was bought an umbrella

For our analysis this kind of disparity is not a problem; on the contrary, it shows the secondary nature of the benefactive constructions, supporting our view that the latter are based on the conceptually simpler 'give' constructions.

Perhaps the strongest syntactic evidence for our analysis comes from cases in which the syntax of benefactives mirrors that of 'give' constructions quite accurately, such that even certain peculiar properties of the latter are reflected in the former. Japanese offers one such case. Japanese has two verbs for 'give'—one (*yaru*) that takes a non-speaker as the recipient and the other (*kureru*) that takes the speaker (and those belonging to the speaker's in-group) as the recipient. One crucial syntactic difference is that *kureru* 'give me/us' allows an expression with an omitted recipient, presumably because it is speaker-oriented by nature and therefore the recipient is almost uniquely recoverable. This is not so in the case of the other verb, *yaru* 'give,' which requires explicit mention of the recipient unless its identity is clear from the context. Thus, in an out-of-the blue context, (35*b*) is not possible, whereas (36*b*) is perfectly well-formed.

(35*a*) Kyoo Taroo ga Hanako ni hon o yatta
      today   NOM   DAT book ACC gave
      'Today, Taro gave Hanako a book'
(35*b*) *Kyoo Taroo ga hon o yatta
      today   NOM book ACC gave
      '(lit.) Today, Taro gave a book'
(36*a*) Kyoo Hanako ga boku ni hon o kureta
      today   NOM I   DAT book ACC gave
      'Today, Hanako gave me a book'

(36*b*) Kyoo Hanako ga   hon o   kureta
today   NOM book ACC gave
'Today, Hanako gave (me/us) a book'

When benefactives are formed using these 'give' verbs, they follow the same syntax; that is the speaker-oriented form *kureru* does not require an overt beneficiary expression. Indeed, the syntaxes of the basic uses of the 'give' verbs as illustrated in (35) and (36) are exactly parallelled in the syntaxes of the benefactives using the same verbs, as the comparison of (35–6) and (37–8) reveals.[7]

(37*a*) Kyoo Taroo ga Hanako ni   hon o   yonde yatta
today   NOM   DAT book ACC read gave
'Today, Taro read Hanako a book'
(37*b*) *Kyoo Taroo ga   hon o   yonde yatta
today   NOM book ACC read gave
'Today, Taro read (someone) a book'

(38*a*) Kyoo Hanako ga   boku ni hon o   yonde kureta
today   NOM I   DAT book ACC read gave
'Today Hanako read me a book'
(38*b*) Kyoo Hanako ga   hon o   yonde kureta
today   NOM book ACC read gave
'Today, Hanako read (me/us) a book'

The syntactic property of the 'give' construction plays a crucial role with regard to cognate object verbs. As seen in (8g), (20g), and (26), Chicheŵa, English, Indonesian, and many other languages do not permit benefactive forms based on the intransitive versions of cognate object verbs. However, these are grammatical if cognate objects are explicitly mentioned, resulting in structures with three NPs matching the 'give' schema.

(39*a*) Msōdzi   a-ku-phík-ír-a   aná
1-fisherman IS-PRES-COOK-APPL-FV 2-children
nyêmba (Chicheŵa; cf. (8g))
10-beans
'The fisherman is cooking beans for the children'
                              (Alsina and Mchombo, 1991)
(39*b*) I sang Mary a song (cf. (20g))
(39*c*) Saya   menari-kan Ana rumba (Indonesian; cf. (26a))
I   dance-BEN
'I danced Ana a rumba'

7 See Shibatani (1994*a*) for a detailed discussion on Japanese benefactives.

This treatment of cognate object verbs in these languages is particularly interesting in that it shows that the satisfaction of the semantics of the schema is not enough for a benefactive to obtain. Cognate object verbs are 'transitive' in meaning with implied objects, yet they do not yield acceptable benefactives in a large number of languages.[8]

Thus, the syntax of the schema plays a crucial role in benefactive formation. This, however, does not mean that the syntax of benefactives always parallels that of the schema. Indeed, due to extension or generalization of the construction, the benefactive structure may depart from the schema upon which it was originally based. And this is what we see in the case of benefactives based on intransitive verbs, in which there are only two NP's present (see (27), (29), and (30) above). This possibility may seem to render our approach practically non-falsifiable. But this is not the case, for we expect the pattern of syntactic disagreement to be such that the generalized constructions always include those expressions that follow the schema closely rather then excluding them. Thus a true counter-example to our claim is the one that goes against this predicted pattern of extension.

Recall, furthermore, that cross-linguistic variation is more random in intransitive-based benefactives.[9] Prototype approaches to cross-linguistic patterning reveal that whereas those forms that closely conform to a prototype show cross-linguistic consistency, those that deviate from the prototype tend to exhibit a random pattern of cross-linguistic variation (see Croft, 1991). Our findings of the cross-linguistic syntactic patterns of benefactive constructions are consistent with this general observation.

7.4.4.2. *The semantics of benefactive constructions.* The semantics of the 'give' construction also plays a crucial role in benefactive formation. As shown in (31), 'give' can be analyzed in terms of the meaning postulate 'NP1 CAUSES NP2 TO HAVE NP3.' From this postulate we

---

[8] The same is true in German. Thus, while *Die Mutter hat mir ein neues Kleid genäht* 'Mother sewed me a new dress' is well formed, **Die Mutter hat mir genäht'* (lit.) Mother sewed me' is not.

[9] This statement should not be taken to mean that everything has been said about intransitive-based benefactives. The facts in Chicheŵa, as gleaned from Baker (1988) and Alsina and Mchombo (1990), are not entirely clear, and a thorough study of intransitive-based benefactives in Chicheŵa and other languages is needed. It might be pointed out that Warlpiri is another language that may allow intransitive-based benefactives rather freely. Observe the following from Simpson (1991: 381): Karnta ka-rla kurdu-ku parnka-mi (woman PRES-3DAT child-DAT run-NPAST): 'The woman is running for the sake of the child'.

obtain the series of semantic characteristics of the construction enumerated in (31). Most of the well-known facts about benefactive constructions follow from these semantic properties.

First, that NP2 of the 'give' construction is typically human is carried over to benefactives, and it is responsible for the ill-formedness of the following examples.

(40a) *I sent Moscow some books (*cf.* I sent Leonid some books)
(40b) *Er baut dem Auto eine Garage[10] (German)
       'He builds a garage for the car'
       (cf. Er baut Karin ein Häuschen 'He builds Karin a small house')

Secondly, oft-noticed contrasts between the meanings of benefactives and their paraphrases, as seen below, are due to the second semantic property referring to the notion of 'possession' associated with the verb 'give.'

(41a) Maurice sent Mary a book
(41b) Maurice sent a book to Mary

(42a) Maurice taught Mary French
(42b) Maurice taught French to Mary

That is, the semantic fact that (41a) implies that Mary actually came into possession of the book and that (42a) implies that Mary has learned some French follows from the second semantic characteristic of the schema: that the beneficiary exercises (potential) possessive control over some entity.

Indeed, this is a most important semantic property determining the well-formedness of benefactive expressions. The cross-linguistic lack of intransitive-based benefactives mainly come from this property of the schema. That is, in intransitively coded situations there is no object involved that can be possessed by the beneficiary. In other words, intransitively expressed situations, lacking an object corresponding to NP3 of the schema, are least construable according to the schema.

For the most part transitivity is a necessary condition, but it is not sufficient. Transitive events, such as throwing away garbage or killing a centipede for someone's sake, which do not result in the possession of objects by the beneficiary, do not conform to the schema. Contrast the situation of killing a centipede or a cockroach with that of killing

---

[10] As an institution such as a library can be assimilated to the human recipient, the matter here is pragmatic such that, as pointed out by Sandra Thompson (p.c.), a car enthusiast might be able to accept this kind of form. In fact, the following is acceptable: *Er baut dem Hund eine Hütte* 'He builds the dog a house.'

a chicken or a goat. The latter in many cultures may result in the possession of the prepared meat. In these cultures, the expressions corresponding to *I killed him a chicken* or *I killed him a goat* would be perfectly well formed (e.g. Chinese *Wǒ gěi tā shā le jī* 'I killed him a chicken;' i.e. 'I served him a chicken'), whereas killing of a centipede or a cockroach under normal circumstances wouldn't render the situations construable in terms of the 'give' schema (see (12*d*) and (24*b*)).

The characterization of 'NP2 exercises potential possessive control over NP3' requires some explanation. First, the qualification of 'potential' over 'possessive control' is needed because of negative benefactives such as *I didn't buy him anything* and *They denied John the right to vote.*

Secondly, the notion of 'possessive control' is interpreted rather abstractly in many instances. Thus, in expressions like (42*a*) above and *I read him a book* and *I danced him a rumba*, there are no concrete objects that are 'possessed,' yet the situations are construable. What is involved here is a metonymic construal, as what is actually transferred is the knowledge of French, the content of the book, or the performance of a rumba. Situations allowing metonymic interpretations can be highly specific, and they provide an interesting insight into the role of the meaning–form–context triad in semantic interpretation. Benefactive expressions portraying the situations of opening of the door or the window for someone provide a good case study for this.

As opposed to the opening of the door, neither Japanese nor Italian yields unequivocally acceptable benefactives expressing a window-opening situation. The forms in (44) also contrast with the unequivocally ill-formed expressions in (45), where the door- or window-closing situations are portrayed.

(43*a*) Boku wa Hanako ni   to   o   akete   yatta (Japanese)
        I   TOP   DAT door ACC open   gave
        'I opened the door for Hanako'
(43*b*) Ho aperto la porta a Mario (Italian)
        have opened the door to
        'I opened the door for Mario'

(44*a*) *?Boku wa Hanako ni   mado   o   akete   yatta (Japanese)
         I   TOP   DAT window ACC open   gave
         'I opened the window for Hanako'
(44*b*) *?Ho aperto la   finestra   a Mario (Italian)
          have opened the   window   to
          'I opened the window for Mario'

(Cf. Ho aperto la finestra per Mario 'I opened the window for Mario')

(45a) *Boku wa Hanako ni   to/mado   o   simete
       I   TOP   DAT door/window   ACC close

yatta (Japanese)
gave
'I closed the door/window for Hanako'

(45b) *Ho chiuso la porta/finestra a Mario (Italian)
      have closed the door/window to
      'I closed the door/window for Mario'

The equivocal nature of the forms in (44) comes from the fact that they may express situations construable according to the schema. Indeed, these forms are more readily accepted when they are describing situations where the beneficiaries were trying to throw themselves out of the window and I helped them by opening the window, or where the beneficiaries were trying to sneak in through the window and I let them in by opening the window. The crucial factor here is whether or not the literal expression of 'giving someone a window' is easily interpretable metonymically. When such an expression is matched with a situation in which a beneficiary actually exercises a 'possessive control' over a specific effect—e.g. going through the passage created by the window opening—a metonymic interpretation succeeds. In the case of closing the door (45) or opening the window for getting fresh air, no immediate controllable effect is created; thus it is more difficult to apply a metonymic interpretation to these expressions, and sentences such as (45) are deemed ungrammatical, or, to be more accurate, uninterpretable as benefactive expressions.

It is worth noting the extent to which an informant automatically supplies a conventional situation in interpreting a sentence. Native speakers of both Japanese and Italian never question the acceptability of the sentences in (43), despite the fact that they cannot be used in expressing non-conventionalized benefactive scenes. That is, these sentences are only possible for the context in which the beneficiaries went through the door; they cannot be used for a situation where I opened the door for them just to get fresh air or to let in their cat (see Section 7.4.4.3).

As far as the cut-off point in the continuum of benefactive expressions is concerned, German is similar to Japanese and Italian in allowing the door-opening situation and disallowing the door-closing situation. But German provides us with clear cases of the semantic transitivity effect. When the expression conveys low transitivity in the sense that a particular effect, e.g. creation of an object, is not so strongly implicated, then the benefactive expression is not easily accepted in opposition to the counterpart form with high transitivity. The contrast seen below is brought about by the difference in verb meaning similar to that observed between the English expressions *shoot someone* and *shoot at someone*.

(46a) Otto baut Emil ein   Häuschen
              build   one   small.house
      'Otto builds Emil a small house'
(46b) *Otto baut Emil an   einem   Häuschen
               build   at   one   small.house
      '(lit.) Otto builds at a small house for Emil'

With these observations as background, we may speculate on the cognitive motivation for the contrast seen earlier between (18) and (19), where verbs of instantaneous causation of ballistic motion, e.g. *throw*, contrast with verbs expressing accompanied motion, e.g. *push* (hence *I threw him the ball* vs. **I pushed him the box*). Our study is based on the idea that a benefactive expression is more plausible as the situation becomes easier to be construed in terms of the schema that specifies the notion of possession. This would lead us to speculate that the contrast seen here is due to the difference in the ease of 'coercing' the situations into the schema. That is, while the ballistic motion entails an instantaneous separation of an object from the former possessor, the accompanied motion does not; accordingly, situations involving ballistic motions are easier to construe in terms of the schema that stipulates the possession of an object by a new owner.

The overall benefactive reading—that a possessive situation is created as a favor to the beneficiary—and the specific 'on behalf of' reading associated with certain benefactive constructions derive from the third semantic characteristics of the 'give' construction. Namely, unlike *get* or *obtain*, *give* states that a possessive situation is created by someone other than the possessor. Furthermore, a possessive situation, i.e. having something, is construed as beneficial to the possessor. In other words, creating this favorable state on behalf of the possessor renders the giving situation highly desirable to the recipient. Thus, while an unfavorable situation can sometimes be expressed by the verb 'give' in English, as e.g. in *The police gave me a ticket*, the 'give' verbs in general typically express situations favorable to the recipient, and this as well is carried over to benefactive constructions. In this connection recall Green's (1974) remarks that the sentence *She burned John a steak*, if accepted at all, is understood with the implication that John likes his steaks burned (see also Goldberg, 1995)[11].

Certain languages that liberally countenance benefactive expressions yield those that are specifically associated with the 'on behalf of' reading, in which the beneficiary is not a possessor of a transferred object. In fact, this reading obtains when the benefactive expression does not match the syntax of the 'give' schema. For example:

(47a) Saya mengirim-kan Ana paket   ke Jakarta (Indonesian)
      I   send-BEN   package   to
      'I sent a package to Jakarta on behalf of Ana'
(47b) Aku ngedol-ne Ana pelem   neng   tamu (Javanese)
      I   sell-BEN   mango   to   customer
      'I sold mangoes to the customer on behalf of Ana'

These sentences would yield the regular benefactive readings if there were no additional goals specified, thereby conforming to the 'give' schema. That is, the regular benefactive reading does not obtain and only one aspect of the benefactive reading obtains when the expression does not match the schema. Interestingly enough, intransitive-based benefactives, which, with only two NPs, again do not match the three-place 'give' schema, also yield the 'on behalf of' reading, if the language permits such benefactives at all. This is the case with the benefactives based on intransitive cognate object verbs in Javanese and those based on true intransitives in Spanish (30d) and Chicheŵa.

(48a) Aku   narek-ne Ana (Javanese)
      I   dance-BEN
      'I danced for Ana/on behalf of Ana'
(48b) Aku   nyanyue-ne Ana
      I   sing-BEN
      'I sang for Ana/on behalf of Ana'
(49a) Yêsu   a-ná-f-ér-s   anthu   ônse (Chicheŵa)
      I-Jesus IS-PAST-die-APPL-FV   2-people all
      'Jesus died for all people'

---

[11] As pointed out by John Haig (p.c.), on closer examination it seems possible to get the malefactive reading out of this kind of sentence—e.g. she did it out of revenge. Perhaps this is a residue of the earlier malefactive use of the double-object construction in English; see Pinker (1989: 116) and the discussion of the German malefactive dative below, as well as n. 14 below.

(49*b*) Mtolankhâni   a-na-thámáng-ir-á   chíphadzûwa
       1-journalist   IS-PAST-run-APPL-FV   7-beauty queen
       'The journalist ran for the beauty queen'

Again, for the forms in (48) to have the regular benefactive readings, they must be made to conform to the 'give' schema by explicitly mentioning the cognate objects, as below:[12]

(50*a*) Aku   narek-ne Ana rumba (Javanese)
      I   dance-BEN
      'I danced Ana a rumba'
(50*b*) Aku   nyanyue-ne Ana 'Bungawan Solo'
      I   sing-BEN
      'I sang Ana "Bungawan Solo" '

The above discussion shows that the syntax of the 'give' schema affects the semantic interpretation of benefactive constructions. In this connection German datives provide us with an interesting case of an interplay between the 'give' schema and the semantic interpretations of dative forms. Among the various uses of the dative form in German, what is known as Dativ Commodi yields the benefactive reading, and what is known as Dativ Incommodi the malefactive (adversative) reading. A point of interest is that the benefactive reading obtains just in case the situations expressed are construable according to the 'give' schema, i.e. situations involving three participants and where there is an entity or effect 'possessible' by the beneficiary. Thus, (51*a–b*) below yield the benefactive (Dativ Commodi) readings, and (51*c–d*) yield the malefactive (Dativ Incommodi) readings, while (51*e*) can be interpreted either way since the malefactive, Dativ Incommodi reading, being independent from the 'give' schema, is possible with both transitive and intransitive situations.[13]

---

[12] We noted a certain degree of syntactic inconsistency in the treatment of intransitive-based benefactives. Semantically, too, they are not entirely consistent. It appears true that in Javanese, the primary reading of benefactives such as (48) based on intransitive forms of cognate object verbs is the 'on behalf of' reading, with a remote possibility of the true benefactive reading of e.g. 'I sang Ana (a song),' in which the beneficiary is the 'recipient' of the implied cognate object. But in the case of the Spanish cognate object benefactive *Le canté* 'I sang for her' given in (30*a*), the primary reading is the true benefactive reading of 'I sang her (a song).'

[13] Again, to a great extent, what is happening here is pragmatic. (51*a*) would yield a malefactive reading, if it were the case that having a house built were to affect Emil negatively for some reason.

Semantic transitivity also plays a role in the malefactive, Dativ Incommodi constructions. It is easier to form the construction with verbs with strong implications of resultative states than with those that emphasize process aspects. Cf. *Mir zerbrach die Vase*

(51*a*) Otto baut Emil ein   Häuschen
             build   one   small.house
        'Otto builds Emil a small house'

(51*b*) Otto öffnet dem   Kind die Tür
            open   the.DAT child the door
        'Otto opens the door for the child'

(51*c*) Otto schliesst dem   Kind die Tür
            close   the.DAT chid   the door
        'Otto closes the door on the child'

(51*d*) Mir   rutscht die Hose
            I.DAT slip   the trousers
        'The trousers slip (down) on me'

(51*e*) Man hat   dem Emil den ganzen Garten umgegraben
            they have the.DAT   the   entire   garden   dug up
        'They dug up the whole garden for/on Emil'

7.4.4.3. *Language-internal continua and cross-linguistic variation.* In our approach to benefactives in terms of the 'give' schema, language internal continua are easily accounted for. The situations that approximate the schema are expressible as benefactives, while those that are harder to construe according to the schema become harder to express as benefactive expressions. The continuum obtains because the matches between the real-world situations and the schema form a continuum. Individual variation also obtains because people's assessments of the situations (or their abilities to imagine unconventional situations) vary.

What is more difficult to explain is how to account for the cross-linguistic variation, i.e. how a particular speech community reaches a consensus as to what is and what is not construable in terms of the given schema. As Allerton's (1978) survey shows, individual variation in the acceptability ratings of various benefactive expressions is observable within a given community. Yet a large majority of English speakers find the expression **I opened Mary the door* unacceptable, while the speakers of Japanese, German, Italian, and some others find the counterpart forms of their languages perfectly acceptable. A cross-linguistic variation of this type is perhaps not much different from a cross-linguistic difference observable with respect to metaphors and metonymies, where different cultures respond somewhat differently to the task of representing abstract concepts in terms of concrete ones.

'The vase breaks into pieces on me' vs. **Mir brach die Vase* 'The vase broke on me'. (See Shibatani, 1994*b* on Dativ Incommodi Constructions.)

Answering this question, therefore, requires us to investigate how a given linguistic pattern is innovated and how it spreads within a speech community.[14]

Yet even a cursory survey like the present one points to a certain pattern of development in the generalization and spread of the benefactive construction that seems to reflect the conventionality of different situations. Languages like Spanish, Indonesian, and Sinhala permit a wide range of transitive-based benefactive expressions, to the extent that no transfer of an object to a beneficiary actually occurs (see (23–5)). But the acceptability of transitive-based benefactives varies according to the conventionality of benefactive situations. That is, while sweeping a yard for someone, for example, is a highly conventionalized benefit-giving activity in many cultures, killing a centipede for someone occurs only sporadically and is not a conventionalized benefit-giving activity easily susceptible to benefactive coding (see the contrast between (24*a*) and (24*b*)).

A general survey like the present one does not permit us to investigate details of individual languages, but again it is clear that languages impose specific restrictions as well as specific conditions under which the construal in terms of the give-schema is suspended. We noted earlier that English imposes morphophonological and semantic restrictions on the formation of benefactives (see section 7.4.1). Similar language-specific restrictions may be responsible for the difference in acceptability displayed by the following closely related languages. (The Dutch data is due to Melissa Bowermann, p.c.)

(52*a*) *He said me something nice

(52*b*) Er sagt mir etwas Gutes (German)

(52*c*) Hij zei mij iets leuks (Dutch)

(53*a*) Mommy made me a dessert

(53*b*) Mutter machte mir einen Nachtisch

(53*c*) ??Mamma maakte mij toeje

---

[14] In many cases what is actually happening may be a narrowing of the domain of the relevant constructions. Between Javanese and Indonesian, for example, the more conservative is Javanese, which allows a wider range of benefactive constructions. The difference between German and English may be the same; i.e. English benefactives may be shrinking from what used to be much more general constructions.

The case of narrowing is highly interesting in that it shows that, even if a construction type becomes quite general and appears to be fairly independent from its original schema, it is still connected with the schema such that, when a narrowing process occurs, it proceeds by shedding first those uses that are remote from the schema.

(54a) Anna knitted him a sweater
(54b) Anna strickte ihm einen Pullover
(54c) ??Anna breide hem een trui

We have all along assumed that intransitive-based benefactives are difficult to form across languages. This is generally true, but certain languages permit them under specific conditions: Japanese, Korean, and Nepali allow intransitive-based benefactives when the beneficiary is not overtly coded, as shown by the contrast in acceptability below:

(55a) *Taroo wa Hanako ni   itiba   e   it-te   yat-ta
           TOP   DAT market to go-CONJ give-PAST
      'Taro went to the market for Hanako'
(55b) Taroo wa   itiba   e   it-te   yat-ta
           TOP   market to   go-CONJ give-PAST
      'Taro went to the market (for some identifiable person)'

As detailed in Shibatani (1994a), this suspension of the construal by the 'give' schema interacts with a number of interesting problems in the interpretation of benefactive expressions. Resolution of such problems requires a formal framework in which the notion of the construal can be formulated in a rigorous manner.

7.4.5. *Toward a formal treatment of the schema-based approach*

Languages such as Japanese and Korean that actually involve verbs of giving as auxiliaries are more readily amenable to a formal treatment.[15] For these languages, one of the tasks that a formal treatment must accomplish is the unification of the thematic structures of the main verb and the auxiliary verb of giving. Benefactive expressions in these languages do not convey two discrete activities of, for example, buying an apple and subsequently giving it to a beneficiary. Rather, the benefactive construction as a whole yields a unified benefactive sense that combines the meanings of (i) an activity carried out by an agent, (ii) a favor directed to a beneficiary, and (when applicable) (iii) a transfer of a concrete object to a beneficiary. Readers are referred to Shibatani (1994a) and Shibatani *et al*. (1994) for the details of

---

[15] A typological difference between lexicalization patterns of the Japanese-type language and the English-type language must be addressed. Unlike the former, which lexicalizes both main verb and auxiliary verb, the latter type incorporates the concepts expressed by auxiliary verbs into main verbs. The difference between the Japanese pattern of *katte yaru* ('buy, give') and the English *buy* incorporating the 'give' concept is paralleled elsewhere; e.g. *eki e aruite iku* 'go to the station by walking' vs. *walk to the station*, in which the motion verb corresponding to *iku* 'go' is not lexicalized.

attempts on Japanese, Korean, and Chinese; but just to show the feasibility of a formal treatment, a brief account is given here.

While the discussion above concentrated on the role of the 'give' schema in the construal of the outside scenes and their possible encoding as benefactive expressions, in the formal treatment focus is shifted toward the role of the schema in semantic construals of the thematic structure involved in benefactive expressions. For the purpose of examining the thematic structure of benefactive constructions, the 'give' schema given in (31) can be rewritten as in (56), where the Japanese instantiation of the schema is shown in the format highlighting the aspects of the thematic structure and its syntactic mapping.

(56) *The 'give' schema*

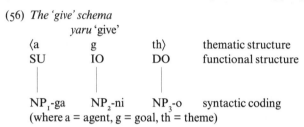

(where a = agent, g = goal, th = theme)

The minimal assumption that one can make with regard to the thematic structure of the auxiliary versions of verbs of giving is that it is identical with that of the basic verbs of giving: they countenance three thematic roles. However, an assumption must be made regarding change in the content of the theme role accompanying the grammaticalization of the main verb 'give' to an auxiliarized benefactive verb. That is, whereas the theme role of the main verb 'give' is instantiated by a concrete object, that of the auxiliary 'give' is instantiated by an event carried out as a favor for someone, so that the basic benefactive notion of doing someone a favor is represented by the main verb. These assumptions yield a complex thematic structure, as in (58) for the benefactive expression (57).

(57) Hanako ga Taroo ni   ringo   o   kat-te   yat-ta
                 NOM   DAT   apple   ACC   buy-CONJ   give-PAST
     'Hanako bought Taro an apple'

(58) *kat-te*   *yat-ta* 'bought, give'
     $\langle a_1\, th_1\rangle_1$ $\langle a_2\, g_2\, th_2\rangle_2$

Here the assumption is that, along with the discussion above, theme$_2$ of *yaru* represents the event expressed by the main verb. In the standard transformational approach this is translated into the analysis that involves the verbs of giving as higher three-place predicates that embed the structure representing the event of the main verb.

The proposed formal analysis makes crucial use of the 'give' schema in (56). That is, benefactive expressions are construed in terms of the schema, such that particular readings, which are consistent with the schema, are imposed upon them. Just to get an idea, consider a case of ungrammatical intransitive-based forms, represented by (59a), whose theta structure and its syntactic realization are given in (59b).

(59a) *Taroo wa   tuma ni   sin-de   yat-ta
            TOP   wife DAT   die-CONJ   give-PAST
      '(intended as) Taro died for his wife'

(59b) *sin-de*   *yat-ta*

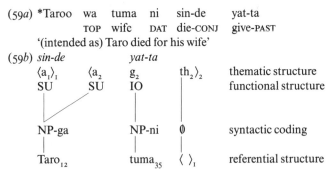

In this type of structure the agent role of the main verb, a_1, and that of the auxiliary, a_2, are co-instantiated by the subject noun phrase. The goal of the auxiliary verb is instantiated by an indirect object nominal. Let us assume that the numbered referential expressions represent specific referential entities. When they lack index numbers, they are assumed to be indefinite. The theme role of the auxiliary verb, which represents the event expressed by the main verb—hence the same subscript as that of the theta frame of the main verb—has no syntactic realization. This event-theme should be distinguished from a theme representing a concrete object specified in the 'give' schema. This difference plays a crucial role in the construal. Now, when we say that structures involving the auxiliary verbs of giving are construed in terms of the 'give' schema, we are imposing a semantic interpretation in accordance with the thematic structure of the schema, which, besides an agent role, calls for a concrete theme associated with a goal. A construal is successful when the entire thematic structure contains a substructure matching the thematic structure of the schema, namely $\langle a, g, th \rangle$, where the theme is instantiated by a concrete object.

For practical purposes we only need to concentrate on finding an appropriate concrete theme and associating it with the goal role of the auxiliary verb. (59b) has no concrete theme that can be associated with the goal role; therefore, the construal fails, and the structure is characterized as ill-formed, as desired.

Let us look at (60), a structure in which the construal is successfully executed.

(60a) Hanako ga Taroo ni   ringo o   kat-te   yat-ta
                NOM   DAT   apple ACC buy-CONJ   give-PAST
       'Hanako bought Taro an apple'

(60b)   *kat-te*   *yat-ta*

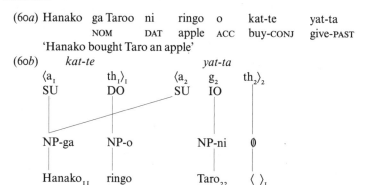

In this structure we find a concrete theme that can be associated with the goal of *yaru*. Let us formally represent the construal by indexing the theme with the same subscript as that of the goal with which it is associated. In other words, when the construal succeeds, as in this structure, we obtain the following post-construal structure.

(61) kat-te   yat-ta
     $\langle a_1\, th_{1/2} \rangle_1$ $\langle a_2\, g_2\, th_2 \rangle_2$

The thematic structure with subscripted theta frames and the co-subscripted roles is to be interpreted in such a way that a_1, for example, is interpreted as an agent of the event expressed by the co-subscripted theta frame, namely $\langle\ \rangle_1$. In the representation in (61), the theme of the theta frame of the verb *kau* is given two subscripts, indicating that it is a theme associated with the two theta frames involved. It therefore receives the interpretation that it is a theme of the buying activity in relation to a_1, and that it is also a theme of the giving activity in relation to a_2 and g_2. The point that figures importantly in a detailed examination is the fact that $th_{1/2}$ is now associated with a goal, in accordance with the pattern of the 'give' schema. At any rate, (61) is the correct thematic structure for (60a), which means, among other things, that the theme 'apple' is both a theme of buying and a theme of giving, and that the referent of g_2 is both the goal of the theme 'apple' and the goal toward which the activity expressed by th_2 is directed.

So far we have been assuming that the construal by the 'give' schema is forced; when the structure fails to be construed, the corresponding sentence is unacceptable, and when the construal goes through, an acceptable benefactive expression results. But there are circumstances under which the construal need not be forced. That is when the goal role is not overtly expressed, or null-instantiated.

Languages like Japanese need not syntactically encode anaphoric elements, which means that in these languages a theta role may be either lexically instantiated or null-instantiated. In a representation incorporating a thematic structure and a matching referential structure, no surface syntactic representation of an anaphoric element is needed, such as a zero pronoun in the Government and Binding (GB) framework. Now when the goal of the auxiliary verbs of giving is null-instantiated, even the intransitive-based benefactive expressions are possible, indicating that the construal by the 'give' schema is not forced. That is, when the structure has the configuration shown in (62), the construal is not forced:

(62a) (Tuma$_{12}$ no koto o   kangaete) Taroo$_{23}$ wa
      wife   of thing ACC   thinking   TOP
      sin-de   yat-ta
      die-CONJ   give-PAST
      '(Considering his wife) Taro died (for her)'

(62b) *sinde*   *yatta*

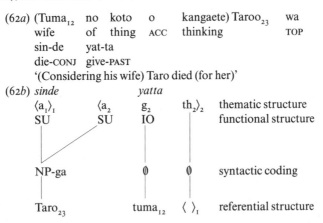

Without the construal by the 'give' schema, the thematic structure receives the conventional interpretation: the theta roles are associated only with their respective theta frames. Thus, in (62b) g$_2$ is the goal of only th$_2$ with no associated concrete theme. Indeed, the reading of (62a) is what (62b) represents: that Taro's dying was done as a favor directed to his wife, without any implication of transfer of a concrete object. Contrast this reading with the one associated with the case of executed construal in (60–1), as well as with the one in which the construal is forced and fails (59).

The approach outlined here formally incorporates an important finding in the studies of grammaticalization: a form undergoing grammaticalization may display at a certain point in its development both its innovative character and its older property (see Heine *et al.*, 1991). That the theme role of an auxiliarized verb of giving represents an event expressed by the main verb is an innovative property acquired in the grammaticalization process. The requirement that the structure containing the verb of giving must be submitted to construal by the 'give' schema reflects the older character of the auxiliarized verb, which, as a main verb, used to involve a concrete theme representing a transferred object in the giving scene.

7.5. CONCLUDING REMARKS

The general account of benefactive constructions offered above is much more falsifiable compared to formal accounts hitherto offered in terms of GB subtheories (e.g. Theta theory, Case theory) or relation-changing within the Relational Grammar framework. In order to falsify our account, we only need to show (1) that benefactive constructions are structurally distinct from the 'give' construction and (2) that benefactive constructions obtain more easily for the situations remote from what is described by the 'give' construction than for ones that are closer to the schema. Our account, in other words, makes much stronger claims than the formal accounts hitherto offered.

It has also been shown above that, contrary to a general feeling that cognitive studies are intuitive and vague, formalization of a schema-based approach is highly feasible. Indeed, as shown in Shibatani (1994*a*) and Shibatani *et al.* (1994), formalization is necessary to bring into sharper focus a number of intricate problems involved in the semantic interpretations of benefactive constructions.

Our basic program has been to seek a correlation between a simple structure and a complex structure in a perspective informed by the recent findings in the studies of grammaticalization. An attempt to correlate a complex structure with a simple structure is not new. In the discussion of causative constructions, it is customary to consult the structural possibilities of simple transitive sentences in order to determine the range of possible causative constructions, e.g. whether or not a double object causative construction is included.[16] But I have tried

[16] See Aissen (1974) and also the more recent attempt by Kemmer and Verhagen (1994), which is highly similar in spirit to the present paper.

to show in this paper that simple sentences do much more than simply provide structural templates. They actively interact with the ways in which we apprehend and interpret real world situations.

Our proposal brings the three elements of grammar—speakers, situations, and structures—into the focus of analysis, thereby obviating the grammar–real world interface problems. I have argued here for the view that certain linguistic expressions are based on specific schemata, which function as construals of scenes or situations. Grammatical schemata represent conceptual archetypes grounded in the experiential domain. Some schemata are abstract or schematic in nature, while others are quite specific. As a representative of the former, I suggested the transitive prototype, which functions as the schema for applicative constructions. In the case of benefactive constructions, more specific 'give' constructions have been shown to function as schemata.

Finally, the variation and gradations exhibited by the data above do not seem to differ much from the prototype effects that Rosch and her associates have discovered (see Rosch, 1977). Just as different types of bird, for example, show differences in 'birdness' and show a gradation from the prototypical (or the most representative) to the least prototypical, benefactives too show a gradation of prototypicality defined along the features of the schema. Also, just as the birdness rating on, say, a pelican can vary from one individual to another, the grammaticality judgment of a marginal benefactive expression can vary. If our way of looking at benefactives is correct, then, contrary to the Chomskyan position, linguistic structure is intimately connected with general cognition.

REFERENCES

AISSEN, J. (1974). 'The Syntax of Causative Constructions.' Ph.D. dissertation, Harvard University.

—— (1983). 'Indirect Object Advancement in Tzotzil,' in D. Perlmutter (ed.), *Studies in Relational Grammar* i. Chicago: University of Chicago Press.

ALSINA, A., and Mchombo, S. (1990). 'The Syntax of Applicatives in Chicheŵa: Problems for a Theta Theoretic Asymmetry,' *Natural Languages and Linguistic Theory* 8: 493–506.

ALLERTON, D. J. (1978). 'Generating Indirect Objects in English,' *Journal of Linguistics* 14: 21–33.

ANDERSON, J. (1980). *Cognitive Psychology and Its Implications*. San Francisco: Freeman.

BAKER, M. (1988). *Incorporation: A Theory of Grammatical Function Changing*. Chicago: University of Chicago Press.

BOLINGER, D. (1977). 'Transitivity and Spatiality: The Passive of Prepositional Verbs,' in A. Makkai, V. B. Makkai, and L. Heilman (eds.), *Linguistics at the Crossroads*, 57–78. Padua: Liviana Editrice/Lake Bulff: Jupiter Press.

BRESNAN, J., and Moshi, L. (1990). 'Object Asymmetries in Comparative Bantu Syntax,' *Linguistic Inquiry* **21/2**: 147–85.

CROFT, W. (1991). *Syntactic Categories and Grammatical Relations*. Chicago: University of Chicago Press.

DRYER, M. (1986). 'Primary Objects, Secondary Objects, and Antidative,' *Language* **62**: 808–845.

FILLMORE, C. J. (1965). *Indirect Object Constructions in English and the Ordering of Transformations*. The Hague: Mouton.

—— (1977). 'The Case for Case Reopened,' in P. Cole and J. M. Sadock (eds.), *Syntax and Semantics* viii: *Grammatical Relations*, New York: Academic Press. 59–81.

—— and KAY, P. (1992). *Construction Grammar Course Book*. Dept. of Linguistics, University of California at Berkeley.

GOLDBERG, A. (1995). *Constructions: A Construction Grammar Approach to Argument Structure*. Chicago: University of Chicago Press.

GOLDSMITH, J. (1980). 'Meaning and Mechanism in Grammar,' in S. Kuno (ed.), *Harvard Studies in Syntax and Semantics* iii, 423–49.

GREEN, G. (1974). *Semantics and Syntactic Regularity*. Bloomington: Indiana University Press.

HEINE, B., CLAUDE, U., and HÜNNEMEYER, F. (1991). *Grammaticalization: A Conceptual Framework*. Chicago: University of Chicago Press.

HUDSON, R. (1992). 'So-called 'Double Objects' and Grammatical Relations,' *Language* **68**: 251–76.

KEMMER, S., and VERHAGEN, A. (1994). 'The Grammar of Causatives and the Conceptual Structure of Events,' *Cognitive Linguistics* **5**: 115–56.

LANGACKER, R. (1991). *Foundations of Cognitive Grammar* ii. Stanford: Stanford University Press.

MATISOFF, J. A. (1991). 'Areal and Universal Dimensions of Grammatization in Lahu,' in E. Traugott and B. Heine (eds.), *Approaches to Grammaticalization* ii, 383–454. Amsterdam: John Benjamins.

OEHRLE, R. (1977). Review of *Semantics and Syntactic Regularity* by G. Green. *Language* **53**: 198–208.

PINKER, S. (1989). *Learnability and Cognition*. Cambridge, Mass.: MIT Press.

RICE, S. (1978). 'Towards a Cognitive Model of Transitivity.' Ph.D. dissertation. University of California at San Diego.

RUDE, N. (1986). 'Topicality, Transitivity, and the Direct Object in Nez Perce,' *International Journal of American Linguistics* **52**: 124–53.

ROSCH, E. (1977). 'Human Categorization,' in N. Warren (ed.), *Studies in Cross-cultural Psychology* i, 1–49. London: Academic Press.

SHIBATANI, M. (1994a). 'Benefactive Constructions: A Japanese–Korean Comparative Perspective,' *Japanese/Korean Linguistics* **4**: 39–74.

—— (1994b). 'An Integrational Approach to Possessor Raising, Ethical Datives and Adversative Passives', *Proceedings of the Twentieth Annual Meeting of the Berkeley Linguistics Society*, 401–56.

—— Z. Qín, and L. Tāo (1994). 'Chinese Benefactive Constructions: Toward a Formal Analysis of the Schema-Based Cognitive Approach,' in M. Chen and O. Tzeng (eds.), *In Honor of William S.-Y. Wang: Interdisciplinary Studies on Language and Language Change*, 459–77. Taipei: Pyramid Press.

SIMPSON, J. (1991). *Warlpiri Morpho-syntax: A Lexical Approach*. Dordrecht: Kluwer.

WIERZBICKA, A. (1988). *The Semantics of Grammar*. Amsterdam: Benjamins.

8

Two Ways to Travel: Verbs of Motion in English and Spanish

Dan I. Slobin

Any aspect of the study of usage which requires mention of particular linguistic forms—as opposed to merely mentioning meaning—belongs properly to the study of grammar.

Charles J. Fillmore (1989: 35)

Fillmore has broadened our vision of semantics, placing word meanings in cognitive frames. In a recent formulation, Fillmore and Atkins (1992: 76) propose—and demonstrate—that 'a word's meaning can be understood only with reference to a structured background of experience, beliefs, or practices, constituting a kind of conceptual prerequisite for understanding the meaning.' The present study is an attempt to apply the insights of cognitive linguistics to uses of verbs of motion in two types of language. I propose to extend the notion of 'frame' in two ways: a motion verb is situated in the *discourse frame* of an account of a *journey*; and, at the same time, it is situated in a *typological frame* that provides and limits the means of expressing components of a motion event in a particular language. In order to characterize the linguistic encoding of such events, then, one must attend to usage, as constrained by typology.

The usage context that I will be concerned with is that of *narrative*—both artificially elicited narratives and the work of novelists. In both types of narrative, the form and content of descriptions of journeys are heavily shaped by the typology of lexicalization patterns. The typological contrast at issue is clearly demonstrated by a comparison of English and Spanish. These two languages represent opposite poles of a typological dichotomy that Leonard Talmy (1985; 1991) has characterized as *satellite-framed* versus *verb-framed*. Consider Talmy's prototypical example—descriptions of a bottle floating out of a cave:

The bottle floated out versus *La botella salió flotando* 'the bottle exited floating.' In English, a satellite to the verb, *out*, conveys the core information of the path of movement, whereas in Spanish it is the verb itself, *salir* 'exit,' that conveys this information. Note also that 'supporting information' about manner of movement is conveyed by the verb in English but by the gerundive *flotando* 'floating' in Spanish. These patterns are quite pervasive in the two languages (with the exception of the use of Latinate verbs of motion in English). Thus English has a large collection of verbs of motion which convey manner, but not directionality (*walk, run, crawl, fly*, etc.), combinable with a large collection of satellites (*in, up to, across*, etc.). Spanish prefers verbs of inherent directionality (*entrar* 'enter,' *bajar* 'descend,' *subir* 'ascend,' etc.), with more restricted use of nondirectional verbs of motion and some verbs of manner (as discussed below).

The typological contrast explored here with regard to verbs of motion is part of a larger set of contrasts analyzed by Talmy, including the conceptual domains of aspect, change of state, action correlation, and event realization. In addition, Talmy proposes that the typological dichotomy is a universal one, dividing languages into those that express the 'core schema' (in this instance, motion) by means of verbs or satellites (Talmy 1991: 486):

Languages that characteristically map the core schema into the verb will be said to have a *framing verb* and to be *verb-framed* languages. Included among such languages are Romance, Semitic, Japanese, Tamil, Polynesian, most Bantu, most Mayan, Nez Perce, and Caddo. On the other hand, languages that characteristically map the core schema onto the satellite will be said to have a *framing satellite* and to be *satellite-framed* languages, and included among them are most Indo-European minus Romance, Finno-Ugric, Chinese, Ojibwa, and Warlpiri.

The present examination of English and Spanish verbs of motion, then, is part of a broader typological framework that embraces a range of conceptual domains and presumably applies to all languages. However, detailed narrative analysis requires two additions to this framework. We will see that Spanish does not always behave like Talmy's characterization of a verb-framed language. And we will see that a new set of issues arises when we go beyond the isolated clause. An examination of narrative data requires one to attend to the extended depiction of motion across clauses, and to go beyond the simple motion event to what I will call the 'journey.' Analysis of elicited picture-book narrations in English and Spanish sets the stage for a comparison of novels written in several English- and Spanish-speaking countries, with some unexpected literary consequences.

8.1. MOTION EVENTS IN ELICITED NARRATIVES

My colleagues and I have devoted a good deal of attention to the study of a special collection of texts that we have come to call 'the frog stories' (Berman and Slobin, 1994). These stories now exist in a number of languages, though they are not translations of an original text. Rather, they have all been elicited by the same wordless, picture story-book, *Frog, Where Are You?* (Mayer, 1969). The texts provide a unique body of data for comparative linguistic and narrative analysis, in that there is no 'original version' from which the others derive, yet all follow the same events and plotline. Our original interest was in language development, and we have gathered frog stories from children of preschool and school age, in addition to adults, in a number of countries. However, my focus here is not on development but, rather, on the typological comparison described above.[1]

The events depicted in *Frog, Where Are You?* invite a rich array of motion descriptions. A pet frog escapes from its jar and a boy and his dog go looking for the lost frog. Their search involves falling from a window, climbing and falling from a tree, climbing a rock and getting entangled in the antlers of a deer who throws the boy and dog over a cliff into some water, and finally climbing out of the water and over a log to discover the runaway frog. (As the reader may have noticed,

[1] The overall study ('A Crosslinguistic Investigation of the Development of Temporality in Narrative') was designed by Dan I. Slobin, in collaboration with Ruth A. Berman, Tel Aviv University, Israel, using a method developed by Michael Bamberg (1987). It is reported in detail in Berman and Slobin (1994) as well as in numerous papers and several dissertations. Of particular relevance to the current paper are Sebastián and Slobin, 1994; Slobin, 1991; Slobin and Bocaz, 1988. *Method*: The person was first shown the book, informed that it 'tells a story,' and then allowed to look through the entire series of 24 pictures. Following that, s/he was asked to tell the story to the investigator, again following the book picture by picture. *Investigators*: Spanish data were gathered in Madrid by Eugenia Sebastián and in Santiago de Chile and Buenos Aires by Aura Bocaz. *Support*: The study was supported by the US–Israel Binational Science Foundation (Grant 2732/82, to R. A. Berman and D. I. Slobin), the Linguistics Program of the National Science Foundation (Grant BNS-8520008, to D. I. Slobin), the Sloan Foundation Program in Cognitive Science (Institute of Cognitive Studies, University of California, Berkeley), the Max Planck Institut für Psycholinguistik (Nijmegen, The Netherlands), the Institute of Human Development (University of California, Berkeley), and the University of Chile (Grant H2643–8712 to Aura Bocaz).

this summary is packed with typical satellite-framed constructions.)
The data come from stories elicited in Berkeley and Madrid, with 12
narrators in each of the following age groups: 3, 4, 5, 9, and adult (college students).

8.1.1. *Verbs*

First consider the entire collection of motion verbs used in the 60
stories in each language. These include verbs of self-movement and
caused movement. A plus sign following an English verb indicates
that it was used with one or more satellites (verb particles).

> (1a) *English verbs*: buck+, bump+, buzz+, carry, chase+, climb+, come+,
> crawl+, creep+, depart, drop+, dump+, escape, fall+, float+, fly+, fol-
> low, get+, go+, head+, hide, hop+, jump+, knock+, land, leave,
> limp+, make-fall, move, plummet, pop+, push+, race+, rush+, run+,
> slip+, splash+, splat+, sneak+, swim+, swoop+, take+, throw+, tip+,
> tumble+, walk+, wander+
>
> (1b) *Spanish verbs*: *acercarse* 'approach,' *alcanzar* 'reach,' *arrojar* 'throw,'
> *bajar(se)* 'descend,' *caer(se)* 'fall,' *correr* 'run,' *dar-un-empujón*
> 'push,' *dar-un-salto* 'jump,' *entrar* 'enter,' *escapar(se)* 'escape,' *hacer
> caer* 'make fall,' *huir* 'flee,' *ir(se)* 'go,' *llegar* 'arrive,' *llevar(se)* 'carry,'
> *marchar(se)* 'go,' *meterse* 'insert oneself,' *nadar* 'swim,' *perseguir*
> 'chase,' *ponerse* 'put oneself,' *regresar* 'return,' *sacarse* 'remove oneself,
> exit,' *salir* 'exit,' *saltar* 'jump,' *subir(se)* 'ascend,' *tirar* 'throw,'
> *traspasar* 'go over,' *venir* 'come,' *volar(se)* 'fly,' *volver(se)* 'return'

A comparison of (1a) and (1b) shows a greater variety in English:
there are 47 types, in comparison with 27 types in Spanish. This is due
to the variety of English verbs that conflate motion and manner
(*crawl, creep, plummet, splat, swoop*, etc.). But the imbalance is even
greater when we consider all of the possible combinations of English
verbs with satellites. Talmy (1991: 486) defines 'satellite' as 'the grammatical category of any constituent other than a nominal complement
that is in a sister relation to the verb root.' In English, satellites are
verb particles. For example, in *He ran out of the house*, *out* is a satellite
and *of the house* is a prepositional phrase. Combining the verbs in (1a)
with the satellites that are used in the 60 English frog stories results in
123 types, as shown in (2).

> (2) *English verbs + satellites*
> buck + off
> bump + down

buzz + out
chase + after, in
climb + down, on, out, over, up, up in, up on
come + after, down, off, on, out, over, up
crawl + out, over, up
creep + out, up
drop + down, off
dump + in, off
fall + down, in, off, on, out, over
float + off
fly + after, away, off, out, over, up
get + away, down, in, off, on, out, over, past, up, up on
go + down, down out, home, in, off, out, outside, over, through, up
head + for, to
hop + in, on, out, over
jump + down, off, out, over, up
knock + down, down out, in, off, out
limp + in
pop + out, up
push + down, off, off in, out
race + after, away
run + after, along, away, by, from, in, off, out, over, through
rush + out
slip + on, over
sneak + out, over, up
splash + in
splat + in
swim + out, over
swoop + down
take + away, off with
throw + down, down in, in, off, over, over in
tip + off over
tumble + down, out
walk + along, down, over to
wander + out

The diversity of English verb + satellite constructions is impressive. Does this diversity, however, make for English narratives that are richer in movement description? This possibility can be explored in several ways, beginning with the use of locative phrases in association with verbs. In addition to 'bare verbs' such as *fall* or *caer(se)* 'fall,' both languages use prepositional phrases to indicate source and goal—regardless of the language-specific means of expression for paths. For example, (3*a*) and (3*b*) are roughly equivalent expressions in the two languages:

(3*a*) They fell in the water. [age 9]
(3*b*) *Se cayeron al agua.* 'They fell to the water.' [age 9]

Do both languages show comparable tendencies to prefer such constructions to the use of bare verbs such as *They fell* or *Se cayeron*? Table 8.1 compares the two languages in this regard, examining the episodes in the frog story in which a character or object falls or is thrown downward (dog from window, beehive from tree, boy from tree, boy and dog over cliff into pond). The analysis includes all of the verbs used to describe downward motion and caused motion in these scenes (mainly versions of 'fall' and 'throw'). At issue is whether the verb occurred alone or with some kind of locative addition—a particle, prepositional phrase, or adverbial expression indicating downward direction, source, or goal of motion. 'Bare verbs' thus provide no elaboration of path beyond the inherent directionality of the verb itself.

TABLE 8.1. *Percentages of downward motion descriptions with bare verb*

	Preschool (3–5 yrs.)	School (9 yrs.)	Adult
English	16	13	15
Spanish	56	54	36

At all ages, English-speakers add locative detail to motion verbs far more often than Spanish-speakers. Although there is essentially no change with age in English, Spanish adults provide elaboration more frequently than children. Nevertheless, they use bare verbs more than twice as often as English-speaking adults. It would appear, then, that descriptions of movement tend to be richer in English than in Spanish.

8.1.2. *Phrases*

The comparison can be made in another way. Table 8.1 lumps together expressions such as *fell down* and *fell in the water* as instances of path elaboration (non-bare verbs). In a sense, however, *fall* and *fall down* are both equivalent to Spanish *caer(se)*, since nothing is communicated about the **ground** (source or goal of movement). Another

---

analysis, therefore, sorts verbs as to whether they are accompanied by prepositional phrases referring to the ground (e.g. *fell out of the window, fell into the water*). Table 8.2 presents figures based on *all* verbs of motion in the frog stories, along with comparable figures from novels (described in detail below). 'Minus-ground clauses' consist of bare verbs or verbs with satellites indicating direction of movement; 'plus-ground clauses' have, in addition, one or more prepositional phrases encoding source and/or goal.

TABLE 8.2. *Percentages of minus-ground and plus-ground clauses*

Age (yrs.)	English		Spanish	
	Minus-ground	Plus-ground	Minus-ground	Plus-ground
3	47	53	48	52
4	46	54	56	44
5	40	60	50	50
9	38	62	39	61
Adult	18	82	37	63
Novels	4	96	19	81

The overall tendency is for English narratives to use more ground adjuncts with regard to verbs of motion than Spanish narratives. The differences between the languages are most marked for mature speakers/writers: for adult frog-narrators the comparison is 82 per cent versus 63 per cent of motion verbs, and for novel-writers it is 96 per cent versus 81 per cent. The developmental patterns are also interesting, showing an advantage for English at several points. There is no difference at age 3, but English-speaking children begin to develop towards more ground-marked clauses during the preschool period, whereas Spanish-speaking children show no development until school age. They do not develop further between age 9 and adulthood, whereas there is a considerable English growth spurt after 9. So, overall, it appears that English-speaking narrators may pay more attention to path details than do Spanish-speakers.

8.1.3. *Journeys*

Up to this point we have taken the verb or the clause as the unit of analysis for motion description, following a long linguistic and psycholinguistic tradition. However, in narrative discourse the movements of a protagonist from place to place are *situated* in a physical setting and temporal flow of events. Narrators need not limit a path description to a single verb and its adjuncts. Linguistic analyses typically deal in terms of a *path* or *trajectory* lying between *source* and *goal* ('ground,' 'landmark'). In describing real-world or fictional events, however, a narrator may present a series of linked paths or a path with way-stations. I will call a complex path a *journey*—that is, an extended path that includes *milestones* or *subgoals*. In addition, a path can be situated in a *medium* (*along a road, through the water*, etc.). A good example of a journey with several components is offered by one of the falling scenes from the frog story. The boy is standing on a rock holding onto what he thinks are branches and sets off on an unexpected journey. A journey can be narrated in a sequence of clauses, as in the following very elaborate adult English version.

(4) What the boy took to be branches were really antlers of a deer on which he gets caught. The dog, oblivious to all this, is looking behind the rock. The deer takes off with the boy strewed across his antlers, and the dog runs at his feet yelling at him to stop it. They're approaching a cliff, and the deer stops abruptly, which causes the boy to lose his balance and fall with the dog down into the stream. [age adult]

The segment in (4) is highly analytical. The narrator makes specific mention of the cliff as a milestone along the way to the goal of the stream. It is also possible for a narrator to compact components of a journey into a single clause, as in the satellites and prepositional phrases appended to the verbs *tip* and *throw* in the following examples from a 9-year-old and a 5-year-old. Here milestone and goal are appended to a single verb.

(5a) He [= deer] starts running and he tips him off over a cliff into the water. And he lands. [age 9]
(5b) He threw him over a cliff into a pond. [age 5]

Using these two means—clause-chaining and clause-compacting—it is possible to distribute attention to path segments that make up a journey. The Spanish approach seems to be rather different from the English. The two languages can be compared in terms both of *what* is said and of *how* it is said.

First consider how Spanish makes use of locative prepositional phrases with verbs of motion. There is nothing about verb-framed typology that should prevent Spanish speakers from using similar expressions to those in (5); yet, although they are common in English, there are only two examples in the entire corpus of 60 Spanish frog stories. In addition, we have recently more than tripled the Spanish sample with data gathered by Aura Bocaz in Chile and Argentina, covering ages 3, 4, 5, 7, 9, 11, and adult. In 156 Latin American frog stories, there is only one clause that mentions both source and goal in relation to a single verb. The three Spanish examples are given in (6). They come from a 5-year-old, a 9-year-old, and an adult—suggesting that this is not a developmental issue.

(6a) *Se cayó de la ventana a la calle.*
'[The dog] fell from the window to the street.' [age 5, Spain]

(6b) *El perro . . . hace un movimiento tal que se precipita al suelo, desde la ventana . . .*
'The dog . . . makes a movement such that he plummets to the ground, from the window . . .' [adult, Chile]

(6c) *Lo lleva campo a través hasta un barranco.*
'[The deer] carries him across (the) field to a cliff.' [age 9, Spain]

It appears, then, that Spanish speakers tend to limit themselves, when using a prepositional phrase with a verb of motion, to one piece of information about the ground (source, goal, or medium).

I will return, in discussing novels, to propose why Spanish narrators make such little use of the extended construction type represented in (6). But first let us see if Spanish provides other means for providing details of paths and journeys. Do the languages differ with regard to *what* is narrated? One possible difference might lie in the degree of analysis of a journey into separate clauses, as in the English example in (4). The scene of the fall from the cliff is a useful one to examine from this point of view. It consists of six narrative segments, separately expressed in various versions: deer starts to run; deer runs, carrying boy; deer stops at cliff; deer throws boy (off of antlers/down); boy and dog fall; boy and dog land in water. Perhaps Spanish narrators mention ***more segments*** of the journey, rather than expressing the journey compactly in English fashion. But this is not the case. Here we consider only 9-year-olds and adults, since preschoolers do not tend to provide many details in their stories. Only 40 per cent of Spanish 9-year-olds provided three segments, and none of them provided more than three. By contrast, 92 per cent of American 9-year-olds provided three or more segments, and, of these, almost half provided more than three segments. Of the adult narrators, 100 per cent of the Americans and only 75 per cent of the Spaniards provided three or more segments of the journey. In sum, Spanish speakers do not seem to 'compensate' for minimal use of source-goal clauses by means of a series of separate action clauses that analyze a journey into its components.

8.1.4. *Settings*

To sum up thus far: in comparison with English-speakers, Spanish narrators use a smaller set of motion verbs; they mention fewer ground elements in individual clauses; and they describe fewer segments of a journey. Yet their narratives, overall, seem to 'tell the same story' as English accounts. Although we have extended the analysis from verbs of motion to include associated locative phrases, and have gone from individual motion verbs to series of clauses, the focus has remained on descriptions of *movement*. However, movement always takes place within a physical setting. The two languages seem to differ, further, in relative allocation of attention to movement and setting. English, with its rich means for path description, can often leave setting to be inferred; Spanish, with its sparser path possibilities, often elaborates descriptions of settings, leaving paths to be inferred. For example, the trajectories described in (5a) and (5b) allow one to infer that there is a cliff located above some water: *over a cliff into a pond, over a cliff into the water.* Compare this to the following Spanish narrative segments:

(7a) *Los tiró a un precipicio donde había harta agua. Entonces se cayeron.*
'[The deer] threw them at a cliff where there was lots of water. Then they fell.' [age 7, Chile]

(7b) *El ciervo le llevó hasta un sitio, donde debajo había un río. Entonces el ciervo tiró al perro y al niño al río. Y después, cayeron.*
'The deer took him until a place, where below there was a river. Then the deer threw the dog and the boy to the river. And then they fell.' [age 9, Spain]

(7c) *Lo tiró. Por suerte, abajo, estaba el río. El niño cayó en el agua.*
'[The deer] threw him. Luckily, below, was the river. The boy fell in the water.' [age 11, Argentina]

In these accounts, we are told that the deer 'threw' them and that they 'fell', ending up in the water. We can infer that the trajectory went from some elevated place to the river because of the *static* descriptions: 'a cliff where there was lots of water,' 'a place where below there was a river,' 'below was the river.' In comparison with English, Spanish frog stories have an abundance of such static descriptions of settings, suggesting a different allocation of attention between description of movement and description of states. In a sense, the Spanish narrators *are* providing ground information—but it is in separate clauses rather than adjoined to verbs of motion. However, it should be noted that even by this criterion Spanish frog stories devote less explicit attention to movement and ground—broadly conceived—than do English versions. Table 8.3 summarizes the percentages of the 12 narrators in each age group in Spain and the US who provided static scene setting descriptions in the scene of the fall from the cliff. There is essentially no development in English, and this option is not taken by any adult narrators at all. In Spanish there seems to be a major development from ages 5 to 9, but only three of the adult narrators take this option.

TABLE 8.3. *Percentage of narrators providing extending locative elaboration in describing the fall from cliff*

	5 yrs.	9 yrs.	Adult
English	8	8	0
Spanish	8	42	25

In sum, analysis of the frog stories reveals a distinct contrast in *rhetorical style* between English and Spanish. English-speakers may devote more narrative attention to the dynamics of movement because of the availability of verbs of motion (often conflated with manner) that can readily be associated with satellites and locative prepositional phrases to trace out detailed paths in relation to ground elements. Spanish-speakers, by contrast, seem to be led (or constrained) by their language to devote less narrative attention to the dynamics and perhaps somewhat more attention to static scene-setting.[2] These are, however, bold claims to advance on the basis of an artificial task, in which narratives were elicited to a single picture storybook. Therefore I have begun to explore literary fiction—with

[2] These differences in rhetorical style may apply to satellite-framed and verb-framed languages generally. The English patterns seem to be true of the other satellite-framed languages in our frog-story data—German and Russian—and the Spanish patterns seem to be repeated in the other verb-framed languages—Hebrew and Turkish (Berman and Slobin, 1994; Slobin, 1991). In a recent NSF-sponsored workshop (Linguistic Institute, University of New Mexico, Albuquerque, July 1995), the patterns reported here seem to appear in frog stories in the following range of languages: *satellite-framed languages:* Dutch, English, German, Icelandic, Polish, Russian, Serbo-Croatian, Swedish, Warlpiri; *verb-framed languages:* Arabic (Moroccan), French, Hebrew, Italian, Japanese, Portuguese, Spanish, Turkish.

preliminary results that seem surprising. (As Chuck Fillmore once said: 'Everybody who has worked with actual corpora has found things they couldn't possibly have dreamed up merely by relying on their own linguistic introspections.')

8.2. MOTION EVENTS IN NOVELS

The findings reported below are tentative, based on a limited sample. Thus far, however, the differences that have shown up in the frog stories are also present in comparing the narration of motion events in ten twentieth-century novels.[3] The choice of novels was unsystematic, partly determined by availability of translations (which also figure in the analysis below). The authors come from a range of English- and Spanish-speaking countries:

English
Daphne Du Maurier (England): *Rebecca* (1938)
John Fowles (England): *The French Lieutenant's Woman* (1969)
Ernest Hemingway (US): *For Whom the Bell Tolls* (1941)
Doris Lessing (Southern Rhodesia, England): *A Proper Marriage* (1952)
James Michener (US): *Chesapeake* (1978)

Spanish
Isabel Allende (Chile): *La Casa de los Espíritus* [The House of the Spirits] (1982)
José Donoso (Chile): *Coronación* [Coronation] (1983)
Gabriel García Márquez (Colombia): *Cien Años de Soledad* [One Hundred Years of Solitude] (1967)
Ernesto Sabato (Argentina): *El Túnel* [The Tunnel] (1988)
Mario Vargas Llosa (Peru): *La Tía Julia y el Escribidor* [Aunt Julia and the Scriptwriter] (1977).

The unit of analysis is a ***motion event***, defined as the description of the movement of a protagonist from one place to another. Simple appearances and disappearances from the scene were excluded, as were nondirectional paths (e.g. turning around, pacing up and down). Motion events could be either a simple trajectory or a journey. The

[3] In a seminar at Berkeley in 1995, the patterns reported here for English and Spanish novels were found in another satellite-framed language (3 Russian novels) and 3 more verb-framed languages (1 French novel, 2 Japanese novels, 3 Turkish novels).

only criterion was thus that the protagonist ended up in a different place within an uninterrupted stretch of narrative. My procedure was to open a book at random and read until finding a motion event, collecting twenty such events from each novel (thus resulting in 100 motion events in each language). There were no striking differences between the five novels in each language; therefore the 100 English and Spanish events are treated as two databases in the following analyses.

As a first, impressionistic observation, I found that I often had to open a Spanish book several times to find a page with a motion event, whereas this was hardly ever the case for the English novels. I have not quantified this impression, but it seems clear that—at least for this sample—the English writers are quite concerned with moving their characters from place to place, whereas the characters in the Spanish novels often simply appear at a new place.

We have already seen in Table 8.2 that English novelists, like English frog-narrators, rarely move their protagonists without mentioning some ground object relative to the path. Only 4 per cent of the motion events in the English novels are represented by bare verbs, compared to 19 per cent in the Spanish novels. Table 8.4 shows that when an author does make reference to ground (source, goal, medium), English authors are far more likely than Spanish authors to refer to two or more ground locations, and Spanish authors never refer to more than two.

TABLE 8.4. *Percentages of motion events with ground references*

Language	No. of ground elements referred to			
	0	1	2	3+
English	4	61	26	9
Spanish	19	73	8	0

When we turn to the verbs themselves, it is curious that the number of *tokens* is almost identical for the two samples of 100 motion events: 165 in English and 163 in Spanish. However, recall that the English motion events tend to have more locative phrases per verb. In addition, the motion events tend to include more ground elements in English. Quantitatively, the English novels mention an average of 2.24 ground elements per motion event and the Spanish novels mention an average of 1.52. Thus the novels, like the frog stories, show English narrations to be richer in encoding path details—both per verb and per motion event.

Furthermore, as in the frog stories, there is a considerable difference in terms of *types* of verbs of motion: 60 in English to 43 in Spanish. (The type-token ratios [TTR] are .36 for English and .26 for Spanish.) English shows greater lexical diversity than Spanish—primarily due to the richness of verbs that conflate motion and manner. Compare, for example, the verbs used to simply indicate motion on foot in the two languages:

(8a) crawl, creep, go, hasten, hurry, march, move, run, rustle, scurry, slip, speed, step, stomp, storm, stride, stroll, walk, wander

(8b) *andar* 'walk,' *caminar* 'walk,' *correr* 'run,' *deslizarse* 'slip,' *dirigirse* 'go,' *ir* 'go,' *lanzarse* 'dash'

These several comparisons are all the more interesting in that the fiction-writers, unlike the frog-narrators, are not constrained by a common set of events to narrate. Each of the novelists happens to be writing about whatever motion events are important to the particular narrative, yet writers using English seem to attend more to this semantic domain—in several different ways.

As an initial qualitative comparison, consider the following two narrations of journeys that lead the protagonist into a new room or building. In Du Maurier's *Rebecca*, the narrator uses four verbs— *went, turn, pass, went*—to move along a path with seven milestones. Note constructions such as *went through . . . and up, passed through . . . and along . . . to*. There are no static descriptions of the locations of the milestones, but their locations relative to one another can be easily inferred:

(9) I went through the hall and up the great stairs, I turned in under the archway by the gallery, I passed through the door to the west wing, and so along the dark silent corridor to Rebecca's room. I turned the handle of the door and went inside. (p. 225)

In Allende's *La Casa de los Espíritus* we find the longest journey presented in any of the five Spanish novels. The protagonist gets off of the train in an unknown town. There are four motion verbs: two pairs of near synonyms—*andar* 'walk,' *caminó* 'walked,' *acercarse* 'approach,' *se aproximó* 'approached'—and a 'negative' motion verb, *se detuvo* 'stopped.' These five verbs relate to five milestones. (Some of the non-locative, inner-state descriptions are omitted.)

(10) *Tomó sus maletas y echó a andar por el barrial y las piedras de un sendero que conducía al pueblo. Caminó más de diez minutos . . . Al acercarse al caserío vio humo en algunas chimeneas . . . Se detuvo a la entrada del pueblo, sin ver a nadie. En la única calle cercada de modestas casas de adobe, reinaba el silencio . . . Se aproximó a la casa más cercana, que no tenía ninguna ventana y cuya puerta estaba abierta. Dejó sus maletas en la acera y entró.* (p. 49)

'He took his suitcases and started to walk through the mud and stones of a path that led to the town. He walked more than ten minutes . . . On approaching the hamlet he saw smoke in several chimneys . . . He stopped at the entrance to the town without seeing anybody. In the only street lined with modest adobe houses, silence reigned . . . He approached the closest house, which had no window and whose door was open. He left his suitcases on the sidewalk and entered . . .'

In this narration, path and ground march along together, verb by verb. There is a characteristic Spanish use of a relative clause to predicate part of the path of a noun, rather than adjoin it to a verb: *un sendero que conducía al pueblo* 'a path that led to the town' (cf. English *walked along a path to the town*). The path itself is described as one that would be difficult to walk on, but where an English writer might make use of a verb of manner, such as *stumble, plod,* or *trudge,* the verbs of motion themselves are neutral as to manner, and the reader can infer the type of walking required by such a path from the description.

8.2.1. *Translations*

The statistical comparisons point clearly to overall cross-linguistic differences, but one must be wary of qualitative comparisons of selected examples. A more useful way to explore the 'rhetorical slants' of two languages is to compare a translation with an original, asking how each language accommodates itself to the demands of the other with regard to the same content. In examining motion events, the most informative comparisons come from Spanish translations of English. How do Spanish translators cope with the abundance of English locative detail? By contrast, English translators of Spanish should have an easier job (and may even seek to enrich the original version). I have examined translations of four of the English novels (with the exception of Hemingway) and three of the Spanish novels (with the exceptions of Donoso and Sabato). Thus we can compare 80 English motion events with their Spanish equivalents and 60 Spanish motion events with their English equivalents.[4] Translations can be compared in terms of fidelity to both path-ground and manner descriptions. For both categories, English loses more in translation than does Spanish. The overall comparisons are summarized in Table 8.5.

TABLE 8.5. *Percentages of faithful translations of motion events*

	Trajectory	Manner
English to Spanish	76	51
Spanish to English	92	77

8.2.1.1. *Trajectories.* English translators have an easy task: they almost always follow the original, and sometimes even add a bit. Spanish translators, however, make changes to English trajectories 24 per cent of the time, and of these changes the majority are reductions of the full path-ground depiction. My impression is that a faithful translation is either not readily accessible, due to lexical and syntactic constraints, and/or it would be too extended, thereby foregrounding material that is naturally backgrounded in the original. Consider several examples in which path segments are omitted in translation.

In the following two examples, the reader knows that the path moves upwards, on the basis of preceding description. The translator simply omits vertical directionality. (Translations are given in italics.)

(11) Gradually he worked his way up to the foot of the bluffs . . . (Fowles, 1969: 136)
   Poco a poco, fue acercándose hasta el pie de los riscos . . .
   'Gradually he was approaching the foot of the bluffs . . .' (Fowles, 1981: 143)
(12) I . . . climbed up the path over the cliffs towards the rest of the people. (Du Maurier, 1938: 236)
   Tomé el sendero que conducía al lugar donde estaba la gente.
   'I took the path that led to the place where the people were.' (Du Maurier, 1959: 339)

The Du Maurier translation also omits a milestone, the cliffs. This translation is 'bumpy' enough without adding the additional information contained in the original. Note also that—like the Allende passage in (10)—the translator describes the 'path' as a static entity,

---

4 Citations for translations follow references to the originals in the bibliography.

by means of a relative clause, rather than using a verb to predicate motion along that path.[5]

The problem facing the Spanish translator, in these instances and many others, is whether or not to allot a separate clause to each of the path segments that are associated with a single verb in the English original. This is due not only to the verb-framed nature of Spanish, but also to the lexicon, which contains verbs that conflate motion and path. In short journeys it is sometimes felicitous to simply break up one English construction into two:

(13) I went through the drawing-room to the morning-room. (Du Maurier, 1938: 221)
Pasando por el salón, fui al gabinete.
'Passing through the drawing-room, I went to the morning-room.' (Du Maurier, 1959: 318)

(14) Martha walked through the park and along the avenues . . . (Lessing, 1952: 71).
Martha cruzó el parque y paseó a lo largo de las avenidas . . .
'Martha crossed the park and promenaded along the avenues . . .' (Lessing, 1979: 84)

Sometimes, however, the translator is more concerned to move the protagonist on, without slowing the pace of the narration with 'obvious' or 'unnecessary' detail, as in the following two examples. In such cases, the Spanish reader simply is not informed of the entire journey.

(15) He strolled across the room to the door . . . (Du Maurier, 1938: 329)
Se dirigió a la puerta . . .
'He went to the door.' (Du Maurier, 1959: 446)

(16) . . . she moved out into the sun and across the stony clearing . . . (Fowles, 1969: 165)
. . . la muchacha salió al claro rocoso . . .
'. . . the girl exited to the stony clearing . . .' (Fowles, 1981: 173)

At some points in a translation, however, a particular journey is too important to be seriously reduced. The following example is from a

---

[5] Such relative clauses are especially frequent with regard to words meaning 'path.' In fact, it could be that English locative prepositional phrases following 'path' words are perceived by Spanish speakers as relative clauses. Compare for example: 'We walked up the drive to the front door . . .' (Du Maurier, 1938: 340) and its Spanish translation, *Echamos a andar por el camino enarenado que conducía a la puerta de la casa . . .* 'We started to walk along the sanded drive that led to the door of the house . . .' (Du Maurier, 1959: 482). It wasn't until reading this translation that I realized that the English version is amenable to an alternate structural analysis: ((We) (walked up) ((the drive) (to the front door))).

critical episode in *Rebecca*. In order to maintain reference to six of the seven milestones (omitting 'the door to the west wing'), the Spanish translator requires six verbs to the original four.

(17) I went through the hall and up the great stairs. I turned in under the archway by the gallery. I passed through the door to the west wing, and so along the dark silent corridor to Rebecca's room. I turned the handle of the door and went inside. (Du Maurier, 1938: 225)

Pasé el hall y subí la escalera principal, doblé la esquina, pasé bajo el arco apuntado junto a la galería, por el pasillo, oscuro y silencioso, hasta llegar al cuarto de Rebeca. Hice girar el picaporte y entré.

'I went through the hall and ascended the main staircase, turned the corner, passed under the pointed archway by the gallery, along the corridor, dark and silent, until arriving at Rebecca's room. I turned the door handle and entered.' (Du Maurier, 1959: 323)

Nothing of this degree of path elaboration occurs in any of the five Spanish novels. We will return to this paradox in the discussion: Spanish writers do not seem to make full use of the devices that are available in their language, as evidenced in such translations.

8.2.1.2. *Manner.* As suggested by the percentages in Table 8.5, manner of movement is far more salient in English narratives than in Spanish. Spanish translators omit manner information about half of the time, whereas English translators actually **add** manner to the Spanish original in almost a quarter of their translations. This is due both to the considerable lexical differences between the two languages and the associated syntactic means of expressing manner. Lexical gaps in Spanish can account for translations such as:

(18) The three women drifted inertly down the hot street . . . (Lessing, 1952: 17)

Las tres mujeres siguieron, pausadamente, calle abajo . . .

'The three women continued, slowly, down the street . . .' (Lessing, 1979: 25)

(19) He stomped from the trim house . . . (Michener, 1978: 607)

Salió de la pulcra casa . . .

'He exited from the trim house . . .' (Michener, 1980: 452)

(20) . . . he bounded up the stairs after her, overtaking her in the bedroom . . . (Michener, 1978: 615)

. . . subió tras ella, alcanzándola en el dormitorio . . .

'. . . he ascended after her, reaching her in the bedroom . . .' (Michener, 1980: 458)

In addition, the English preference for non-Latinate vocabulary can account for translations *from* the Spanish such as the following. (Note also the translator's addition of a more vivid expression in (22).)

(21) Don Federico avanzó sin apresurarse . . .
'Don Federico advanced without hurrying . . .' (Vargas Llosa, 1977: 181)
Don Federico walked unhurriedly towards her . . . (Vargas Llosa, 1982: 150)

(22) Se dirigió a la casa, abrió la puerta de un empujón, y entró.
'He directed himself [= went] to the house, opened the door with a push, and entered.' (Allende, 1982: 51)
He walked up to the house, gave the door a single forceful push, and went in. (Allende, 1985: 49)

In other instances of translation into Spanish, the translator has to decide whether to simply omit a detail of manner or to preserve it in an adverbial clause, thereby giving it more narrative weight than in the original.[6] In the following examples, two translators came to different solutions for the verb *rustle*.

(23) Mrs Tranter rustled forward, effusive and kind. (Fowles, 1969: 101)
Mrs Tranter se adelantó, efusiva y amable.
'Mrs Tranter moved forward, effusive and kind.' (Fowles, 1981: 109)

(24) She rustled out of the room . . . (Du Maurier, 1938: 204)
Salió del cuarto, acompañada del susurro siseante de sus ropas . . .
'She exited from the room, accompanied by the swishing rustle of her clothing.' (Du Maurier, 1959: 293)

Finally, it should be noted that some verbs that conflate motion and manner can be used in identical fashion in both languages, even though Spanish is a verb-framed language:

(25) They ran downstairs . . . (Lessing, 1952: 133)
Corrieron escaleras abajo . . .
'They ran stairs downwards . . .' (Lessing, 1979: 152)

---

[6] As Talmy (1985: 122) has pointed out: 'A theoretical perspective that encompasses both sections 1 [verbs] and 2 [satellites] pertains to *salience*: the degree to which a component of meaning, due to its type of linguistic representation, emerges into the foreground of attention or, on the contrary, forms part of the semantic background where it attracts little direct attention. In this regard, there appears to be a universal principle. Other things being equal . . . a semantic element is backgrounded by expression in the main verb root or in any closed-class element (including a satellite . . .). Elsewhere it is foregrounded.'

(26) ... he slipped among the trees ... (Michener, 1978: 23)
... *se deslizó entre los árboles* ...
'... he slipped among the trees ...' (Michener, 1980: 14)

(27) Suddenly she was walking, almost running, across the turf towards the path. (Fowles, 1969: 124)
De pronto, echó a andar, casi a correr, a través del prado hacia el camino.
'Suddenly she started to walk, almost to run, across the meadow towards the path.' (Fowles, 1981: 131)

8.3. DISCUSSION

It is important to try to distinguish those characteristics of Spanish that are definitional of a verb-framed language from those that may result from typological factors but not be a necessary consequence of them. Spanish is verb-framed in that the core meaning of a motion event—its directionality—tends to be expressed by the verb itself (e.g. *entrar* 'go in,' *bajar* 'go down,' *cruzar* 'go across'). We have already noted, though, that Spanish also has verbs that are neutral with regard to directionality, and that some of these also encode manner of movement (e.g. *ir* 'go,' *correr* 'run'). Some of these verbs also occur with what appear to be satellites (e.g. *correr abajo* 'run down'). As is almost always the case, typologies leak. In addition, both types of language—verb-framed and satellite-framed—have constructions in which locative phrases can be used with verbs of motion to indicate landmarks. Why, then, are there such large differences in the degree of narrative attention paid to motion events in the two languages?

I think the answer can be found in another type of constraint in Spanish. Jon Aske (1989: 6), in a qualification to Talmy's typology, has pointed out that there are two types of path phrase: (1) a *one-dimensional locative path phrase* 'which adds the "location" (i.e. the path or one-dimensional region) in which the activity took place' and (2) a *telic path phrase* which 'predicates ... an end-of-path location/state of the Figure.' Both types are possible in English—e.g. (1) *He ran along the road/across the lawn/through the tunnel*; (2) *He ran into the house/off of the bridge*. Only the former, however, are possible in Spanish. (Aske points out (p.c.): 'The problem in Spanish is expressing the resulting state—the telic state—in the same clause' as a non-telic verb of motion.) Aske attributes this to a general constraint in Spanish. The telic path phrase acts as a *non-verbal predicate* (Fillmore, 1988)—that is, it predicates both path and the location of the figure (he ran into the house *and* he is in the house as a consequence). Aske proposes that Spanish has a general restriction against resultative nonverbal predicates, accordingly excluding these motion constructions along with others. He notes, for example, that Spanish 'has nothing comparable to *Pat kicked the door open, We stood the pole erect,* or *She knocked the door down*' (Aske 1989: 6). Thus, in addition to being a verb-framed language, Spanish also has a further restriction on the types of path phrases that can occur with verbs of motion.[7]

The consequence for the encoding of motion events is that a single verb can accumulate path phrases only if they are nontelic. This seems to be true both of the Spanish novels and of the Spanish translations, as well as of the frog stories. In the novels there are only three instances of a verb of motion occurring with phrases indicating two ground elements. All three are nontelic, describing only the path itself or the arrival at a goal, without predicating an end-state (or crossing a boundary).

(28) *Los llevó a través de un laberinto de helados corredores hasta la sala que había preparado* . . .
'He led them through a labyrinth of icy corridors to the room that he had prepared.' (Allende, 1982: 213)

(29) . . . *Miguel se arriesgaba a entrar de día, arrastrándose entre los matorrales, como un ladrón, hasta la puerta del sótano* . . .
'. . . Miguel dared to enter by day, crawling through the bushes, like a thief, to the door of the basement . . .' (Allende, 1982: 294)

(30) . . . *pude caminar, sin grandes dificultades, por el callejón de entrada, entre los eucaliptos.*
'. . . I was able to walk, without great difficulty, along the entry lane, between the eucalyptus trees.' (Sabato, 1988: 129)

Note that, in all three instances, the first ground is the medium (and also the second in 30)—that is, it constitutes part of the path itself ('through a labyrinth of corridors,' 'through the bushes,' 'along the entry lane between the trees'). The goal in (28) and (29) is only approached, and therefore its particular locative features are neutral

---

[7] More recently, Slobin and Hoiting (1994), following a suggestion from Talmy (p.c.) have proposed that Aske's telic verbs all involve paths in which the figure crosses a boundary, such as 'exit,' 'enter,' and 'cross.' They find that, across a range of verb-framed languages, verbs of manner can occur with path expressions as long as the path does not cross a boundary (American Sign Language, French, Japanese, Korean, Sign Language of the Netherlands, Turkish). In this same collection of languages, resultative changes of state must also be expressed in separate clauses, as in Spanish: *El hombre abrió la puerta de una patada* 'The man opened the door of [= with] a kick.'

with regard to the verb. The phrase is marked by *hasta*, which means 'up to' or 'as far as' ('up to the room,' 'up to the door'). These journeys are thus nontelic in Aske's sense, or non-boundary-crossing in the sense of Slobin and Hoiting. (The same is true of (6c) from a frog story.)

There are an additional eight Spanish examples of such descriptions of journeys in the translations. All of them either encode details of the path itself, as in (30), or only approach the goal—indicated by *hasta* or *hacia* 'towards.' Some of these even specify three ground elements—indicating that this is possible in Spanish, though it does not occur in any original Spanish examples. For example:

> (31) . . . *echó a correr sendero abajo, entre los setos, hacia el coche.*
> '. . . started to run down the path, through the bushes, towards the car.'
> (Lessing, 1979: 72).
> (32) . . . *los tres hombres caminaron . . . por las calles, desde la cárcel, hasta el extremo de la marisma . . .*
> '. . . the three men walked . . . through the streets, from the jail, to the tip of the marsh . . .' (Michener, 1980: 764)

Such accumulations of locative phrases are not possible with a single motion verb in Spanish if the phrases are telic. Thus the following English journey is broken up into two separate telic phrases in Spanish translation:

> (33) I went into the hall and through to the dining room. (Du Maurier, 1938: 243)
> *Entré en el hall y pasé al comedor.*
> 'I entered in the hall and passed to the dining room.' (Du Maurier, 1959: 348)

Aske examines isolated clauses and presents his constraint in syntactic terms. However, in the analysis of multiclause journeys, it seems to be a rhetorical constraint as well. Consider the journeys described in (13) and (14) above. The first clause in each, taken alone, seems to have a nontelic path phrase: *went through the drawing-room*, *walked through the park*. That is, there is no nonverbal predicate that indicates a particular 'end-of-path location/state of the Figure' (Aske, 1989: 6). Yet these phrases become telic by virtue of the following phrase, which begins another path segment: *went through the drawing-room → to the morning-room*; *walked through the park → and along the avenues*. The second segment assigns an end-state to the first, thus providing a nonverbal predicate by implication. (Following the suggestion of Slobin and Hoiting, 1994, these paths involve a boundary crossing, as indicated by the arrows in the examples.) Accordingly, these single-verb journeys are translated with two-clause constructions: *Pasando por el salón, fui al gabinete* 'Passing through the drawing-room, I went to the morning-room;' *Martha cruzó el parque y paseó a lo largo de las avenidas* 'Martha crossed the park and promenaded along the avenues.'

Given these constraints, Spanish speakers and writers have apparently developed a 'rhetorical set' that favors separate clauses for each segment of a complex motion event. A series of separate clauses, however, retards the fluent depiction of a journey, perhaps leading to a preference to limit the specification of path details unless absolutely necessary. This may be why the average number of verbs per motion event is the same for the Spanish and English novels: something like one to two verbs may represent a comfortable narrative rhythm. Because manner generally requires an additional verb in Spanish, depiction of manner is also curtailed in comparison with English, where it can come along as part of the verb of motion. In addition, each separate main clause demands attention as a foregrounded proposition, thus militating against a proliferation of main clauses, and perhaps favoring subordinate and adverbial clauses in order to maintain a foreground/background contrast. These rhetorical constraints may lead Spanish speakers to make more use of adverbial constructions to encode manner, and more use of descriptive locative constructions such as relative-clause constructions to encode setting.

Once such a rhetorical set has become established in a language, speakers may be loath to go beyond the norm even when there are no syntactic or semantic constraints that block particular expressions. This may explain the findings that only two out of 216 Spanish and Latin American frog-story narrators used the equivalents of 'the dog fell from the window to the ground/street'; that only one used the equivalent of 'he carried him across the field to a cliff;' and that only 8 per cent of motion events in Spanish novels mention two ground elements in one clause. These few examples, along with more extended examples from the translations, demonstrate that some types of construction with two or more locative phrases in a clause are, indeed, possible in Spanish. Yet they 'go against the grain' of the rhetorical use of the language.

There is thus a multifaceted answer to the question of why Spanish narrations of motion events seem so sparse from an English point of view. Part of the answer has to do with characteristics of a verb-framed language. These characteristics also interact with the particular type of lexicon in the language and with general constraints on the types of construction that are licensed. Finally, all of these factors 'train' the speakers—at least from late preschool age onwards—in the development of a particular rhetorical style (Berman and Slobin, 1994). Once established in the discourse and literature of a language, such a style can apparently maintain itself across dialects, and probably across discourse types and genres as well.

Fillmore has pointed to various types of evidence for 'the connection between linguistic forms and matters of rhetoric and usage' (1989: 35). I offer this analysis of the constructions associated with motion events as another piece of evidence for the pragmatic functions of grammar. And, further, I suggest that typologies of grammar have consequences for 'typologies of rhetoric.' The effects of such typologies on usage may be strong enough to influence speakers' narrative attention to particular conceptual domains. And, as a consequence, the meanings of verbs of motion in a given language must be considered in the light of both the typological frame of the language and the discourse frames in which such verbs occur.

REFERENCES

ASKE, J. (1989). 'Path Predicates in English and Spanish: A Closer Look,' *Proceedings of the Fifteenth Annual Meeting of the Berkeley Linguistics Society*, 1–14.

BAMBERG, M. G. W. (1987). *The Acquisition of Narrative: Learning to Use Language*. Berlin: Mouton de Gruyter.

BERMAN, R. A., and SLOBIN, D. I. (1994). *Relating Events in Narrative: A Crosslinguistic Developmental Study*. (Hillsdale, NJ): Erlbaum.

DIETRICH, R., and GRAUMANN, C. F. (eds.) (1989). *Language Processing in Social Context*. Amsterdam: Benjamins.

FILLMORE, C. J. (1988), 'On Grammatical Constructions.' Unpublished paper.
—— (1989). 'Grammatical Construction Theory and the Familiar Dichotomies,' in Dietrich and Graumann (1989: 17–38). Amsterdam: Elsevier.
—— and ATKINS, B. T. (1992). 'Toward a Frame-Based Lexicon: The Semantics of RISK and its Neighbors,' in Lehrer and Kittay (1992: 75–102).

LEHRER, A., and KITTAY, E. V. (eds.) (1992). *Frames, Fields, and Contrasts: New Essays in Semantic and Lexical Organization*. Hillsdale, NJ: Erlbaum.

MAYER, M. (1969). *Frog, Where Are You?* New York: Dial Press.

SEBASTIÁN, E., and SLOBIN, D. I. (1994). 'Development of Linguistic Forms: Spanish,' in Berman and Slobin (1994: 239–84).

SHOPEN, T. (ed.) (1985). *Language Typology and Syntactic Description* iii: *Grammatical Categories and the Lexicon*. Cambridge: Cambridge University Press.

SLOBIN, D. I. (1991). 'Learning to Think for Speaking: Native Language, Cognition, and Rhetorical Style,' *Pragmatics* 1: 7–26.

—— and BOCAZ, A. (1988). 'Learning to Talk About Movement Through Time and Space: The Development of Narrative Abilities in Spanish and English,' *Lenguas modernas* 15: 5–24.

—— and HOITING, N. (1994). 'Reference to Movement in Spoken and Signed languages: Typological Considerations,' *Proceedings of the Twentieth Annual Meeting of the Berkeley Linguistics Society*, 487–505.

TALMY, L. (1985). 'Lexicalization Patterns: Semantic Structure in Lexical Forms,' in Shopen (1985: 36–149).

—— (1991). 'Path to Realization: A Typology of Event Conflation,' *Proceedings of the Seventeenth Annual Meeting of the Berkeley Linguistics Society*, 480–519.

Novels

ALLENDE, I. (1982). *La Casa de los Espíritus*. Barcelona: Plaza & Janes. (1985). *The House of the Spirits*, trans. M. Bogin. New York: Bantam.

DONOSO, J. (1983). *Coronación*. Barcelona: Seix Barral.

DU MAURIER, D. (1938). *Rebecca*. New York: Modern Library. (1959). *Rebeca*, trans. F. Calleja. Barcelona: Plaza & Janes.

FOWLES, J. (1969). *The French Lieutenant's Woman*. Boston: Little, Brown. (1981). *La Mujer del Teniente Francés*, trans. A. M. de la Fuente. Barcelona: Argos Vergara.

GARCÍA MÁRQUEZ, G. (1967 (1982 edn.)). *Cien Años de Soledad*. Madrid: Espasa-Calpe. (1970). *One Hundred Years of Solitude*, trans. G. Rabassa. New York: Bard.

HEMINGWAY, E. (1941 (1976 edn.)). *For Whom the Bell Tolls*. London: Grafton.

LESSING, D. (1952). *A Proper Marriage*. New York: New American Library. (1979). *Un Casamiento Convencional*, trans. F. Parcerisas and A. Samons. Barcelona: Argos Vergara.

MICHENER, J. A. (1978). *Chesapeake*. New York: Fawcett Crest. (1980). *Bahia de Chesapeake*, trans. A. Martín. Barcelona: Plaza & Janes.

SABATO, E. (1988). *El Túnel*. Barcelona: Seix Barral.

VARGAS LLOSA, M. (1977). *La Tía Julia y el Escribidor*. Barcelona: Seix Barral. (1982). *Aunt Julia and the Scriptwriter*, trans. H. R. Lane. New York: Avon.

9

Reasoning, Mappings, and Meta-metaphorical Conditionals

Eve Sweetser

Charles Fillmore's work on conditional constructions (1986; 1990*a*; 1990*b*) has laid out ways in which verb forms and other aspects of conditional structure are mapped onto different aspects of conditional semantics and pragmatics. In some of my own work (Sweetser, 1990) I have examined aspects of conditional interpretation, and even (Sweetser, forthcoming) attempted to build on Fillmore's analysis, and to find added compositionality in the relationship between the forms and meanings of the varied manifestations of conditionals in English. This particular paper is about a class of conditionals which has not to my knowledge been considered in the literature, and which affords a unique glimpse of the power of conditionals in building cognitive structures. In particular, I shall argue that examples like (1–4) provide interesting evidence that metaphorical statements share crucial properties of reasoning structure with literal statements.

(1) If the Île de la Cité is the heart of Paris, the Seine is the aorta
(2) If life is a candle-flame, then people are moths burned on the flame
(3) If Moriarty is the Napoleon of crime, then Holmes is a civilian Wellington[1]
(4) If Scarlett O'Hara is a red rose, then Melanie Wilkes is a violet[2]

Barbara Dancygier and Gilles Fauconnier, both of whose work inspired this paper in crucial ways, have been helpful critics throughout. George Lakoff should also be thanked for his commentary on earlier drafts. The paper's debt to Charles Fillmore will be evident to all readers who know his work: the author's general debt to Fillmore's work and teaching is, however, far greater than can be acknowledged here.

[1] Sherlock Holmes refers to his arch-enemy, the criminal gang leader Professor Moriarty, as 'the Napoleon of crime' (Sir Arthur Conan Doyle. 'The Final Problem'). In this story, Holmes succeeds in finishing off Moriarty, who—rather like Napoleon—is apparently back in business after the British police thought they had destroyed his whole gang. Holmes is thought to have died with Moriarty, but turns out to have survived.
[2] Scarlett O'Hara is the beautiful, strong-willed, and self-centered heroine of

What do all of these conditionals have in common? First, the conditional relationship is clearly not at what I have called the level of *content* (Sweetser, 1990): these sentences do not express conditional dependence of one event or state in the world on another. Melanie won't be a different person if Scarlett is different: rather, we might metaphorically describe Melanie differently if we don't describe Scarlett as a rose. These examples are thus not *content conditionals* like (*a*), but more nearly resemble *epistemic conditionals* such as (*b*), where the conditional relationship is between the speaker's belief in the truth of the protasis and the speaker's conclusion about the apodosis.

(*a*) If Susan gets here in time, we'll go to the party
      (The party-going event will be enabled by the arrival event.)
(*b*) If he typed her thesis, he loves her
      (The loving is not conditioned by the typing, BUT
      belief about the loving is conditioned by knowledge about the typing.)

In the meta-metaphorical conditionals, it is specifically a choice of a metaphorical cognitive mapping which conditions the choice of another such mapping.

Second, the two clauses in each example are presented as harmonious rather than discordant pairings of mappings between mental spaces. Since I intend to make use of Fauconnier's (1985) theory of mental spaces in this paper, it will be useful at this point to distinguish the term *mental space* from other potentially related concepts such as *domain* or *possible world*. As used by Fauconnier, *mental space* is a broad term, in that it covers entities which might indeed be traditionally called domains (such as 'flowers' or 'colors' or 'famous detectives') and others which are more similar to possible worlds. The distinguishing characteristic of mental spaces is that they are structured groupings of cognitive entities and beliefs about those entities, with the possibility of creating mappings and connections between different groupings. Fauconnier explicitly differentiates mental spaces from possible worlds in that not only are mental spaces non-objective, but they are partially rather than completely structured objects. Thus, for example, when I say, 'It would be perfect if only John could come to the meeting,' I don't mean that a world identical to the present one (complete with famines, economic recession, and racial bigotry) would be perfect. I am only evoking a partial cognitive structure, and

Gone With the Wind; Melanie Wilkes—quiet, unglamorous, and good—is her successful rival for Ashley.

trusting the listener to construct the right parts of it and not the wrong ones (for example, that we would expect to get more done at the meeting, or that we would enjoy seeing John). A representation, such as a picture or a story, also creates a partial cognitive structure rather than a full possible world: this cognitive structure is also seen by Fauconnier as a mental space. A very partially structured mental space may indeed be what has traditionally been called a *frame* (Fillmore, 1982) or a *schema*, rather than even resembling a filled-out possible world. Mappings between mental spaces can create counterpart relations between entities in two spaces: for example, between a depiction and the object depicted, or between a literary heroine and a red rose.

Returning to my conditional sentences, then, examples like (1–4) are used specifically to mark conditional relationships between two mappings between one mental space and another. Although other interspace mappings behave very similarly, it is of particular interest that these seem to involve metaphorical mappings—that is, actual viewing of one domain in terms of another via mappings between elements in the two domains. Thus, in (3) there is a mapping between the world of famous criminals and the world of famous military and political figures. (3) states that if we map Moriarty onto Napoleon (here taken to be a prototype of the powerful, brilliant, and evil empire-building military leader), then we should also map Holmes, Moriarty's lifelong opponent, onto Wellington (another great military leader who devoted much of his life to the frustration and eventual defeat of Napoleon's imperialistic expansion). (1) says that if we are metaphorically talking about the Île de la Cité as the heart of Paris, then we should call the Seine the aorta of Paris. Here the two domains are the human body and the city of Paris, and once again, one submapping is conditional on the other.

So the first observation is that conditional forms can be used to refer to the structure of inter-domain metaphorical mappings. The examples above are not talking about conditional relationships between events or states, but purely between mappings from one domain or mental space to another. These mappings are viewed as having a relationship of contingency. Why should one metaphor be contingent on another? Why should conditional forms be used at all for these examples? I shall return to these issues. But let us first examine a little more data.

In many cases, unlike standard conditionals, these conditional pairings of mappings are easily reversible:

(5) If the Seine is Paris' major artery, the Île de la Cité is its heart
(6) If humans are moths, life is the flame on which they burn their wings
(7) If Melanie is a violet, Scarlett is a red rose

Others are not:

(8) If Paris is a body/person, the Île de la Cité is its heart
(9) ?If the Île de la Cité is the heart of Paris, then Paris is a person
(10) ??If the Seine is an artery, then Paris/France/Europe is a person

Crucially, however, other formally similar conditionals would be as obviously 'false' or inappropriate as these are 'true' or appropriate. It is no novelty, in fact, to argue that metaphorical statements can be true or false. Since much of our ordinary everyday language is metaphorical, utterances such as *Prices went up* (when nothing physical moved upwards) or *My heart sank* could not be true or false, without it also being possible to decide whether or not metaphorical conditionals are true.[3]

We are typically more willing to make judgments about the truth of metaphorical statements when the metaphors involved are more conventional (as are the uses of *sink* and *go up* just cited): however, even quite artistic and novel metaphors can be so judged. (11–12), for example, contain metaphorical protases and apodoses which are false because the mappings are not in fact appropriate ones: the submappings represented by the individual clauses are not ones that speakers are likely to accept. Scarlett is *not* a violet, nor Melanie a rose. (This is assuming an interpretation of (11) which involves a false portrayal of Scarlett as a quiet person and Melanie as a flamboyant one: other, potentially true and/or sensible interpretations might be devised, of course.) As is normally the case with a conditional whose protasis is false, it is difficult for speakers to make truth or falsity judgments about the whole conditional statement. These cases contrast with (4) and (1), which involve appropriate mappings between the same domains as those involved in (11) and (12).

(11) If Scarlett is a violet, then Melanie is a rose
(12) If the Île de la Cité is the aorta of Paris, then the Seine is the heart

(13–15) are false, and unsensible, because they involve mappings that are not between the same pair of domains. There is no frame

---

[3] Gentner and Gentner (1983) is a classic article, giving strong evidence not only that we have cognitively real metaphorical models but that the inference structures which come from knowledge of the source domain influence our reasoning about a target domain seen in terms of that source domain.

involving elephants and candle-flames, to be mapped onto the frame of people and human life. Macavity the Mystery Cat does not belong to the same frame as Sherlock Holmes and Moriarty. Telegraph Avenue is an 'aorta' of Berkeley, if of any place—surely not of Paris. The protasis and apodosis are thus not in fact connected, and the conditional relationship is false, as it would be in a non-metaphorical case such as *If you come home by five o'clock, then the nation's economy will recover today*. We cannot readily think of a causal link between coming home at five o'clock and national economic recovery, but in order to interpret this sentence, we set up a context involving such a link. Of course, it may well be a patently false context, and we may assume that the speaker is therefore lying to or kidding the addressee.

(13) ??If Macavity the Mystery Cat is the Napoleon of Crime, then Holmes is a civilian Wellington[4]

(14) ??If life is a candle-flame, humans are elephants

(15) ??If the Île de la Cité is the heart of Paris, Telegraph Avenue is its aorta.

Perhaps most interesting of all, there are some cases where it is apparently acceptable to link metaphorical statements from distinct (but, as we shall see, related) domains, in acceptable and potentially 'true' conditional constructions.

(16) If the Île de la Cité is the heart of Paris, then Columbia is the brain of New York, and Wall Street is the digestive tract

9.1. CONDITIONALS AND MENTAL SPACES

Conditionals create coherent mental spaces, in Fauconnier's (1985) sense of the term. A conditional construction may be used precisely to indicate that the apodosis holds true in the same mental space as the protasis, indeed in a mental space defined by the truth of the protasis. But in these metaphorical cases, the 'coherent' space is a meta-space where the two mappings are done, and we can note that they map counterparts in the two spaces. So the conditional relationship is something like the following. Set up a meta-metaphorical space which is defined by the fact that, in mapping between the space of military

---

[4] Macavity is a character in T. S. Eliot's *Old Possum's Book of Practical Cats*. He is a feline 'master criminal who can defy the law.'

heroes and that of criminals, we are viewing (e.g.) Moriarty as
Napoleon. In this space we are also viewing Holmes as Wellington.

9.1.1. *Reasoning patterns in nonmetaphorical conditionals*

But why are some of the reversed examples of meta-metaphorical conditionals meaningful and reasonable, while others are simply strange,
and not very sensible-sounding? The answer lies, I think, in the
relationship between our reasoning processes (as marked by the conditional form) and metaphorical mappings. The use of meta-
metaphorical conditionals, I would like to claim, gives us evidence
about how we reason via metaphor.

First of all, let us examine some of our usual ways of reasoning with
non-metaphorical conditionals.

From a larger generalization to a sub-case ('Modus Ponens'):

(17) If all Cretans are liars, then this particular Cretan is a liar

not typically from a subcase to a larger generalization:

(18) ??If this particular Cretan is a liar, then all Cretans are liars

But if a subcase is prototypical, central to the category, it may be used
to reason about the category:

(19) If the orange tree likes sun, all citrus trees like sun

Sometimes this kind of reasoning remains implicit, so that a larger
generalization is never stated but simply assumed, permitting another
kind of reasoning, from one subcase to another *via* an assumed larger
generalization:

(20) If the orange tree likes sunshine, so will the lemon tree
      (Assumption: Citrus trees all require similar growing conditions.)
      (Or: the orange tree is a *representative* example of citrus trees.)

If the added premise above is that citrus trees are all similar in their
requirements, then the logic is mathematically allowable. If, however,
the assumption is that the orange is a prototypical citrus, the logic is
anything but standard. Rosch (1978) showed that people do indeed
reason this way: told that robins catch a certain disease, they will be
more likely to conclude that birds in general (and hence chickens, or
eagles) catch it, than if they were told that ostriches catch it. This is because a robin is a more prototypical bird than an ostrich. So our
reasoning is influenced not only by subset relations between categories (like standard logic), but also by the complexities of cognitive

category structure.[5] I will argue that the same is true of our reasoning about metaphorical structures.

Nonmetaphorical conditionals are thus often irreversible, but not always. As we have seen, it is not normally possible to reverse a general-to-specific conditional like (17) and produce a specific-to-general conditional like (18). But given the right kind of category structure, reasoning from specific to general, and sometimes reasoning from specific to another specific case via a general statement (which may be unstated) can be possible. However, the general-to-specific pattern of reasoning should in principle *always* be possible.

9.1.2. *Meta-metaphorical reasoning patterns*

One class of meta-metaphorical examples, like (8) ('If Paris is a body, the Île de la Cité is its heart'), involve reasoning from a higher-level mapping to specific counterpart mappings that are constituents of the higher-level one. The reasoning is that if the whole-to-whole mapping is in place, the corresponding part-to-part mappings which constitute it must also be in place. Thus, if Paris is a body, then the Île de la Cité is the heart.

A second class of examples, like (4) ('If Scarlett O'Hara is a red rose, then Melanie Wilkes is a violet'), are cases where a familiar higher-level metaphorical mapping sanctions reasoning from one submapping to another. Thus, if we already have a higher-level conventional metaphor that WOMEN ARE FLOWERS, then we can evoke that higher-level mapping in comparing Scarlett to a rose, and once it is evoked, we can conclude that Melanie should also be mapped onto a counterpart in the domain of flowers. This discussion has not, of course, motivated the choice of counterparts between domains. It seems clear that Scarlett and Melanie's flower-counterparts could not just be reversed. But my assumption is that these mappings are subject to the same constraints that metaphors are subject to in general. My attempt here is not to explain these particular mappings, but only the structural relations among them.

A third class of examples are essentially cases of one mapping between counterparts being seen as conditional on another such mapping, with some higher-level mapping partly provided by the

[5] See also Mervis and Rosch (1981) and other work by these authors. Lakoff (e.g. 1970; 1987) has given extensive attention to issues of nonstandard logical structure in linguistic categories and in the natural-reasoning structures typically represented in natural language.

linguistic statement of the metaphors. In (1), the protasis 'If the Île de la Cité is the heart of Paris' provides not only one submapping but also half of the higher-level mapping PARIS IS A HUMAN BODY. It is thus not too surprising to find that we can reason from this to another submapping, namely 'the Seine is the aorta.' In general, what Turner (1991: ch. 9) has called 'XYZ' metaphors (metaphors of the form 'X is the Y of Z') fill exactly the functions of giving a submapping and sufficiently indicating a higher-level mapping by giving the relevant target domain.[6] The assumption seems to be that the source domain will be readily identifiable at the higher level, given the rest of the information provided.

Both the Seine–artery mapping and the Île–heart mapping are connections between elements in the two broader domains constituted by our understandings of Paris and of a human body. They are coherent because they both appeal to the same higher-level mapping. The conditional form indicates their coherence. These conditionals are reversible, because the two halves are coequal: one can reason just as well in either direction, as long as the higher-level mapping between Paris and a human body is available as an added premise in the reasoning process.

Perhaps even more interesting are cases like (16), 'If the Île de la Cité is the heart of Paris, then Columbia is the brain of New York, and Wall Street is the digestive tract.' Here lower-level part-to-part mappings are allowed to evoke a higher-level mapping which is superordinate to the whole-to-whole mapping. This superordinate mapping is in turn allowed to evoke part-to-part mappings within other whole-to-whole mappings which it implicitly evokes. Thus, if the Île is Paris's heart, we know (partly from explicit material) that PARIS IS A HUMAN BODY, and if we further assume that Paris is a prototypical (or possibly stereotypical) great city, then we might reason to LARGE CITIES ARE HUMAN BODIES. From this we can get by standard general-to-specific reasoning to NEW YORK IS A HUMAN BODY, and from there to COLUMBIA IS NEW YORK'S BRAIN.

[6] Thus e.g. *Cambridge is the Berkeley of the East* sets up not only a mapping between Cambridge and Berkeley but a target domain for the mapping. The source domain, discoverable without difficulty, is *the West*. Or *The wages of sin is death* provides not only a mapping between death and wages but also another part of the domain within which we are to be construing death, namely its relationship with religion and sin. Our spiritual life, involving sin, is thus mapped onto some relevant source domain which includes wages—presumably the domain of financial exchange. Simply saying *Death is wages* would not give us relevant domains, and would probably thus be unsuccessful at conveying the content of the XYZ metaphor.

The particularly interesting part about the above example is that it shows clearly that metaphorical reasoning patterns are shaped by category structure, like literal reasoning patterns. We would not reason from a metaphor about the structure of Stratford-upon-Avon or College Station, Texas, to metaphors about the structure of New York City, because Stratford and College Station are far from being prototypical examples of large cities.

The metaphorical reasoning pattern that is apparently disallowed is the *explicit* reasoning from part-to-part mappings to whole-to-whole or superordinate mappings. It seems odd to say, 'If the Seine is the main artery of Paris, then Paris is a body.' Is this oddness simply due to obviousness, to the fact that 'X is the Y of Z' partially prespecifies the higher mapping, so why should we state it? If so, we would expect (21) to be sensible:

(21) ???If the Seine is an artery, Paris/France/Europe is a body/person

But (21) is, if anything, worse than the XYZ counterpart. It is hard to pick a higher level of mapping to reason to (several possibilities present themselves), and none of the possibilities makes a very good conditional utterance. Even worse would be an example like:

(22) ???If the Seine is an artery, then cities/countries are people/bodies

In this case, we are attempting to reason from a submapping, not to the whole-to-whole mapping, but directly to a superordinate mapping. This is quite difficult to process, because it is not a reasoning pattern we expect, or see as sanctioned by general rules without further premises being provided. In general, the only reasonable interpretation is one where the superordinate mapping is assumed as part of the basis for the protasis, and therefore it seems redundant to derive it *from* that protasis. Alternatively, to a speaker not already conventionally equipped with a CITIES ARE BODIES metaphor, the protasis of (22) would be hard to process, and the apodosis underivable therefore. If we see metaphorical conditionals as being structured by the same reasoning processes as literal ones, then there is no mystery in the problem of interpreting such examples.

9.1.3. *Some parallel cases*

There are some other examples of conditionals which essentially set up mappings as dependent on each other. Consider, for example, a director doing casting who says (23).

(23) If Andy is Hamlet, then Susie is Ophelia

The director is expressing a dependency relationship, not between two events or states within a space (as he would if he said, *If Andy could act, then he might play Hamlet*), but between two mappings between spaces. In a higher meta-space, there is a coherence between the mapping of Andy (in the 'real-world' or base space) and Hamlet (in the drama space), and another mapping between Susie and Ophelia. The director, of course, is setting up actor–character relationships, not metaphorical mappings between domains.

Fauconnier (to appear) has focussed on another interesting set of examples, which he calls analogical counterfactuals. An example (taken from Fauconnier) is that of a film character who seems callous about the case of a murdered prostitute. An interlocutor says, 'What if it were your sister?' and the unsympathetic character answers, 'I don't have a sister, but *if I did, she wouldn't be a hooker.*' The purport of the conditional here appears to be putting limits on the co-occurrence of mappings between spaces: if you map this character into the imaginary world, and give him a sister there, you still cannot map a dead prostitute (in particular, her status as a prostitute) onto the same individual.

In both of these cases, as with the meta-metaphorical conditionals, the contents of the conditionals cannot be said to have objective truth or falsity. Like the meta-metaphorical conditionals, these examples assert coherence between mappings, and may also establish such coherence in a declarative manner.

Dancygier's (1992; 1993) *metalinguistic conditionals* also provide some close parallels to meta-metaphorical cases. Basic examples of metalinguistic conditionals can be seen in (24–25); the basic function of these conditionals is to conditionally use some particular linguistic form.

(24) If you'll pardon my language, that's *bullshit*
(25) She's practicing her *solfeggio*, if I have the term right

Cases where the metalinguistic comment involves conditional dependence of one linguistic usage on another can be exemplified in (26–8).

(26) If I was a *bad* carpenter, I was a *worse* tailor[7]

---

[7] Example from Defoe's *Robinson Crusoe*, cited by Dancygier (p.c.), who is citing it from Jespersen. The italics are mine.

(27) If he is a *liberal*, then she is a *radical*
      (i.e. If we call him a liberal, the only term left for her is *radical*.)
      [Assumption: She is much further left than he is on the political spectrum, so the same term cannot be used for both.]
(28) If Ann's exam was *brilliant*, we don't even have a word for Sally's
      [Assumption: Sally's exam was much better even than Ann's.]

Since the meta-metaphorical conditionals can be interpreted both as meaning that two cognitive mappings are in a conditional dependency relationship and (simultaneously, in many cases) that one metaphorical expression is likely to be used if another is used, it is not surprising that they show similarities in behavior to both epistemic and metalinguistic conditional expressions.

Another related set of examples which has been discussed in the literature is Akatsuka's (1986) observations on the way in which conditionals like 'If you're the Pope, then I'm the Empress of China' are related to standard conditional reasoning structures. She very intelligently observes that truth value alone cannot be the crucial factor in setting up these reasoning structures—'If you're so smart, why aren't you rich?' is quite similar in reasoning structure, yet questions do not have truth values.[8] Here is another case where conditionals cannot be seen as traditional truth-conditional reasoning structures, yet are regular representations of structured reasoning processes.

9.2. CONCLUSIONS

The central conclusion of this paper is simply that meta-metaphorical and other meta-mapping conditional uses are normal conditional uses, and are subject to interpretation via the same kinds of reasoning processes that we use to interpret literal conditionals which refer to real-world ('content') conditional relationships between events or states. It is my hope that not only will there be further exploration of the interaction between mapping processes and reasoning, but also that these observations have contributed to our general understanding of metaphor as not separable from logic and reasoning.

Given the data mentioned above, *If* and *then* can't simply mean what we once thought they did, and the cognitive structure of 'better-behaved' conditionals—that is, ones that seemed more amenable to

---

[8] Cf. Sweetser (1990) for some further observations on these structures, considered as a class of speech-act conditionals.

objective logical analysis—is called into question as well. If we reason via metaphor and analogy, using mental spaces and pragmatic inferences as basic interconnections in our logical processes, then the motivation for the entire structure of logic and human reasoning needs a serious re-examination.[9]

REFERENCES

AKATSUKA, N. (1986). 'Conditionals Are Discourse-Bound,' in *On Conditionals*, E. C. Traugott, A. Ter Meulen, J. S. Reilly, and C. A. Ferguson (eds.), *On Conditionals*, 333–52. Cambridge: Cambridge University Press.

DANCYGIER, B. (1992). 'Two Metatextual Operators: Negation and Conditionality in Polish,' *Proceedings of the Eighteenth Annual Meeting of the Berkeley Linguistics Society*, 61–75.

—— (1993). 'Interpreting Conditionals: Time, Knowledge and Causation,' *Journal of Pragmatics* **19**: 403–34.

FAUCONNIER, G. (1985). *Mental Spaces: Roles and Strategies*. Cambridge, Mass.: MIT Press; repr. Cambridge University Press, 1994.

—— (forthcoming). 'Analogical counterfactuals,' in G. Fauconnier and E. Sweetser (eds.), *Spaces, Worlds, and Grammars*. Chicago: University of Chicago Press.

FILLMORE, C. J. (1982). 'Frame Semantics,' in Linguistic Society of Korea (ed.), In *Linguistics in the Morning Calm*, 111–37. Seoul: Hanshin for the Linguistic Society of Korea.

—— (1986). Varieties of Conditional Sentences, *Eastern States Conference on Linguistics* **3**: 163–82.

—— (1990a). 'Epistemic Stance and Grammatical Form in English Conditional Sentences,' *Papers from the Twenty-Sixth Regional Meeting of the Chicago Linguistic Society* i: *The Main Session*, 137–62.

—— (1990b). 'The Contribution of Linguistics to Language Understanding,' in A. Bocaz (ed.), *Proceedings of the First Symposium on Cognition, Language, and Culture* (University of Chile), 109–28.

GENTNER, D., and GENTNER, D. R. (1983). 'Flowing Waters or Teeming Crowds: Mental Models of Electricity,' in D. Gentner and A. L. Stevens (eds.), *Mental Models*, 99–129. Hillsdale, NJ: Erlbaum.

JOHNSON, M. (1987). *The Body in the Mind: The Bodily Basis of Meaning, Reason, and Imagination*. Chicago: University of Chicago Press.

LAKOFF, G. (1970). *Linguistics and Natural Logic*. Ann Arbor: University of Michigan Linguistics Dept.; repr. in D. Davidson and G. Harman (eds.), *Semantics of Natural Language*. Dordrecht: Reidel, 1972.

[9] Cf. Lakoff and Johnson (1980), Johnson (1987), for claims about the basis of rationality in physical experience and in metaphorical mappings.

—— 1987. *Women, Fire and Dangerous Things: What Categories Reveal About the Mind*. Chicago: University of Chicago Press.

LAKOFF, G., and JOHNSON, M. (1980). *Metaphors We Live By*. Chicago: University of Chicago Press.

MERVIS, C., and ROSCH, E. (1981). 'Categorization of Natural Objects,' *Annual Review of Psychology* **32**: 89–115.

ROSCH, E. (1978). 'Principles of Categorization,' in E. Rosch and B. B. Lloyd (eds.), *Cognition and Categorization*. Hillsdale, NJ: Erlbaum.

SWEETSER, E. (1990). *From Etymology to Pragmatics: Metaphorical and Cultural Aspects of Semantics*. Cambridge: Cambridge University Press.

—— (forthcoming). 'Mental Spaces and the Grammar of Conditional Constructions,' in G. Fauconnier and E. Sweetser (eds.), *Spaces, Worlds and Grammars*. Chicago: University of Chicago Press.

TURNER, M. (1991). *Reading Minds: The Study of English in the Age of Cognitive Science*. Princeton, NJ: Princeton University Press.

10

The Windowing of Attention in Language

Leonard Talmy

INTRODUCTION

Using the perspectives and methods of Cognitive Linguistics, this paper sets forth the system with which languages can place a portion of a coherent referent situation into the foreground of attention by the explicit mention of that portion, while placing the remainder of that situation into the background of attention by omitting mention of it. Terminologically, the cognitive process at work here is called the *windowing of attention*, the coherent referent situation with respect to which the windowing must take place is an *event-frame*, the portions that are foregrounded by inclusion are *windowed*, and the portions that are backgrounded by exclusion are *gapped*. In engaging this subject, the paper treats a number of phenomena. It examines five generic types of event-frame—a path, a causal chain, a cycle, a participant interaction, and an interrelationship—and it considers the cognitive factors that constitute and bound such event-frames. It examines the properties of the windowing process, including its capacity for embedding or for multiple co-occurrence, as well as the functions that this process may serve within the overall organization of cognition. It investigates a number of concomitant cognitive phenomena including the nature of attention; foregrounding and backgrounding; conceptual alternativity; cognitive splicing; goal-schema constancy; causal transparency and the sense of causal immediacy versus distance; conceptual contrast frames; and the systematic relationship of factuality to affect states and explanation types. It speculates on correlations between the windowing structure in language and comparable structuring in perception and motor control, including the ways in which these are manifested in the experiments of virtual reality. And it observes

For their advice and assistance, my thanks go to Kean Kaufmann, Ruth Shields, Robert Van Valin, and David Wilkins.

the commonality of windowing structure in spoken language and in the sign-language systems spontaneously developed by certain deaf children, a commonality that testifies to the fundamental character of the cognitive structure presented here.

The windowing of attention is just one fragment of the much vaster cognitive system constituting the conceptual structuring of language. Specifically, the windowing of attention—along with level of attention, center of attention, scope of attention, and network of attention—is part of the larger cognitive structural category in language that we have termed the *distribution of attention*. In turn, the category of the distribution of attention is an *imaging system*, and this—along with other imaging systems such as configurational structure, location of perspective point, force dynamics, and cognitive state—together constitute the fundamental delineation of conceptual structuring in language.[1]

10.1. THE NATURE OF ATTENTIONAL WINDOWING

Linguistic forms can direct the distribution of one's attention over a referent scene in a certain type of pattern, the placement of one or more *windows* of greatest attention over the scene, in a process that can be termed the *windowing* of attention. In this process, one or more portions of a referent scene—where each portion has internal continuity but is discontinuous from any other selected portion—will be placed in the foreground of attention while the remainder of the scene is backgrounded. The most fundamental formal linguistic device that mediates this cognitive process is—straightforwardly—the inclusion in a sentence of explicit material referring to the portion or portions of the total scene that are to be foregrounded, and the omission of

[1] A brief note can help place the present paper within the context of the author's publications. The general framework for the representation of conceptual structure in language is set forth in Talmy (1988*a*). That paper includes the description of one portion of the imaging system that concerns the distribution of attention. The present paper consists of new material that describes an additional portion of that imaging system, while still further portions are scheduled for written description. The plan is next to combine these latter separate descriptions into a single article on the whole imaging system of the distribution of attention. This article in turn will then be combined with works on the other imaging systems. This last unification would then constitute an updated overall description of the framework for the representation of conceptual structure in language, in an analysis that would now be organized around the imaging systems.

material that would refer to the remainder of the scene intended for backgrounding. This device is the only one to be treated here and the one for which the term 'windowing' will be reserved.[2] Although only a certain portion or portions of the referent scene are explicitly specified when thus windowed, it is understood as part of the nature of the windowing process that—given the appropriate context—the addressee will be able to infer the remainder of the scene. Generally, the same referent scene can be windowed in any of several different ways— that is, different patterns of selected windows can be placed over the scene. This latitude is another manifestation of the fundamental linguistic property of *conceptual alternativity* described in Talmy (1983), and it will be exemplified in all the categories of windowing treated below.

To introduce some of the terminology employed below, a referent scene that is sequential in nature or that has been sequentialized conceptually can have a window of strongest attention placed over its beginning, middle, or end portion—or, as will be said here, may have *initial, medial,* or *final windowing.* On the other hand, such a scene can have a particular portion without a window upon it, backgrounded by the lack of sentence constituents referring to it, and accordingly here be said to have *initial, medial,* or *final gapping.*

10.1.1. *The event-frame*

To be viable, the concept of windowing requires a basis on which to distinguish between two kinds of material missing from a sentence: a kind whose referent would indeed be understood as belonging to the represented scene, and another kind whose referent would be felt as peripheral or incidental. Serving such a function, something like the following consideration is needed. Arising from whatever causes, whether in part innately universal ones or in part linguistically or culturally specific ones, language-users apparently tend to conceive

---

[2] This factor, the presence versus the absence of overt language material, is only one linguistic device for the setting of attentional salience. Other devices, to be treated in subsequent work, include the following: hierarchy among grammatical categories, hierarchy of grammatical relations, positioning at certain sentence locations instead of other locations, head versus non-head constituency within a construction, degree of morphological autonomy, solo expression versus joint conflation, phonological length, and degree of stress. While most of these other devices can place attention along a gradient, windowing is taken to set attentional salience at two discrete levels: relatively foregrounded or backgrounded.

certain elements and their interrelations as belonging together as the central identifying core of a particular event or event type. Other elements, which on other grounds might have seemed to share an equally intimate involvement in the event, are instead conceptualized as peripheral or incidental.

A set of conceptual elements and interrelationships that in this way are evoked together or co-evoke each other can be said to lie within or to constitute an *event-frame*, while the elements that are conceived of as incidental—whether evoked weakly or not at all—lie outside the event-frame. Prominent examples of event-frames include the so-conceived entirety of an object's path, that of a causal chain, and that of an interchange of entities (including an exchange of possessions, as in Fillmore's 'commercial event'). Typically *not* included within an event-frame, however, are, for example, the day of the week on which an event occurred, the geographic locale in which the event occurred, the ambient temperature of the space in which the event occurred, or the state of health of a participant in the event—even though such factors can be fully or even necessarily as much involved in an event as those factors which do get treated as part of the event.

This notion of an event-frame is very close to Fillmore's (e.g. 1982) concept of a frame or scene when applied to an event, but there appear to be several differences of emphasis or of conceptual basis. First, where Fillmore emphasizes mainly the copresence of certain interrelated conceptual elements, our notion of an event-frame is intended to stress as well the exclusion of other conceptual elements from the privileged core. Second, a frame for Fillmore seems to represent a concept or phenomenon that may be specific to a particular language or set of languages and that may be determined only within a particular sociocultural context. Our event-frame, however, is generally understood as a more generic category that is quite likely universal across languages, that at least in part corresponds to the structuring in other cognitive systems such as visual perception, and that may well be innately determined. Such a generic status is thus assumed for the event-frame types treated below—hence, for the path, the causal-chain, the cycle, the participant-interaction, and the interrelationship event-frames. Fillmore's commercial scene, which involves an exchange of possessions, thus might under further investigation come to be seen as constituting only one particular form of a generic type of event-frame that consists of an interchange of entities and that is demarcated in accordance with some general factor such as reciprocity or symmetry.

It remains to be determined whether there are relatively general conceptual factors or cognitive principles that govern which clusterings of conceptual material are felt to constitute coherent eventframes of particular types. To this end, the analysis below successively posits a number of factors that may contribute to the demarcation of different types of event-frame. To preview them, we can at this point indicate the factors that will be proposed. First, in an eventframe of motion, the so-conceived entirety of an object's path may be demarcated by periods of stationariness that temporally bound the period of motion; by 'path singularities,' i.e. abrupt qualitative shifts in the path direction or in the surrounding medium; by a normative scope of perception; by the analysis of a path complex into an embedded structure of one path nested within another; by the spatial coincidence of two points of a path when this path is closed; or by two bilaterally symmetric elements that represent corresponding points in a reflection about a central axis. Second, in an event-frame of agentive causation, the so-conceived entirety of a causal chain may be demarcated by the initiating volitional act of an agent and by the final goal that the agent intends as a result of this act, where this act and goal mark the beginning and the end of the agent's scope of intention. Third, in a cyclic event-frame, the so-conceived entirety of a cycle is generally demarcated by two temporal points that bear the same phase relation to two congruent stretches of occurrence, where these two points are conceptualized as part of a 'home' phase. Fourth, in a participant-interaction event-frame, the occurrence of two distinct punctual events that are extrinsic to a certain circumstance which extends through time can mark out a portion of that circumstance and establish that portion conceptually as an event-frame. And, finally, an interrelationship event-frame can be demarcated by the coentailment of its component elements; by the complementary relationship of its component elements where there are only two of these; or by the capacity of its component elements to function as alternative conceptualizations juxtaposed within a single comparison frame.

Given such relatively general factors that help determine those portions of conceptual material that will be felt to constitute unitary coherent event-frames, is there any still more general cognitive principle that runs in common through these factors or that characterizes the ways in which they function to demarcate the event-frames? Such a principle seems to be that the organizing factors function to establish what is conceptualized as a ***boundary*** around the portion of conceptual material constituting the event-frame. This boundary separates that portion from other conceptual material. As might be expected, such a boundary—and hence an event-frame in general—exhibits various prototype effects such as those described by Rosch (1978) and Lakoff (1987). For example, the boundary might not be a sharp line but a gradient zone, and its particular scope and contour—hence, the particular quantity and portions of material that it encloses—might vary in accordance with the specific context or type of context. Nevertheless, some sense of boundary appears to be present across the relevant cases and to govern certain associated characteristics. First among such characteristics is the definitional one that the material enclosed within the boundary is felt to constitute a unitary coherent conceptual entity distinct from the material outside the boundary. Second, there seems to be some sense of *connectivity* throughout the material enclosed within the boundary and, contrariwise, some sense of *discontinuity* or *disjuncture* across the boundary between the enclosed and the external material. Such conceptualized connectivity and disjuncture might be spatial, temporal, or causal, for example, or might further pertain to information or to perception. Heuristically, thus, it might be spatial, where within the boundary there is access from any one point to any other point without blockage but where the boundary acts as a barrier to movement from points within to points outside; or temporal, where the material within the boundary extends through a continuous period of time without gaps, but where this material is conceptually excerpted from the surrounding flow of time; or causal, where effects can freely propagate within the boundary but not beyond it. Further, it might be informational, where information or knowledge about particular phenomena held at one point is available at other points within the boundary but not to or from points outside the boundary; or perceptual, where there is perception of all points within the boundary from any point also within it, but not perception of points or from points outside the boundary. Third, the various portions of the material within the boundary are felt to be *corelevant* to each other, whereas the material outside the boundary is not relevant to that within. This sense of relevance may be able to override the different forms of connectivity, e.g. in a commercial scene, bringing together just those participants during those periods of action that constitute the exchange of goods and money, excerpted from their spatio-temporal surround.

10.1.2. *Event-frames and complement structure*

Undoubtedly, something of this sense for what lies inside and what lies outside a conceptual event-frame has motivated syntacticians, beyond purely formal evidence, to distinguish between 'complements' and 'adjuncts,' respectively. But the explicit positing of the event-frame as a linguistic entity permits an elaboration of complement structure theory that might not otherwise be possible. Current theory recognizes two types of complement to a lexical item that represent its semantic arguments: an obligatory complement, which must accompany the lexical item, and an optional complement, which may or may not do so. To these two types of complement we could add a third type, a ***blocked complement***, to be adduced where a predicate arguably has an associated argument that cannot be expressed in construction with the particular lexical item.[3] In our terms, such an argument would be felt to be an intrinsic part of a particular conceptually coherent event-frame, an argument that might be expressed in construction with some other lexical item that refers to this event-frame but one that cannot be expressed in construction with the lexical item in question. Fig. 10.1 shows these relationships. Here, the large rectangle represents a particular event-frame; inside the rectangle, the solid-line square represents an obligatory complement, the dotted-line square an optional complement, and the X-line square a blocked complement; and outside the rectangle, the dotted-line square represents an element that can be optionally expressed as an adjunct.

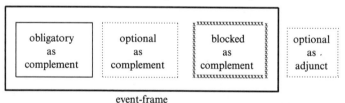

event-frame

Fig. 10.1. Types of linguistic realization of conceptual elements inside and outside an event-frame

All three types of complement, as well as adjuncts, can be illustrated for the verb *spend*, which invokes the Fillmorean commercial scene

---

[3] Some precedent for the notion of a blocked complement is present in Jackendoff's (1990) 'constant argument,' which can be expressed in an optional complement when specific but which, in effect, is blocked in standard speech when generic. An example of a constant argument is the argument pertaining to money in connection with the verb *buy*. Thus, one can say *I bought the book for $50*, but not **I bought the book for money*.

that includes as arguments a seller, a buyer, goods, and money. Thus, the sentence in (1) shows in italic the verb's obligatory complements, the buyer as subject, and the money as object; shows in parentheses an optional complement, the goods as prepositional object; shows in square brackets a blocked complement, the seller in an attempted oblique constituent; and shows in braces two optional adjuncts referring to locale and day of week.

(1) *I* spent *fifty dollars* (for/on this book) [*from/by/to/for/. . . the clerk] {at that store} {last Friday}.

To illustrate the potential extent of complement blockage, we can consider what may be posited as the event-frame for force dynamics (Talmy, 1988b), which necessarily includes an Antagonist and an Agonist, the two main entities engaged or potentially engaged in an opposing-force interaction. The verb *permit* refers to one such force-dynamic event-frame and requires complements referring to both of the force entities—the Antagonist as subject and the Agonist as direct object—as seen in (2a). But, in their force-dynamic usage, the English modals regularly block expression of the Antagonist, requiring solely the Agonist as subject. This is seen in (2b) for the modal *may*, which refers to the same type of force dynamic event-frame as *permit*.

(2a) I permit you to go to the park
(2b) You may go to the park (*by / from / . . . me)

The force-dynamic event-frame further serves as the event-frame for a more extended form of complement-blocking. In one of its constructions, the verb *require*, like *permit*, refers to a particular type of force-dynamic event-frame and requires complements referring to both of the force entities—again, the Antagonist as subject and the Agonist as direct object—as seen in (3a). The modal *must*, which refers to the same type of force-dynamic event-frame as *require*, can participate in the usual modal construction just seen in (2b)—blocking expression of the Antagonist and requiring expression of the Agonist as subject—as in (3b). But most modals can participate in a still further construction, characterized in Talmy (1988a) as involving 'Agonist demotion,' that exhibits an extreme case of complement blockage: it blocks complements referring both to the Antagonist and to the Agonist—that is, it blocks the entire substantive core of the force-dynamic event-frame, as illustrated for *must* in (3c).

(3*a*) I require that you let the cat stay in the box
(3*b*) You must let the cat stay in the box (*by / from . . . me)
(3*c*) The cat must stay in the box (*by / from / . . . you, *by / from / . . . me)

To argue out some of the theoretical issues, we note that one view concerning the complement structure of a lexical item holds that this structure—its requirements, allowances, and exclusions—is exactly consonant with the semantic structure of the lexical item, if that semantic structure is assessed adequately. On this view, there can be no such thing as a blocked complement, since the semantics of the lexical item could have no component which lacks a corresponding syntactic component. For example, a proponent of this view might argue, on the basis of sentences like *I spent fifty dollars and a hundred hours of my time on that modem kit*, that the verb *spend* does not really involve the notion of a seller but rather refers to a frame more generic and smaller than a full commercial scene, one that contains an agent expending possessed resources in order to attain a desired goal, so that it is no surprise that the verb's complement structure would exclude reference to a seller. But a closer inspection reveals that when *spend* is used to refer to the outlay of money, as against other kinds of resource, that money must in fact go to a seller engaged with the agent in a standard commercial transaction. For example, in the preceding illustrative sentence, the verb *spend* could not have been used if the fifty dollars had not been given to a seller in exchange for the kit but rather, say, was used as paper ignited to melt solder. Further, the verb *spend* cannot even be used, say, in **I spent fifty dollars on their ritual mask*, if in exchange for the mask the money was given to native tribespeople who wanted it for its esthetic or curiosity value rather than as part of our standard commercial transaction (as observed by Kean Kaufmann). Thus, when applied to money, the verb *spend* still requires the participation of a knowing seller, even though this participant cannot be expressed by a complement of the verb.[4] With evidence such as this, we

---

[4] This argument is further strengthened by the fact that it has been conducted over examples containing the more liberal of the two prepositions—*on* instead of *for*—that *spend* permits with its goods-specifying complement, for instance, above with *that modem kit*. With *on*, not only can the expenditure of non-monetary resources be mentioned, but the money itself could have been used either to buy the goods mentioned or to purchase other things—e.g. paint, tools, insurance, expert advice—for use in the maintenance of the goods. But the use of the alternative preposition, *for*, permits reference only to money used in exchange for the goods and precludes reference to the expenditure of other resources: *I spent fifty dollars (*and a hundred hours of my time) for that modem kit*.

would therefore maintain the contrary view that, while there is generally much correspondence in language between the system of formal syntactic structure and the system of semantic structure, the two systems nevertheless each have at least in part their own independent structuring patterns and principles. One possibility is that the semantic structure which pertains to event-frames derives from, or is simply composed of, the structure of our conceptual organization, a structure that perhaps is in part innate and universal, while the syntactic complement structure of particular lexical forms in a language can either directly reflect that semantic structure or partially deviate from it in a kind of frozen grammaticization.

We now examine in sequence several different types of event-frame for the forms of attentional windowing that they support.

10.2. PATH WINDOWING

The first type of event-frame considered is that of the so-conceived entirety of a path of motion, here termed a ***path event-frame***, with respect to which the windowing process can be termed ***path windowing***. This windowing process can be treated with respect to three different categories of paths—open paths, closed paths, and fictive paths—all of which can exhibit a cognitive process called cognitive splicing.

10.2.1. *Open path*

An *open path* here will refer to a path that is described by an object physically in motion in the course of a period of time, that is conceptualized as an entire unity thus having a beginning and an end, and whose beginning point and ending point are at different locations in space. To illustrate open-path windowing, the example in (4) pertains to a single particular instantiation of the open-path type but with various patterns of windowing and gapping imposed on it. Thus, (4a) presents the event with maximal windowing over the whole of the conceptually complete path, while (4b) presents three forms of gapping over one portion of the path and (4c) presents three forms of windowing over one portion of the path. It is understood here that the gapped portions are attentionally backgrounded relative to the foregrounded windowed portions but that, given sufficient context, a hearer would reconstruct each of the partially gapped paths in (4b c) into the same conceptualization of a complete path.

(4) The crate that was in the aircraft's cargo bay fell—
    (*a*) with maximal windowing over the whole of the so-conceived entire
        path:
        —out of the plane through the air into the ocean
    (*b*) with gapping over one portion of the path:
        1. medial gapping = initial + final windowing
        —out of the plane into the ocean
        2. initial gapping = medial + final windowing
        —through the air into the ocean
        3. final gapping = initial + medial windowing
        —out of the airplane through the air
    (*c*) with windowing over one portion of the path:
        1. initial windowing = medial + final gapping
        —out of the airplane
        2. medial windowing = initial + final gapping
        —through the air
        3. final windowing = initial + medial gapping
        —into the ocean

We can suggest factors that may play a role in the putative cognitive processes by which an open path becomes conceptualized as an event-frame, i.e. as a unitary event bounded off from surrounding material of space, time, or other qualitative dimensions. One such factor might be the scope of perception that one might imagine as being normatively or canonically available at the referent scene. For instance, in generating or in interpreting the sentences of the preceding example, a speaker or a hearer might imagistically locate a viewpoint for themselves at a canonic position between the aircraft and the ocean whence the crate's path from the plane to the ocean would fall within the available scope of perception and thereby be treated as a unity. Since from such a viewpoint the crate would not be visible either in its prior motion while in the cargo bay or in its subsequent motion through the water to the ocean floor, such additional surrounding paths of motion would be excluded from the event-frame in the operation of the putative scope-of-perception factor.

Another possible cognitive factor would function to frame together a sequence of phenomena that was assessed as having one qualitative character and separate that off from otherwise adjoining sequences assessed as being qualitatively different. One form of this factor, involving stationary boundary periods, would treat a period of stationariness as qualitatively distinct from a period of motion, so that the attribute of unitary entityhood could be cognitively ascribed to a period of continuous motion that was bounded by two stationary periods. Although perhaps otherwise frequent, this form of the factor would not play a role in the preceding aircraft example, since the crate is in fact in motion both before and after the path represented in the sentences. However, the factor of qualitative difference may have other forms, ones that would apply to the example. One such form might be the treatment of a conceivedly abrupt shift in path direction as marking the distinction between two qualitatively distinct paths and the conceivedly sharp-angled point of the shift as marking the boundary between the two paths. Such a 'path singularity' form of the factor could be at work in the aircraft example to mark the beginning-point of the crate's fall. Another form of the qualitative factor might address any abrupt shift in the character of the space surrounding a path, e.g. a change in the ambient medium. This form of the factor could then apply in the example to the passage of the crate's path from air to water, treating that as the endpoint of the preceding portion of motion. When they have the requisite character, certain qualitative shifts in a path complex may lead to a conceptual reanalysis of the path into an embedded structure consisting of one smaller distinct path nested within a larger path that can then act as a background reference frame. Thus, though the crate in the aircraft example may be assumed to have objectively traced out a complex path consisting of a horizontal segment followed by a descending parabola, a hearer of the example sentence would probably reconceptualize the motion situation as involving an attentionally salient straight downward vertical path that is abstracted out as separate from an attentionally back-grounded horizontal forward path that preceded the vertical plummet and that the aircraft maintains after dropping the crate. The simpler parts of such a conceptually nested path structure would tend to be demarcated by the so-conceived singularity points located at qualitative shifts.

10.2.2. *Closed path*

The second kind of path, here termed a *closed path*, will refer to the same kind of entity as the open path described in the preceding section with the exception that its beginning-point and endpoint coincide at the same location in space, so that the path now constitutes a circuit. If this single starting-and endpoint is treated as lying outside the motional path itself and hence outside the event-frame, then the initial, medial, and final portions of the event can be additionally identified as being the 'departure,' the 'away,' and the 'return' portions of the path. The cognitive factors for demarcating an event-frame that were adduced in the preceding section might all serve in bounding a closed path as well, with perhaps the factor pertaining to stationary boundary periods as the likeliest to play a role. In the case of a closed path, however, we can perhaps adduce an additional factor, that of spatial coincidence—i.e. the fact that two points of the path occupy the same location in space—which permits the conceptualization of the stretch of path looping to and from this location as a unitary entity. This closed-path type will figure below as well in the treatment of cycles with phase windowing.

Illustrating this closed-path type is the example in (5). Given the context, the whole event in (5a) can effectively be evoked by any of the alternatives of windowing indicated in (5b): basically, all the possibilities occur except windowing of the departure portion alone. Again, the windowed portions are foregrounded in attention while the gapped portions are backgrounded.

(5a) [I need the milk.]
     (1) Go (2) get it out of the refrigerator (3) (and) bring it here
(5b) The whole can be represented by:
    A. 2:   Get it out of the refrigerator
    B. 3:   Bring it here
    C. 1 + 2:   Go get it out of the refrigerator
    D. 2 + 3:   Get it out of the refrigerator and bring it here
    E. 1 + 3:   Go bring it here
    F. 1 + 2 + 3: Go get it out of the refrigerator and bring it here

10.2.3. *Fictive path*

A spatial configuration that is otherwise understood as static through time can often be alternatively conceptualized so as to be rendered 'conceptually sequentialized' and to include a path of 'fictive motion' (as characterized in Talmy, 1988a; 1990; forthcoming). One type of such a *fictive path* is the 'trajectory' exhibited by a person's focus of attention shifting over a conceived scene. When the linguistic formulation of a sentence is of the sort that can direct a hearer's attention along such a trajectory, this indication of a fictive path is amenable to the same windowing patterns as is a reference to a path of physical motion. One English construction that directs one's attentional focus along a spatial path in this way is 'X BE across Y from Z.' This construction is comparable to the construction 'X BE between Y and Z' in that both specify a complex spatial schema that includes two reference points (the Ground objects Y and Z). (For our 'Figure' and 'Ground' notions, see section 10.6.1 or Talmy, 1978.) But the 'between' construction calls for a stationary distal perspective point with global scope of attention over the spatial schema as a whole, whereas the 'across from' construction specifies a moving proximal perspective point with local scope of attention upon elements of the schema taken in sequence. In particular, the construction directs that one's focus of attention describe a path that begins at point Z, that next traverses the extent of Y, and that lastly terminates at point X. This construction thus specifies a fictive equivalent of an open path. The construction is exemplified for two different referent scenes in (6), shown with full windowing, medial gapping, and initial gapping, respectively.

(6a) with maximal windowing:
      My bike is across the street from the bakery
      Jane sat across the table from John
(6b) with medial gapping:
      My bike is across from the bakery
      Jane sat across from John
(6c) with initial gapping:
      My bike is across the street
      Jane sat across the table

In the (b) forms, the spatial complex is medial-gapped by the omission of the Y component of the construction. Here, the gapped portion is backgrounded and its identity is generally provided by the context or by convention, while the discontinuously windowed portions, the Figure and 'initial Ground,' are conceptually abutted against each other (as described further in the next section). In the (c) forms, the spatial complex is initial-gapped by omission of the entire 'from Z' constituent. In this case, again, the backgrounding of the initial reference point is associated with the assumption that its identity is clear from the context or from convention. To illustrate and elaborate this idea with a sentence like *The injured cow is across the field*, the implicit initial point is typically (a) a location already in reference (e.g. across from where I had said the tractor had broken down), or (b) the current deictic center (e.g. across from where we are now standing), or possibly (c) a canonical location (say, across from the only gas station on the road).

Again, the cognitive factors for demarcating an event-frame that were adduced earlier for an open path of physical motion might all serve in bounding a fictive open path. However, in the case of the 'across from' schema and certain other fictive path types, one may perhaps adduce an additional factor of bilateral symmetry, where the two X and Z elements that can be understood as bounding the event-frame can in some respect be taken to represent corresponding points in a reflection about a central axis. A factor of this sort seems more evident where the two elements have reversed geometries, e.g. have fronts pointing in opposite directions so as to face each other, as would generally be inferred for the scenes represented by sentences like *Jane sat across from John* or *The couch was located opposite the armchair*. But even in the scene represented by the sentence *My bike is across the street from the bakery*, the bike and the bakery can in some sense be regarded as the bilaterally symmetric 'bookends' at either end of a path that lies a bit beyond either side of a geometric strip (the street).

10.2.4. *Conceptual splicing*

With particular regard to the attentional backgrounding that takes place for the medial path portion, consider together all the medial-gapped forms of path windowing above: *The crate fell out of the plane into the ocean, Go bring the milk here, My bike is across from the bakery*, and *Jane sat across from John*. For these and similar cases, the medial portion of the path in some hearers' cognitive representations may reduce to so minimal a state in conscious conceptualization that the discontinuous initial and final phases may seem to run together contiguously, perhaps even seamlessly. This cognitive phenomenon can be termed *conceptual splicing*, and may be taken to constitute a particularly significant cognitive process. The next section will present further forms of conceptual splicing and will explore its cognitive ramifications.

10.3. CAUSAL-CHAIN WINDOWING

What on other grounds and in other cognitive systems can be understood as a 'causal continuum' is, instead, in the conceptual organization that seems to underlie much of the linguistic and, no doubt, additional cognitive systems, prototypically conceptualized as a sequence of linked 'events,' or 'subevents'—i.e. the equivalent of a so-conceived chunking of the continuum into relatively discrete packets—in which the sense of causality may be associated only with the boundary between each subevent and its linked successor.[5] A causal chain can constitute another type of sequential event-frame, a *causal-chain event-frame*, that exhibits windowing of attention, in what may be termed *causal-chain windowing*. Analyzed in the way that seems to underlie much linguistic structure and possibly other cognitive structure as well, the type of causal chain that is understood to be initiated by an intentional agent progresses through the sequence of subevents characterized next and schematized in (7) (cf. Talmy, 1976): The cognitive agent first intends that a particular event will occur and that it will result from his action. The agent thereupon generates an act of volition, a subevent that will cause a certain whole-body or body-part motion in the case where the intended outcome is in the physical realm. The resulting bodily motion is a subevent that will then—in the case where it is not itself the final intended outcome—cause a second physical subevent. To this point, three levels of initiation can be distinguished: the agent's original conceiving of an intention can be regarded as the event that initiates the entire processual complex, with its identifying of a goal and the steps that can lead thereto; the volitional act can be regarded as the subevent that initiates the full causal sequence of subevents; and the bodily motion can be regarded as the subevent that initiates the physical portion of this causal sequence. Resulting from the subevent of bodily motion, there may then ensue an intermediate, causally linked chain of subevents that will lead to the penultimate subevent. Resulting from the body-motion subevent or from the last in an intermediate chain of subevents, there may next occur a penultimate subevent, which would thus constitute the immediate cause of the final result. Finally, caused by one of the preceding subevents, there takes place the final resulting subevent, that is, the goal that the agent originally aimed for as the end of his scope of intention.

(7) semantic composition of a physical causal chain with an initiatory intentional agent:

---

[5] In less prototypical conceptualizations, the causality can encompass not only direct causation but also allowance or enablement, and it can occur not only at the boundary marking the end of one subevent and the start of another subevent (onset causation) but also throughout the duration of a single subevent (extended causation) (cf. Talmy, 1976; 1988*b*).

agent's scope of intention

[————————————→]

[1] → [2] → [3] → [4] → [5]

sequence of causally chained subevents

[1]: agent's act of volition that activates bodily motion

[2]: bodily motion of the agent (particular body part(s) or whole body) that initiates the physical causal chain

[3]: intermediate causally chained subevents

[4]: penultimate subevent = immediate cause of final result

[5]: final resulting subevent = agent's intended goal within scope of intention

NB: (*a*) [3] may be absent

     (*b*) [3] may be absent and [2] may coincide with [4]

     (*c*) [3] and [4] may be absent and [2] may coincide with [5]

With regard to factors that might function to cognitively demarcate an event-frame of the causal-chain type, certainly in the present kind involving an initiatory agent, the straightforward determiner of such demarcation would be the agent's scope of intention. More specifically, the event-frame would consist of that sequence of occurrent or projected causal subevents, beginning with the agent's volitional act and ending with the agent's goal, which is encompassed within the scope of intention that is assumed for, attributed to, or claimed by the agent.

10.3.1. *Discontinuous windowing over agent + result (+ immediate cause)*

What is noteworthy about the characteristic or grammaticized structure of constructions that refer to causal chains in most familiar languages is that the entire medial portion of the sequence is gapped, with discontinuous windows solely upon the initiatory agent and the finally resulting subevent. For example, a standard English causative construction like *I broke the window* refers to the initiatory agent, 'I,' and to the final subevent, 'the window broke,' and indicates that the former intended to, and did, bring about the latter. But there is no indication of what bodily motions the agent undertook to execute the intention—say, my bending down and moving my hand to grasp a rock on the ground, straightening up and lifting the rock with my hand, swinging my arm while holding the rock in my hand, and releasing the rock from my hand thus propelling it forward; nor of what intervening causally linked subevents might have occurred—say, the rock's sailing through the air followed by the rock's making contact with the window; nor of what the immediate cause of the final result might have been—say, the rock's forcefully impacting with the window.

Of the material characteristically gapped from the middle of a causal chain, the portion that seems cross-linguistically to have the next-most-ready means for expression is the penultimate subevent of the causal chain, i.e. the immediate cause of the final intended result. In English, this penultimate subevent is readily expressed in a *by*-clause, as in the case where the situation in which I intentionally lift, swing, and propel a rock through the air into a window to break it can be expressed by a sentence like *I broke the window by hitting it with a rock*, shown in (8g). This *by*-clause, however, does not accommodate any other subevents in the whole causal chain, from the act of willed bodily motion to the antepenultimate subevent, as seen in the unacceptability of (8a–e). For many speakers, even a *by*-clause like that in (8f) is not acceptable, and those speakers who do accept it do so because they feel that the clause contains within it reference to the penultimate subevent in which the rock actually impacts the window.[6]

(8) English *by*-clause reserved for penultimate subevent:
I broke the window—
   (*a*) *by grasping a rock with my hand
   (*b*) *by lifting a rock with my hand
   (*c*) *by swinging a rock with my arm
   (*d*) *by propelling a rock through the air
   (*e*) *by throwing a rock toward it
   (*f*) ?by throwing a rock at it
   (*g*) by hitting it with a rock

[6] Although this formulation in terms of a requirement for penultimacy may lie in the right direction, refinements and emendations are clearly needed. For example, although the sentence *?I broke the window by throwing a rock* seems rather marginal, its close kin, *I broke a window by throwing rocks*, seems relatively acceptable. In search of an explanation, we can note that, in general, a contributing factor in acceptability may be the issue of granularity or chunking—for example, the amount of the causal continuum that is conceptually framed together for consideration as a penultimate event. Thus, in the more acceptable sentence here, since the window did not break as a result of my aiming some particular rock at it, but rather as a chance consequence of my hurling rocks in various directions, the relevant chunk size of the penultimate event may be felt to extend from the act of throwing to the chance impact of one of the missiles with a window—a larger subevent that perhaps metonymically can be referred to as 'throwing rocks.' Further sentences pose additional challenges—e.g. why it is fine to say *He killed himself by jumping out the window* instead of *He killed himself by throwing himself onto the pavement*—and it is not clear if the factor of granularity alone can resolve them.

Supporting the next-most-privileged status of the penultimate subevent in a causal chain is the fact that some languages do in fact characteristically or obligatorily identify that event in a causative construction. Thus, in Atsugewi, in most cases a verb root requires a prefix, selected from a set of some two dozen, that specifies the penultimate subevent (cf. Talmy, 1972; 1985). For example, consider a situation in which I used my hands to build a fire with which to destroy a house. To refer to this situation, I can use the verb root -*miq-* '(to cause) an architectural structure to lose its structural integrity' together with the instrumental prefix *mu:-* 'by acting [on the Patient] with heat/fire.' But I cannot use that verb root together with the instrumental prefix *ci-* 'by acting [on the Patient] with one's hands.' The reason is that the former prefix refers to the mandated penultimate subevent whereas the latter prefix refers to an earlier subevent.

In a comparable way, in the characteristic English verb + satellite construction in which the satellite expresses the final resulting event and the verb expresses a prior causal subevent, this causal subevent must again be the penultimate one, and nothing earlier (cf. Talmy, 1991). Thus, if I have grasped a lever and then used it to pry a lid off a box so as to open the box, I can refer to this causal sequence with *I levered the box open* but not with **I grasped the box open*. Similarly, the previous arson situation—in which I have lit a fire so that a house would catch fire from that and proceed to become consumed in flames to the point of its destruction—can be referred to by the sentence *I burned the house down*, but not by a sentence whose verb expresses any causal subevent prior to the penultimate one, as in **I lit/kindled the house down*.

10.3.2. *Windowing of causal chains with intermediate cognitive agents*

Following the activities of an initiating Agent, an ensuing causal chain can include additional cognitive entities whose agency is essential in the sequence leading to the final reported result (cf. Talmy, 1976). However, to the extent that material referring to such intermediary agents is gapped from a sentence, the intentions, volitional acts, and effects of these agents are attentionally backgrounded, conceptually neglected, and thereby rendered causally 'transparent'—i.e. subject to the conception of a causal continuity progressing directly through such agents rather than stopping at each agent and being renewed by a fresh act of intention and volition. This effect is seen, for example, in the sentence *I'm going to clean my suit at the dry-cleaning store on the corner*, which omits mention of the cleaners whom the speaker will engage to do the job. Further, the amount of the neglectable intervening material can be enormous, as seen in the referent of a sentence like (9a), which, though mediated by a whole society over decades, can still be conceptualized in terms of a juxtaposition of an individual initiator and a final result.

(9a) The Pharaoh built a pyramid for himself/*him
(9b) The Pharaoh had a pyramid built for himself/him
(9c) The Pharaoh had his subjects build a pyramid for *himself/him

This example further allows us to note that the syntax of the reflexive in English, though usually treated in solely formal terms, nevertheless can be seen to correspond to actualities of conceptualization. In this regard, we can observe that the form in (9a), which windows only the initiator and the final result and distracts little attention onto intermediary factors, requires the reflexive in referring back to the initiator and excludes any use of the nonreflexive for this purpose. However, the (9b) form, whose '*have* + *-en*' construction adds a window onto the presence of an intermediary agency, though not onto its identity, permits *either* the reflexive *or* the nonreflexive. Further, the (9c) form, with a construction that now also refers explicitly to an identified mediating agency, requires the nonreflexive and excludes use of the reflexive.

In this sequence of forms, we can discern the presence of clines in three different linguistic systems—syntax, semantics, and conceptual structure—and of correlations across these clines. Thus, with respect to syntax, there is a dual cline that involves both a successively lengthening verb complex and a shift along an obligatory–optional axis. In particular, proceeding through (9) above, the cline progresses from a simplex 'V' (*build*) with a requirement for the reflexive in (a); through the form '*have* -EN + V' with the allowance of either the reflexive or the non-reflexive in (b); to the complex '*have* + NP + V' with a requirement for the nonreflexive in (c). In correlation with this syntactic cline, there is a cline in referential semantics—that consisting of the specification of the intermediary agency—which ranges from null specification in (a), through indication of the presence of such agency without specification of its identity in (b), to specification of both its presence and its identity in (c). And, in correlation with these syntactic and semantic clines, there is an attentional–conceptual cline with dual aspects. In this cline's progression from (*a*) to (*c*), there is an increase in the strength of attention directed to the presence of the intermediary agents (as distinguished from the mention and identification of them that was treated in the preceding cline). Further, there is a qualitative shift in the conceptualization of the relationship between the initiator and the final outcome that ranges from a sense of direct causal immediacy in (*a*)—another case of the cognitive splicing effect—to a sense of causal distance in (*c*).

The lexico-semantic 'logic' here is presumably that a reflexive form suggests a more direct connection between two references to a single entity, thus according better with the conceptual immediacy of the initiator–outcome relationship in (9*a*), whereas a nonreflexive form suggests a more distant connection between two references to a single entity, thus according better with the conceptually greater causal distance between the initiator and the final outcome in (9*c*). The middle form, (9*b*), is the most telling for a demonstration that the role of semantics is here more determinative than that of syntax. For while there may be solid syntactic arguments for the necessity of the reflexive in (9*a*) and for the nonreflexive in (9*c*), there is no immediately obvious non-*ad hoc* syntactic justification for open use of either the reflexive or the nonreflexive in the (9*b*) form. But the semantic–conceptual account involving a gradient in the cognitive salience of the intermediate causal factors does accord neatly with the overt linguistic behavior.[7]

10.3.3. *Cognitive underpinnings of causal windowing and gapping*

Again, what is cognitively noteworthy in the characteristic medial gapping of causal sequences is the great degree to which the middle portion is reduced in one's field of attention, and sometimes seemingly eliminated from it, in the cognitive process of conceptual splicing noted earlier.

With its patterns of causal windowing and gapping, language structure here appears to reflect a cognitive structuring in which a sentient agent's intention for the occurrence of a particular state or event and its actual occurrence are characteristically conceptualized together as a kind of melded unity in the foreground of attention, with little or no attention directed to the intervening mediating stages. This conceptual

---

[7] Kuno (1987) has extensively investigated the conceived degree of immediacy or distance between two references to the same agent.

arrangement would seem to match a presumed kind of experience, recurrent from earliest age onwards, in which an intention and its realization, both in awareness, feel seamlessly linked, and which includes little or no awareness of mediating actions and events—ones which, if considered, might be taken for granted as automatic bodily movements and expectable physical occurrences.[8]

One may speculate that biological evolution has resulted in this form of cognitive structuring of attention for its selective advantages, namely, that it constitutes a functionally relevant type of invariant or constancy in cognition while allowing for other forms of necessary plasticity. The constancy here is the goal of achieving a correspondence between an intention to effectuate some particular circumstance and seeing to it that that circumstance in fact becomes realized through whatever activities prove necessary. Where cognitive organization must remain plastic is in the determination and marshalling of such necessary activities, since the conditions attendant on realizing some purpose can vary greatly. There are two main categories of such variation. First, the physical and functional constitution of any individual organism can change, whether by ontogenetic development or by environmental impact, including injury. Second, the characteristics of the surroundings, both physical and social, that an organism encounters can vary and change. The overall function of the cognitive processes here posited to be in operation would thus be to maintain a goal schema as constant and to execute it through variously appropriate means across constitutional and environmental variety and change.

To illustrate these notions, consider as a candidate for a commonplace cognitive invariant the intention to move forward while avoiding obstacles. With respect to constitutional change through ontogeny, as a human individual develops from an infant into an adult, he will replace crawling on all fours by bipedal walking to effectuate this forward-motion intention, thus ontogenetically changing the means marshaled while maintaining the goal schema intact. As for constitutional change due to external impact, if that individual were to suffer the loss of a leg, the baby crawling on three limbs or the adult walking with crutches would now execute a new movement pattern while still

---

[8] One indicator of the degree of backgrounding of the medial causal material is the fact that even linguistic analyses of agentive expressions failed to explicitly note the necessary presence of a bodily act by the agent until this was pointed out in Wierzbicka (1975) and Talmy (1976).

effectuating the same goal of forward motion with avoidance of obstacles. To exemplify environmental variety, if the adult learns to drive a car, he replaces the use of alternating leg movements for that of a slight pressure of the right foot on a pedal to effectuate the same goal of forward motion, and he replaces judging lateral clearance for the span of his shoulders by assessing instead the clearance for his car's fenders in maintaining the same goal of avoiding obstacles.

In fulfilling the function of maintaining goal-schema constancy, the degree of plasticity of execution can clearly be enormous, as evidenced, for example, by a human's ability to learn to move forward across a range of implementations as disparate as crawling on all fours, limping along on crutches, driving a car, swimming underwater, or propelling himself in the microgravity of a space shuttle. In all such cases, the primary attentional window can remain constant, encompassing only the intended goal and its realization, and once proficiency has been achieved, little or no attention may be directed to the particular physical means and movement patterns engaged in to execute this goal. A cognitive concomitant of this attentional restriction can be an experience in the individual of the maintenance or continuation of a single 'sense of body' across all the variation of physical means for executing the goal—or, from a dynamic perspective, an experience in the individual of the projection of his baseline sense of body into the divergent new means employed to execute the goal. This phenomenon is evident, for example, in the way that a driver can invest his car with the experiential property of being an extension of his body or even of constituting his body, or in the way that the operator of a remote robotic device (such as a mechanical arm) often has the experience of being present at the distal location in what has come to be termed 'telepresence.'

Note further that the implementational range of the disregarded intermediate causal phenomena can encompass the role not only of the body and mechanical extensions of the initiating agent but also of the voluntary cognitive and physical contributions of other mediating sentient agents. Linguistic evidence of this expanded plasticity was given in the preceding section. Comparably, for the preceding conceptual case of intended forward motion, an individual who has, say, taken a bus part of the way in getting to town can experience his going into town in terms of his intention to do so and its realization, with little or no attention directed to his reliance on a bus-driver to transport him in the bus over a portion of the path. Evidently, our cognitive

system of executional plasticity can include the utilization of the actions of other agents so that these, too, subserve our cognitive constancy system for intentions and their realization.

Given the familiar examples of plasticity in motor execution and in bodily identification noted above, little surprise should be caused by the recent successes of computer-based 'virtual reality' in placing an individual in circumstances unusual for perception and motor control. Virtual reality simply makes extended use of plasticities long since selected for and everywhere evident. If anything, virtual reality systems at present are still shy of incorporating certain commonplace capabilities of our everyday executional plasticity, for example, our subsumption of the actions of other agents in addition to our control over our bodies and their direct extensions. Where the techniques of virtual reality can in fact prove most instructive is, complementarily, in ascertaining the constraints on and limitations of human plasticity. For example, would it be feasible for a subject in a virtual-reality system to adapt to conditions where the more slowly he moves, the faster the scene shifts, and vice versa, or where the softer the pressure he exerts, the more forcefully the objects in the scene behave, and vice versa? Could a subject learn to bodily identify with an octopus figure depicted in the virtual scene, integratedly controlling each of the eight limbs with eight different kinds of motion of his own body?

The perspectives and evidence arrayed above argue for the selective advantage in the evolution of a cognitive system of intentional constancy—which maintains certain abstract schemas of intention and its realization—beside a cognitive system of executional plasticity. In the same way that cognitive linguistics has proposed other close correspondences between linguistic structure and the structure of nonlinguistic cognitive systems, the thesis proposed here is, specifically, that the portion of an agentive causal chain characteristically windowed in linguistic structure corresponds to the cognitive system of intentional + realizational constancy, while the characteristically gapped material corresponds to the cognitive system of executional plasticity.

10.4. PHASE WINDOWING

A further type of event-frame consists of an event that iterates in a cycle—what will here be termed a *cycle event-frame*.

A sentence referring to such an event can direct the positioning of a window of strongest attention over a particular phase of that iterating cycle—a cognitive process that is here termed *phase windowing*. The overall event comprised of an iterating cycle is sequential, but may have no clear beginning, middle, or end portions in reference. However, each component cycle when abstracted out can be thought to have the usual initial, medial, and final portions of a sequential event. Further, though, now that this sequence repeats and can be interpreted as additionally having a rest state between iterations, it can be considered to have an *initial, medial,* and *final phase* as well as a *base phase* that occurs after the final and before the initial phase. In the specific case where the overall event is a motion event and one component cycle constitutes in particular a closed path of the type treated in Section 10.2.2, then the earlier distinctively labeled portions of a closed path now become its 'departure phase,' 'away phase,' and 'return phase,' while the base phase can now be distinctively labeled as its *home phase* and be understood as constituting the state of locatedness at the spatially coincident point of the closed loop.

The conceptual event-frame associated with a cyclic occurrence may have a hierarchical structure, unlike previous cases. Rather than comprising a larger frame that directly spans the overall event, it would seem instead to consist of a frame around just one cycle's worth, but with the sense that successive iterations of this cycle are superimposed on each other within the single smaller frame. Thus, with respect to the factors that can cognitively define an event-frame, one can here posit a still further factor, that of the part-for-part congruence of one segment of occurrence with another—a property of direct mappability between segments—which can function to cognitively delimit a portion of occurrence that can constitute such a segment and that can thus be conceptualized as a unit event. Here, any two temporal points that bear the same phase relation to two such congruent stretches of occurrence can be taken to constitute the boundaries of one cycle's worth. And, in particular, points of this sort that occur within what can be conceptualized as the 'basic' or 'home' portions of occurrence have a privileged status for constituting the boundaries of a cycle.

To illustrate cycles with an iterated closed path, the sentences in (10) can all—given a sufficiently constrained context—be taken to pertain to the same cyclic event-frame in which the home phase consists of a pen lying on a table, the departure phase consists of the pen falling off the table onto the floor, the away phase consists of the pen lying on the floor, and the return phase consists of my picking the pen up from the floor and placing it back on the table. Exhibiting alternative options for attentional windowing, however, the sentence in (10a) windows greatest attention on the departure phase of this cycle (or, more precisely, on just the earlier portion of the departure phase, comprising the pen's falling down off the table but not down onto the floor), leaving the remainder of the cycle in the background of attention. The sentence in (10b) windows only the return phase (or, more precisely, only the later portion of the return phase, comprising my lifting the pen up onto the table but not up off the floor). And the sentence in (10c) places discontinuous windows over the departure and return phases while leaving the remainder of the cycle in the background—as schematized in Fig. 10.2(a). Thus, here as before, the language affords the speaker alternatives of attentional windowing upon essentially the same event-frame, with the addressee feasibly able to infer the different gapped portions for each alternative so as to reconstruct back to the same single event-frame. Further, the sentence in (10c) can be taken to induce cognitive splicing in the hearer by conceptually running together the departure and return phases, with the extreme backgrounding or loss now not only of the medial phase but also of the base phase (i.e. of the static home and away phases).

(10a) with departure-phase windowing:
       The pen kept falling off the table
(10b) with return-phase windowing:
       I kept putting the pen back on the table
(10c) with departure-phase plus return-phase windowing:
       The pen kept falling off the table and I kept putting it back

In this paper's examples, including the preceding example, alternatives of windowing constitute different attentional patterns, but these patterns are placed over what can otherwise be the same single referent. However, the cycle event-frame can also support referentially nonequivalent phase windowings. This can arise where a particular phase window is established by some reported external coincident event, rather than by the speaker's predilection. To illustrate, the main cyclic event could be an iterated closed path undertaken by a Mr Smith with respect to his office: being in the office (home phase), leaving it for another location (departure phase), being at that other location (away phase), and going from that location back to his office (return phase). And the external coincident event could be my repeated telephoning of Mr Smith always during the same particular phase of his path cycle. The three sentences in (11) express such a co-incidence for three different phases of this cycle while Fig. 10.2(*b*) schematizes the coincidence pattern for sentence (11*c*).[9] The phase windowings selected out in this way are clearly part of three referentially distinct situations.

(11) Whenever I phoned,
    (*a*) Smith was always just about to step out of his office
    (*b*) Smith was always just stepping out of his office
    (*c*) Smith had always just stepped out of his office

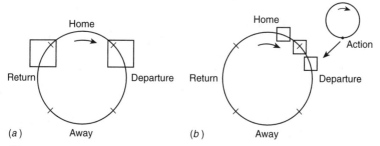

Fig. 10.2.

10.5. PARTICIPANT-INTERACTION WINDOWING

Consider a complex situation that consists of two parts: (1) a primary circumstance, and (2) some participant(s) interacting with that circumstance at least twice. A 'participant' here can be a participant either of the expressed referent event or of the current speech event. A participant's interaction with the circumstance can be direct, as in observing or considering the circumstance, or indirect, as in asking another participant about the circumstance. In referring to the whole of such a situational complex, some languages have provision for the alternative placement of a window of heightened attention over one or another of these interactions. In particular, linguistic devices direct one to adopt one of the participant interaction times as the point at which to locate one's temporal perspective point, and to place around

---

[9] Actually, these sentences exhibit an additional factor beyond windowing, 'direction of viewing.' The window in (11*a*) is located in the latter portion of the home phase, but it includes a prospective viewing ahead to the initial point of departure, while the window in (11*c*) is located in the earlier portion of the departure phase but includes a retrospective viewing back to the initial point of departure.

the interaction there an attentional window that could include such elements of the interaction as the activity, the surrounding scene, or the cognitive content of the participant. The whole situational complex can be understood to constitute a new type of event-frame, the *participant-interaction event-frame*, which permits alternatives of *participant-interaction windowing*. This type of event-frame shares a characteristic with the preceding types (and in this respect all these types differ from the type treated next): it constitutes a sequence of phenomena differing through time and, accordingly, the alternative windows of attention differ with respect to their temporal placement. Considering again the kinds of factor that can demarcate the boundaries of an event-frame, the present type of event-frame may exhibit a further such factor: the occurrence of two distinct punctual events that are extrinsic to a certain circumstance which extends through time can mark out a portion of that circumstance and establish that portion conceptually as an event-frame. Here, in particular, a portion of the primary circumstance is marked out by two participant interactions with it.

For a first illustration, the two short segments of discourse in (12) can be interpreted as referring to a single situational complex that is of the sort just outlined.

(12*a*) John met a woman at the party last week. Her name was Linda
(12*b*) John met a woman at the party last week. Her name is Linda

Here, the primary circumstance is the temporally unbounded state of a certain woman's having the name Linda. And it can be argued for (12*a*) and perhaps even more strongly for (12*b*) that each of these segments of discourse equally evokes the same concept of a pair of participant interactions with this circumstance. The first interaction, an indirect one, is that of John with the primary circumstance of a woman's being named Linda, namely, his encounter at the party last week with the woman bearing that name. He may have asked and/or been told her name, or the discourse may be providing that information without his having learned it. The second interaction, a direct one, is my (i.e. the speaker's) consideration of the woman's name at the present moment of speaking. In the second sentences of (12*a* and *b*) referring to the woman's having a name, the use of the past tense in (12*a*) and of the present tense in (12*b*) then signals the differential placement of an attentional window over one or the other of these interactions. This past tense in (12*a*) might on one score seem peculiar, since the past tense is largely associable with an event that has terminated before the present moment, whereas in fact the state of the woman's bearing her name is continuous. The explanation for the use of the past tense here, we would argue, is that, despite the overt syntax, it does not apply to the main referent of the sentence, i.e. to the woman's being named Linda, but rather to the time of the first participant interaction, i.e. to John's encounter with the woman. The window of attention placed around that temporal point would then include aspects of the interaction, some of them inferred or imagined, such as John's interchange with the woman or the surrounding party scene. On the other hand, the present tense of (12b) signals the adoption of the temporal perspective of the second participant interaction, i.e. the present moment, and directs the placement there of an attentional window that includes something of the interactional context— such as my contemplation of the woman's name-bearing state either in its current relevance or in its ongoing unbounded character. Accordingly, we have here in the participant-interaction case a type of windowing rather comparable to those in the preceding sections where each of two formulations evokes the entirety of a particular event-frame while explicitly indicating only certain subportions of that event-frame and thus establishing a selective window of attention upon it.

Although it was just argued that each of the discourse sequences in (12) at least implicitly evoked a pair of participant interactions with the primary circumstance, nothing in the sequences explicitly specified the duality of interaction. But in (13), the word *again* unmistakably indicates that there were at least two interactions in the situation.

(13a) What was your name again, please?
(13b) What is your name again, please?

In the situational complex here, the primary circumstance is the unboundedly continuous state of your having a particular name. The two interactions with this circumstance are, at an earlier moment, your or someone's saying your name in my presence, perhaps with my having asked you for it, and, at the present moment, my asking you for your name. The initial interaction would have been in the present tense, consisting e.g. of my asking you *What is your name?* or of your saying *I'm Linda*, or of someone's saying *This is Linda*. But my subsequent question to you would need to be something like one of the forms in (13) because, by the requirements of English for reflecting the pragmatic circumstances here, if I have forgotten or didn't catch your name the first time and assume that you and I remember my prior presence at the name's utterance, then my subsequent asking must include a marker specifically acknowledging the repetition, such as the word *again* or the English 'echo question' intonation pattern. Thus, both sentences of (13) explicitly indicate that the present question is the second of two interactions with the same intent on my part to learn your name. But this second-question formulation with *again* permits the use of either the past or the present tense. And, as before, the past form may at first seem paradoxical in its usage with a temporally unbounded referent (your having a name). However, the explanation of this behavior, as posited previously, is that the choice of tense in the main verb does not pertain to the overt referent of the clause but rather to my two interactions with that referent—i.e. the earlier or the later instance of my hearing or asking about the referent. In particular, the past tense of (13a) selects the time of my initial interaction as the point at which one is to locate one's temporal perspective so as to place a window of heightened attention over that interaction, while the present tense of (13b) requires the performance of the same cognitive processes for my later interaction, the one occurring at the present moment of speaking.

Certain observations can serve to reinforce and refine our analysis that attentional windows are placed over participant interactions with the primary circumstance. First, the view that the past and present tenses in the preceding examples direct the placement of windows only over the two participant interactions cited is buttressed by our clear English-speaker intuition that they could not refer to other bounded temporal periods. Thus, the past in (12a) could not refer to a moment between the time of last week's party and the present moment—say, to a moment three days ago—or to some time before the party. Comparably, the past in (13a) could not refer to a point between the last time I heard your name and the present moment, nor between any previous occasions of my hearing your name if there were more than one of these.

Second, since the overt tense that has been selected for a sentence is expressed as part of a reference to the primary circumstance rather than as part of some explicit reference to the posited participant interaction, there may be some preference to see an alternative analysis in terms of the primary circumstance alone. Such an analysis might hold that a delimited portion of the unbounded primary circumstance is conceptually marked out for consideration in isolation, and that it is only this portion that is placed in a tense relation with the present moment. However, the primary circumstance does not have to be continuous and unbounded, as it has been in the previous examples, but can also be a punctual event that occurs only once—yet here, too, the account in this section will still hold. Thus, each of the sentences in (14) equally reflects two interactions I have had with you over your knowledge of a plane schedule, and they would seem to differentially window respectively the earlier interaction and the present interaction, but there is now no possibility of interpreting the tense as applying to some marked-out subportion of the primary referent, which is now the punctual and upcoming plane departure.

(14a) When was her plane going to leave again tomorrow?
(14b) When is her plane going to leave again tomorrow?

Further, if there really were a tense-located referent of the sentence that indeed consisted of a temporally delimited subportion of an otherwise unbounded circumstance, then that referent portion should be compatible with an overt constituent that explicitly refers to the delimited time period in question. But such additional constituents, on the contrary, render the sentence unacceptable, as seen in (15). The unacceptability of these sentences further indicates that the use of a past or present tense in the example sentences of this section cannot be accounted for simply as some automatic syntactic reflex involving, say, some sequence-of-tense rule that is triggered by some other time-specific constituent but, rather, must genuinely reflect a semantic option.

(15a) John met a woman at the party last week. Her name was Linda
*while he was there. / *when he asked her for it. / *when she told him
(15b) What was your name again
*when I asked you for it before? / *when you told me it before?

Note that some participant-interaction-type sentences can support an alternative 'evidentiary' reading that does permit temporally specific adjuncts. Thus, the segments of discourse in (16a, b) would probably first be read in accordance with the participant-interaction analysis of earlier examples—with the unbounded iterative activity of a geyser's spouting replacing the unbounded static state of bearing a name. In this reading, the two segments would refer to approximately the same situational complex and differ only in their pattern of attentional windowing. But in addition, they can have evidentiary readings with meanings substantially different from each other. Under such readings, in (16a), I report only what I witnessed during my visit and suggest no inferences about activity outside that scope. But in (16b), I use what I witnessed as evidence to confirm the general notion that there is continuous unbounded activity. And, in (16c), a temporally delimiting constituent, of the type seen above to be unacceptable, here appears compatibly with the past-tense form. Such new readings and sentence forms do not instantiate participant-interaction event-frames or windowing and, accordingly, their tenses apply directly to the overtly expressed referent in the usual way.

> (16a) I was in Yellowstone Park last year. Old Faithful spouted regularly
> (16b) I was in Yellowstone Park last year. Old Faithful spouts regularly
> (16c) I was in Yellowstone Park last year. Old Faithful spouted regularly
> (—at least) while I was there

In all the preceding examples of this section, the primary circumstance that is in reference is unchanging through the progression of time. However, reference to a circumstance that does change with time can constitute a further case that looks like participant-interaction forms but in which the choice of tense applies directly to the primary referent, rather than to a participant interaction, and in which a temporally specific adjunct is compatible. This can be seen in (17a), where the changing primary circumstance is the time of day.

> (17a) The time was 10:53 when I asked for it
> (17b) *The woman's name was Linda when I asked for it

Accordingly, with the *again*-question frame used earlier, if I am now asking you for the time of day for the second time, where the first time I asked was sufficiently earlier to render the answer you then gave pragmatically useless, then I cannot felicitously use the past tense, as in (18a), but must rather use the present, as in (18b). On the other hand, I can felicitously wish to know the answer you delivered on the earlier occasion—e.g. where I was recording in a notebook the on-going results of an experiment—in which case the past tense would be acceptable and could now be used with an overt constituent explicitly referring to the past moment in question, as seen in (18c).[10]

---

[10] Note that the *again* in the sentences of (18) still pertains to the speaker's dual interaction with the primary circumstance, namely, to the fact that I have now twice heard or asked you for the time. But—unless the time of my first interaction is pragmatically

(18a) #What time was it again, please?
(18b) What time is it again, please?
(18c) What time was it again when I asked you before?

Finally, consider again the original examples of participant-interaction windowing. Here as elsewhere, although the choice of window placement does not affect the principal situational complex that is in reference, it does have further semantic consequences. Thus, the tense that is used can suggest the relevance that the primary circumstance has to current concerns, with the past suggesting lack of relevance and the present suggesting the presence of relevance. For example, the past tense in (12a) can suggest that John's association with the woman last week at the party ended there, while the present tense in (12b) can suggest that their association has continued to the present and is of current relevance.

10.6. INTERRELATIONSHIP WINDOWING

A frequent type of language-relevant cognitive entity is a conceptual complex which contains or comprises parts that are not autonomous in themselves but are intrinsically relative with respect to each other, where the presence of one such part necessarily entails the presence of the other parts.

A conceptual complex of this sort is here called an *interrelational complex* and can constitute a further type of event-frame, the *interrelationship event-frame*. Such an internally self-entailing complex could logically be considered a single-unit entity, but our conceptual and attentional systems are so organized as to be able to conceptualize the whole as if portioned out into quasi-independent elements to which heightened attention can be differentially directed. With respect to its linguistic expression, such a complex can be conceptually partitioned—in a way that may be universal—into parts expressed by syntactically distinct constituents. Frequently, a language will permit alternatives of windowing over one or another part of such a complex, while mention of the remaining parts is omitted—although their presence is still understood. Such alternatives of *interrelationship windowing* allow the selection of a locus of strongest attention within

recent enough, in which case the tenses in (18a, b) can revert to their participant-interaction windowing usage—the tense can now no longer be used to window one of these interactions, since its use is pre-empted for pertaining to a particular subportion of the changing circumstance.

a complex or the adoption of a particular perspective over the complex while—given the appropriate context—still conveying the whole of the complex.

Note that the earlier types of windowing do not seem to fit this notion of an intradependent interrelationship—for example, for path-windowing, a later path segment is not entailed by an earlier one but is rather represented as being additionally present. By contrast, in interrelational complexes, the relevant components codefine each other. Accordingly, once again considering the factors that can function to demarcate an event-frame, it appears that the boundaries of an interrelationship event-frame can be determined by a new factor, that of co-entailment. Apart from these differences, however, what is common to both the earlier types and the present type is that each event-frame type supports alternatives of the placement of attentional windows over it, and the gapped portions are largely recoverable by the hearer—whether by inferences involving entailment or by inferences involving familiarity with other event-frame-determining factors at work in a particular context.

We examine here two kinds of interrelationship event-frame, one based around Figure and Ground roles, and the other around factual and counterfactual conditions.

10.6.1. *Figure–Ground interrelationship*

As they are characterized in Talmy (1978) for their function in language, the Figure and the Ground in a spatial scene are relative concepts necessarily characterized with respect to each other. The Figure is a moving or conceptually movable entity within the scene whose site, path, or orientation is conceived of as a variable of which the particular value is the relevant issue and which is characterized with respect to the Ground. The Ground is a stationary reference entity within the scene with respect to which the Figure's site, path, or orientation is characterized. As described in Talmy (1985), the Figure and Ground are components of an event of Motion (covering both motion and location) that includes two further components, as in the semantic structure in (19).

(19) [Figure + Fact-of-Motion + Path + Ground]

This Motion event well exemplifies the kind of conceptual entity that is intrinsically irreducible—i.e. of which no part can exist without the rest—but which in general is conceptually and linguistically parti-tioned into components that can be treated differentially as to atten-tional distribution. This conceptual entity, then, constitutes a particular type of interrelationship event-frame, the *Motion event-frame*, and it can support a particular type of attentional alternativity, *Figure–Ground windowing*

To illustrate this type of windowing, consider a scene in which paint is peeling off a wall, where the paint would be understood to function as the Figure relative to the wall as Ground. For mention of both the Figure and the Ground within a single sentence, English often has available two counterpart constructions (analyzed in detail in Talmy, 1972: ch. 10), one in which the Figure appears as the subject and the Ground in an oblique phrase, as in (20*a*), and another in which these grammatical relations are reversed, as in (20*b*).[11]

(20*a*) The paint is peeling from the wall
(20*b*) ?The wall is peeling of its paint

If there were a need to gap reference to the Figure or the Ground, the constituent referring to it would have to be omitted. Since English does not generally permit the omission of a subject NP but can often omit an oblique constituent, as here, (21) shows two further counter-part constructions based on the preceding pair but with the oblique constituents missing. Given the appropriate context, then, (21*a*) refers to the original scene but with windowing of the Figure (plus the activ-ity) and gapping of the Ground, whereas (21*b*) windows the Ground (plus the activity) while gapping the Figure.[12] Thus, with such altern-ative constructions, one can refer to basically the same interrelational spatial complex of codependent Figure/Ground elements and select-ively window one or the other of those elements.

---

[11] Although the inclusion of the oblique Figural phrase in (20*b*) is awkward for this example, other examples readily exhibit all four of the construction types treated in (20) and (21), e.g. the less pleasant forms in (i) and (ii) below. The Figure or Ground roles of the noun phrases are here indicated symbolically.

    (i) (*a*) His blood [F] slowly drained from his veins [G].
        (*b*) His veins [G] slowly drained of their blood [F].
    (ii) (*a*) His blood [F] slowly drained.
        (*b*) His veins [G] slowly drained.

[12] This analysis shows a point neglected in previous work (e.g. Keenan and Comrie, 1977) which posited the advancement or demotion of a term along a hierarchy of grammatical relations. That work emphasized advancement as a process for increasing the prominence of a referent, but spoke little of demotion as a process for getting a refer-ent into an oblique constituent that could then be deleted in order to background that referent.

(21*a*) The paint is peeling
(21*b*) The wall is peeling

10.6.2. *Factual-counterfactual interrelationship*

A linguistic construction can have the semantic property of presenting the referent of its overtly expressed material as being the case or, alternatively, as not being the case. In traditional terminology these are, respectively, factual and counterfactual constructions.

Further, a language can have a pair of constructions, one of them factual and the other counterfactual, such that if their overtly expressed materials are positive–negative counterparts of each other, then both constructions make the same overall statement. Given the availability of a particular doublet of such paired constructions, a speaker can make the same overall statement in choosing either one of the constructions, but the speaker would also thereby select whether to direct greater attention to something that was the case or to something that was not the case. Since each member of such a pair of counterpart factual–counterfactual construction types entails the other, their referent types together can be considered to constitute a certain kind of interrelationship event-frame, a *factuality event-frame*, and the directing of heightened attention to one or the other of these referent types can be called *factuality windowing*.

A factuality event-frame exhibits a still further property. Under selective attentional windowing, it can support not only the exclusive consideration of one chosen alternative by itself but also the placement of the two alternative conceptualizations within a single frame of consideration, so that, although main attention is on only one of the alternatives, the other alternative is still present in a backgrounded way to act as a foil for comparison. An event-frame that in this way evokes larger-frame juxtapositions of alternative conceptualizations can be further said to constitute a *comparison frame*. The characteristic of constituting a comparison frame can then function as one further factor for demarcating an event-frame, and the factuality event-frame seems to derive some of its characterizability as an event-frame from this factor. Certain constructions and lexical forms in a language tend to evoke comparison frames, and the following are ones which do so for the occurrence versus the non-occurrence of some referent.

First, a syntactically negative clause (e.g. *I didn't go to John's party last night*) overtly names something that did not take place but tends to evoke consideration of the corresponding unrealized positive event—and in this respect it differs from a simple positive clause, which tends not to evoke consideration of its negative counterpart. Second, even a syntactically positive main clause, when it is adjoined by a *because*-clause (e.g. *I went to the movies last night because they were playing my favorite film*), tends to evoke its unrealized counterpart (a failure to go to the movies), since the offering of a reason or cause that has given rise to some realized phenomenon suggests that, for want of that cause, the phenomenon would not have occurred. Third, a nonsimple positive clause that additionally includes a constituent which places the referent event at some point along a scale of certainty or realizedness (e.g. *Sue may have gone to John's party last night,/Perhaps Sue is at John's party now,/I just barely got to the movies last night*) brings into consideration the existence of such a scale and thereby evokes the consideration of points nearer the opposite pole of the scale. Fourth, an interrogative form, even of an otherwise simple positive clause (e.g. *Did Sue go to John's party last night?*), has as its main semantic point the issue of the occurrence or non-occurrence of the situation it refers to and, of course, thus naturally contrasts the occurrence status of its overtly expressed material against the opposite occurrence status. And fifth—the topic of this section—a grammatically counterfactual construction (e.g. *I would have gone to John's party last night if I had had the time*) overtly names a counterfactual event that did not take place, (*I. . . have gone to the party*) but also evokes its factual complement, what actually took place (my staying away from the party). Among sentence types, perhaps mainly it is a simple positive factual declarative clause (e.g. *I went to the movies last night*) that raises in consciousness only the named event without the backgrounded accompaniment of its unrealized alternative. Although it may be the case that a positive statement of this kind is generally made only if its referent is taken to be news to the hearer, unanticipated relative to some baseline of expectation, nevertheless it seems that such a statement is not usually experienced as an assertion averred contrastively against the potential of its non-occurrence. There is apparently at work here a cognitive asymmetry that accords to the positive and to the factual the status of having primacy and of being basic, so that the negative and the counterfactual are on the contrary conceptualized as secondary and nonbasic, perhaps as somehow derived from the basic by some cognitive process of reversal.

In addition to construction types like those above, certain lexical items seem to incorporate within their lexicalization a scope encompassing both realization and nonrealization. Thus, the verb *miss*, as in *I missed the target*, seems not to simply refer directly to a projectile's passing to one side of a target, but rather to evoke a two-stage bipartite conceptualization consisting first of the projectile's hitting the target and then the denial of such an occurrence, with a conceptual shifting of the projectile's path off to one side. Comparably, the verb *regret*, as in *I regret that I lent him money*, though referring directly to an actually occurrent event, nevertheless conjures up the wished-for non-occurrence of that event. Similarly, the use of the verb *succeed*, as in *I succeeded in opening the window*, shares in common with its non-use, as in *I opened the window*, a reference to an actually occurring event, but its use differs from its non-use in that (among other effects) it sets this occurrence of the event within a comparison frame for a contrast with the possibility of the event's non-occurrence.

As indicated earlier, given that a construction can evoke within a single comparison frame both the factual and counterfactual alternatives of a situation, the issue of windowing enters where the same situation can be referred to by either of two constructions, where one construction names the factual form of the situation while evoking its counterfactual alternative, and where the other construction does the opposite. Why might languages afford ready syntactic means for focussing on what has not occurred? In explanation, one can adduce for the systems of discourse or narrative such factors as the motivation to achieve a heightened effect by specifying a goal that was vainly sought (in the case where the non-occurrent was preferable to the occurrent), or by specifying a danger that was avoided (in the case where the non-occurrent was less desirable than the occurrent).

Notationally in the specific analyses that follow, the symbol A, as a mnemonic for 'Actual', will represent any particular factual alternative, while the symbol ~A will represent the corresponding counterfactual. For any particular example, in addition, a P may be used to indicate a clause whose overt syntactic form is positive, while not-P would indicate a syntactically negative clause. Thus, the sentence *I didn't go to the party* can here be represented symbolically as A (not-P) to suggest a paraphrase like 'What actually happened is that it was not the case that I went to the party.' In truth-value terms, A and ~A entail each other with the sign of their proposition reversed—i.e. A (P) is equivalent to ~A (not-P), and A (not-P) is equivalent to ~A (P)—but in terms of conceptual organization, it is necessary to discriminate an A/~A factual–counterfactual parameter separately from a P/not-P syntactically positive–negative parameter. The symbols A/~A are chosen over the symbols T/F of truth-conditional semantics for several reasons. First, the truth-conditional symbols are used in an objectivist system of reference, whereas the orientation here is of a conception-based system of reference, whose theoretical distinctness can be better kept in attention by the use of distinct symbols.[13] Second, it is clearer to show explicitly the counterpart relationship between a matched factual–counterfactual pair with the use of a reversal-type operator like ~ than with the use of two separate symbols like T and F, which obscures the fact and the nature of their interrelationship. Third, the assignment of the simpler symbolic representation, A, to the factual and of the more complex and derived representation, ~A, to the counterfactual corresponds to the cognitive asymmetry that accords basic status to the factual and nonbasic, possibly derived, status to the counterfactual.

10.6.2.1. *Affective states associated with factuality states.* Our first specific demonstration of a factuality interrelationship is of the linguistic representation of the counterpart affective states that are experienced with respect to a pair of factual and counterfactual complements. We first consider the case where the counterfactual circumstance is held to be more desirable than the actual circumstance. Here the affective pattern consists of two emotional states: 'regret' over what factually happened and a 'wish' for what counterfactually did not happen. These two states are understood to refer to the same single situation, as represented in (22), and to differ essentially only as to their placement of attention.

(22)   ~A more desirable than A—associated affective states:
       regret over A '=' wish for ~A

---

[13] Truth-value semantics and logic assume, or proceed as if assuming, the view that there is a direct relation between a linguistic expression and what is held to be its counterpart (its 'referent') in the world. Cognitive linguistics, on the other hand, maintains that the relation between a linguistic expression and something in the world cannot be direct but must, in effect, 'pass through' the mind of the language user. In particular, the relevant primary relationship is between the linguistic expression and the mind of the language-user, who must first cognize the expression. Thus, a linguistic expression must first evoke a particular conceptual content in the language-user's mind, there entertained by the imaginal cognitive system. This content can then be further related to other conceptual contents in the same mind, including concepts about the world.

(23*a*) *windowing A, i.e. what did take place*
    I regret that I didn't go to the party
    I regret not having gone to the party
    It's too bad I didn't go to the party
(23*b*) *windowing ~A, i.e. what did not take place*
    I wish I had gone to the party
    If only I had gone to the party/Would that I had gone to the party
    I should have gone to the party

That is, as we typically understand them, each of these emotions conjures up the full comparison frame of the factual–counterfactual interrelationship, but focusses attention on only one of the alternative factuality states while evoking the other as a background comparand. In the terms used above, each of these states windows attention on one alternative of the interrelational complex. English constructions that represent these two affective states and their attentional windowings are shown in (23*a*) and (23*b*) respectively, here exemplifying a case where the factual circumstance is an absence of activity ('I didn't go to the party').

We next consider the inverse condition where the counterfactual is held to be *less* desirable than the actual. With the desirability thus reversed, the associated emotions—again, ones whose character must depend on bringing both factuality alternatives into a single frame of comparison—would seem to be, on the one hand, pleasure over the actual realization of what has occurred considered against the possibility of its not having occurred and, on the other hand, hypothetically contemplated displeasure over what did not occur considered against the knowledge of what has in fact occurred, as indicated in (24). In English, at least, it is evident that there are fewer constructions and lexicalizations that represent this arrangement of factors than in the case where the non-occurrent alternative was the preferable one. Some of the most serviceable forms that do occur for this poorly represented pattern are given in (25)—here, again, illustrating a case where the factual circumstance is an absence of activity ('I didn't go to the lecture').

(24) A more desirable than ~A—associated affective states:
    pleasure at realizing A as against ~A
    '=' hypothetically contemplated displeasure with ~A as against A
(25*a*) *windowing A, i.e. what did take place*
    It's a good thing that I didn't go to the lecture
    I am (sure) glad that I didn't go to the lecture

(25*b*) *windowing ~A, i.e., what did not take place*
    It would have been too bad if I had gone to the lecture
    I would/could have gone to the lecture to my misfortune

The differential favoring of the former case (the counterfactual as preferable) over the latter case (the factual as preferable) is evidenced not only by the greater availability of open-class lexical forms that directly lexicalize the favored affectual patterns—e.g., here, the existence in English of the fully specific *regret* and *wish* for the first case as against nothing but the partially serviceable *sure glad* or the too general *glad* for the second case. In addition, rather, the favored case exhibits a greater representation by closed-class forms, which, as Talmy (1988*a*) argues, collectively represent the fundamental conceptual structuring system of language. Thus, many languages express the 'wish' notion by subjunctive-like morphemes or by unique constructions like the English *would that* and *if only* or by specific modal forms comparable to English *should*. And the 'regret' notion has at least some closed-class representation, e.g. in Yiddish by the particle form *nebekh*, which could be glossed as 'poor me/you/him/. . .' (hence comparable to English *alas* except for being fully syntactically integrated within the sentence) as in *Ikh bin nebekh nisht gegangen oyf der siimkhe*, 'I alas didn't go to the party.' But closed-class representation for the unfavored patterns—the 'sure glad that' and 'would have been too bad if' notions—is not immediately apparent. This difference in closed-class representation can be highlighted by noting that the favored pattern can be represented (as it was in (23*b*)) by a basic member of the modal system, *should*, whose meaning can be approximately characterized as 'would to one's betterment, benefit, and pleasure' (cf. Talmy 1988*b*). However, the unfavored pattern has no counterpart modal with the meaning 'could to one's worsening, detriment, and displeasure,' which could have fit into a sentence in (25*b*), as if to express something like '*I would-to-my-misfortune [= Modal] have gone to the lecture.'

This observation of more and less favored affective patterns suggests a program of investigation. This program would involve (i) first isolating the factors that, occurring together in patterns, appear to underlie affective and cognitive states with obvious lexical or constructional representation; (ii) then recombining those factors so as to generate a full array of potential patterns; (iii) then searching various languages for lexical or constructional representation of all such generated patterns; and (iv) finally seeking explanations for the apparent distribution of well and poorly represented patterns.

10.6.2.2. *Explanation types associated with factuality states.* Our second specific demonstration is in the general semantic domain of *explanations*—in which one circumstance, A, is proposed to account for another circumstance, A—where we observe that complementary explanation types can be associated with the two complementary factuality states.

The basic equivalence of explanation types across the factual–counterfactual distinction can be formulated as in (26).

(26) A because A'
     '=' ~A-[conditional] if ~A'

This generic formulation can be considered to encompass distinct subtypes of explanation on the basis of additional parameters, such as whether A or ~A is held to be the preferable circumstance and whether there is an Agent either in A or in A' who is deemed to be responsible for or in control of the specified event by dint of his intentions and actions. However, at least in English (though other languages must be checked), the explanation constructions generally do not overtly mark any such subtypes—unlike the affect constructions, which explicitly distinguish different affective states. Accordingly, the different explanation types proposed next generally correspond to constellations of solely inferrable factors. However, given the ascription of a particular explanation type to a presented construction, there will be a specific counterpart explanation type to be ascribed to the construction whose factuality is complementary to that of the first construction.

As before, we begin further analysis with the case where what has not occurred, ~A, is held to be more desirable than what has occurred, A. Consider in addition the case where a particular cognitive agent is deemed to be responsible for A but not for A'. Here, then, an actual circumstance A' that is outside a particular agent's control and that is offered to account for another actual but undesired circumstance for which the agent is responsible, A, can be construed to constitute an *excuse* for A. Complementarily, explicit reference to the non-occurrent but desired circumstance ~A can be construed as *reassurance* (or *bravado* for a first-person report) about the agent's capacity to realize ~A in the potential case where cause A' remains non-occurrent as ~A'. These relationships are symbolized and illustrated in (27).

(27) ~A more desirable than A—associated explanation types where:
     an Agent is responsible for A but is not in control of A'

(*a*) *structure of the explanation types*
excuse for A: A because A'
'=' reassurance (bravado) as to ~A: ~A-[conditional] if ~A'

(*b*) *example with A: I didn't catch the frisbee, A': the car was in the way*
factual: excuse:
I didn't catch the frisbee because the car was in the way
A (not-P) because A'(P')
counterfactual: reassurance/bravado:
I would have caught the frisbee if the car hadn't been in the way
~A-[conditional] (P) if ~A' (not-P')

Proceeding now to the case where the occurrent A is held to be more desirable than the non-occurrent ~A, we further consider the case in which a specified agent is in control of A' but not of A (an unspecified agent is in control of A). Here, A can be understood as the compensation or *reward* that follows from the agent's execution of A'. Correspondingly, any potential non-execution of A' by the agent would be understood to result in the non-occurrence of A, hence to constitute the *threat* of non-compensation—relationships that are symbolized and exemplified in (28).

(28) A more desirable than ~A—associated explanation types where:
a specific agent is in control of A' but not of A (which another agent controls)

(*a*) *structure of the explanation types*
A as a reward: because A'
'=' ~A as a threat: if ~A'

(*b*) *example with A: he got a raise, A': he worked hard*
factual: reward:
He got a raise because he worked hard
A (P) because A' (P')
counterfactual: threat:
He wouldn't have gotten a raise if he hadn't worked hard
~A-[conditional] (not-P) if ~A' (not-P')

The explanation types that are complementary with respect to factuality states also bear specific relations to each other with respect to force dynamics (cf. Talmy, 1988*b*)—i.e. the semantic component of language that pertains to the interactions of opposing forces such as an object's intrinsic tendency toward motion or rest, another object's opposition to this tendency, resistance to such opposition, the overcoming of resistance, and the impingement, disimpingement, or non-impingement of blockage. Employing the terminology of Talmy

(1988*b*), we can note that, for all the explanation types, the A circumstance functions as the Agonist, i.e. the force-bearing entity of focal attention, while the A' circumstance functions as the Antagonist, i.e. the opposing force-bearing entity; that the Agonist has an intrinsic tendency toward rest, i.e., here, toward non-occurrence; and that the Antagonist is the stronger of the two circumstances. In the factual explanation types, e.g. the excuse and reward types, the Antagonist circumstance impinges upon the Agonist circumstance and thus overcomes its tendency toward rest, i.e. forces it into occurrence. On the other hand, the counterfactual explanation types, e.g. the reassurance and threat types, depict a potential world in which the Antagonist circumstance does not impinge upon the Agonist circumstance, which is thus free to manifest its intrinsic tendency toward rest, i.e. toward non-occurrence.

Although abbreviated, the analysis in this section serves to demonstrate the existence of an integrated system that interrelates four semantic–syntactic domains that might otherwise have been thought to be independent: the windowing of attention, factuality states, affective–cognitive states, and force dynamics. It further shows that factuality and counterfactuality are complementary states within a single conceptual interrelationship, and that languages afford devices for placing a window of primary attention over either of the two states.

10.7. MULTIPLE AND NESTED WINDOWING

Although the windowing process has so far been treated separately for each type of event-frame, in fact multiple instances of windowing can occur at the same time, each with respect to several concurrent event-frames. In some cases, one instance of windowing would have to be understood as nested within another, whereas in other cases, two instances of windowing would have either an indeterminate hierarchical relationship or an equipollent status. The sentences in (29) exhibit a successively greater number of instances of windowing.

(29*a*) The ball rolled off the lawn back onto the court
(29*b*) The ball rolled back onto the court
(29*c*) The ball rolled back
(29*d*) I rolled the ball back

(29*e*) I kept rolling the ball back
(29*f*) If I hadn't kept rolling the ball back, there would have been no game

Sentence (*a*) here exhibits a simple path event-frame, complete perhaps except for a medial gapping. Sentence (*b*) refers to the same path event-frame but now with initial and medial gapping, hence windowing only the final portion of the path. Sentence (*c*), treating the path event-frame as an interrelationship event-frame—in particular, as an event of motion with a Figure and a Ground—retains the Figure (the ball) within its windowing but gaps the Ground (the court). Sentence (*d*) now adds an agent-initiated causal chain to the previous already gapped motion event, thus representing a causal-chain event-frame, and, as is typical for English, windows only the agent and the final resulting subevent, while gapping specification of all the intervening causal actions. Sentence (*e*) puts the previously gapped referent into an iterated cycle, thus representing a cycle event-frame, but windows solely that referent as the return phase of the cycle, while gapping mention of the home, departure, and away phases of the cycle. Finally, sentence (*f*) places the windowing complex to this point within a comparison frame, in particular, within a factuality event-frame that windows consideration of the counterfactual while gapping consideration of the factual.

To consider one entire windowing complex that results from the concurrent or nested application of several distinct windowing processes, take sentence (*e*) as an example. Of the entire event that it refers to, this sentence windows the presence of a path but has gapped virtually the entirety of its particulars except for an indication that it is a return path (*back*); it windows the presence of a motion event and, within that, the Figure (*the ball*), but has gapped the Ground; it windows the presence of an agent-initiated event-frame, but within this it windows only the agent (*I*) and the final resulting subevent (rolled the ball back) while gapping mention of all the intervening actions such as my volitionally bending down, grasping the ball, and propelling the ball into motion; and it windows the presence of an iterated cycle (*kept*), and within this the return phase, but gaps the remainder of the cycle, including the ball's use within the court, its path from the court to the lawn, and its resting on the lawn. It is thus evident that a sentence can allude to quite an extensive referential complex while gapping an enormous amount of conceptual material from this complex.

10.8. SOME EVIDENCE FOR THE FUNDAMENTAL
CHARACTER OF THE WINDOWING PROCESS

A range of types and alternative patterns of windowing are exhibited by the communicative signing systems that are generated spontaneously and autonomously by deaf children in certain circumstances. As studied by Susan Goldin-Meadow, such children have hearing parents who aim without success to communicate aurally and who employ gestural indications no more extensively or elaborately than most hearing parents use with their hearing children. To express themselves to their parents, such deaf children develop their own signing systems, ones whose structure and components are largely not based on any external exemplars. Accordingly, one may interpret the characteristics of such systems as reflecting fundamental properties of cognition and of conceptual organization, where perhaps these properties are themselves innately determined. Thus, the fact that windowing figures prominently in such spontaneous signing systems argues for the conclusion that the cognitive processes of attentional windowing and gapping are sufficiently fundamental that they are not specific to spoken languages but appear at least through the whole cognitive domain of natural communication systems.

To illustrate, we can describe the alternatives of path-windowing patterns and of causal-chain-windowing patterns exhibited by a deaf child, David, observed between the ages of 2; 10 and 4; 10 (Goldin-Meadow, 1979; Goldin-Meadow and Mylander, 1990; Goldin-Meadow, p. c.). Consider first the circumstance where David would want another person to move a particular object from where it was located to a new location. One way he indicated this idea was first to point to the particular object by extending an index finger at the object and then retracting the finger a bit, and next, with the hand reoriented, to point in the same way to the new location. The initial pointing was aimed directly at the object, whether this was resting at some inanimate location or was already in the grasp of the other person. The subsequent pointing was aimed directly at the new location if this was an inanimate site, with the whole gesture perhaps adequately translated with the English verb *put* as in *Put that there*. But if a person—whether a third person or David himself—was to be the recipient or new possessor of the object, the subsequent pointing gesture was aimed at the person's chest, not hands. The whole gesture is now perhaps well translated with the English verb *give* as in *Give that to him/me*. It is not clear whether for David the conceptualization under-lying the initial pointing was of the object alone or of the object at its initial spatial location, and it is further unclear whether subsequent pointing at a person's chest was conceptualized solely as marking that person as a recipient or also as a spatial location. Nevertheless, the fact that the overall gesture does indicate initial and subsequent regions of the surrounding space that approximate and are temporally iconic with the beginning and ending points of a desired motion and the fact that the gesture does not indicate any intermediate regions of the space suggests that the gesture is much like a spoken-language indication of a path with initial and final windowing and with medial gapping.

Another way David would represent a desired object transfer was to begin as before by pointing at the object but then to indicate the path through the surrounding space that the object should follow. He would trace out this path usually again with his index finger, now re-extended, or, on occasion, with a new hand shape that represented how the other person might hold the particularly contoured object while moving it (e.g. a fist shape for holding a long thin object such as a spoon). He might then finish by pointing at the desired post-transfer location, or simply stop after a sufficient execution of the path-tracing gesture where the continued trajectory and terminus of this path could be inferred. Accordingly, to continue the comparisons, this gestural complex without the final pointing would seem to correspond to spoken-language forms of initial plus medial path windowing with final gapping, while the gestural complex that included the final point-ing would seem to correspond to a full-path windowing. Thus, David demonstrated a process of selection among alternative patterns of windowing over a path event-frame.

David employed a still further type of gesture to express a desired object transfer, one exhibiting yet another path windowing pattern. For example, to indicate to the experimenter that she should put her coat in the closet, David, without any initial point at the coat, began his gesture with a flat hand held palm downward (a hand shape used to signal carrying an object so as to place it) moving in a line toward the closet, and finished by pointing at the closet. We can now interpret this further gestural type as exhibiting medial plus final windowing with initial gapping.

David's gestural communication also exhibited what may be inter-preted as alternative patterns of causal-chain windowing. Consider, for example, the two ways in which he would represent his using drumsticks to beat his toy drum. He could clench his hands as if each were holding a drumstick and alternately swivel his hands as if swinging the drumsticks repeatedly down onto and up off a drumhead. Alternatively, he could extend the index finger of each hand as if these were the drumsticks themselves and alternately swivel his hands as if his fingertips—the ends of the 'drumsticks'—were hitting the drumhead. It seems likely that David formed both these gestural complexes out of the one framework of a single conceptual structure, an event-frame of the causal-chain type. This causal chain would have consisted of a precursor subevent [0], consisting of an intentional Agent's exercise of volition on his body; the resulting bodily movement [1], which is the initial subevent of the physical part of the causal chain that here consists of the hands clenching and alternately swiveling; the resulting medial subevent [2], consisting of the drumsticks alternately swinging; and the resulting final subevent [3], consisting of the tips of the drumsticks alternately hitting the drumhead at the bottom of their arc. By a narrow windowing interpretation, that is, where solely the overtly visible gesture is taken to be within the window, David's first gestural complex windows only the initial subevent [1] of the causal chain, i.e. the subevent in which the hands clench and swivel (or, if one takes the first gestural complex to include the whole of David's person as well as his hands, then it windows together the precursor subevent [0]—that is, the agent exercising volition—along with the initial subevent of the causal chain). By the narrow interpretation, the second gestural complex would then window the medial subevent [2] of the causal chain, i.e. the subevent in which the drumsticks swing. A wider windowing interpretation would include in a window the overt gesture plus its most directly suggested concomitant. Under this interpretation, the first gestural complex windows both the initial subevent [1] of the clenching swiveling hands, which it shows overtly, plus the directly suggested medial subevent [2] of swinging drumsticks—i.e. it windows the initial plus medial portion of the causal chain. Comparably under a wide interpretation, the second gestural complex windows both the medial subevent [2] of drumstick-swinging, which it shows overtly, plus the directly suggested final subevent [3] of drumstick tips hitting the drumhead—i.e. it windows the medial plus final portions of the causal chain. Under either the narrow or the wide interpretation, it is strongly to be inferred that David was windowing only portions of a full causal event-frame while intending to communicate the whole of the event-frame, and was thus spontaneously exhibiting the cognitive windowing process in the causal domain much as in the spatial path domain before. Such spontaneous and autonomously generated manifestations of a windowing process acting on implicit event-frames, occurring in a gestural system in a way that seems fully parallel with the same phenomena earlier demonstrated for spoken language, strongly suggest that these attentional phenomena are a fundamental part of conceptual structuring in the human cognitive system for communication, and perhaps also in much of human cognition in general.

10.9. LINGUISTIC WINDOWING AND THE COGNITIVE SYSTEM OF ATTENTION

We can now briefly consider the functions that the linguistic windowing process serves with respect to the overall organization of cognition, looking in particular at the functions served by windowing, by gapping, and by the alternatives of patterning that these can enter into. Since the fundamental characteristic of windowing is the selective distribution of attention with respect to a conceptual complex, we must first consider more closely the nature of attention before we can determine the cognitive functions of the windowing process. Our view is that the faculty of attention is the operation of a particular cognitive system. This attentional system is able to establish active connections with aspects of other cognitive systems. The attentional system appears to have extreme flexibility as to what it is able to link up with in this way (perhaps as much flexibility as any cognitive system has), and it seems able to shift these linkups with great rapidity.

In a linkup of this sort, the attentional system lends its own processing properties to the usual functioning of the other system. These properties may be quantitative as well as qualitative and executive in character. Thus, quantitatively, the posited attentional system may include an especially fine-grained and finely differentiated set of neural connections that allow it to function in the following ways: to enhance the processing of the other linked-up system; to differentiate factors in the other system in a more fine-structural fashion; and to process concurrently a greater number of factors present in the other system than it alone can do. In addition, the attentional system may have certain special processing capabilities that allow it to function qualitatively and executively in the following ways: to select certain factors within the other linked-up system for special processing; to compare and contrast various factors in the other system with each other; to detect incompatibilities across such factors and bring them into an encounter for potential resolution; to bring in processing from still other cognitive systems to form a larger field of integrated processing; and, in the execution of this last function, to modulate or bring about interactions between such other cognitive systems whose forms of processing might otherwise have little or no compatibility. It is possible that different proportions of the attentional system can be engaged in a link-up with another cognitive system in a process that gives rise to attentional gradience.

The operations of the other cognitive system would thus be able to occur over a range: more in the foreground or more in the background of attention. It is assumed that the attentional system is able to link up at any given moment with only limited portions of other systems, so that its distinctive processing capabilities are in effect a limited cognitive resource.

We can now apply these observations to windowing in language. The establishment of a linguistic window over certain portions of a conceptual complex correlates with the linkup of the attentional system with the corresponding aspects of the cognitive system which is processing that conceptual complex. On the positive side, one function served by this establishment of windows of attention over certain portions of a conceptual complex is that the enhanced processing capabilities of the attentional system can thereby be associated with only those conceptual areas that are currently taken as the most relevant or important relative to larger concerns and goals.

In a complementary fashion, the gapping of certain portions of a conceptual complex permits certain conceptual areas that are considered less relevant, more redundant, or more obvious (i.e. capable of being filled in by the hearer) to continue unenhanced at their usual background level of processing. In addition, gapping allows the limited resource of the enhancement system to be reserved for the more important areas. These two properties of gapping thus subserve the function of the efficiency of communication of conceptual material.

By this analysis, the phenomenon of alternativity in linguistic windowing would clearly arise from the flexibility characteristic of the attentional system. If the attentional system were rigidly connected with the system processing a conceptual complex, one could attend only to certain portions of that complex, never to other portions. The function served by this alternativity is that approximately the same conceptual complex can be differentially adapted to different patterns of concerns that occur within different contexts.

10.10. CONCLUSION

The present paper has examined a fundamental form of conceptual and attentional organization as this is evidenced primarily in language, though its more general cognitive counterparts have also been addressed. We have seen that human cognition appears to systematically segment the occurrence of phenomena into certain types of unitary coherent conceptual packet, here termed *event-frames*, where each type of event-frame includes certain kinds of conceptual material but not other kinds. We posited a number of conceptual factors that help determine which phenomena are in this way packeted together into an event-frame. A common cognitive principle was posited as running through these different factors: we conceptualize an event-frame as demarcated by a boundary, one that encloses a region of coherence, corelevance, and connectivity. The different types of event-frame are understood to constitute generic conceptual categories that are probably universal across languages, possibly innate, and apparently in correspondence with conceptual structures present in cognitive systems outside that of language. This paper has treated several types of event-frames: a path, a causal chain, a cycle, a participant interaction, and an interrelationship. This last type of event-frame includes both the Figure–Ground interrelationship and the factual–counterfactual interrelationship, and in the latter we demonstrated a systematic relationship that affect states and explanation types bear to factuality.

Our cognition has the further capacity to select particular portions out of an event-frame and to direct greatest attention to those portions while placing the remainder of the event-frame in the background of attention. This cognitive process has here been termed the *windowing of attention* when it is realized in language by the inclusion of explicit linguistic material for the portions to be foregrounded (*windowed* portions) and the exclusion of any explicit material for those portions to be backgrounded (*gapped* portions). As part of a general cognitive capacity here termed *conceptual alternativity*, we are further able to perform the selective windowing process in different patterns for the same event-frame. Several event-frames are able to co-occur or to be embedded one within another, each with its own windowing pattern, so as to form a rather extensive referential complex with a corresponding complex of composite windowing.

For any event-frame, those portions that are selected for placement in the foreground of attention may be experienced as forming a seamless continuous unity in a cognitive process here termed *cognitive splicing*. This process may well constitute one of the major psychological constancies, though one perhaps little recognized. Such a constancy could have evolved for the selective advantage of (among other things) maintaining a single goal schema, consisting of a particular intention plus its realization, invariant across a wide range of executional variation.

Finally, we observed the strong parallels between windowing in spoken language and what seems to be a fully comparable process in the spontaneously developed signing systems of certain deaf children. Here, as well as in the parallels between linguistic windowing and perception or motor control, and in several further respects, the linguistic structures examined in this paper can be seen as reflecting general and fundamental forms of cognitive organization.

REFERENCES

FILLMORE, C. J. (1982). 'Frame Semantics,' in Linguistic Society of Korea, (ed.), *Linguistics in the Morning Calm*, 111–37. Seoul: Hanshin Publishing Co.

GOLDIN-MEADOW, S. (1979). 'Structure in a Manual Communication System Developed Without a Conventional Language Model: Language Without a Helping Hand,' in H. Whitaker and H. A. Whitaker (eds.), *Studies in Neurolinguistics* iv. New York: Academic Press.

—— and MYLANDER, C. (1990). 'Beyond the Input Given: The Child's Role in the Acquisition of Language,' *Language* **66/2**: 323–55.

JACKENDOFF, R. (1990). *Semantic Structures*. Cambridge, Mass.: MIT Press.

KEENAN, E. L., and COMRIE, B. (1977). 'Noun Phrase Accessibility and Universal Grammar,' *Linguistic Inquiry* **8**: 63–99.

KUNO, S. (1987). *Functional Syntax: Anaphora, Discourse and Empathy*. Chicago: University of Chicago Press.

LAKOFF, G. (1987). *Women, Fire and Dangerous Things: What Categories Reveal About the Mind*. Chicago: University of Chicago Press.

ROSCH, E. (1978). 'Principles of Categorization,' in E. Rosch and B. Lloyd (eds.), *Cognition and Categorization*, 27–48. Hillsdale, NJ: Erlbaum.

TALMY, L. (1972). 'Semantic Structures in English and Atsugewi' Dissertation, University of California at Berkeley.

—— (1976). 'Semantic Causative Types,' in M. Shibatani (ed.), Syntax and Semantics vi: *The Grammar of Causative Constructions*, 43–116. New York: Academic Press.

—— (1978). 'Figure and Ground in Complex Sentences,' in J. H. Greenberg (ed.), *Universals of Human Language* iv: *Syntax*, 625–49. Stanford, Calif.: Stanford University Press.

—— (1983). 'How Language Structures Space,' in H. L. Pick, Jr., and L. P. Acredolo (eds.), *Spatial Orientation: Theory, Research, and Application*, 225–82. New York: Plenum Press.

—— (1985). 'Lexicalization Patterns: Semantic Structure in Lexical Forms,' in T. Shopen (ed.), *Language Typology and Syntactic Description* iii: *Grammatical Categories and the Lexicon*, 57–149. Cambridge: Cambridge University Press.

—— (1988a). 'The Relation of Grammar to Cognition,' in B. Rudzka-Ostyn (ed.), *Topics in Cognitive Linguistics*, 165–205. Amsterdam: Benjamins.

—— (1988b). 'Force Dynamics in Language and Cognition,' *Cognitive Science* 12: 49–100.

—— (1990). 'Fictive Motion and Change in Language and Cognition,' plenary address at Conference of the International Pragmatics Association, Barcelona.

—— (1991). 'Path to Realization: A Typology of Event Conflation,' *Proceedings of the Seventeenth Annual Meeting of the Berkeley Linguistics Society*.

—— (forthcoming). 'Fictive Motion in Language and "Ception": The Emanation Type,' in P. Bloom *et al.* (eds.), *Language and Space*. Cambridge, Mass.: MIT Press.

WIERZBICKA, A. (1975). 'Why "Kill" Does Not Mean "Cause to Die": The Semantics of Action Sentences,' *Foundations of Language* 13: 491–528.

11

The Case for 'Effector': Case Roles, Agents, and Agency Revisited

Robert D. Van Valin, Jr. and David P. Wilkins

INTRODUCTION

Although they may call them case roles, participant roles, thematic roles (θ-roles), thematic relations, proto-roles, or role archetypes, most current theories of grammar have some account of semantic roles and their relation to syntax. As Newmeyer (1986: 106) notes: 'Fillmore and the case grammarians deserve credit for impressing upon the linguistic community the importance of these roles.' Further, in all discussions of the 'semantic side' of grammar, beginning with Fillmore 1968 and Gruber 1965, 'agent' plays a central part. Since virtually every theory which incorporates a thematic-relations component invokes this role, its status as one of the vital elements in linguistic theory and description has gone largely unchallenged. The purpose of this paper is to argue against this view of agent as primary and pivotal and to show that agent, in the sense in which it has typically been used in recent linguistic theory, is a derivative notion which is not as essential to grammar as has previously been suggested. We will argue that it is better understood as being derived from the interaction of a number of morphosyntactic, lexical, semantic, and pragmatic factors which coalesce at the level of the contextualized interpretation of the utterance, and that the more basic role arising from verb semantics is what we call *effector*, roughly, the dynamic participant doing something in an event. This thematic relation underlies agent, force, and instrument, roles which are normally taken to be distinct but related in some way. Our goal is to demonstrate the basicness of the effector relation and to show how agent, force, and instrument interpretations derive from it.

We would like to thank Cliff Goddard, Karin Michelson, Masayoshi Shibatani, Len Talmy, and Lindsay Whaley for their comments on previous versions of this paper.

The discussion will proceed as follows. In Section 11.1 several different accounts of 'agent' will be briefly summarized and critiqued. In 11.2 the Role and Reference Grammar [RRG] (Van Valin, 1993) view of case roles in general and agent in particular will be presented, and it will be shown why the account given in earlier work in the theory is, like many of the proposals reviewed in 11.1, flawed. In 11.3 the theory of agent as a pragmatic implicature largely triggered by properties of the argument nominal in interaction with verb semantics is presented, starting from the revised RRG analysis of agent put forth in Holisky (1987), and the derivation of force and instrument as variants of the more basic relation of effector will be presented. Conclusions are given in 11.4.

It is important to recognize that all the work to be discussed in this paper has contributed in varied and substantial ways to our knowledge of the semantic side of grammar, and all of it owes a great debt, whether acknowledged explicitly or not, to the pioneering work of Fillmore on case, case roles, and lexical semantics.

11.1. VIEWS OF AGENTS, AGENCY, AND SEMANTIC ROLES

In this section we briefly outline the views of eight linguists with respect to the notion of agent, agency, and semantic roles. The main purpose is to present a representative overview of the different positions that have been taken as far as the semantics of 'agent,' and its role in grammar, are concerned. The primary focus of this overview is semantic, rather than syntactic, in nature, and so the summaries highlight the various semantic features that have been proposed as definitional for 'agents' and 'agency.' Where relevant, we also discuss various authors' views on issues which feature prominently in later sections of the paper. These other issues include the nature of causation, the notion of 'instrument,' the notion of 'force,' and the purpose of semantic roles.

For the purposes of this paper, post-Fillmorean approaches to case roles can be divided roughly into two groups. The first, the 'cognitivist' camp, is a much more homogeneous group, represented by such linguists as Talmy, Langacker, Croft, and DeLancey. Very generally, this group is associated with the following views:

(1) linguistic meaning is a property of mind, not objective reality;
(2) in the mind there is no independent level of linguistic semantics, since semantics is not distinct from basic cognitive structure (i.e. there is a level of cognitive structure, but no level of semantic structure);
(3) syntactic structure follows largely from cognitive structure;
(4) there is no significant distinction between semantics and pragmatics.

On top of this, the 'cognitivist' camp can be said to eschew strong formalism and have only the most general of schemas for lexical semantic representation.

By contrast, the 'semanticist' group is more heterogeneous, and members are primarily identified by their not sharing in some of the assumptions of the 'cognitivists.' In particular, the 'semanticists' are viewed as identifying a level of semantics independent of basic cognition and syntax and favoring strong formalism, with a richer system for lexical decomposition. This group includes Dowty, Jackendoff, and Ravin. While Jackendoff may seem a controversial inclusion, his conceptual-structure module, which is responsible for the creation and interpretation of language-specific lexical conceptual structures, and which takes input from other cognitive modules such as vision, counts in our terms as a clearly articulated independent level of semantics.

After reviewing Fillmore's original proposal, the 'semanticists' and the 'cognitivists' will be discussed in turn.

11.1.1. *Fillmore (and Case Grammar)*

In the context of 1960s Transformational Grammar, Fillmore's (1968) 'The Case for Case' was a radical shifting of theoretical gears. Its main purpose was to change the base component by replacing syntactically defined grammatical relations like subject and object, which Fillmore did not believe were cross-linguistically valid, with semantically defined case roles, like agent, which he believed were universal and probably innate. In his introduction to the paper, Fillmore writes (pp. 2–3):

My paper will plead that the grammatical notion 'case' deserves a place in the base component of the grammar of every language. . . . what is needed is a conception of base structure in which case relationships are primitive terms of the theory and in which such concepts as 'subject' and 'direct object' are missing. The latter are regarded as proper only to the surface structure of some (but possibly not all) languages.

The paper was meant to demonstrate the viability of Fillmore's vision of a 'semantically justified universal syntactic theory'—a vision which would necessitate a drastic rethinking of the basic premises of TG. For Fillmore, it was (and remains) of importance that commonalities between languages be real and discoverable, rather than merely stipulated by theory, and a semantically driven deep structure seemed more viable for representing and explaining these commonalities than did a syntactically driven one. With regard to the nature of the Chomskian level of syntactic deep structure as it was construed in the immediately post-*Aspects* period, Fillmore (1968: 88) asserted:

It is an artificial intermediate level between the empirically discoverable 'semantic deep structure' and the observationally accessible surface structure, a level the properties of which have more to do with the methodological commitments of the grammarians than with the nature of human languages.

It is in this theoretical context that Fillmore's frequently criticized use of the term 'case' is to be understood. Fillmore's 'case' properly resided in semantic deep structure as an inherent relationship between a verb (more precisely, a predicate) and the noun phrases (more precisely, the arguments) associated with it. Primitive case roles would not typically be easily identifiable by some overt surface morphosyntactic marking, but instead would need to be discovered using the same methods that Whorf had developed for discovering other covert categories. Fillmore thus introduced the distinction between case-marking (i.e. case forms) and (deep) case relations (i.e. case roles). He writes (1968: 21):

We may agree, then, for our present purposes, with Hjelmslev, who suggests that the study of cases can be pursued most fruitfully if we abandon the assumption that an essential characteristic of the grammatical category of case *is expression in the form of affixes on substantives*. I shall adopt the usage first proposed, as far as I can tell, by Blake (1930), of using the term *case* to identify the underlying syntactic-semantic relationship, and the term *case form* to mean the expression of a case relationship in a particular language—whether through affixation, suppletion, use of clitic particles, or constraints on word order. [*Emphasis in original.*]

Fillmore has always been interested in investigating how natural languages reflect and relate to the way human beings construe their universe, and the basic case roles that he proposed were meant to capture 'certain types of judgements human beings are capable of making about the events that are going on around them, judgements about such matters as who did it, who it happened to, and what got changed' (p.24). For the purposes of our discussion we need only present the definitions he gives (pp.24–5) for three of his proposed set of cases, 'agentive', 'instrumental', and 'objective.'[1]

Agentive (A), the case of the typically animate perceived instigator of the action identified by the verb.

Instrumental (I), the case of the inanimate force or object causally involved in the action or state identified by the verb.

Objective (O), the semantically most neutral case, the case of anything representable by a noun whose role in the action or state identified by the verb is identified by the semantic interpretation of the verb itself; conceivably the concept should be limited to things which are affected by the action or state identified by the verb. The term is not to be confused with the notion of direct object, or with the name of the surface case synonymous with accusative.

Even at the outset there were questions about the appropriate characterization of *agentive*, even though, as we shall see, it is one of the more general characterizations in the literature. Fillmore (1968: 24) himself notes that '*typically* animate' is an unsatisfactory 'escape qualification,' which is used because of his 'awareness that contexts which I will say require agents are sometimes occupied by "inanimate" nouns.' The main features of this definition are *animacy*,[2] *instigation*, and *action*, and it is clear from Fillmore's discussion that his agentive case is as likely to be found with intransitive as with transitive verbs. Indeed, in recasting Sapir's typology of pronominal systems in Native American languages into his own framework, Fillmore basically highlights the issue of what has since come to be known as split intransitivity, and proposes that one set of intransitive verbs is associated with an underlying 'agentive' case (i.e. unergative verbs) while the other set is associated with an underlying 'objective' case (i.e. unaccusative verbs). Given that a number of later theorists identify 'agent' as one member in a binary opposition, it is worth pointing out that in Fillmore's characterization of the 'agentive' and 'objective' cases they

---

[1] Other cases originally proposed in Fillmore's (1968) paper are Dative (D), Factitive (F), and Locative (L). He acknowledged that this list was probably incomplete, and at various points in this paper he discusses other possible candidates.

[2] Fillmore eventually argued, in 'The Case for Case Reopened' (1977), that the problems inherent in using the notion of 'animacy' as definitional for cases were too great and it should be abandoned.

are not treated as semantic opposites. Each is described in terms which are independent of the other.

The notion of 'instrument' which Fillmore uses is also much broader than that of many linguists and covers forces, like *The wind* in *The wind opened the door*, as well as more prototypical instruments, like *the key* in *John opened the door with the key*. Instrument is not merely the inanimate version of agentive, since it, unlike agentive, is necessarily '*causally* involved in the action *or state.*'

One of the main premises of Fillmore's Case Grammar was that the case roles assigned to NPs remained constant through transformations. Thus, while the surface syntactic grammatical status of a particular NP may vary, its deep semantic role does not. Sentences like the following were used to illustrate this point (1968: 25).

(1*a*) John opened the door
(1*b*) The door was opened by John
(1*c*) The key opened the door
(1*d*) John opened the door with the key
(1*e*) John used the key to open the door

In these sentences, *John* remains the agent whether he is presented as subject (*a*, *d*, *e*) or in the *by*-phrase of a passive (*b*). Similarly, *the key* is always instrument, even though it is the subject of example (*c*), the object of example (*e*), and in a prepositional phrase in example (*d*). Finally, while the NP *the door* surfaces both as object (e.g. *a*, *c*, *d*, *e*) and as subject (e.g. *b*), it is always understood to manifest the objective case role.

The 1968 version of Case Grammar stipulated that every NP in a sentence could bear one, and only one, case role, and that predicates could not assign the same case role to different NPs in the sentence. In this respect, Fillmore had already formulated what became known in GB as the Theta-Criterion (Chomsky, 1981).[3] As a consequence of this assumption, it was possible to represent in the lexicon the set of case roles that the NPs associated with a particular verb could fill, since no case role would be repeated, and every NP would be associated with one of the designated case roles. These representations are the well-known case frames of Case Grammar. Verbs can differ as to whether a certain case role is obligatorily or optionally associated with

---

[3] Fillmore (1977) presents a modified version of this position which, like the Gruber–Jackendoff position, allowed arguments to take composite roles (e.g. agent-source with a verb like *sell*).

it, and optional case roles were placed in parenthesis in the case frame. The case frame for the verb *open*, for example, was given as +[__O(I) (A)]. In other words, the case frame states that while the verb *open* may optionally assign agentive case, or instrumental case, or both, it must always occur with an NP manifesting objective case, and this can be the only NP that the verb occurs with. This case frame is based on the following example sentences.

(2a)	The door opened	[__O]
(2b)	John opened the door	[__O + A]
(2c)	The wind opened the door	[__O + I]
(2d)	John opened the door with a chisel	[__O + I + A]

The above sentences can also be used to illustrate a further point of significance. Fillmore observed that for kernel sentences there was a preference as to which case role would appear at surface in subject position—what he called (1968: 33) the 'unmarked' subject choice. The rule he proposed is as follows:

If there is an A, it becomes the subject; otherwise, if there is an I, it becomes the subject; otherwise, the subject is the O.

This is clearly an early version of the various thematic relations hierarchies proposed by a number of different theories. We can represent this particular hierarchy as follows:

agentive > instrumental > objective

With respect to the sentences in (2), Fillmore's rule correctly predicts that if the NP filling the objective case role is the only NP to occur with *open*, then it will be treated as subject (2a). However, if there is a second NP filling either the instrumental or the agentive case role, then this NP must occur as subject (2b–d). Finally, if there are three NPs, then it is the NP in the agentive case relation which appears as the subject (2d).

These, then, are the main features of Case Grammar as first outlined in Fillmore's foundational paper. Given that the current standpoint of a number of linguists, including the authors of this paper, would be that the attention to semantic considerations in case grammar was insufficient, there is a kind of irony in Fillmore's (1968: 88) statement that 'one criticism of case grammar that has been brought to my attention is that it is too strongly motivated by semantic considerations.' Although Case Grammar claimed that a complete lexical entry would contain the semantic representation of the meaning of a form, no attention was given to detailing the nature of these semantic representations, nor was there any clear suggestion as to how the case frames would relate to the basic semantic structure of verbs. Furthermore, the semantic nature of the case roles was never made completely clear. For instance, what precisely is meant by 'perceived instigator' in the definition of agentive case, and how would we identify the presence of this feature? Finally, there seem to be some questionable calls as far as the treatment of certain verbs are concerned. Is it really sufficient, or even accurate, to say that *kill* differs from *murder* in that *kill* requires that either an instrument or an agent be present, while *murder* requires an agent? Are *like* and *please* in fact nearly synonymous, and do they truly manifest the same case frame (i.e. +[__O + D])? Later, in his 1971 paper 'Some Problems for Case Grammar,' Fillmore noted that in many situations the determination of case roles was based on 'intuitive decisions,' and for a number of sentences his intuitions failed. While intuitions play an important role in semantic research, these intuitions must be validated by some other independent means. The above criticisms notwithstanding, the importance of Fillmore's Case Grammar is indisputable.

11.1.2. *'Semanticist' approaches*

Ravin (1990) argues strongly for a model of semantic representation which is fully independent of syntactic representation, and observes (p.32): 'owing to the absence of an independent level of semantic representation, Fillmore's Case grammar is inadequate in its representation of the semantic relations that hold between predicates and arguments.'

Decompositional Theory (DT), the model of semantic representation that Ravin adopts and expands, derives from Katz's theory of semantic decomposition. In this view, semantics is an autonomous level of grammar bounded on one side by pragmatics and on the other by syntax (1990: 113). It is claimed (p.117), although nowhere adequately substantiated, that the concepts utilized in the decompositions are 'universal semantic notions that are independent of the vocabulary of any particular language.' Given that thematic relations, or case roles, are by definition both semantic and syntactic in nature, they are deemed to be 'superfluous concepts' and rejected by Ravin. If 'agent' is in fact the conjunction of properties such as animacy, causation, and action, then, Ravin argues (pp.170–1), it can be represented by the semantic markers and tree of relations given in Fig. 11.1. A verb that contains this structure in its representation (e.g. *swallow*) might then be said to assign thematic agent, but, as Ravin correctly points out, very few verbs explicitly specify the conjunction of these properties (e.g. *put*, which does not require animacy, but is often said to take an agent). So, while the semantic content typically attributed to *agent* can be captured in Ravin's system, there is no evidence that this is an especially significant cluster of properties at the level of verb decomposition.

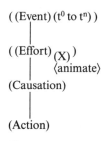

Fig. 11.1

Dowty (1991), by contrast, tackles the question of the theoretical status of thematic roles from the perspective of model-theoretic semantics. He investigates argument selection as a first strategy for gathering the kind of linguistic evidence appropriate for identifying role types correctly. As a methodological principle, he proposes (p. 562) that only those semantic distinctions that can definitely be shown to be relevant to argument selection somewhere in some natural language can count as relevant data for the definition of role types. As a consequence of this position, it turns out that 'all roles are event-dependent in meaning' (p. 564), but they never have discourse- or viewpoint-dependent meanings.

For Dowty, the most general notion of thematic role type, from the point of view of model-theoretic semantics, is 'a set of entailments of a group of predicates with respect to one of the arguments of each' (p. 552). The entailments that he discusses derive directly from the meanings of nonlogical predicates (i.e. basic verbs), and are termed 'lexical entailments.'

Dowty goes on to argue that traditional approaches to thematic roles have failed because they attempt to treat the roles as discrete categories. He proposes, instead, that thematic roles are cluster concepts which allow different degrees of membership, and so are essentially prototypes evidencing membership and centrality gradience. Having taken this position, he goes on to claim that only two roles (i.e. two cluster concepts) are needed to account for argument selection, and these are dubbed *proto-roles*. These two proto-roles, 'proto-agent' and 'proto-patient,' are characterized by the independent verbal entailments (1991: 572) listed in Table 11.1.

TABLE 11.1.

Contributing properties for the agent proto-role	Contributing properties for the patient proto-role
volitional involvement in the event or state	undergoes change of state
sentience (and/or perception)	incremetal theme[4]
causing an event or change of state in another participant	casually affected by another participant
movement (relative to the position of another participant)	sationary relative to movement of another participant
(exists independently of the event named by the verb)	(does not exist independently of the event, or not at all)

An examination of the entailments for proto-agent reveals most of the same definitional features that are proposed for agents by other writers on this subject (i.e. volition, entailed animacy, causation, motion, and change in another entity). In order to head off the possible criticism that the above entailments are as unclear as the traditional thematic roles, Dowty (p.575) puts forward two weak arguments in support of his position. The first, and less satisfactory, is that these entailments are 'not any less clear' than traditional thematic roles. The second argument makes the grandiose, and difficult to prove, claim that the entailments 'are more straightforwardly relevant to human life.'

Although the proto-roles may be nondiscrete, Dowty (p.577) notes that verb meanings 'can be as precise as you like, with definite criterial definitions.' While he acknowledges that the position he argues for may be compatible with theories like RRG in which thematic relations

---

[4] 'Incremental theme' is a new role category proposed by Dowty to refer to the entity in a telic event which undergoes a definite change of state, and undergoes this change via distinguishable separate stages (1991: 567–571).

are derived from argument positions in the logical structure of verbs, he remains sceptical as to whether his entailment properties can be derived from, or identified with, the primitive verbs of the logical structure definition.

The fullest development of a theory of thematic relations in generative grammar is found in Jackendoff's work (e.g. 1972; 1976; 1983; 1990), which takes off from the proposals in Gruber (1965). Jackendoff (1976; 1990) proposes a theory of thematic relations in which semantic role notions are derived from decompositional representations of verbs rather than being independently existing relations which are assigned to verbs. Thus, to take a very simple example from Jackendoff (1976), in the representation GO (x,y,z), which would be used for a sentence like *The ball rolled from the table to the wall*, the x argument position defines the theme role, y the source role, and z the goal role. The definition of agent is rather more complex, as it involves both the basic 'motion tier' of roles, as in [CAUSE (w), GO (x,y,z)]], and what he calls the 'action tier,' e.g. AFF (x,y), where AFF = 'affect', x = actor, and y = patient. He summarizes it as follows:

To sum up the dissection of the notion Agent, we see that it breaks down into three semi-autonomous parts: doer of the action (first argument of AFF), volitional Actor (first argument of AFF$_{+vol}$), and extrinsic instigator (first argument of CAUSE).

Like other analysts, Jackendoff recognizes that agent involves the notions of doer, volition, and causer, and he also notes the importance of the lexical properties of the NP involved:

there are plenty of verbs that require [+vol] Actors; some, like *die*, require [- vol] Actors. When a verb is unmarked for volitionality (like *roll*), an animate subject is preferably interpreted as volitional, although this preference is easily overridden by other information. Finally, if the Actor is inanimate, [- vol] must be selected for consistency. (1990: 129)

In claiming that a sentence like *Bill rolled down the hill* has three representations which differ at the level of their action tiers, i.e. *Bill* would be willful doer, nonwillful doer, and undergoer, it is not clear whether this is meant to be a claim about the conceptual structure of the English verb *roll* or the conceptual structure of the whole clause.

One issue that the 'semanticist' group does not adequately address is the nature of the interaction between the semantic level, the syntactic level, and the pragmatic level, and the type of information that each level provides. This leaves open the question of where some of the basic semantic features in their description come from, and allows the possibility that 'agent' could be viewed as a coherent (nonsuperfluous) notion that arises as a function of the interaction of these levels.

11.1.3. *'Cognitivist' approaches*

Talmy's work on semantic causative types (1976) and force dynamics (1988) has set the foundations for much of the work on semantic roles within the 'cognitivist' camp. His research program takes as its beginning point of focus the cognitive structure of complete conceptualizations of events before they are packaged into linguistic form. One of Talmy's goals is to investigate how a single conceptualization of an event can be differentially packaged within one language as well as cross-linguistically. Talmy views causation at its simplest as being non-agentive and as minimally involving two events, the causing event and the caused event. These two events could otherwise be viewed as autonomous events, but are crucially linked by a perceived causal relation to constitute a macro-event. To support the position that it is events, and not individuals, which cause other events, he notes (1976: 53) that while *The ball broke the window* can be paraphrased by *The window's breaking resulted from a ball's sailing into it*, it is not possible to simply say **The window's breaking resulted from a ball*. As for agency, he notes (1988: 9):

The inclusion of an agent in a sentence, though often yielding a syntactically simpler construction, actually involves an additional semantic complex. An agent that intends the occurrence of a particular physical event, say, a vase's breaking, is necessarily involved in initiating a causal sequence leading to that event. This sequence must begin with a volitional act by the agent to move certain parts or all of his body, and this in turn leads either to the intended event or to a further event chain, of whatever length, that leads to it.

Thus, for Talmy, an agent is an entity whose volitional act initiated an intended causal sequence leading to a final intended event. From our perspective, it is very important that he does not claim that this conjunction of properties necessarily resides in one element or another of the linguistic structure. Agent in this view is at the level of unified conceptualization, or unified interpretation, and the individual properties that make it up may be distributed across distinct elements of the sentence or may be evoked pragmatically in context or may not be present in the linguistic signal or context at all. Talmy himself, however, does not indicate exactly how this constellation of features may correspond to elements of linguistic structure. A further aspect of Talmy's research is the observation that, cross-linguistically, the preferred syntactic pattern for representing agentive causation is to 'permit expression merely of the agent and of the final event,' while gapping out the details of the causal event. Talmy (this volume) has called this 'windowing of attention' and 'gapping of attention.' The insight is that, by a process we are calling *metonymic clipping*, the agentive NP stands in for the whole causing-event sequence, and the subevent that is highlighted in an utterance is the final result state intended by the agent.

DeLancey (1984; 1990a; 1990b; 1991), Langacker (1987; 1990) and Croft (1991) follow Talmy in recognizing that agentivity is to be understood 'in terms of its place in the model of causation and event structure' (DeLancey, 1990a: 312). Further, like Dowty, these three scholars argue for what is essentially a prototype treatment of agents and agentivity. However, while the characteristic properties of Dowty's proto-agent are extensional, those proposed by the 'cognitivists' are clearly intensional. Finally, all three take essentially the same position that, in the broadest sense, an agent will be identified as the ultimate identifiable cause in the cognitively structured set of causal events that are understood to be present in the scenario evoked by a clause. Croft (1991) and Langacker (1990) independently argue for a model of semantic roles based on the perceived energy flow within an event, and 'agent' is the ultimate source of energy. Within this model, Langacker sets up a hierarchy of archetypal roles that is almost identical to that proposed in Fillmore (1968) but is defined by the flow of energy along an action chain (1990: 238):

Agent > Instrument > Patient/Mover/Experiencer

So, in this view, the definition of the 'instrument' role is as the intermediate entity in a flow of energy from 'agent' to 'patient.'

While there are these similarities in the work of Langacker, Croft, and DeLancey, there are also differences, especially between Langacker and DeLancey. Within the theoretical framework of Cognitive Grammar which Langacker has developed, *role archetypes* replace the notion of case roles or thematic relations. Role archetypes differ from these other constructs in that they are considered to be 'part of our general conceptual apparatus' and are 'not viewed as being solely or specifically linguistic in nature' (1990: 236). These archetypes are said to organize our conception of events, and so at this level play a role in semantics which has consequences for grammatical packaging and morphosyntactic coding. Langacker (p.210) notes: 'Descriptions of these roles read very much like Fillmore's classic definitions of semantic "cases" (1968), and some of the same terms are appropriate, but I must emphasize that we are not yet talking about specifically linguistic constructs.'

The roles that Langacker (p.236) considers archetypal, on the basis of cross-linguistic significance, are agent, instrument, experiencer, patient, mover, and absolute. It is important to emphasize that these roles of Cognitive Grammar do not form an exclusive set of role conceptions; they are only meant to delineate the most salient points in the conceptual space devoted to framing events. The archetypal 'agent' role is considered to be in polar opposition to the 'patient' role, and is conceived of as 'a person who volitionally carries out physical activity which results in contact with some external object and the transmission of energy to that object' (p.210). In the prototypical scenario the 'patient' role is an inanimate object which absorbs the energy originally transmitted from the 'agent' and undergoes some change of state because of this.

DeLancey's earlier position was that prototypical agents were (ultimate) volitional acting causers (1984: 185). However, he (1990*a*) notes that this position was unable to accommodate certain natural language data, and identifies the attempt to characterize the agent prototype independently of other relevant constructs as the source of the problem. In its narrowest sense, an agent is the 1st person, since 'a volitional action represents the most elaborated possible version of a causal schema' and, thus, 'the full agentive prototype can be experienced only subjectively' (1990*b*: 146). However, to get to the broader (more minimalist) conception of 'agent', DeLancey (1991: 342–3) advocates that case roles be 'defined and assigned in terms of tightly-constrained event schemas, rather than being assigned with reference to the larger more amorphous scenarios found in the lexical semantics of verbs.'

The event schema which yields 'agent' is: Agent CAUSE Theme GOTO Loc. Within a localist model, this schema is identified as underlying almost any clause which has an encoded 'cause'. Taking on Croft's (1991) notion of 'agent' as the first cause ('autonomous cause'), DeLancey then argues that what have originally been considered 'instrument subjects' (e.g. _the key_ opened the door), 'natural-force subjects,' and other inanimate subjects are 'agents.' This is because of DeLancey's controversial, and to our minds misguided, proposal that only one basic schema is manifested in any verb/clause and that 'all elements of a schema must be referred to in a clause which encodes that schema' (1991: 343). In the famous sentence *The key opened the door*, a causal schema is identified; such a schema must have a surface representative of 'agent,' and '[t]hat Agent can only be *the key*; there is no other candidate in the clause' (p. 348). DeLancey has completely abandoned Fillmore's insight that an entity can be seen to play a constant semantic role within an event, independent of the syntactic function of the NP that encodes it, and he has essentially turned Fillmore's view of the hierarchical nature of case-role accessibility to subject position into a hierarchy of accessibility of expressed causal entities to the 'agent' role in the basic causal-event schema.

Thus, we find, especially in DeLancey's approach, but also in that of Croft, a very stripped down notion of 'agent,' devoid of notions such as 'volition' or 'animacy.' But DeLancey fails to demonstrate how the factors he proposes interact to determine attributions of different degrees of agent and agentivity. In part, this may be a function of the fact that there is no means for representing anything but the grossest details of semantic structure. Moreover, he has never abandoned the position that some role called 'agent' plays a pivotal role in the characterization of grammar and in the understanding of of the similar notions such as 'natural forces' and 'instruments.' It is our contention that Talmy has the correct view of 'agent' as an important conceptual-level notion arising as a function of the total integration of information in a clause, and that the term 'agent' should be reserved for this; but a new role is needed in semantic structure (whose independent existence 'cognitivists' fail to recognize) to explain the facts that DeLancey and Croft use their stripped down notion of 'agent' to explain.

11.1.4. Discussion

Fillmore's (1968) paper set the foundations for much of the debate over semantic roles in general, and agent(ive) in particular. Are semantic roles primitive or derived? Are they discrete concepts or cluster categories? How many roles are there? Are they essentially semantic notions, or hybrid semantico-syntactic notions, or extralinguistic cognitive-conceptual structures, or mere figments of the analyst's imagination? If they are semantic notions, are their properties extensional or intensional? What is the proper way to characterize the relations between the event structure coded by verbs and the roles which are realized by NPs? Do the roles contribute to the interpretation of a clause, or do they arise as the function of the interpretation of a clause? Why do we need semantic roles anyway?

The positions presented above vary widely as to the answers they provide for these, and other, questions. However, all the authors, except Ravin, take some notion of agent to be crucial for the explanation of grammatical phenomena in natural languages. They also share the fact that whatever characterization of agent or agentivity they present, the properties identified tend to be a mix of prototypically nominal properties (e.g. animacy and volition) and prototypical event properties (e.g. activity and causation). Moreover, the primary interests of most of these authors has been to characterize verbs and/or event structures, pushing aside the question of the proper treatment of NPs and their contribution to the clause and to role interpretation. Finally, while many of the authors acknowledge similarities between agents, natural forces, and instruments, and opposition between agent and patient (undergoer), there is no fully accepted view as to the source of these similarities and how they are to be described.

If we were to amalgamate all the properties of agents or agentivity suggested by the above authors, the list would look very similar to the cluster of fourteen properties which Lakoff (1977: 244) isolates for prototypical uses of prototypical agent–patient sentences. This is significant, since his features are meant to cover a typical sentence type, not a particular role or verb type. As noted above, these properties can be divided into those which may be considered more 'entity'-related (i.e. NP-related) characteristics, as opposed to more event- or state-related (i.e. verb-related) characteristics. Thus, *singularity, definiteness, volition, animacy, responsibility, having perceptual faculties, self-controlling,* and *self-energetic* (i.e. energy source) may be seen as the entity-related properties often associated with 'agents,' while *activity (of agent), causality, manipulation of body parts or instruments, movement, change of state (in patient), spatio-temporal overlap between agent's activity and patient's change of state,* and *flow of energy from agent to patient* may be seen as the relevant event-related (or verb-related) properties.

11.2. THE VIEW FROM ROLE AND REFERENCE GRAMMAR

Role and Reference Grammar (RRG) (Van Valin, 1993) is in many respects a direct descendent of Fillmore's original Case Grammar, as many of its central features have antecedents in the 1968 model. RRG takes the same fundamental view of the nature of grammar: there is a direct mapping between the semantic representation and the syntactic structure, and case roles play an important part in the mapping. One difference between Case Grammar and RRG is that discourse pragmatics also has a crucial role in this mapping in RRG. In terms of specific features of the two theories, the Case Grammar 'S' rule, S → Modality + Proposition, is reflected in RRG in the distinct treatment of predicates, arguments, and adjuncts on the one hand and operators (e.g. tense, aspect, modality) on the other; it is also seen in the projection grammar representation of the clause, in which constituents (predicates, arguments, and adjuncts) are represented in one projection and operator categories are represented in another (see Johnson, 1987; Van Valin, 1990; 1993). The hierarchy of case roles underlying the subjectivalization and objectivalization rules in Case Grammar is the ancestor of the Actor–Undergoer Hierarchy and linking rules in RRG. In the original model there was no commitment to grammatical relations like 'subject' and 'object' as necessarily universal features of natural language, and the lack of universality of grammatical relations has been an important focus of research in RRG since its inception.[5]

In earlier work in RRG (e.g. Foley and Van Valin, 1984), the treatment of agent followed that in Dowty (1979), which was in turn derived from the analysis in Ross (1972). A fundamental feature of the RRG approach to case roles is the distinction between specific thematic relations like agent, theme, and patient, and generalized case roles called *semantic macroroles*. There are two macroroles, Actor and Undergoer, and each subsumes a number of specific thematic relations.[6] All case roles involve generalizations over the specific semantic

---

[5] Finally, on a rather different note, the original conversations which led to the development of RRG began during Thanksgiving dinner at Fillmore's house in 1974.

[6] Dowty's proto-roles bear a striking resemblance to RRG macroroles, as he himself acknowledges. There are, however, important differences between them. Proto-roles are not a 'status' or 'role' that an argument actually bears to a predicate; rather, they are clusters of properties of arguments which affect subject and object selection with verbs. To say that an argument is proto-agent is to say that it is the one that is to be realized as subject in a clause containing that verb; the only formal syntactic or semantic relation

properties of particular arguments with particular verbs, and this is illustrated in Fig. 11.2. Thematic relations such as experiencer are generalizations over the the cognizer arguments of cognition verbs like *think, believe*, and *know* on the one hand, and the perceiver arguments of perception verbs like *see, hear*, and *smell*. A macrorole such as actor is a further generalization across experiencer, agent, possessor, and other such roles. Finally, all these semantic contrasts are neutralized in syntactic grammatical relations.

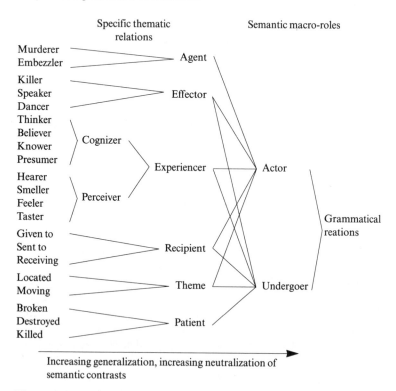

Fig. 11.2.

In the RRG decompositional system of lexical representation adapted from Dowty and the theory of semantic relations used, case

that the argument has is that of subject. In RRG, on the other hand, macroroles are roles that arguments bear, and they are a central component of the system linking semantic and syntactic representations. In addition, macroroles are discrete categories, while proto-roles are not. See Van Valin (1993) for detailed discussion.

roles are derived from argument positions in lexical representations of verbs (following the general approach of Gruber, 1965, and Jackendoff, 1976), and agent is defined as the first argument of the abstract operator DO (originally proposed as an abstract higher predicate in Ross, 1972). In the continuum of thematic relations posited in RRG, agent anchors one endpoint and patient the other; it is considered the prototype thematic relation for the macrorole Actor.

Since DO is an abstract operator, it can co-occur with a number of different argument types, yielding a number of composite case roles. Examples are given in (3–6); only the relevant argument is discussed.

(3a) John smiled (instinctively)   **smile'** (x), x = effector
(3b) John smiled (intentionally at the pretty girl)   DO (x, [**smile'** (x)]), x = agent-effector
(4a) The boy broke the window (accidentally)   [do' (x)] CAUSE [BECOME **broken'** (y)] x = effector
(4b) He broke it (on purpose)   [DO (x, [**do'** (x)])] CAUSE [BECOME **broken'** (y)] x = agent-effector
(5a) Mary slipped (on the ice)   **slip'** (x), x = theme
(5b) Mary slid (into second base)   DO (x, [**slip'** (x)]), x = agent-theme
(6a) The girl saw the picture   **see'** (x, y), x = experiencer
(6b) The girl looked at the picture   DO (x, [**see'** (x, y)]), x = agent-experiencer

In this scheme, the fact that an argument is interpreted as an agent is represented in the lexical representation ('logical structure') of the verb by DO; if a verb may, but need not, take an agent, as with *smile* and *break*, then the two lexical entries can be unified by indicating that the DO is optional (cf. Foley and Van Valin, 1984: 97).

There are several problems with this approach to agents and agency. First, this scheme attributes the property of 'agency' entirely to the verb, when it in fact is related in part to properties of the NP argument. For example, if the relevant argument of *break* were inanimate, e.g. *the rock*, there would be no possibility of a DO interpretation, but if this is true, then it cannot be the case that being an agent is solely a verbal property. Moreover, in Van Valin (1993) it is argued that case roles (thematic relations) are nothing more than mnemonics for argument positions in lexical representations, and that they derive their semantic content entirely from these representations; hence they are not independent relations with their own meaning separate from the verbs they occur with. On this view, if agency is not entirely a lexical property of a particular verb, then it cannot be represented in the logical structure for that verb. Second, given the complexity surrounding the interpretation of agency, representing agent in the logical structure of the verb can lead to counterintuitive results. For example, in Foley and Van Valin (1984) it is argued that a sentence like *Joan broke the glass* has three different interpretations with respect to the issue of intention, volition, and control, all of which are central components of agency: (i) she could have accidentally done something and not intended for that action to lead to the breaking of the glass; (ii) she could could have done something intentionally but not intended for that action to lead to the breaking of the glass; and (iii) she could have intentionally done something and intended for her action to lead to the breaking of the glass. Each of these readings would require a different lexical representation for *break*, leading to a proliferation of logical structures for *break* in the lexicon, an unfortunate result, and it is not at all clear that these differences in interpretation should be a direct function of the lexical representation of a verb. Third, there is no account of the conditions governing when DO may or may not occur with a verb with which is it 'optional.' Fourth, the RRG system of lexical representation and semantic roles treats agent as being on a par with other case roles, e.g. effector, experiencer, theme, and patient, but this is in fact misleading: while there are arguments which are 'pure' effectors, themes, and experiencers, there are no 'pure' agent arguments, because agents are always *composite*, i.e. an agent is always also an experiencer, effector, theme, etc. Hence, unlike the other roles, agent is always a *secondary interpretation* added to other, lexically determined roles. Finally, the representations in (1–4) simply make the wrong predictions in some instances. For example, if the main difference between *see* and *look at* is agency, then *look at* + agency-cancelling adverbial should be equivalent to *see*, but this does not seem to be the case, as shown in (7).

(7a) Max accidentally looked at his neighbor's test and was accused of cheating ≠
(7b) Max saw his neighbor's test and was accused of cheating

It is important to note that many of the arguments given here to demonstrate problems with the original RRG approach to agents and agency are also applicable to a number of theories outlined in Section 1, most particularly that of Jackendoff. In addition, verbs which clearly take an agent argument, e.g. *murder*, do not easily co-occur with adverbs like *accidentally* or *inadvertently*, as in (10b) below; yet *look at* seems to quite readily, which suggests that its actor is not an agent like that of *murder*. There are thus serious problems with the account of agent and agency, like the one sketched here.

11.3. AGENTS, EFFECTORS, FORCES, AND INSTRUMENTS

11.3.1. *Agent as a pragmatic implicature*

In a very important paper, Holisky (1987) analyzes the coding of intransitive 'subjects' in Tsova-Tush (Bats) and proposes a radically different account of agent from those discussed in the previous two sections. On the basis of variable interpretation of the single argument of intransitive verbs as agentive or non-agentive, she puts forth the following claim:

I would argue that the meaning of agent is often not a property of the semantic structure of the predicate at all. (It does not always correspond to the operator DO.) Agent interpretation often arises, rather, from the intersection of the semantics of the clause (the semantics of both the actor NP and the predicate) and general principles of conversation (cf. Grice, 1975). It particular, it derives from the pragmatic principle proposed in [8].

[8] Pragmatic principle: You may interpret effectors and effector-themes which are human as agents (in the absence of any information to the contrary). (pp.118–19)

The basic insight of Holisky's analysis is that most verbs are simply unmarked for agency, and that the interpretation of an argument as an agent is a pragmatic inference or implicature and not an inherent property of the verb's semantic representation. Consider the examples in (9).

- (9a) Larry killed the deer
- (9b) Larry intentionally killed the deer
- (9c) Larry accidentally killed the deer
- (9d) The explosion killed the deer

The sentence in (9a) is neutral with respect to whether the actor is an agent or not; there is no explicit indicator to force an interpretation one way or another. In terms of (8), the default reading would be that of an agent. The default reading is confirmed in (9b) by the occurrence of the adverb *intentionally*. However, the addition of the agency-cancelling adverb *accidentally* in (9c) does not result in a contradiction of any kind; rather, it acts as 'information to the contrary' and cancels the inference in (8). In (9*d*) principle (8) cannot apply and the inference cannot arise, because the actor is inanimate. Hence, it must be concluded that a verb like *kill* does *not* have an agent argument in its semantic representation; rather, it has an effector argument which may be interpreted as an agent according to pragmatic principle (8).

There are verbs in English which have an agent in their semantic representation, but they are very few.[7] The prime example of such a verb is *murder*, whose actor must be an agent, and its logical structure would contain DO. With verbs such as these, the occurrence of an inanimate actor or the addition of an agency-cancelling adverb is either deviant semantically or at the very least highly marked.

(10*a*) Larry murdered his neighbor
(10*b*) *Larry inadvertently murdered his neighbor
(10*c*) *The explosion murdered Larry's neighbor

This approach avoids all the problems with positing agents in the semantic representation of most verbs noted in the previous section. First, it locates the agent reading for most verbs in the interaction of the lexical properties of the NP argument with the semantics of the verb in the context of the clause as a whole. Hence, the problem of a different semantic representation for every possible construal of agency in a clause simply does not arise. Second, it is no longer necessary to indicate that DO is optional with a verb; it occurs only with verbs which lexicalize agency, e.g. *murder*; with other verbs the agent interpretation is derived via principle (8). Third, the nature of agent as an overlay on lexically determined case roles is naturally captured. Finally, in the case of *see* and *look at*, the contrast between these two verbs would not be captured in terms of DO, since *look at* need not have an agentive experiencer, as (5*b*) shows, but rather in terms of the contrast between state and activity perception verbs. This would be represented as in (11).

(11*a*) State: *see* see' (x, y)   x = experiencer
(11*b*) Activity: *look at* do' (x, [see' (x, y)])   x = effector-experiencer[8]

---

[7] Languages vary with respect to how often agency is lexicalized in verbs. For example, Hasegawa (1992) shows that Japanese verbs like 'kill' and 'break (transitive)' take true agent arguments, not simply effectors, unlike their English counterparts. Hence it appears that agency is lexicalized in more Japanese verbs than English verbs.

[8] *do'* in the RRG system is a generalized activity verb, and it is completely neutral with respect to agency. Its first argument is an effector. Also, this representation should not be taken to be complete in any sense; it is merely intended to represent the contrast between the two types of perception verb.

One piece of evidence for this contrast comes from the following question–answer pair.

(12a) What is John doing?
(12b) He's looking at/*seeing the picture

The agent interpretation with perceptual activity verbs like *look at* and *listen to* derives via principle (8), just as with other activity verbs (or verbs containing an activity component in their logical structure, e.g. *kill*). There is no DO in their semantic structure.

An important facet of the context of the clause as a whole for the interpretation of agent is the grammatical construction(s) involved.[9] A grammatical construction may impose a particular interpretation on the effector argument which can lead to a strong agent reading or can preclude it. Two constructions with this property are causative and purposive constructions. In monoclausal causative constructions of the type found in many languages, e.g. French, Italian, Jacaltec, Japanese (but not English), the causee may or may not be interpreted as an agent, and this interpretation is often constrained by the morphological case it bears. The following French examples are from Hyman and Zimmer (1976) and the Bolivian Quechua examples are from Bills *et al.* (1969).

(13a) J'ai   fait   nettoyer les toilettes au   général   (French)
      I-have made clean   the toilets to.the general
      'I made the general clean the toilets'
(13b) J'ai   fait   nettoyer les toilettes par le général
      I-have made clean   the toilets by the general
      'I had the general clean the toilets'
(14a) Nuqa   Fan-ta   rumi-ta   apa-ci-ni   (Bolivian Quechua)
      1SG   Juan-ACC rock-ACC   carry-CAUSE-1sg
      'I made Juan carry the rock'
(14b) Nuqa   Fan-wan   rumi-ta   apa-ci-ni
      1SG   Juan-INST rock-ACC   carry-CAUSE-1sg
      'I had Juan carry the rock'

In the (*a*) examples the causee (*le général* in (13), *Fan* in (14)) is not normally interpreted as an agent, whereas in the (*b*) examples it can be so understood. The only difference between the sentences in each pair

9 RRG, like Fillmore's Construction Grammar (1988), recognizes grammatical constructions as central to linguistic analysis and description, but they differ quite substantially in terms of how constructions are to be analyzed and formally represented. See Hasegawa (1992) for a detailed presentation of how the two approaches can be integrated.

is the case-marker borne by the causee NP, and so we may conclude that in the French opposition of *à* vs. *par* and Quechua opposition of ACC versus INST, *à* and ACC block the agent implicature based on (8), while *par* and INST permit it. These contrasts highlight another deficiency in the lexical representation system in (3–6): if agent were part of the lexical representation of the verb, then the causative constructions in (13*a*) and (14*a*) would involve changing the thematic relation of the causee (i.e. from agent to effector), while those in (13*b*) and (14*b*) would not. In the analysis proposed here, there is no change in the thematic relation of the causee at all; rather, the agent implicature is allowed in one case and blocked in the other.

Purposive constructions require that the main clause subject want or intend for the situation in the purposive clause to come about, and therefore it forces an agent interpretation. Consider the following examples

(15*a*) John rolled down the hill
(15*b*) The ball rolled down the hill
(16*a*) John rolled down the hill in order to get to the road before the bikers got there
(16*b*) *The ball rolled down the hill in order to bounce into the lake

The first sentence in (15) is ambiguous with respect to whether *John* is an agent or not; the situation could be one in which he threw himself down the hill or one in which he tripped and fell. The (*b*) example is not ambiguous, by virtue of the inherent lexical content of the subject *ball*. Adding a purposive clause renders (*a*) unambiguous and (*b*) nonsensical, as the sentences in (16) show clearly. The interpretive requirements of purposive constructions are so strong that they can override the normal implications of the lexical meaning of a verb and impose an agentive interpretation where it would otherwise be impossible. This is exemplified in (17).

(17) Jesus died to save us from our sins

Die is often taken to be the prototype of a *patient*-taking verb, and yet in (17) it is occurring with a purposive clause, with its subject receiving a quasi-agentive reading. This is not an odd fact about English; in Tsova-Tush (Holisky, 1987) and Acehnese (Durie, 1985), the single argument of *die* can receive agent-marking in the context of religious martyrdom. It would be extremely *ad hoc* and unrevealing to say that there is a separate verb *die* which takes an agent rather than a patient argument and occurs only in the context of religious martyrdom; rather, it is clearly preferable to say that there is only one verb *die*, and that this interpretation is imposed by the purposive construction, just as in (16*a*).

There are, then, three factors in the determination of whether an argument will be interpreted as an agent: the lexical semantic properties of the verb, the inherent lexical content of the NP argument, and the grammatical construction in which the verb and NP co-occur. In terms of lexical semantic properties of verbs, those with an activity predicate in their logical structure admit an agentive interpretation for their actor more readily than those without one; in other words, activity/accomplishment > achievement > state.[10] The factor of inherent lexical content of the NP is extremely complex; the major parameters involved are summarized in Fig. 11.3.[11]

The fundamental insight in this figure is that there are at least two competing, and interlinked, hierarchies of properties which can be used to predict whether the referent of a particular NP is likely to be conceived of, and/or treated, as an agent in an actional event. From left to right, along the top, the properties delineate what is essentially an animacy hierarchy. In this hierarchy, for instance, +*human* implicates, but does not entail, *rational*, which in turn implicates *intentional*, which in turn implicates *volitional*, and so on. In the philosophical and linguistic literature, *volition* has a diverse range of characterizations, but for our purposes it is a property of entities which manifest nonconscious basic acts of will (such as a baby crying for milk). *Intention*, on the other hand requires consciousness of wills, and ability to plan, and *rationality* adds to these components that the entity is knowledgeable about what the resulting consequences of its acts will be. If we compare the two sentences *The looter broke the window* and *The baby broke the window*, we can see directly the effect of these entity

[10] Achievements outrank states here because there are achievement verbs which are inchoate activities, e.g. Georgian *aṁyerdeba* 'start singing' (Harris, 1981) or Hausa *ruugàa* 'start running' (Abdoulaye, 1992).

[11] This figure originally appeared in Wilkins (1990). There it was argued that many of the basic properties that are identified here correspond to semantic primitives proposed by Wierzbicka (1988; 1992). 'Speaker' corresponds to Wierzbicka's (1992) 'I,' 'addressee' to 'you,' 'other socially relevant humans' to 'someone,' '+entity' to 'something,' '+animate' to something which can 'feel' and 'do,' 'volitional' to 'want,' 'intentional' to something which can 'thing' and/or 'say,' and 'rational' to something which can 'know.' We would suggest that Wierzbicka include a primitive 'move' or 'go' which corresponds to 'motive' in this schema. It should also be acknowledged that the hierarchical sets of features given here has been heavily influenced by Silverstein (1976; 1981).

Typology of Argument Properties
Relevant to 'Agency' Assignments
in Natural Languages
(i.e. an overview of dependency relations amongst
the semantically encoded or entailed properties of
certain nominals/nouns which can detemine distinct
morphosyntactic/grammatical treatments in
different natural languages)

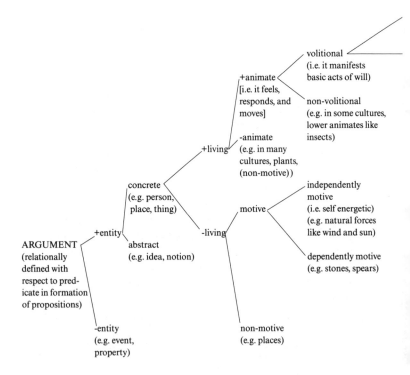

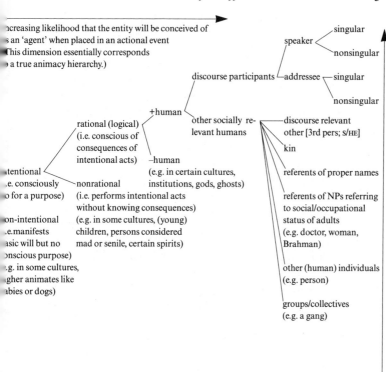

increasing likelihood that the entity will be conceived of as an 'agent' when placed in an actional event. This dimension essentially corresponds to a true animacy hierarchy.)

speaker — singular / nonsingular

discourse participants — addressee — singular / nonsingular

+human — other socially relevant humans

rational (logical) (i.e. conscious of consequences of intentional acts)

intentional (i.e. consciously do for a purpose)

nonrational (i.e. performs intentional acts without knowing consequences)

−human (e.g. in certain cultures, institutions, gods, ghosts)

non-intentional (i.e. manifests basic will but no conscious purpose) (e.g. in some cultures, higher animates like babies or dogs)

(e.g. in some cultures, (young) children, persons considered mad or senile, certain spirits)

discourse relevant other [3rd pers; S/HE]

kin

referents of proper names

referents of NPs referring to social/occupational status of adults (e.g. doctor, woman, Brahman)

other (human) individuals (e.g. person)

groups/collectives (e.g. a gang)

increasing likelihood that the entity will be conceived of as an 'agent' when placed in an actional event. This dimension corresponds very roughly to proposed empathy and topicality hierarchies.)

properties on the canonical interpretation of agency in the sentence. Although both sentences can be modified by *accidentally*, showing that there is no entailment that the act was intentional, the default interpretation of the sentence with the noun *looter* is that this person is a true intentional and rational agent who broke the window on purpose. The semantics of *looter* is such that it entails a human entity who willfully, intentionally, and rationally breaks into places in order to destroy things and take the things they want; thus agency is strongly implicated by the co-occurrence of this noun and the verb 'break.' *Baby*, by contrast, refers to an entity that is too young to look after itself and to do things on its own, and may, therefore, be considered nonrational, and non-intentional. So it is not surprising that the default interpretation of *The baby broke the window* is that the baby accidentally instigated the act, and so is not considered a 'true' agent.

In the vertical dimension, two entities may be of the same animacy type, but will be differentiated in terms of their ability to trigger agency attributions when occurring in an actional context, because they differ in some vaguer notion of 'experiential salience.' More 'experientially salient' entity notions tend to be higher on the vertical axis. The type of notion we are trying to get at can be exemplified by the fact that *rock* and *tornado* are both nonliving, physical entities, but *tornado* is more likely to be treated like an agent in an actional event, because it is independently motive (i.e. has its own energy source). The tornado is not more animate than the rock, it just happens to share one of the properties which also characterizes animates, self-movement (self-energetic). Similarly, the first person is no more animate than the second person, but, as DeLancey (1990*b*) and Langacker (1990) suggest, one can be sure of one's own volition, intention and rationality, but not of that of another person's. As noted in Section 11.1.3, DeLancey (1990*b*: 146) suggests that 'the full agentive prototype can be experienced only subjectively.' This vertical dimension might be best described using Langacker's (1990: 248) proposal that such hierarchical organization in the attribution of agency could be explained by an empathy hierarchy which he describes as reflecting 'a person's assessment of his relation to other sorts of entities.' It should also be pointed out that, at least for the human entities, the vertical hierarchy closely corresponds to proposed topicality hierarchies.

Finally, the influence of grammatical constructions on the interpretation of an argument as an agent is significant, but it has not been explored in the same depth as the other two factors. This is an important topic for future investigations.

11.3.2. *The derivation of instrument and force from effector*

It has been argued throughout this paper that agent, force, and instrument are but allo-roles of the more basic role of effector, and in the previous section we showed how agent derives from effector for most verbs. In this section, the nature of force and instrument will be investigated.

Forces are inanimate effectors which share two crucial properties with human and animate effectors: they are capable of independent motion and action, and they are not subject to the control of another effector, animate or inanimate. In terms of Fig. 11.3, they are [concrete, –living, motive]. Wind, rain, storms, floods, earthquakes, and lightning act on their own, without any kind of external instigation. Moreover, forces instigate causal chains which can have an intermediate effector, e.g. *The storm did most of its damage with its large hail and high winds*. Instruments lack both of these properties: they are inanimate entities which are not capable of independent motion or action and are subject to the control of another effector. Even where they appear to be the first segment in a causal sequence, e.g. *The rock broke the window*, the sentence must be understood to have an unspecified instigator which caused the rock to come into contact with the window, be it a boy, the wind, or a truck tire.[12]

The RRG system of logical structure representations make it possible to capture the distinction between instigator effectors and non-instigator effectors in a straightforward way. Consider the accomplishment logical structure in (18).

(18) $[\ [\textbf{do}' (x) \ ] \text{CAUSE} [\textbf{do}' (y, [...]) \ ] \ ] \ ] \text{CAUSE} [\text{BECOME } \textbf{pred}' (z) \ ]$

In (18), effector x induces an action by y, which may be unspecified (if the second argument of the second *do'* is unspecified (as indicated by $\emptyset$)) or which may be 'come into contact with z' if this argument is

---

[12] The view of instrument presented here is consistent with the first three components of Wierzbicka's (1980: 6–7) candidate for a universal definition of the 'instrumental case': something happened to Y/because something happened in IN/because X did something. Thus, something happened to the window (it broke), because something happened to the rock (it moved through the air), because the boy/the wind/the truck tire did something (threw the rock/blew it through the air/flicked it from the ground into the air).

[BECOME **be-at'** (z,y)], or which may represent a different event, and this sequence in turn induces a change of state in *z*. The 'come into contact with' event is the canonical case of a manipulated instrumental entity in a causal sequence. In Section 11.1.3 we introduced the term *metonymic clipping*, which is explicitly represented in these logical structures by a $\emptyset$ in the second argument position of the first **do'**. Some examples of forces and instruments with their logical structures are given in 19.[13]

(19a) The typhoon destroyed the village

(19a') [[**do'** (typhoon, $\emptyset$)] CAUSE [**do'** ($\emptyset$, $\emptyset$)]] CAUSE [BECOME **destroyed'** (village)]

(19a'') *[[**do'** ($\emptyset$, $\emptyset$)] CAUSE [**do'** (typhoon, $\emptyset$)]] CAUSE [BECOME **destroyed'** (village)]

(19b) The boy broke the window with the rock

(19b') [[**do'** (boy, $\emptyset$)] CAUSE [**do'** (rock, [BECOME **be-at'** (window, rock)]]] CAUSE [BECOME **broken'** (window)]

(19c) The rock broke the window

(19c') [[**do'** ($\emptyset$, $\emptyset$)] CAUSE [**do'** (rock, [BECOME **be-at'** (window, rock)]]] CAUSE [BECOME **broken'** (window)]

(19c'') *[[**do'** (rock, $\emptyset$)] CAUSE [**do'** ($\emptyset$, $\emptyset$)]] CAUSE [BECOME **broken'** (window)]

(19d) The boy broke the window

(19d') [[**do'** (boy, $\emptyset$)] CAUSE [**do'** ($\emptyset$, $\emptyset$)]] CAUSE [BECOME **broken'** (window)]

(19e) The terrorists destroyed the car with a bomb

(19e') [[**do'** (terrorists, $\emptyset$)] CAUSE [**do'** (bomb, [BECOME **exploded'** (bomb)]]] CAUSE [BECOME **destroyed'** (car)]

(19f) The bomb destroyed the car

(19f') [[**do'** ($\emptyset$, $\emptyset$)] CAUSE [**do'** (bomb, [BECOME **exploded'** (bomb)]]] CAUSE [BECOME **destroyed'** (car)]

(19f'') *[[**do'** (bomb, [BECOME **exploded'** (bomb)])] CAUSE [**do'** ($\emptyset$, $\emptyset$]] CAUSE [BECOME **destroyed'** (car)]

A force argument, then, is the inanimate but independently motive effector of the first CAUSE in a causal sequence, while an instrument is the inanimate effector-theme (it is both the first argument of **do'**, which defines effector, and the second argument of **be-at'**, which defines theme) which occurs as in the second argument of the first CAUSE in a causal sequence. We could define the notion of 'instigator' as the effector of the first CAUSE in a causal sequence. Note that this is

---

[13] The expanded logical structures proposed herein follow the program of richer lexical decomposition for RRG outlined in Van Valin and Wilkins (1993).

not a thematic relation like effector or theme but rather a label for a subclass of effectors. The contrast among agent, force, and instrument may be summarized as in (20).

(20a) Agent: animate (preferably human), effector (preferably instigator)
(20b) Force: inanimate (motive), effector, instigator
(20c) Instrument: inanimate (nonmotive), effector, non-instigator

One consequence of this analysis is that force arguments only occur in causal sequences; that is, *the wind* is a force in *The wind blew down the tower* but not in *The wind is blowing briskly*, in which it is merely an effector. NPs like *the bomb* in (19e, f) are instruments, not forces, in this analysis; while they may have their own energy, they are not independently motive and must be planted by an instigating effector. Examples with *bomb* are misleading, due to the nature of the noun; the same causal structure can be seen in the pair *The pranksters stunk up the classroom with the rotten eggs* and *The rotten eggs stunk up the classroom*, in which the instruments have no real independent energy which makes it seem that they are somewhat force-like. The characterization of instrument in (20c) applies equally to less prototypical instances of instrument, as in e.g. *The woman looked at the parade with binoculars*, in which *binoculars* is not part of a causal sequence but is simply an accessory. In the prototypical case, however, the instrument is an effector-theme, as in (19b).

11.4. CONCLUDING REMARKS

We have argued that, contrary to the conventional wisdom of the field, agent is not a basic or fundamental semantic role at all and that very few verbs actually lexically require an agent argument. Rather, most of the relevant verbs take effector arguments which may under the appropriate circumstances be interpreted as an agent in the context of the sentence as a whole. The reason that agent has seemed to be so important and so prevalent is that most verbs denoting actional situations take effector arguments, and these arguments are very often human; given this high frequency of human effectors in action sentences, the default interpretive principle in (8) yields sentences with subjects interpreted as agents. When we dissect the notion of agent, to use Jackendoff's appropriate phrase, we find that in the vast majority of these cases the actual lexical requirement of the verb is that its subject be a doer (effector) and not necessarily an agent. This has important implications for the notion of an 'agent prototype' and the idea that relations like force and instrument are just 'less good' members of the category of which agent is the central member. The features in question do not in fact define a prototype, but rather constitute the relevant information on the basis of which the agent implicature is made. Moreover, force and instrument are not variants on agent at all but rather are variants of the effector role which underlies agent as well. All three roles are doers which differ in certain crucial ways along the dimensions of the lexical properties of the NP and their position in the causal sequence defined by the verb.

REFERENCES

ABDOULAYE, M. L. (1992). 'Aspects of Hausa Morphosyntax in Role and Reference Grammar.' Ph.D. dissertation, SUNY Buffalo.
BAKER, M. (1985). Review of Fillmore's 'The Case for Case', in B. Levin (ed.), *Lexical Semantics in Review* 63–73. Cambridge, Mass.: MIT Center for Cognitive Science.
BILLS, G., BERNARDO VALLEJO, C., and TROIKE, R. (1969). *An Introduction to Spoken Bolivian Quechua*. Austin: University of Texas Press.
CHOMSKY, N. (1981). *Lectures on Government and Binding*. Dordrecht: Foris.
CROFT, W. (1991). *Syntactic Categories and Grammatical Relations: The Cognitive Organization of Information*. Chicago: University of Chicago Press.
DELANCEY, S. (1984). 'Notes on Agentivity and Causation,' *Studies in Language* 8: 181–214.
—— (1990a). 'Ergativity and the Cognitive Model of Event Structure in Lhasa Tibetan,' *Cognitive Linguistics* 1: 289–322.
—— (1990b). 'Cross-linguistic Evidence for the Structure of the Agent Prototype,' *Papers and Reports on Child Language Development* 29: 141–7.
—— (1991). 'Event Construal and Case Role Assignment,' *Proceedings of the Seventeenth Annual Meeting of the Berkeley Linguistics Society*, 338–53.
DOWTY, D. (1979). *Word Meaning and Montague Grammar*. Dordrecht: Reidel.
—— (1991). 'Thematic Proto-roles and Argument Selection,' *Language* 67: 547–619.
DURIE, M. (1985). *A Grammar of Acehnese*. Dordrecht: Foris.
FILLMORE, C. J. (1968). 'The Case for Case,' *Universals in Linguistic Theory*, in E. Bach and R. T. Harms (eds.), 1–88. New York: Holt, Rinehart & Winston.
—— (1971). 'Some Problems for Case Grammar,' *Monograph Series on Languages and Linguistics* 24: 35–56.
—— (1977). 'The Case for Case Reopened,' *Grammatical relations*, in P. Cole

and J. Sadock (eds.), *Syntax and Semantics* viii: 59–81. New York: Academic Press.

—— (1988). 'The Mechanisms of Construction Grammar,' *Proceedings of the Fourteenth Annual Meeting of the Berkeley Linguistics Society*, 35–55.

FOLEY, W. A., and VAN VALIN, R. D., JR. (1984). *Functional Syntax and Universal Grammar*. Cambridge: Cambridge University Press.

GRICE, H. P. (1975). 'Logic and Conversation,' *Speech Acts*, in P. Cole and J. Morgan (eds.), *Syntax and Semantics* iii: 41–58. New York: Academic Press.

GRUBER, J. (1965). 'Studies in Lexical Relations.' Ph.D. dissertation, MIT.

HARRIS, A. (1981). *Georgian Syntax*. Cambridge: Cambridge University Press.

HASEGAWA, Y. (1992). 'Syntax, Semantics and Pragmatics of *te*-linkage in Japanese.' Ph.D. dissertation, University of California at Berkeley.

HOLISKY, D. A. (1987). 'The case of the intransitive subject in Tsova-Tush (Batsbi),' *Lingua* 71: 103–32.

HYMAN, L., and ZIMMER, K. (1976). 'Embedded Topic in French,' in C. N. Li (ed.), *Subject and Topic*, 189–211. New York: Academic Press.

JACKENDOFF, R. S. (1972). *Semantic Interpretation in Generative Grammar*. Cambridge, Mass.: MIT Press.

—— (1976). 'Toward an Explanatory Semantic Representation,' *Linguistic Inquiry* 7: 89–150.

—— (1983). *Semantics and Cognition*. Cambridge, Mass.: MIT Press.

—— (1990). *Semantic Structures*. Cambridge, Mass.: MIT Press.

JOHNSON, M. 1987. 'A New Approach to Clause Structure in Role and Reference Grammar,' *Davis Working Papers in Linguistics* 2: 55–9.

LAKOFF, G. (1977). 'Linguistic gestalts,' *Papers from the Thirteenth Regional Meeting of the Chicago Linguistic Society*, 236–87.

LANGACKER, R. (1987). *Foundations of Cognitive Grammar*, i. Stanford, Calif.: California University Press.

—— (1990). *Concept, Image and Symbol: The Cognitive Basis of Grammar*. Berlin: Mouton de Gruyter.

NEWMEYER, F. J. (1986). *Linguistic Theory in America*, 2nd edn. New York: Academic Press.

RAVIN, Y. (1990). *Lexical Semantics Without Thematic Roles*. Oxford: Clarendon Press.

ROSS, J. R. (1972). 'Act,' in D. Davidson and G. Harmon (eds.), *Semantics of Natural Language*, 70–126. Dordrecht: Reidel.

SILVERSTEIN, M. (1976). 'Hierarchy of features and ergativity,' in R. M. W. Dixon (ed.), *Grammatical Categories in Australian Languages*, 112–71. Canberra: AIAS.

SILVERSTEIN, M. (1981). 'Case marking and the nature of language,' *Australian Journal of Linguistics* 1: 277–44.

TALMY, L. A. (1976). 'Semantic Causative Types,' in M. Shibatani (ed.), *Syntax and Semantics* vi: *The Grammar of Causative Constructions*, 43–116. New York: Academic Press.

—— (1988). 'Force Dynamics in Language and Cognition,' *Cognitive Science* 12: 49–100.

VAN VALIN, R. D., JR. (1990). 'Layered Syntax in Role and Reference Grammar,' in M. Bolkestein *et al.* (eds.), *Layers and Levels of Representation in Language Theory: A Functional View*, 193–231. Amsterdam: Benjamins.

—— (1993). 'A Synopsis of Role and Reference Grammar,' in R. D. Van Valin, Jr. (ed.), *Advances in Role and Reference Grammar*, 1–164. Amsterdam: Benjamins.

—— and WILKINS, D. P. (1993). 'Predicting Syntactic Structure from Semantic Representations: "Remember" in English and Its Equivalents in Mparntwe Arrernte,' in Van Valin (ed.), *Advances in Role and Reference Grammar*, 499–534. Amsterdam: Benjamins.

WIERZBICKA, A. (1980). *The Case for Surface Case*. Ann Arbor, Mich.: Karoma.

—— (1988). *The Semantics of Grammar*. Amsterdam: Benjamins.

—— (1992). 'The search of universal semantic primitives,' in M. Pütz (ed.), *Thirty Years of Linguistic Evolution*, 215–42. Amsterdam: Benjamins.

WILKINS, D. (1990). 'Notions relevant to the discussion of "agents" and "agency" as coded in natural languages.' Ms, University of California at Davis.

The Interpretation of Deverbal
Nouns in Tepehua

James K. Watters

INTRODUCTION

There are several issues that face us in any attempt to account for the interpretation of deverbal nouns. Among these are the following: the relation of the argument structure of the base verb to that of the derived noun and the diachronic and synchronic narrowing or specification of meaning. The purpose of this paper is to briefly explore these issues with reference to nominalization processes found in Tepehua (Totonacan, Mexico), a language with a rich word-formation component, including extensive nominalization.[1]

Tepehua (like other Totonacan languages) has several processes which form nouns from verbs so that a verb stem often has various corresponding derived nominal forms. Note the following examples derived from *ča ʔa·-* 'wash':

(1) ča ʔa·-na·   'washer (person)'
    t ʔa·-ča ʔa·-na·   'fellow washer'
    ɬi·-ča ʔa·-ti   'laundry (still dirty)'
    ča ʔa·-n-ti   'laundry (cleaned)', 'act of washing'
    ɬa·-ča ʔa·-n   'scrubber, wash water'
    pa·-laq-ča ʔa·-n   'washing basin'
    pa·-ča ʔa·-n   'washboard, washing stone'

---

[1] The data discussed here are from the Tlachichilco (Veracruz) dialect area, called *ɬi·ma·sipihni* by the speakers. The other two dialects of Tepehua, Huehuetla (*ɬi·maq ʔaɬqama ʔ*) and Pisa Flores, manifest rather extensive differences in the lexicon, both in form and meaning. Thus while the derivational processes discussed here are for the most part reflected in the grammars of all three dialects of Tepehua (and to a lesser degree in Totonac dialects; see McQuown, 1990), I cannot claim that the discussion of finer points applies throughout the language area. I am indebted to various Tepehua friends and co-workers for their help and patience.

> pu·-ča?a·-kan   '(any) washing instrument'
> ?iš-ča?a·-ka [NP]   'the washing of [NP]'

Some of the processes which derive nouns from verbs in Tepehua involve applicative affixes that I have discussed elsewhere at some length (Watters, 1988; 1989; 1995): *ɬi·-* 'direction', *pu·- ~ pa·-* 'route', and *t?a·-* 'comitative'. Though there are several nominalization processes in Tepehua, I will not pursue the formal details of the grammar of nominalization here (discussed in Watters, 1988). I will focus instead on the semantic-pragmatic aspects of four of the different nominalization types, including those which manifest the applicative prefixes *ɬi·-* and *pu·- ~ pa·-*.

Traditional linguistic notions such as compositional semantics and determination of argument structure are necessary steps in determining the meaning of deverbal nouns, but they are only part of the story. This is obvious for lexicalized forms with their specialized meanings; but I will show that it is also true for the more productive nominalization processes in Tepehua. To account for the meaning of a deverbal noun one must appeal to its FRAME.

Much of the linguistic and AI literature that refers to frames (or scenes, or scripts, etc.) focuses on a higher level, a discourse frame. Fillmore's work in frame semantics (e.g. 1968; 1975; 1977; 1982; 1985; Fillmore and Atkins, 1992), while acknowledging the existence of higher-level frames, focuses largely on frames associated with lexical items.

Following Fillmore, I will consider a lexical item's frame to be the 'background' associated with that lexical item: the prototypical scene evoked by the word, knowledge of which is part of knowing what the word means. When we are dealing with derived words, the schematic compositional semantics contributed by the morphology is interpreted against this background.

12.1. ARGUMENT STRUCTURE

Accounting for the interpretation of a deverbal noun begins, however, with an account of argument structure. One general mapping procedure operates across nominalization types in Tepehua, mapping the argument structure of the base verb onto that of the derived noun. Before presenting an explicit account of the mapping, a few preliminary points need to be made.

Tepehua deverbal nouns typically have only one argument, in the usual sense of the term. As in Spanish or English, that argument fully assimilates to NP syntax and so occurs as the possessor of the nominal (cf. Comrie and Thompson, 1985: 370 f.) However, we can assume, following Williams, 'that every noun has an [additional] argument (R) by virtue of which it can be used referentially (the "x" in the logician's "man(x)")' (1987: 367).[2] This then gives us two arguments for each deverbal noun in Tepehua, one realized as the possessor of the nominal and the other as the argument that corresponds to the referent of the nominal. Thus in the following form one argument corresponds to Juan, the other to the action of bathing:

(2)   ʔiš-paša·-ka   Juan
      3POSS-bathe-PASS (NMLZR)   Juan
      'the bathing of Juan'

Now, there are usually at most three arguments filling the positions in a verb's argument structure that are available to serve as arguments of the derived nominal: the subject, the argument of the base verb (if it is transitive), and the argument of one of the applicative prefixes. These map onto the syntactic positions for the arguments of the derived noun as shown in Table 12.1.

TABLE 12.1. *Argument structure of derived nouns (map one to one, from top to bottom)*

Arguments of base verb	Arguments of derived nominal
Subject	
	Possessor
Argument of prefix	
	R of noun
Argument of verb root	

The highest-ranking argument of the verb maps onto the highest argument position in the derived noun, the possessor. The next-highest argument of the verb (if there is one) then maps onto the other argument position of the derived noun, R (i.e. it corresponds to the referent of the noun). If there is only one argument of the base verb it

---

[2] For Williams this is the 'external argument': 'In nominalization . . . n-place predicates are taken to (n + 1)-place predicates—the verbal θ-roles are internalized, and the derived nominal is supplied a nominal external argument' (1989: 284).

is realized as possessor of the derived noun and the referent of the noun is simply the activity or state denoted by the verb.[3]

Consider how the mapping posited above applies to the following examples:

(3) ʔiš-pu·-maqni·-kan   pʔašni
    3POSS-VIA-kill-PASS (NMLZR)   pig
    'an instrument for killing pigs'

(4) ʔiš-pa·-maqni·-n   Pedro
    3POSS-VIA-kill-DT (NMLZR) Pedro
    'Pedro's killing instrument'

(5) ʔiš-maqni·-ka   pʔašni
    3POSS-kill-PASS (NMLZR) pig
    'the killing of a pig'

(6) ʔiš-ʔača-ti   Pedro
    3POSS-be.happy-NOM Pedro
    'Pedro's happiness'

In (3) the passive suffix *-kan* is present, with the result that the notional object functions as the subject and thus maps onto the possessor position in the derived nominal. The argument of the applicative prefix *pu·-*, the instrument in this case, then maps onto the R position of the derived nominal.

In (4) the detransitivizing suffix *-nVn* is present,[4] with the result that the direct argument of the verb root is absent. The subject of the verb and the argument of the instrumental prefix, *pa·-*,[5] map onto the possessor and R of the derived nominal, respectively.

The NP in (5) demonstrates by far the most productive nominalization process in Tepehua: the passive suffix, *-kan*, is present; as in (3), however, there is no applicative prefix. As a result the subject (the notional object) maps onto the possessor position of the derived nominal and the activity denoted by the verb is realized as the R of the noun.

In (6) the subject of the intransitive verb root maps onto the possessor position and the derived noun refers to the state denoted by the verb.

---

[3] In the case of agent nominals (not discussed in this paper) the subject of the verb maps onto the R of the noun. This is the only nominalization type which violates the mapping, but it reflects the fact that, although the other nominals are most often possessed, the agent nominals are rarely possessed.

[4] A rule of *n*-truncation applies in most deverbal nominalizations in Tepehua: (*a*) $V_1nV_2n \rightarrow V_1n$; (*b*) CVn → CV. Following the Elsewhere Principle, (*a*) is disjunctively ordered before (*b*). Thus the suffix *-nVn* appears as *-nV* (from (*b*)) or *-n* (from (*a*)).

[5] See Watters (1988) for discussion of the two forms of the route-instrumental prefix *pu·-* and *pa·-*.

The mapping procedure gives the correct results in each instance and proves to be a major factor in accounting for the interpretation of deverbal nouns. However, as noted earlier, the interpretation doesn't stop at the correct determination of argument structure. At least two complications arise. First, the applicative prefixes (especially *pu·-* ~ *pa·-* and *ɬi·-*) have varying semantic functions due to the fact that the particular schema associated with each prefix may be applied to spatial, temporal, or other domains (see Watters, 1988; 1995). Second, as derived forms the deverbal nouns are lexical items and subject to semantic narrowing (as well as phonological idosyncracies) typical of lexical items. In both cases the frame associated with the base verb plays a major role.

12.2. ACTION AND OBJECT DEVERBALS

Consider the difference between nonprefixed deverbal nouns (such as the one in (6)), which require an intransitive verb base (inherently intransitive or detransitivized by the suffix *-nVn*), and the *ɬi·-* prefixed deverbals, which may have either a transitive or intransitive base. The two classes of nouns overlap in semantic category. Nonprefixed deverbals most commonly refer to the state or activity but at times refer to an object. The *ɬi·-*prefixed deverbals most commonly refer to objects but sometimes refer to activities. Some verbs that lack a nonprefixed deverbal have a *ɬi·-*prefixed deverbal that serves a similar function of denoting an activity:

(7) tapaca·-y   ɬi·tapaca
    work-IMPF   work, job
    la-y   ɬi·lati
    do, be.able-IMPF   work, things to do
    paš-a   ɬi·pašati
    bathe-IMPF   bathing, bath

The semantic role of the argument of *ɬi·-* is most basically that of 'direction,' giving spatial readings of 'toward' and, in some contexts, 'away from' (Watters, 1988). The central notion in this concept of 'direction' is the object, state, or event toward which the action is directed; however, the schema clearly extends into nonspatial domains. In the temporal domain the argument of *ɬi·-* is typically a proposition or term that refers to an event that is future in relation to the event denoted by the verb which has the *ɬi·-*prefix. In the following example, the argument of *łi·-* is the fiesta, the presence of the prefix marking that the bread 'ran out before the fiesta:'

(8) maka·-ł   pa·n   para   la·kʔa·tan pero wa· ni·man
    make-PFV bread for   fiesta   but FOC immediately
    łi·-miʔo·-ł,   ha·ntu ka-lakača·-ł   kʔa·tan
    DIR-run.out-PFV NEG   IRR-last/reach-PFV fiesta
    'S/he made bread for the fiesta but right away it ran out before it, it didn't last for the fiesta'

Although verbs with *łi·-* typically take an 'extra' argument, the prefix does not always incorporate another argument into the logical structure; it may 'overlay' its semantic role on an argument of the base verb.

(9) cakʔa-y   łi:-cakʔa-y
    bite-IMPF   DIR-bite-IMPF
    'X bites Y'   'X bites toward/snaps at Y'

These facts, along with the fact that the *łi·-*deverbal does not require previous detransitivization of a transitive verb base, help to account for the interpretation of this class of nominals. Following Fig. 12.1, the two arguments in the argument structure of the verb that will be realized as arguments of the noun are the subject and the argument of the prefix. The subject will be realized as the possessor of the derived noun. The referent of the derived noun, then, will correspond to the argument of *łi·-*. With an intransitive verb base, this referent will usually be the activity or an object toward which the activity is directed; with transitive verbs, the referent will usually correspond to the direct object of the base verb. Compare the action (nonprefixed) deverbals and object (*łi·-*) deverbals of the following verbs:

(10) ma·stakʔa·-y   ma·stakʔa·nti
     greet-IMPF   greeting
                       łi·mastakʔa·ti
                       person greeted
(11) ma·payni·-y   ma·payni·nti
     pity-IMPF   mercy, compassion, pity
                       łi·ma·payni·ti
                       one who's pitied
(12) ma·ša·nan   ma·ša·nti
     be.ashamed (IMPF) shame, embarrassment
                       łi·ma·ša·n
                       what/who one is ashamed of

However, when the referent of a ɬi·-prefixed deverbal is the activity, it differs from the corresponding nonprefixed deverbal in that reference is consistently to the activity as 'lacking' or 'not yet done:'

(13) wa·wa·-y   ɬi·wa·wa·ti
     feed-IMPF   feeding (undone), one to be fed
                 wa·wa·nti
                 action of feeding
(14) ʔah-ya   ɬi·ʔahati
     dig-IMPF   digging (that needs to be done)
                 ʔahnati
                 digging (done), diggings

Similarly, when both the nonprefixed deverbal nominal and the ɬi·-nominal refer to objects, the former refers to the object that has undergone or results from the activity, the latter to the object which has not yet undergone the action:

(15) čeʔe-y   ɬi·čeʔeti   čeʔenti
     break-IMPF what.is.to.be.broken what.is.broken
     čʔi·-y   ɬi·čʔi·ti   čʔi·nti
     tie-IMPF   what.is.to.be.tied   what.is.tied
     laqayma·-y ɬi·laqayma·ti   laqayma·nti
     rebuke-IMPF one.not.yet.rebuked who.has.been.rebuked

In the examples we have seen thus far the presence or absence of the applicative prefix ɬi·- is the key to accounting for the distinct intepretations of the deverbal nouns. Significantly, however, the interpretation varies according to whether or not the schema associated with the prefix applies within a temporal domain. As will be seen below, the same is true for the route/instrument deverbals.

12.3. FRAMES AND ENRICHMENT

In the rest of this paper I will try to account for two issues regarding the interpretation of Tepehua deverbal nouns: first, the interpretation of apparently vague or polysemous forms; second, those cases where the meaning of the form has been narrowed to a much more specific sense than that determined by a compositional semantics of the morphology. The first is a problem of synchronic analysis while the second is largely diachronic. However, as will be seen, the verb frame is crucially involved in both accounts.

Nominalized forms such as those discussed here are instances of what have been called 'contextuals' (Clark and Clark, 1979; Aronoff, 1980). They are shorthand or telegraphic expressions with phrasal paraphrases. Often when contextuals are interpreted in isolation, much of the information that is explicit in the phrasal paraphrase must be invoked by the interpreter (Fillmore, 1985: 232).

Some of the processes involved in interpreting deverbal nouns presumably are the same as those used in interpreting other contextuals that have been discussed in the literature. Zimmer's (1971) notion that for a noun–noun compound to occur in English it must be 'appropriately classificatory' can also be used in accounting for both the production and interpretation of other contextuals. That is, a derived form, if it serves more than simply a syntactic recategorization function (Kastovsky, 1986), must be able to label a cognitively salient set of referents.

This is certainly true when we are dealing with nouns derived from verbs. A verb has associated with it a frame which includes the action and the various animate and inanimate participants prototypically associated with the word. In fact, the notion of prototype (Rosch and Mervis, 1975) is a key feature of frames.[6]

Tepehua deverbal nouns represent a process of making different components of that prototypical scene 'discourse manipulable' as nouns (Hopper and Thompson, 1984).[7] Which components are so represented are those most salient. For more innovative, less lexicalized forms, this is largely a matter of salience in the immediate context and is thus determined by the discourse frame. However, forms can come to have a narrow reading due to the frequent pairing of a form with a particular class of referents. Thus they are a reflection of cultural or cognitive salience (as well as of what gaps exist in the lexical repertoire of the language).

---

[6] Hudson seems to overdo the relation between frames and prototypes when he claims: 'What then is the main positive claim of frame semantics? . . . In my opinion . . . it is the claim that stored knowledge is organised in terms of "normalised" entities—in other words, "prototypes" . . . I know of no important difference between the kinds of structure which are discussed in the "frame" and "prototype" traditions . . .' (1986: 86, 87). Cf. the discussion in Fillmore (1975).

[7] In their 1984 article Hopper and Thompson claim that there is a correlation between the degree to which a lexical item displays noun versus verb morphosyntax and the degree to which it has a reading of 'discourse-manipulable participant' versus 'reported event.' This a topic that goes well beyond the concerns of this paper, but the correlation is well supported by the Tepehua data.

Consider the following forms:

(16) šeqe-y 'X grinds (peppers)'; 'X sharpens blade'
      grind-IMPF
(16a) pa·-šeqe-n
      VIA-grind-DT (NMLZR)
(16b) ʔišpa·šeqen María
      'Maria's mortar for grinding peppers'
(16c) ʔišpa·šeqen Juan
      'Juan's stone for sharpening machete'
(17a) ʔiš-pu·-šeqe-kan
      3POSS-VIA-grind-pass (NMLZR)
(17b) ʔišpu·šeqekan pʔin (pepper)
      'mortar for grinding peppers'
(17c) išpu·šeqekan či·tah (machete)
      'stone for sharpening machete'

Here the base verb refers to an action of grinding that applies to both
the grinding of peppers (though not corn or coffee) and to the sharpening of machetes or knives.[8] The deverbal noun in (16) is based on the
intransitive form of the verb (marked by the presence of the final -n;
see n. 5 above), the subject of the base verb maps onto the possessor of
the nominal, and the object of the applicative prefix maps onto the R
of the noun. Here the applicative is the route/instrumental prefix, pu·-
~pa·-, which takes a spatial or temporal 'route' argument or an instrumental argument, in this case the latter. The deverbal noun in (17) is
based on the passive form of the verb. The subject (notional object)
maps onto the possessor position of the noun and the object of the
route/instrumental prefix maps onto the R of the noun.

However, the specific kind of instrument that is being referred to is
only resolved at a level external to the derived nominal, where a more
specific frame is established by the convergence of the verb frame and
the frame of the possessing noun. When the verb šeqe- is applied to
peppers or refers to an action typically carried out by a woman, the
frame includes a mortar that is used for such grinding; when it is
applied to machetes, or refers to an action typically carried out by a

[8] There is another word for grinding machetes and knives, waqa-. In one subdialect
waqa- is the only appropriate term for sharpening blades, šeqe- referring only to grinding chilis, and so pa·šeqen can only refer to a mortar for grinding chili peppers. In the
subdialect from which the examples are drawn, both šeqe- and waqa- are acceptable for
either peppers or blades. The first, according to my consultant, seems to focus on the
grinding or wearing away of the material; the second simply means to rub (usually on or
with a rock). The root for grinding coffee or corn is swaʔa-.

man, the frame includes a certain type of stone that is used for
sharpening machetes. The meaning of the nominal is thus only schem-
atically determined by the mapping rules given above; its full interpretation is crucially dependent on the knowledge contained in the
frames of 'grinding' as applied to peppers and machetes.

Now consider some examples which are somewhat more complex:

(18) tʔal-ay 'X throws.against Y'
      strike-IMPF ('strikes Y with a propelled object'; or 'X hunts Y')
(18a) ʔiš-pu·-tʔal-kan   kafeh
      3POSS-VIA-strike-PASS NMLZR coffee
      'pestle for pounding hulls off coffee'
(18b) ʔiš-pu·-tʔal-kan   tʔu·n
      3POSS-VIA-strike-PASS NMLZR dirt
      'dirt-pounder' (stone to make clay griddle)
(18c) ʔiš-pa·-laq-tʔala-n   María
      3POSS-VIA-MULT-strike-DT NMLZR María
      'María's stone for pounding dirt'
(18d) ʔiš-pa·-tʔala-n   Juan
      3POSS-VIA-strike-DT NMLZR Juan
      'Juan's rifle/pistol'

In these examples we are dealing with two nominalization processes,
both of which typically result in nouns referring to instruments. The
mapping of argument structure is determined in the same manner as
the examples discussed previously.

The deverbal noun in (*a*) is the standard way of referring to the long
pounding pestle used to hull coffee inside a hollowed-out log. The
same noun occurs in (*b*), this time with *tʔun* 'earth/dirt' as the syntactic possessor. This construction is immediately recognized as referring to a hand-sized cylindrical stone used in pounding out dirt to
make a clay griddle. Interestingly, this is not the standard term for this
'dirt-pounder', which is found in (*c*). There we find a different deverbal noun based on the detransitivized, nonpassivized form of the
same verb (with the prefix *laq-*, 'multiple', here signifying striking
'into pieces'). The same noun that occurs in (*c*) appears in (*d*) without
the *laq-* prefix as the standard term for 'firearm.'

Other nouns can also be constructed on the same base verb. As
is the case with all verbs, the acceptable derived nominals include
some that are very common terms and others that are apparent neo-
logisms. Considering the forms in (16), (17), and (18), one possible
account would claim that the lexicon simply lists distinct meanings

for the nominals in (16*b*) and (16*c*) and for (18*a*) and (18*b*). However, that would obviously miss the generalization that a semantic core— determined by the basic meaning of the verb, the applicative prefix, and the principles of argument structure mapping—is shared by both. Furthermore, it is not clear that the form-meaning in (18*b*) could be considered a 'listed' item, since the standard name for the same object is that given in (*c*).

Another approach might suggest the meanings are 'radially' connected (cf. Lakoff, 1987). Each meaning is distinct yet shares some components with a neighboring meaning. In fact, however, the meaning in this case seems not to involve radial categories: rather, the morphology provides a vague schema which is fleshed out by the frames associated with the base verb and the related object (the possessor) in the noun phrase. Examples such as these and those discussed earlier exemplify Fillmore's slogan 'meanings are relativized to scenes' (1977: 59).

Within another tradition, the interpretation of deverbal nouns such as these involve what Sperber and Wilson call 'enrichment' of the semantic representation (1986: 180–93). They claim that enrichment, as well as disambiguation and reference assignment, is brought about by the application of their principle of 'relevance,' the same principle that accounts for how the correct implicatures are deduced from an utterance:

the propositional form the hearer should be interested in recovering is the one that is consistent with the principle of relevance. . . . it is a matter of finding the first accessible enrichment of the concept which will yield an interpretation relevant enough to be consistent with the principle of relevance. (pp. 184, 189)

However, in the approach taken here, cases such as these each involve a frame that is evoked by the lexical item(s). In other words, the hearer does not need to determine the relevant enrichment; the hearer does not need to invoke the correct frame by calculating the ratio of contextual effects to processing costs. The key to interpreting nominals such as these is (contrary to Sperber and Wilson) certainly determined by a process different from that which sorts out the conversational implicatures of an utterance.

The centrality of frames in nominal interpretation can be demonstrated by many other examples, though only a few can be mentioned here. As noted earlier the applicative prefixes *pu·- ~ pa·-* and *ɬi·-*, though basically marking spatial relations, have uses that extend into the temporal domain. This can be seen in the following examples, which involve a temporal use of *pu·-~ pa·*:

(19) pa·-ʔoqštama:-n
VIA-hire-DT (NMLZR)
'time for hiring'
(20) ʔiš-pu·-ʔalin   šaqši
3POSS-VIA-exist (NMLZR)   strangler.fig
'the time when the strangler figs are ripe'
(21) ʔiš-pu·-pa·ʔan   kʔa·tan
3POSS-VIA-fade (NMLZR)   fiesta
'the time when the fiesta has passed'

In each of these cases the only possible interpretation of the derived nominal involves a temporal reading of *pu·- ~ pa·*. The instrumental or spatial readings are ruled out, not by argument structure or by compositional semantics but by the associated frames. The nouns in (19) and (20) are invariably given a temporal reading, but the same noun occurring in (21) is given an instrumental reading when associated with the appropriate frame:

(22) ʔiš-pu·-pa·ʔan   laqčʔi·ti
3POSS-VIA-fade (NMLZR)   clothes
'that by which the clothes fade' (bleach or sun)

Here the frame determines what kind of reading (spatial or temporal or instrumental) should be given the *pu·*-prefix. This, in turn, determines the sense of the derived noun.

12.4. DIACHRONIC NARROWING OF REFERENCE

Consider the action nominal *hatʔalanti*, derived from *tʔal-* 'throw against' (the same verb discussed earlier). Now recall that in Tepehua the nonprefixed nominals often may be used to refer to either (1) the activity or state denoted by the verb or (2) the resulting object of the action. Thus, *hatʔalanti*, should (compositionally) refer to any activity of striking objects with a propelled instrument or to the targeted object which has been struck. Thus it can be used to refer to already hulled coffee:[9]

---

[9] For speakers of the subdialect from which the data were gathered, the prefix *ha-* appears on finite verbs to mark either multiple objects or multiple events; it is also typically required on all noncount nouns. The corresponding forms from speakers of a nearby subdialect, however, very frequently lack *ha-*; thus, *tʔalanti*.

(23) ʔalin   kafeh   yu·   ha-tʔala-n-ti
     exist (IMPF)   coffee   PRO   HA-strike-DT-NMLZR
     'There is some coffee that is hulled-stuff'

However, when it refers to an activity it has only one 'throwing' reading: 'hunting.' Compare the following constructions, the first employing the infinitive form of the verb, the second the derived noun:

(24) ha·ntu   lani-y   tʔal-na·
     NEG   learn-IMPF   throw.against-INF
     'S/he hasn't learned to hunt/hull/throw'
(25) ha·ntu   lani-y   ha-tʔala-n-ti
     NEG   learn-IMPF   ha-throw.against-DT-NMLZR
     'S/he hasn't learned hunting/*hulling/*throwing'

This illustrates the diachronic narrowing of sense that is such an ubiquitous characteristic of lexical items.

In one of his many presentations of frame semantics, Fillmore has stated:

> With respect to word meanings, frame semantic research can be thought of as the effort to understand what reason a speech community might have found for creating the category represented by the word, and to explain the word's meaning by presenting and clarifying that reason. (1985: 234)

Clearly, the search for such reasons involves not only linguistic but cultural issues.

As we have seen, the morphologically determined compositional semantics of a derived form provide a very schematic meaning; however, the derived form often has a much more specific meaning. The challenge is to reconstruct a scenario for how this narrowing of meaning comes about for such a lexical item. Presumably at some previous point the association between the form and a particular scene is a purely pragmatic one, determined by something like Horn's R principle (a 'speaker-oriented' Relevance principle):[10]

> R-based narrowing . . . is not linguistically, but culturally or socially, motivated . . . When *drink* and *smell* take on narrowed readings denoting a particular type of drinking and smelling . . . with the resultant autohyponymy of the lexical item, it is because we can count on an addressee who shares our culture

---

[10] Horn's R principle is not equivalent to Sperber and Wilson's (1986) relevance. A significant difference is that Horn does not attempt to reduce Grice's maxims to one overarching principle; rather, he reduces all the maxims (except Quality) to two principles. The R principle is 'speaker-oriented' ('say no more than you must'), inducing lower-bounding implicata; the Q principle is 'hearer-oriented' ('say as much as you can'), inducing upper-bounding implicata (Horn, 1989: 194).

to be able to figure out just which salient, highly charged member of the extension the speaker would have sufficient reason to avoid naming directly. (1989: 358)

At some point the association of the lexical item with a more specific background leads to the 'attachment' of the relevant frame. The frame then becomes a conventionalized component of the word's semantics.
Consider the following examples:

(26a) sa·-y
hit-IMPF
'X hits Y'

(26b) sa·-nan
hit-DT (IMPF)
'X hits'; 'X plays music'

(26c) ha-sa·-n-ti
HA-hit-DT-NMZLR
'music' (*'hitting')

(27a) šawa·-y
burn-IMPF
'X burns Y'

(27b) yu· oxi pa·-ma·-šawa·-n wa· tus ma·yuh
ART good VIA-CAUS-burn-DT (NMZLR) until May
'The good field-burning-time isn't until May'

(27c) mim-pa·-ma·-šawa·-n
2POSS-VIA-CAUS-burn-DT (NMZLR)
'your field-igniter'

(28a) čʔan
plant (IMPF)
's/he plants'

(28b) pu·-čʔa
VIA-plant (NMZLR)
'planting stick' (not applicable to any other planting instrument)

The deverbal nouns in these examples all have narrower senses than could be derived compositionally from the base and affixes. Any ambiguity present in the base verb has been resolved, and where there is vagueness in the base form, the derived form is specific. In each case one of the subsets of potential referents has become the only one possible, and in each case it involves an activity or object that is culturally highly salient.

Note that the nominalized form of *(ma·)šawa·*- 'burn (trans.)' is given an instrumental reading if possessed (27c) and (usually) a temporal reading otherwise (27b). Significantly, while the base verb can refer to burning anything from a scrap of paper to a whole forest, the nominalized forms only refer to a frame that is culturally highly salient: burning a field in preparation for sowing. The lexical semantics of the derived nominal have thus narrowed. Furthermore, there is a pragmatically driven specification of the same nominal, following Horn's R principle. The prototypical referent of (27c) is a dried corn-stalk which is lit and used to burn the dried cuttings in the field. This is the reading given in isolation, and given by native speakers as part of the meaning of the word. However, this specification-by-implicature can be overridden:

(29) kim-pa·-ma·-šawa·-n   wa· maqa-taun kʔiw
     1POSS-VIA-CAUS-burn-DT (NMZLR) FOC CLAS-one   wood
     'My field-burning-instrument is a stick'

12.5. CONCLUSION

Tepehua deverbal nouns display an argument structure that can be predicted directly from the argument structure of the base verb by means of the mapping procedure. However, the argument structure is only a first step in accounting for the noun's interpretation. The applicative prefixes *ɫi·-* and *pu·-* result in readings of derived nouns that vary according to whether their schemata are interpreted within a temporal or nontemporal domain. Furthermore, the deverbal noun typically has a semantic richness beyond what can be attributed to the compositional semantics.

The frame semantics approach presented here makes claims about the 'enrichment' of lexical items that differ significantly from the picture drawn by Relevance Theory. It appears misguided to claim that enrichment or specification of the bare lexical semantics of a deverbal noun takes place by calculation according to the same maxims or principle(s) that produce conversational implicatures. Rather, a deverbal noun is associated with a frame (based on a prototypical scene denoted by the base verb) which provides the background against which its bare compositional semantics are interpreted.

REFERENCES

ARONOFF, M. (1980). 'Contextuals,' *Language* **56**: 744–58.
BACH, E., and HARMS, R. T. (eds.) (1968). *Universals in Linguistic Theory.* New York: Holt, Rinchart & Winston.

Deverbal Nouns in Tepehua

BALTIN, M. R., and KROCH, A. S. (eds.) (1989). *Alternative Conceptions of Phrase Structure.* Chicago: University of Chicago Press.

CASAD, E. (ed.) (1995). *Cognitive Linguistics in the Redwoods.* Berlin: Mouton de Gruyter.

CLARK, E., and CLARK, H. (1979). 'When Nouns Surface as Verbs,' *Language* **55**: 767–811.

COGEN, C. *et al.* (eds.) (1975). *Proceedings of the First Annual Meeting of the Berkeley Linguistics Society.*

COLE, P., and SADOCK, J. (eds.) (1977). *Syntax and Semantics* viii: *Grammatical Relations.* New York: Academic Press.

COMRIE, B., and THOMPSON, S. A. (1985). 'Lexical Nominalization,' in Shopen (1985: iii. 349–98).

FILLMORE, C. J. (1968). 'The Case for Case,' in Bach and Harms (1968: 1–90).

—— (1975). 'An Alternative to Checklist Theories of Meaning,' in Cogen *et al.* (1975: 123–31).

—— (1977). 'The Case for Case Reopened,' in Cole and Sadock (1977: 59–82).

—— (1982). 'Frame Semantics,' in Linguistics Society of Korea (1982: 111–38).

—— (1985). 'Frames and the Semantics of Understanding,' *Quaderni di semantica* **6**: 222–54.

—— (1986). ' "U"-Semantics, Second Round,' *Quaderni di semantica* **7**: 49–58.

—— and ATKINS, B. T. (1992). 'Toward a Frame-based Lexicon: The Semantics of RISK and Its Neighbors,' in Lehrer and Feder Kittay (1992: 75–102).

HOPPER, P., and THOMPSON, S. A. (1984). 'The Discourse Basis for Lexical Categories in Universal Grammar,' *Language* **60**: 703–52.

HORN, L. R. (1989). *A Natural History of Negation.* Chicago: University of Chicago Press.

HUDSON, D. (1986). 'Frame Semantics, Frame Linguistics, Frame . . . ?', *Quaderni di semantica* **7**: 85–101.

KASTOVSKY, D. (1986). 'The Problem of Productivity in Word Formation,' *Linguistics* **24**: 585–600.

LAKOFF, G. (1987). *Women, Fire, and Dangerous Things: What Categories Reveal about the Mind.* Chicago: University of Chicago Press.

LEHRER, A. and FEDER KITTAY, E. (eds.) (1992). *Frames, Fields, and Contrasts.* Hillsdale, NJ.: Erlbaum.

Linguistics Society of Korea (ed.) (1982). *Linguistics in the Morning Calm: Papers from the SICOL Conference* Seoul: Hanshin.

MCQUOWN, N. (1990). *Gramática de la Lengua Totonaca: Coatepec, Sierra Norte de Puebla.* Mexico: Universidad Nacional Antónoma de México.

NEED, B., SCHILLER, E., and BOSCH, A. (eds.) (1987). *Papers from the Twenty-Third Regional Meeting of the Chicago Linguistic Society.*

ROSCH, E., and MERVIS, C. B. (1975). 'Family Resemblances: Studies in the Internal Structure of Categories,' *Cognitive Psychology* **8**: 382–439.

SHOPEN, T. (ed.) (1985). *Language Typology and Syntactic Description* (3 vols.). Cambridge: Cambridge University Press.

SPERBER, D., and WILSON, D. (1986). *Relevance: Communication and Cognition.* Cambridge, Mass.: Harvard University Press.

WATTERS, J. K. (1988). 'Topics in Tepehua Grammar.' Ph.D. dissertation, University of California at Berkeley.

—— (1989). 'The Syntax of Applicatives in Tepehua,' paper read at the annual meeting of the Linguistic Society of America, Washington, DC.

—— (1995). 'Frames and the Semantics of Applicatives in Tepehua,' in Casad (1995: 971–96).

WILLIAMS, E. (1987). 'English as an Ergative language: The Theta Structure of Derived Nouns,' in Need *et al.* (1987: 366–75).

—— (1989). 'Maximal Projections in Words and Phrases,' in Baltin and Kroch (1989: 280–91).

ZIMMER, K. (1971). 'Some General Observations about Nominal Compounds,' *Working Papers on Language Universals* **5**: 1–21 Stanford, Calif.: Stanford University Press.

Index